D0843279

Full Faith
and Credit

FULL FAITH
AND CREDIT

The Story of
C.I.T. Financial Corporation
1908-1975

WILLIAM L. WILSON

Random House
New York

Grateful acknowledgment is made to the following for permission to reprint previously published material:

Automotive News: Excerpts from an article which appeared in *Automotive Daily News,* p. 1, February 13, 1937.

Fortune Magazine: Excerpts from articles which appeared in *Fortune Magazine,* January 1933 and September 1947.

Nation's Business: Excerpts from page 66 of *Nation's Business,* March 1926. Copyright 1926 by *Nation's Business,* Chamber of Commerce of the United States.

The New York Times: Excerpts from articles which appeared in *The New York Times,* November 20, 1925; February 12, 1926; June 20, 1926; December 4, 1927; December 6, 1927; November 1, 1927; February 12, 1928; December 1, 1929; May 10, 1931. Copyright 1925, 1926, 1927, 1928, 1929, 1931 by The New York Times Company.

The Wall Street Journal: Excerpts from an article which appeared in *The Wall Street Journal,* February 26, 1975. Copyright © 1965 by Dow Jones & Company, Inc. All Rights Reserved.

Library of Congress Cataloging in Publication Data
Wilson, William L
Full faith and credit.
Includes index.
1. C. I. T. Financial Corporation—History.
I. Title.
HG5129.N5W54   332.1'0973   75-318885
ISBN 0-394-40278-2
ISBN 0-394-73164-6 pbk.

Manufactured in the United States of America
98765432
First Edition

Contents

FULL FAITH
AND CREDIT

I

The First Morning

The date was Tuesday, February 11, 1908. At a measured and purposeful pace, the gentleman emerged from his comfortable middle-class residence at 5153 McPherson Avenue, St. Louis, Missouri, part of a four-family, four-story brick structure. He descended the few marble steps to his automobile waiting at the curb. As a streetcar rattled by, he greeted his part-time driver, entered the rear of the auto and was driven off on his important mission of the morning.

The sky was leaden, the air had a winter chill. He noted from the forecast at the top of the front page of the St. Louis *Globe-Democrat,* which he had brought with him from his home, that rain was possible for later in the day, with snow in prospect for the Lincoln's Birthday holiday. As the automobile moved eastward on McPherson Avenue toward the central city and the financial district, the driver took a left jog onto Kingshighway and two short blocks later turned eastward on Olive Street for the direct drive to their destination.

His passenger's attention was centered primarily on the newspaper. The front page was dominated by scandals and the goings-on of international society, material not very much to the liking of that particular reader. There was an account of a disputed will case involving a deceased Colonel Snell, in which the court heard testimony concerning his "orgies" and revelry in Chicago. There was a lead story that Mrs. Cornelius Vanderbilt had become betrothed to a rapscallion Hungarian count. A local member of the U.S. House of Representatives and "one of the most beautiful young women in St. Louis society" had stolen a march on their friends by eloping to Cincinnati. A Shurtleff College (Illinois) student had been shot and one of his classmates who had been with him at the time had attempted suicide. The only front-page story of national or international significance reported an address by Secretary of War William Howard Taft at Kansas City, where he strongly defended the policies and acts of President Theodore Roosevelt in attempting to secure the vote and the full rights of citizenship for the Negroes of the South.

Turning rather impatiently to the financial pages, the reader noted with interest that Thomas A. Edison, the inventor, had settled nine years of patent litigation against an array of motion picture producers by accepting a settlement of $250,000 a year. The New York stock market had continued to decline on Monday, the weakness being attributed to "political uncertainty." The break was said to be the worst since that day in the previous October when a New York bank closed its doors, precipitating a panic throughout the financial community. Elsewhere, the economic news was not good, as it scarcely had been for months. More than 1,500 men had been laid off by the complete closing of the American Car and Foundry Company at Madison, Illinois, which normally employed 4,000 workers. Lack of orders from the railroads "because of the business depression" had wiped out the backlog of the car building plant.

Money was scarce and dear. Six-month commercial paper notes in the St. Louis market commanded a 6% rate. Credit conditions were treacherous. Sunday's *Post-Dispatch* said that Dun & Bradstreet had reported that business failures for the January just passed were "the largest for any month in 11 years and had been exceeded only 7 times in 15 years." The total liabilities involved in these failures were the fourth highest in that fifteen-year period, being $63 million in January 1908, compared with $18 million and $15 million in the two previous Januarys. The 1907 "money panic" or "rich men's panic" and the consequent withdrawal of support from many enterprises by their banks were blamed for the wave of bankruptcies.

The comfortable residential character of the western section of the city gave way to less expensive homes, retail stores and other storefront businesses and then to the rising structures of the downtown financial district, fronting on the Mississippi. At Sixth Street, the passenger automatically looked to the north and reflectively studied the roof outline of the building housing the Famous Department Store at Washington Street. His car turned northward on Fourth Street, and he got out midway in the next block in front of the Fourth Street entrance to the Security Building, standing at the southwest corner of Fourth and Locust Streets. The most magnificent fireproof structure in the West, the building had been completed in 1892 and was still regarded as the city's finest. Constructed of brick and quarried stone in a U-shape, it covered a good part of the block between Olive and Locust. The tenants were a number of leading brokerage, securities, insurance and law firms, with the prestigious Noonday businessmen's luncheon club on the top ninth and tenth floors.

The gentleman entered the vaulted first-floor lobby through 18-foot-high, iron-bound, heavily ornamented doors. A glass dome two stories above cast outdoor light against the lavish marble walls, the mosaic tile floor and wrought-iron staircase of the lobby.

The scene was a familiar one—he had been there a number of times before. Eddie O'Donnell, the sandy-haired, youthful head elevator operator, greeted him with an Irish grin and a respectful "Good morning, sir!"

As they both entered the waiting lift, the gentleman may well have nodded and acknowledged the greeting, then saying, "The sixth floor, please."

"Right, sir!" Eddie may have responded. "I've seen you here in the building before. Are you with the new people who moved in today? We're glad to have you in the building!"

"Yes, I am" may have been the quiet answer as they rode upward.

"Well, sir, here's the sixth floor. Welcome and good luck! Hope you make a million dollars!"

2

The Pioneer

The man who made that journey across the city of St. Louis on February 11, 1908 was a 36-year-old businessman named Henry Ittleson. He was preoccupied that morning because he was making the substance of a dream into reality. He was expecting notification from the office of the Secretary of State of Missouri in Jefferson City that a charter had been granted to a company whose creation represented the results of years of observation and planning on his part for an almost totally new concept of business enterprise.

By birth and for the majority of his working years to that time, Henry Ittleson had been a retail merchant. Yet throughout that period he had repeatedly attempted to get out of retailing. The new enterprise he was establishing might be said to be his boldest attempt to escape from the career of a merchant.

The Ittleson family name was brought to the United States in 1861 by Henry Ittleson's father, Oscar, who was then a penniless youth of 17. Oscar had been born a subject of the Russian czar, reputedly in the Province of Lithuania. Of Jewish parentage, he immigrated to the United States, doubtless to escape the wave of pogroms that forced so many of his faith to seek safety and opportunity in the New World during the middle decades of the nineteenth century. He was a skilled bookbinder and worker in leather. He settled in Philadelphia and was naturalized as an American citizen there on July 6, 1870. His wife, Eva Margaret Stern, had been born in England and had previously been married to a man named Getzlow, so that her son, Maximilian, became Oscar Ittleson's stepson.

Oscar and Eva Ittleson returned to Europe in 1870 for a period of more than ten years, no doubt because he sought a better market for his leather-working trade in the sophisticated cosmopolitan centers of the continent. It was during this period that Henry Ittleson was born—on January 27, 1871, in Berlin. He acquired American citizenship automatically because both his parents were American citizens, but he did not see what became his homeland until the entire family, including Maximilian, 17, Henry and one older and one younger sister, returned to the United States in 1880 and settled in New York City for several years.

There Oscar Ittleson entered the mercantile business. This was the period when the western lands beyond the Mississippi were being opened to development and the crowded eastern cities were alive with stories of the opportunities that existed for those who would migrate westward. Various organizations existed in the Jewish communities of the East to help their compatriots by moving them westward to escape the overcrowding and hard economic lot that was theirs in the major ports of entry on the East Coast.

The Ittleson family may not have been beneficiaries of this program, as some evidence exists that Oscar had accumulated capital. Young Henry, then in his mid-teens, was in school. But his studies were interrupted in 1886 when his father decided to move by covered wagon, with his stock-in-trade, to Dodge City, Kansas, and open a retailing business there.

Selling goods to the ranchers and farmers around Dodge City, largely on credit against the next harvest or sale of cattle, was a hard business. When a severe drought struck Kansas in 1888–89, Oscar Ittleson had had enough. Since arriving in Dodge City, he had acquired a son-in-law, Moses Cohn, who had been a laborer and farmer but joined in the storekeeping enterprise after his marriage to Henry's older sister, Emma. The immigrant aid organizations in New York City had provided financial help to Cohn to enable him to become established in Kansas.

Again exciting news was coming out of the West, this time about the gold and silver strikes around Aspen and Leadville, Colorado. Ittleson and Cohn decided to pack their merchandise on the backs of burros and head for the land of promise.

The emigrant storekeepers traveled into the Rockies, down the Roaring Fork River and halted their journey in Carbondale, Colorado, near Aspen. There they opened a store—O. Ittleson & Company. From the beginning, the enterprise flourished, with Oscar tending to the daily storekeeping business and Moses roaming the countryside with a burro carrying the wares. He sold on an itinerant basis to ranchers, farmers and miners, and made special "deals." In one transaction they anticipated the coming of the Denver and Rio Grande Railroad to the area. The partners bought up stands of trees and arranged to have them felled and cut to railroad-tie measurements. These were sold at a handsome profit to the railroad builders.

But Henry was not a part of all this, for he had chosen to stay in Dodge City. Earlier, he had "helped out" in his father's business but demonstrated little interest in storekeeping and peddling around the countryside. He therefore had begun to read for admission to the bar, in the office of M. W. Soper, a leading Dodge City lawyer. There is also a family legend that for a time he studied to be a rabbi. Handsome and energetic, he took part actively in the bustling frontier life of Dodge City and reputedly wore a pistol, as did almost every other male citizen.

The Carbondale enterprise flourished and within a few months the partners sent for their wives and children, who were able to travel to their new home by train, since the railroad link to Carbondale had been completed.

The departure of the rest of the family from Dodge City put Henry completely on his own, although he maintained very close ties with them. There remains a letter he wrote from Dodge City in March of 1888 regretting that he could not join his loved ones for the approaching religious holidays. Addressed to his sister Emma and her husband, the letter reads in part:

> You know of course that I would like very much to spend that week with you; first on account of the religious importance I attach to it, and second, to see your lovely little angel [Rosie] which dear Emma has so often described to me in her letters. . . . Our court meets here next week and will be in full session during the holidays; and Court time is the busiest time of the year for us in the office, as then we have double the amount of work to do, both in the office and in Court. . . . I am afraid that I will have to forego the pleasure of spending those days with you. . . . I wrote to our dear Mother and father to-day, and told them about the cordial invitation you so kindly extended to me. . . . Received a letter from dear papa and mama this week, and they are all well except our dear mother who is suffering painfully with her rheumatism. I feel

very sorry for her and would help her in any way in my power that I could. Of course I know that I am doing her lots of good by being a good boy and trying to become a useful man in the community. She knows very well that I am doing my best to please her and the rest of our dear family. . . .

Your loving brother,

Henry

Despite his devotion to the law that is reflected in this letter, Henry soon decided that the opportunities offered to a prospective young attorney in a farming community were not for him. The siren tales of the enormous business boom that was sweeping Colorado because of the mineral strikes grew ever stronger. By mid-1888 he decided to quit his law studies and strike out for the central hub of all this new prosperity—Denver.

That fast-growing city was enjoying a real estate boom, touched off by the enormous amounts of mineral wealth being taken from the mountain mines of the surrounding area. Henry became a clerk for Amter and Gottenberg, real estate and financial agents. The following year he was a stenographer for the Denver Real Estate Exchange, and in 1891 went into business for himself with a partner named Rose. This venture is said to have been almost instantly successful, with the firm dealing in buying and selling property in a constantly rising market.

The young real estate broker enjoyed his prosperity, dressed smartly and became very much the young man about town. Dark-haired, handsome and of medium, athletic build, he was popular and in great demand as an extra man for social occasions of all kinds. He began to take an active part in civic life; in *A Centennial History of the Jews of Colorado 1859–1959* Allen Bush tells us that "interest in welfare was the concern . . . of numerous Jews in the late '80's and pressures for some definite community action resulted in a dozen men coming together on November 3, 1889, to seek some solution to the problem. With Henry Frankel in the chair and Henry Itleson [sic] as secretary, the members pondered the question 'of building a Jewish Hospital or Sanatorium in or near the city of Denver.' " This meeting unquestionably was the first formative step in the establishment of the world-renowned National Jewish Hospital at Denver, which formally opened on July 15, 1899.

The May-Shoenberg clan, headed by David May, a merchant, held a prominent position in the social fabric of Denver and were the owners and operators of the May Shoe & Clothing Company, one of the city's most aggressive and fastest-growing retail enterprises. The Sunday luncheon parties at the David May home had become a social fixture and Henry Ittleson, as an attractive bachelor, regularly attended them.

As an historical footnote, the May-Shoenberg retailing interests had developed on lines parallel to the Ittleson-Cohn enterprise, although much more successfully. David May had come to the United States from Germany in 1863, landing in New York as a penniless youth of 26. He began clerking in one small retail store after another while moving westward and then set up so-called tent stores of his own. After ten years, he had achieved a partnership in a dry goods store in Hartford City, Indiana. He suffered from asthma and had heard of the clear mountain air and the fortunes that were being made in the Colorado mining boom. In 1876 he sold his interest in the store for $25,000—a respectable fortune then—and moved on to Leadville, Colorado, which was then a boom town with a population of 25,000, compared with 500 a few years earlier.

With his brother-in-law, Moses Shoenberg, as his partner, he built a thriving retailing business, the May & Shoenberg Company, which took large space ads in the local press in 1881 to proclaim, "We don't advertise what we don't have in stock. Ours is the Boston Square-Dealing, One-Price House!"

David May must have sensed the sudden collapse of the mining boom in 1888. He took notice of an announcement that a Denver dry goods and shoe store had failed and that its merchandise was for sale. He moved swiftly to take a look at the property and in less than twenty-four hours bought the business and inventory for $31,000. May and Shoenberg closed the Leadville store. May was joined in the new venture by two other Shoenberg brothers, Joseph and Louis, who had been operating a separate store in Leadville. Moses Shoenberg moved on to Kansas City, going into a retailing business there with other relatives.

Tradition has it that May and his new partners hired a brass band for the reopening in Denver and sold out the entire stock and replaced it with merchandise of their own choosing within a week. The name of the Denver store was simplified to "The May Company." Thus, one of the great success stories in American merchandising history picked up momentum.

Henry Ittleson's success in real estate lasted for about two years and then the land boom in the Denver area collapsed, probably as a part of the general panic of 1893. His profits, which were in the $25,000 range, were wiped out, and he was struggling to keep his office open.

David May had kept a close and approving eye on young Ittleson, so at this juncture he invited Henry to his office and said bluntly, "Henry, I know you have lost money and your business is in trouble. I've been watching you and I think you've learned a lesson or two and have a good future before you. I want to propose that you close your office and come to work for me. It is time you went into some business that has security, stability and a future where you can use all that business ability of yours. It won't be easy because you'll have to learn our business the only way that's right—from the bottom up. But if you show you have the goods, we'll give you every opportunity to move ahead."

After some hesitation, Ittleson agreed and went to work for the May Company wrapping packages and making deliveries. His progress during the next few years was rapid, as was that of the May Company as well. The company flourished and the proprietors amassed capital rapidly.

In the meantime, Moses Shoenberg had purchased and was operating the Famous Company clothing store in St. Louis, having acquired it after it had suffered a disastrous fire. That business quickly outgrew the limited quarters it occupied at Broadway and Delmar Street in the downtown area, and Moses proposed to expand into much larger quarters at Sixth and Washington Streets. Presumably, this required more capital (and possibly more management assistance) than he had at his command. In 1892, David May and the two other Shoenberg brothers joined him as equal partners in the St. Louis operation, while Moses received an interest in the Denver store.

The Denver partners promptly dispatched their rising young associate, Henry Ittleson, to assist Moses and look after their new St. Louis interests as superintendent of the store there. His efforts were very successful—the Famous soon became the more important of the two stores. The May and Shoenberg families shortly left Denver and moved to St. Louis, where they have held leading positions in the life of the city for many decades.

Young Ittleson, second in command of the Famous store although only in his mid-twenties, roomed in a bachelor boarding house on McPherson Avenue and, through his landlady, met her charming and vivacious niece, Blanche Frank. A swift courtship followed and they were married on April 10, 1898. They set up housekeeping on Lindell Boulevard, and their first son, Henry Ittleson, Jr., was born there on October 25, 1900.

But once again, for reasons that are unknown, Henry Ittleson de-

Henry Ittleson, a rising young merchant

cided to quit the retailing business in spite of his success in it. In 1902, he resigned his position as manager of the May interests and cast his lot with one Alexander D. Nast as manager of A. D. Nast & Company, stock and bond brokers.

Meanwhile, Oscar Ittleson and Moses Cohn, again following a pattern identical with that of the May group, had left Denver and transferred their business to St. Louis, where they operated the West End Bazaar Company.

Henry spent two more years, from 1903 to 1905, with Morris Glaser & Company, stock brokers, as a partner. In that period, the May-Shoenberg interests continued to expand, acquiring a store in Cleveland and, in 1905, the D. Crawford store in St. Louis, which had gone into bankruptcy.

David May had continued to follow Henry Ittleson's activities closely. He noted that his young friend's venture into stock brokerage, which had begun most auspiciously in a booming market, had worsened as prices and investors' interest had virtually collapsed in a sudden market decline. He again made Ittleson an offer of employment—to manage the Crawford acquisition and put it on its feet. A generous salary accompanied the proposition. Ittleson accepted and the store was renamed The May Company and promptly moved into the black.

In the May philosophy of retail management, buying was the primary responsibility of its executives. Everything else was subordinated to combing the markets, particularly in the East, for the most salable and potentially profitable lines of merchandise.

Thus, Ittleson once again became a steady commuter between St. Louis and New York City, as he had been during his days with the Famous store. He became intimately acquainted with scores, perhaps hundreds, of manufacturers and suppliers, learning their capabilities, strengths and weaknesses, and financial affairs. Many of these "resources" began to seek advice from the brilliant young merchant from the Midwest, usually on the subject of the chronic shortage of working capital that plagued so many of them as they sought to expand their businesses or simply meet everyday cash needs.

These suppliers were compelled to offer credit terms to their customers, whether they were large establishments such as the May organization or small and shaky operators. To bring in funds that were badly needed at all times, suppliers offered big discounts for cash, running as high as 7% or 8% for payment by the end of the current month. Such a scale was roughly equivalent to a money cost to them of 100% per year.

Many of these wholesalers had profitable businesses, good personal reputations and a record of successful operations. But being unable to accumulate capital to show on the asset side of their balance sheets, they could not qualify for bank credit in any substantial way. Any other private sources of money would make loans to them only at very high rates of interest.

The chaotic financial condition plaguing so many of these otherwise competent businessmen was something that Ittleson found himself constantly turning over in his mind. He noted there had been no perceptible change since colonial days in the way the "trade" financed itself. Yet elsewhere throughout the nation's economy, sweeping changes were occurring. Inventions, innovations and discoveries in science, manufacturing, transportation, power supply and other areas were remaking the entire style of American life.

As he traveled to and from the markets and pondered the financial shortcomings of the industries selling to retailers, Ittleson thought he saw a great personal opportunity. He discussed the subject with his friend and former associate, A. D. Nast, who had continued his investment business in Chicago. He found that Nast agreed with his conclusions.

In the light of today's commercial practices, the idea seems a fairly simple one. Suppliers were paying the equivalent of as much as 100% per year for funds through the discounts offered to their customers for cash. *Thus, anyone with a sufficiently strong capital position might borrow funds on the open market at approximately 6%, and relend the money to the hard-pressed wholesalers on the collateral of their outstanding billings to their customers.* These loans could be made at a much lower interest rate than such creditors were paying by way of the discount e.o.m. (end of month) practice, and the lender would still earn an excellent return. The catch, of course, was that the personal creditworthiness of the borrowers must be known to be good, and the value of the collateral they tendered must be adequate to secure the risk the lender was assuming. But on these points, with his intimate knowledge of both sides of the market, Henry Ittleson appeared to have few qualms.

This is surprising, for the nation was then passing through one of the most difficult periods of economic recession in its history up to that time. The setback was a sharp and wholly unexpected one. It was touched off on October 23, 1907, when a two-day run by its depositors closed the doors of the Knickerbocker Trust Company in New York and ruined the institution. In the wake of this, runs broke out against banks all over the country. Sixteen national banks went under in the next ten weeks, as did many more trust companies, state-chartered banks and private institutions.

Cash was short everywhere. Currency was hoarded and many banks began to cash checks partly in hard funds and partly in clearinghouse scrip.

Business leaders such as J. P. Morgan issued statements intended to quiet the public's fears, but business conditions continued to worsen even over the Christmas holidays. On February 1, 1908, the large Orient Bank became the second New York institution to go under. The Bowery Mission there was feeding 2,000 more impoverished, unemployed men than ever before in its history. In Cleveland, Chicago, St. Louis and other industrial centers, the employment situation was equally bleak.

About the middle of 1907, the May group had decided to combine its two St. Louis stores, merging the respective store managements into one. This had little appeal for Ittleson, who had been running his own show at the May Company store. He told David May such a move would overburden the top echelon of executives of the one remaining store. Moreover, he said to May, he had been thinking for some time of starting a new type of financing business and had in fact discussed the possibility with a potential partner, A. D. Nast.

To this statement, David May is supposed to have replied, "Henry, you can do anything you want and go into any business you like, but I intend to insist on one thing—whatever you do, we are going to be your partners and furnish you with whatever capital you will need! Don't you go looking anywhere else for partners or money!"

And to that statement, May added, "Besides, why do you want to start such a business with only the little bit of capital you and Nast can put together? And where will you two get more capital as you need it if your business grows as you expect? With our backing, you can have the initial capital to start a really good-sized business and we'll be there to back you with more money when the need arises."

May's logic prevailed, and so it was that a compact was struck and Henry Ittleson prepared to give up his $20,000-a-year salary—a handsome income in those days—and organize a new business to be founded on a single, untested idea.

He embarked on several weeks of intensive activity, helping to arrange the transfer of the May store operations, while launching the plans for his new venture. One of his first decisions was to select a name for the new company. He chose "Commercial Credit and Investment Company," which he immediately shortened for ready reference to "C.C.I. Co."

3

A Billion-Dollar
Scrap of Paper

Henry Ittleson's first expression of his dream—one that was to return more than $1 billion in net profits over the next sixty years, with earnings in the following decade moving toward $100 million annually—was a financial projection, a budget, and an estimate of expected earnings. For this, he took a small piece of buff paper, 2 ½ by 4 inches, torn from a larger sheet and carefully made a penciled calculation of what he visualized as the needs and expectations of his first year's business. His conception had already been carefully plotted in his mind. There were no erasures or corrections in the entire statement.

He had already organized the staff of the company. As general manager, he would receive $8,000 a year, a sharp reduction from his previous earning power. He would take with him from the May Company an associate, Claude L. Hemphill, who had been his office manager there and who would assume the same responsibilities in the new enterprise. There were to be two clerks and an office boy, bringing the total monthly salary bill to $1,248.33. As his legal representatives, he had selected the firm of Stern and Haberman. The Gustave Stern and Henry Ittleson families were near neighbors and close friends. Julia Stern and Blanche Ittleson had gone through their first pregnancies together and had sons born on the very same day in October 1900.

Estimate Expense
1st year 1908. C. C. I. Co

Salaries
                                    CLH.   166.67
                                    Logan   75.00
                                    HJ.   666.66.
                                    Solicitor 200.—
                                    Cons   50—
                                    Boy   30—
                        1248.33   Asst.   60—

Int +
Dist   1166.67   Cap.   416.67
                                    Int ohn
Rent   75   150.000   750.
Ptg P&S   60.
                                    Rent   75
Atty   83.33
                                    Ptg Staty 60.
Sundries   395.   Post

              $3008.33   Atty   83.33
                 12
                 36109.
Keeping avge balance of: Merc Agency 50.
$40.000 = on hand   Telephones   20.
leaves 210.000 loanable   Insurance   125.
210.000 is 80% of 262,5.00   Loss   125.
This loaned on avge 90   Sundries   75.
day maturities will
net @ 4% Disk for 40 days   or 10500 or $42000
per year : net Profit of 6000 =
If we can do instead of 840.000 the 1st year
1.090.000 which means an addl int chgs
on 50.000 of $3000 we can make $10,000 addl
gross or 3000 addl net making total $13000 1st y.
we need $2800 a day in invoices =

The Security Building, St. Louis, Missouri

Ittleson carefully estimated total monthly expenses at $3,008.33, for an annual outlay of $36,000. Included in this amount was an "interest and discount" item of $14,000 to allow the company to have average borrowings during the year of $150,000 at 6%, plus a projected return on capital of $5,000. The amount of capital the May and Shoenberg interests would provide him, as individuals, would be $100,000 to earn the $5,000 return.

On the income side, he projected that his total available capital of $250,000 could produce gross interest charges of $42,000 for the year and a profit of $6,000. To earn this amount, he calculated that $40,000 could be maintained as unused funds, with the remaining $210,000 kept out on loans, earning a 4% discount for 90-day maturities. If the company's total loans for the year were higher than the estimated $840,000 and could top the million-dollar mark (he used a $1,090,000 figure), net profits would reach $13,000. (When the books first were closed on April 30, 1909—after nearly fifteen months of operation— the actual net for the period had more than doubled his forecast.)

One other figure from the projection should be noted. Although the business—and particularly the credit—outlook was bleak indeed, Ittleson intended to run a tight ship from a credit standpoint. Against his substantial $840,000 loan volume, he estimated that losses for the year would be no more than $1,500. (The total charge taken for "Bad and

Doubtful Accounts" was $647 when the first year's books were closed.)

This document, which may be unique of its kind in American business history, has been preserved and remains in the possession of the Ittleson family.

Ittleson was lining up office quarters and equipment while the Stern and Haberman firm filed incorporation papers with the office of the State Secretary of Missouri at Jefferson City. It was in anticipation of the granting of that charter that Henry Ittleson set out for his new place of business on the morning of February 11, 1908.

As he left Eddie O'Donnell's elevator, he had the bright nickel key to the office suite ready in his hand, but it was not needed. Claude Hemphill was already there and was instructing the two new members of the staff in their future duties. Everything was in place, awaiting the arrival of the new general manager. That was wiry, neat, quiet Claude Hemphill's way. He anticipated every responsibility Henry Ittleson expected of him and consistently maintained the impeccable good order of the business throughout the twenty-three years he was the "Mr. Inside" of C.C.I.

4

Open for Business!

The night before, Mr. Ittleson received word from his attorney, "Gus" Stern, that the new company's Articles of Association, which he had signed along with the other founders, David May, Moses Shoenberg, Louis D. Shoenberg, and Sydney M. Shoenberg, had been duly filed in the office of the St. Louis Recorder of Deeds on that Monday, February 10. The only technicality remaining was the actual granting of the Certificate of Incorporation, under the laws governing "manufacturing and business companies," by the Honorable John E. Swanger, Secretary of State of the State of Missouri, at the state capital, Jefferson City.

As was appropriate for the active head of the business, Henry Ittleson had selected the corner office of the three-room suite for his own use. This was Room 623. The remainder of the staff occupied the adjoining Rooms 600 and 601, one of which doubled as a conference room. Ittleson's office was a handsome one with a high ceiling; it offered a fine view of the city and the Mississippi River from four windows.

All hands occupied themselves with various tasks to get ready for business. As the day wore on, the expected message eventually came

from the offices of Stern & Haberman. The incorporation papers had
been approved and Commercial Credit and Investment Company was a
legal entity.

As an historical aside, two other enterprises were incorporated on
that same February 11. They were the Mississippi Valley Reduction
Company and the St. Louis Extraction and Reduction Company. Both
wound up their affairs, in 1910 and 1913 respectively, and have disappeared from the records.

Ittleson had made his plans for the new company well known among
his business contacts and friends through the Midwest and in the East.
He had recruited several individuals as potential sales agents on commission and now informed them that they could proceed to solicit
business in accordance with the plans and rates that he had previously
laid out. However, his main concern for the next two days was to
prepare for the organization meetings of the company's stockholders
and board of directors. Both gatherings had been set for February 18,
in the expectation that the incorporation procedures at Jefferson City
would take longer than they actually did.

The meetings were held as scheduled, in the company's conference
room. The stockholders met first. David May as the acknowledged
senior among the group, chaired the meeting, and Ittleson was secretary. The first business was to note that 1,000 shares of stock had been
subscribed to at a price of $100 per share. David May and his two
brothers-in-law, Louis D. and Moses Shoenberg, each purchased 330
shares and Henry Ittleson and Sydney M. Shoenberg were listed as
holders of five shares each.

In the minutes, it was noted that the company had been organized
and was empowered by its Certificate of Incorporation "to buy and sell
notes, accounts receivable and other commercial securities and pledge
the same, to buy and sell bonds, stocks and other negotiable securities
and pledge the same." This wording is somewhat broader and more
legalistic than the first "commercial notice" the new company published in Gould's *St. Louis Directory:* "We Buy the Active Open Accounts and Cash Daily Sales of Merchants and Manufacturers."

The meeting also approved a set of by-laws, including a definition of
the duties of the office of vice president and general manager, which
Ittleson would fill, as being "to manage the business of the company
and all property of the company shall be in his charge, and to exercise
the powers of the president in the absence of the latter from the state or
his inability to act for reasons of sickness."

Seven directors were elected to serve one-year terms. They were David May, Moses Shoenberg, Sydney M. Shoenberg, L. D. Shoenberg, Morton J. May, Dudley C. Shoenberg and Henry Ittleson.

This board met following the meeting of stockholders. They proceeded to elect David May president, Henry Ittleson vice president and general manager, Louis D. Shoenberg second vice president, and Claude L. Hemphill secretary and treasurer. The Mechanics-American National Bank of St. Louis was designated as the depository for the company's funds.

Now all decks were clear and the moment of embarkation for the new venture had arrived. A week passed before the first piece of business was entered on the books. Certain receivables were purchased from The Providence Jewelry Company, an organization about which existing records are sparse, except that it remained a client of C. C. I. Company for several years and traded with midwestern retail outlets.

It was another week before a second account was acquired, the local Mound City Chair Company. Then business began to come in a rush. In chronological order, to illustrate the wide diversity of the acceptance of the company's new service, the following clients were acquired during the next three months:

J. A. Ruhl Clothing Co. (Agency)
Gram & Glass Cap Co.
Baum Manufacturing Co.
Comfort Suspender Co.
E. Ernst Furniture Mfg. Co.
Delmar Mfg. Co.
Shumate Razor Co.
L. S. Frank Co.
E. & F. Mfg. Co. (Agency)
Adolph Selige Pub. Co.
Adolph E. Wendling Lbr. Co.
Star Upholstering Co.
L. B. Tebbetts & Sons Carriage Co. (Agency)
T. L. Horn Trunk Co. (Agency)
E. J. Schuster Printing Co.
Ferguson Lumber Co.
Monsanto Chemical Works
C. H. L. Beckers
W. C. Manley
Imperial Novelty & Scale Co.
Big Muddy River Cons. Coal Co.
Alf Bennett Lumber Co. (Agency)

Two names on the above list warrant special comment. The L. S. Frank Company was a direct mail, advertising and printers' representative concern located on a lower floor of the Securities Building. Louis Frank was Henry Ittleson's brother-in-law. Ten years younger than his sister Blanche, in later years he reveled in repeating the story of how he pestered Henry and Blanche when they were courting, and would only agree to leave them alone if his sister's suitor would give him "five cents" to clear out.

Louis Frank handled the company's promotional and printing activities from the beginning. Later, when the company headquarters was transferred to New York City, he served as its St. Louis representative, while continuing his own business. He eventually joined the company on a full-time basis in 1921 and, over the years until his retirement in 1951, was responsible at various times for advertising, public relations, personnel relations and office management functions.

The Monsanto Chemical Works went on the books on April 25. It had been founded in 1901 in St. Louis by John Francis Queeny, an employee of a drug distributing firm. Queeny operated his company, to which he had given his wife's maiden name, on a part-time basis, manufacturing saccharin, vanillin, caffeine and other flavoring agents in a 150-by-150-square-foot plant on the outskirts of the city. By 1908 he finally had built his business to a point where he felt justified in resigning from his regular job and devoting all his time to Monsanto. It was at this juncture that C. C. I. Company agreed to ease his tight cash-flow problems by paying cash for his customers' obligations, which were expanding rapidly. Despite the hard times of the period, Queeny's company flourished and went on to great success. As the worldwide Monsanto Company, it commands assets in the $2 billion range, with annual sales exceeding $3 billion.

While there was quite a broad geographical distribution among the firms appearing on this list of the company's first clients, most of them understandably had addresses in the St. Louis area. Some of these clients soon had discounted receivables of customers located in such relatively faraway places as Atlantic City, Pittsburgh, Chicago and Indianapolis, indications of how fast the network of the new credit service spread.

Another early client of the company, one that was to write a notable chapter in the history of the American chemical industry, was the Dow Chemical Company of Midland, Michigan. Herbert Henry Dow had founded this company in 1897 to manufacture bleaching powders, bromines and bromides and by 1905 had won a dominant position in the U.S. market for these products. At that juncture, he decided to enter the world market, which was dominated by a great German chemical combine. Dow received word directly from the German trust that unless he backed down from his plans to sell for export they would invade the American market and ruin him. Dow sent back a sharp rejection of the demand. *The Dow Story,* an official history of the Dow Company, recounts:

> Herbert Dow was feeling the pinch of hard times, too. . . . Perhaps the effects of the depression would not have been so severe had not the Germans continued their pressure on Dow Chemical to force it out of the European market. The price of bromides in the United States was cut from 15 cents a pound to 12 cents and then to 10½ cents. Even though Dow was shipping bromides to Germany and other European countries, profit margins were thin or nonexistent. . . . Dow decided the time had come in the fight with the Deutsche Bromkonvention to go to Germany and see for himself what the situation was. . . . The more Dow saw the more he became convinced that in all important respects the Dow Chemical Company had a more efficient plan than the German bromide makers. He also discovered the world demand for bromides was even greater than he had suspected, and that the overseas market offered tremendous possibilities for his own company. . . . There were some bright spots in that dismal depression year of 1908. Early in January Dow closed a contract with the Eastman Kodak Company to supply 100,000 pounds of bromides a year for five years, the beginning of a long and close business association. . . . Another bright spot for Dow was a report that the Germans were weakening in their offensive to force Dow to an agreement in the bromides war. . . . If a reasonable settlement could be reached, a great deal of pressure would be lifted from him and his company during one of the worst depressions the country had ever known. . . . (Years later a colleague would say: "We were bankrupt, but thank God nobody knew it."). . . . Certainly the Germans were not fully aware of the precarious financial condition of The Dow Chemical Company and Dow had no intention of showing any weakness. . . . The Germans finally withdrew from the American market and Dow gradually halted his shipments of bromides to Germany. The rest of the world market became free competitive territory and remained that way. Prices began to rise in late 1909 to their prewar levels. . . . It was a costly victory for Dow but it had its rewards. . . . He had learned that the market for chemicals which he could produce was a far greater market than he had ever imagined. . . . All this knowledge was not very helpful as the economic depression continued on into 1909.*

David May

The Dow Company's financial resources obviously were hard pressed from the cost of the victory that had been won, and there was much work facing the management to consolidate and normalize its markets. It was at this point, in 1909, that Commercial Credit and Investment Company offered to provide financial support and the Dow name went on the books on October 13, 1909. It remained for a number of years.

Illustrative of the outreach of the C. C. I. Company's sales efforts is the list of other companies approved for credit on the same date as the Dow Company. They included coal companies, glove companies, machine tool companies, knit goods manufacturers, watchmakers and producers or distributors of kitchen ranges, patent medicines, umbrellas and, once again, tools and scrapers.

5

"Being Profit for the Period — $29,373.67"

As the months of 1908 wore on, business flowed into the new company at a steadily increasing pace. The directors approved 27 new contracts in June, 24 more at their next meeting in October, and so on. In February 1909, the first anniversary month, the company acquired $112,148 in receivables. Nearly $900,000 worth of business had been placed on the books in the first year, meeting the founder's original projection.

The purchase of producers' and distributors' receivables, with recourse on the seller, at a discount from the face value of the invoices and for indirect collection obviously was a service for which there existed a large and unanswered need. A vacuum in the nation's financial structure existed and Commercial Credit and Investment Company had moved in to occupy it, as the company's immediate reception and success clearly demonstrated.

Henry Ittleson never claimed that he had discovered an entirely new and unique business technique. Certainly, no organization existed prior to the establishment of C.C. & I. that had its breadth of operations and impact on so many industries. However, there are a scattering of records of earlier undertakings of the same character.

26

Arthur R. Jones and John L. Little, who had been selling books on the instalment plan in Chicago about 1904, began buying up the accounts receivable contracts of other similarly engaged outfits. Their company became the National Trust and Credit Company in 1905, and eventually that company became a significant factor (after changing its name to National Bond and Investment Company) in automobile retail and wholesale financing. National Bond was acquired by Commercial Credit Company of Baltimore in 1941. It is to be noted that the principal emphasis of the National Bond Company was always on handling receivables involving sales of consumer products.

Commercial Credit Company was a principal competitor of Ittleson and his successors from the post-World War I period into the 1970's and remains so. It was founded in 1912 by the late Alexander E. Duncan on the same accounts receivable financing concept as Commercial Credit and Investment Company. Duncan had initiated an abortive entry into the financing business in 1910 and organized Commercial Credit two years later, leading it to great success in the ensuing years. Commercial Credit was acquired by Control Data Corporation in 1968.

At the first anniversary meeting of the directors of Commercial Credit and Investment Company, held on February 9, 1909, all of the officers were reelected and an additional depository relationship with the National Bank of Commerce of St. Louis was opened. This gave the Company three "line" banks—the Mercantile Trust Company had been added the previous April. Of special significance was the authorization given to the management to invest up to $100,000 in piano leases, mortgages and instalment obligations. This action may have marked the company's first entry into true consumer financing.

The employment of a Mr. A. P. Mackie to solicit business for the company on a 12½% commission arrangement was approved, and he was given a drawing account of $350 a month. The company's first potential credit loss was reported to the board. The Ferguson Lumber Company was delinquent on an item of $205.33, and it was noted that the matter was "gone over in detail" by the board members. It was decided to charge the full amount against the reserve for contingencies. It is also interesting to note that this situation was referred to as a "status." That is a word of art that has been used in the C.I.T. organization to this day to describe any account where collectibility is in question.

The next meeting of the directors on April 8, 1909, was notable for the approval of eight new contracts. Most of these were with concerns well outside the immediate St. Louis area, giving evidence of the geographical extension of the company's sales activities. Accounts

approved at this and the previous board meeting included the Mutual
Lumber Company of Kansas City; the Warner Keffer China Company
of East Liverpool, Ohio; the John E. F. Corr Piano Company of Battle
Creek, Michigan; the Claugh, Warren Company of Detroit; the Krell
French Piano Company of Newcastle, Indiana; and the Anderson Car-
riage Manufacturing Company of Anderson, Indiana.

The new company then had its first independent audit by a public
accounting firm, for the period from February 11, 1908, to April 30,
1909. This was conducted by the Investors Audit Company of
Chicago, which reported to the board on the examination of the company's books under the date of June 25, 1909.

On April 30, the company held accounts receivable totaling
$271,145, surpassing Ittleson's most optimistic projection for the first
year of business. All borrowed funds, amounting to $110,000, were
owed to the "Famous" store, otherwise the May-Shoenberg interests.
There had been no bank borrowings. Total assets were $306,994,
including the original paid-in capital of $100,000 that remained un-
changed.

The company had total income for the period of $60,050 and ex-
penses of $30,677. The balance, as the auditors stated, "being profit
for the period of $29,373.67." From this, a dividend of $4,708 was
paid, beginning a series of disbursements to its stockholders that has
continued with unbroken regularity to the present day.

There was absolutely no item for taxes among the expense accounts!
The reserve for "Bad and Doubtful Accounts" was $309. Mackie was
clearly the principal producer of new business outside the company
staff, having rolled up commissions of $1,540 in the first three months
of his employment.

As a general comment, the auditors affirmed to the directors: "The
books and accounts were very neatly and accurately kept and the
system used is well suited to the present business of the Company. The
management appeared to be exceptionally well informed regarding
every detail of the office work, and we have no doubt that your interests are being well and ably guarded."

6

The St. Louis Years

The company's growing business and the accompanying expansion of the office staff soon made the three-room suite in the Security Building uncomfortably crowded. In 1911, a move was made to larger quarters on the third floor of the building. The room numbers were 310–316. The company's archives and the reminiscences of several members of the office force paint a graphic picture of the way of life and tell the story of business success that occurred in those offices of Commercial Credit and Investment Company.

* * *

Advertising notice of Commercial Credit and Investment Company in Gould's *St. Louis Directory* 1911:

> We buy your open accounts for cash. You make your own collections.

* * *

Frank P. Rohlman, early employee, by letter, October 24, 1949:

> You will note in the group picture a number on the door of 312. That door led into a large office which was one of the offices comprising a suite of offices located in the southeast corner of the Security Building, 4th and

Locust. Looking beyond the group you see an open door which led into a small office. That office was Mr. Claude Hemphill's office. In the office with him was his secretary, Elvira Schmidt. Directly across the corridor was Mr. Henry Ittleson's office. His office was on the 4th St. side in the southeast corner of the building. The windows in his office were covered with heavy drapes which he usually kept drawn. The furniture comprised of a mahogany table in back of him and his executive desk. The only light he used in the room was the light on his desk. Directly in front of his desk was a large mahogany table which was used for directors' meetings. Toward the north, along the 4th St. side, was a reception room and switchboard and Mr. Ittleson's secretary. . . .

Our business at that time was strictly financing on Accounts Receivable. Frank Collins and Mr. Kantorwitz were account clerks making up individual cards on each invoice purchased on respective schedules from our clients. Milton Russack and the writer handled all the schedules which were checked against Dun and Bradstreet's credit books. We then checked invoices and evidence of delivery against schedules. After this operation was completed, a check was drawn which we presented to Mr. Ittleson together with schedules and evidences and either he or Claude Hemphill completed the transaction with their signature to the checks.

The rating of these schedules were handled by Ray Noonan who was then our office boy. Returning to the procedure on the purchase schedule, originally the rate was 1/25 of 1% a day. Later it was reduced to 1/30 of 1% a day. We deducted 3% from the face amount of the schedule to cover service charge. We deducted 20% of the face amount of the schedule as a reserve to cover discounts, returned merchandise, slow accounts or bad accounts. We advanced 77% of the face amount of the schedule; that was the amount of the check drawn and sent to our client. . . .

Over and above those duties performed by the writer, I also set up a recapitulation sheet so that I could give Mr. Ittleson instantly any information covering over-all figure or figures covering individual accounts. This recapitulation sheet was very helpful inasmuch as when Mr. Ittleson wanted information, he wanted it now; not after hours of research. From my recapitulation sheet, I was able to tell him the amount of Accounts Receivable purchased up to that respective day of the year together with comparison of the amount of purchases up to the respective day of the previous year together with the amount of reserve together with the amounts of service deducted and also as amounts to service earned. Also these same figures to each respective account.

* * *

Ray J. Noonan, office boy and clerk, from interview, March 27, 1974:

Henry Ittleson was a very responsible man and a very important man and everything had to be just so. The only time you could go in his office was when he called for you. He worked long hours—came in at regular time—till five or six o'clock. We worked a full day on Saturdays.

Mr. Ittleson went to New York quite a bit—on business I would imagine. He didn't take many vacations as far as I remember. His health was fine. He was a big, strong man.

I did mathematics work, ran errands, handled mail. I never went to Mr. Ittleson's home. I never saw his son in the office. All my connections were with Famous-Barr back in those days. I dealt with Mr. Butler, secretary of Famous-Barr. Anything that Mr. Ittleson wanted I would have to take to Mr. Butler, who was secretary to the Shoenbergs and Mays. He reported to them—he was their representative.

Mr. Hemphill was a very gentle man, very well-educated and well-equipped to handle the job. But they were all under the supervision of Mr. Ittleson and whatever he said went, and that was it. He was very fine to the employees.

I left before they moved. I had an inkling they were going to move. I could see they were getting too big for St. Louis.

* * *

Louis S. Frank, longtime C.I.T. executive and brother-in-law of Henry Ittleson, from interview, January 11, 1957:

The original purpose of CCIC—and still one of the prime purposes— was to provide a financial service for people who couldn't get it from any other source. CIT became expert at judging people's moral value—the intangibles of integrity and business acumen and industry—whereas the banks insisted on judging just the cold black-and-white figures of financial value. We loaned money to people who could not get money from conventional sources—not because they were bad risks but because they had difficulty proving by the accepted criteria that they were good risks.

At the beginning, accounts-receivable financing was the basis of the business. Sometimes it was on a notification, sometimes a non-notification, basis. But that wasn't important. We probably weren't the only people offering this kind of credit in those days. There may have been others. But ours was the first successful company. We were successful, first and foremost, because of Ittleson's personality and character and because of the way he molded the company—all the people he gathered about him—to this character. Everything was flexible at CCIC. There were no unbreakable rules—except those of absolute honesty in doing business. Ittleson was a merchandising man, and he could talk the language of the people he did business with. From the beginning, his service was *custom*-tailored to the needs of the people we dealt with. There was no rigid formula that had to be followed, no absolutely standard contract.

* * *

Excerpt from minutes of a meeting of the board of directors, February 8, 1910:

Mr. Ittleson took occasion at this time to speak of the work of the secretary-treasurer, stating that the same had been very satisfactory and that he had had during the two years of Commercial Credit & Investment Company's activities the loyal and diligent co-operation of Mr. Hemphill, which had contributed much toward the progress of the Company.

* * *

Claude L. Hemphill, office manager, letter to Frank P. Rohlman, July 23, 1913:

F.P. Rohlman, Esq.,
c/o Howald Hotel,
Hamilton, O.

Dear Rohlman:

We received the Anderson Tool Company's collections this morning, and also a letter from them explaining the re-organization situation. I wired Mr. Gorman last night and got a reply this morning that he will be in Anderson early Monday morning; so try your best to get through checking the balance and as far as possible in the work by that time.

Meet Giesen at Hanlin Hotel Thursday night 24th—catch 6:18 CH&D train at Hamilton—eat your dinner in the cafe-parlor car on this train— take street car front of station in Cin & get off at Vine St. walking to Hanlin Hotel—return to Hamilton that night. Tell Giesen all the troubles you find—he will help you, if you need any assistance.

* * *

Excerpt from minutes of annual meeting of stockholders, January 10, 1912:

The vice-president and secretary and all subscribers to said increase were, upon motion, directed to execute any and all documents required for carrying into effect the increase of capital stock aforesaid from One Hundred Thousand Dollars ($100,000) to Five Hundred Thousand Dollars ($500,000), said capital when increased to consist of Five Thousand (5000) shares of common stock of the par value of One Hundred Dollars ($100) each, and of which stock all of the same shall be issued.

* * *

Excerpt from minutes of meeting of board of directors, January 10, 1912:

All of this met with the approval of the directors and they expressed themselves as pleased with the showing the Company had made during the preceding eleven months, and on motion of Mr. D. May, seconded by Mr. Thomas May, it was resolved that out of the net earnings for the eleven months ending December 31st, 1911, amounting to $101,212.55, a regular annual dividend of 100 Per Cent of the capital stock, be declared, amounting to $100,000.00.

* * *

Excerpt from minutes of meeting of board of directors, January 14, 1913:

The directors expressed themselves as highly gratified at the success shown by the Company and a vote of thanks was tendered to Mr. Henry Ittleson, vice-president and general manager, for the efficient manner in which the Company's business had been handled.

* * *

Excerpt from minutes of meeting of board of directors, October 31, 1913:

The chairman announced that the first matter for the consideration of the meeting was to consider and vote upon a proposition to increase the capital stock of said Commercial Credit & Investment Company from Five Hundred Thousand Dollars ($500,000.00), its present authorized capital, to One Million, Two Hundred Fifty Thousand Dollars ($1,250,000.00), said capital when so increased to consist of Twelve Thousand Five Hundred (12,500) shares of common stock of the par value of One Hundred Dollars ($100.00) each. A resolution embodying said proposition was thereupon offered by Mr. Henry Ittleson, duly seconded, submitting to the stockholders said proposition for approval, and after the due appointment of canvassers and the due canvassing of votes for and against the proposition, it was declared . . . that the unanimous vote of all of the stockholders was in favor of said proposition, and the same was thereupon duly announced by the chairman to have carried. . . .

The chairman then announced that the next object of the meeting was to consider a report respecting the assets and liabilities of said Company. The following report was thereupon made, showing the present assets and liabilities and net assets of the Company: to-wit:

Assets

Cash	$ 163,157.14
Bills receivable	618,045.28
Accounts receivable	967,149.59
Insurance, etc. paid in advance	1,201.33
Stocks	6,575.00
	$1,756,128.34

Liabilities

Bills payable	$1,224,737.08
Accounts payable	28,272.61
Capital stock	500,000.00
Surplus	3,118.65
	$1,756,128.34

* * *

Excerpt from minutes of meeting of board of directors, January 19, 1914:

Cash on hand, accounts payable, and general resume of the business were gone over in detail, and the secretary reported the following concerns were in financial trouble:

> Ashner-Canmann-Taylor Woodenware Co.
> Burlington Buggy Co.
> J. H. Menge & Sons
> Druss Bros.
> Sibley Menge Brick & Coal Co.

The total amount of money that we have in these accounts aggregates some $4,000, and we expect to collect the majority of this. There will probably be a loss on Sibley Menge Brick & Coal Company and possibly something on J. H. Menge & Sons, but it was estimated the amount would not be over $7,500, the amount left over from previous year which had been set aside to take care of possible credit losses on the Breeden Medicine Co., and Kansas City Scale Sales Company. The collections from debtors, and over $5,000 from the bonding companies, has practically paid out these accounts on our books, hence the $7,500 is available for any possible credit losses on accounts outstanding now.

* * *

Excerpt from minutes of meeting of board of directors, June 11, 1914:

Report was also made to the directors of the efforts that were being made to secure business from auto truck and other manufacturers who sell their product on time payment, securing the indebtedness by lien rights covered by conditional sales contracts and mortgages. The rate quoted on such business would be lower than our regular rate, and in some extreme cases, where the business was highly desirable, it might run as low as 13% or 14% per annum. This met with the approval of the directors.

* * *

Excerpt from minutes of meeting of board of directors, January 12, 1915:

On motion made by Mr. Henry Ittleson, duly seconded by Mr. Morton J. May, Col. Moses Shoenberg was unanimously elected chairman of the board for the ensuing year, Col. Shoenberg not voting. Col. Shoenberg then took the chair.

On motion made by Mr. S. M. Shoenberg, duly seconded by Mr. Thos. May, Mr. Henry Ittleson was unanimously elected president for the ensuing year, Mr. Henry Ittleson not voting.

Over the years, Ittleson's equity in the company had steadily increased. Although he received only 5 shares of the 1,000 issued at the founding of the company, by the time of the annual meeting of 1911 he held 400 of the 1,000 outstanding shares and was the largest stockholder. This holding yielded him a dividend for the year of $40,000. As he assumed the presidency of the company, his equity grew to 5,000 shares out of 12,500 outstanding. The increases in his holdings were derived by acquiring portions of the shares of David May, Moses Shoenberg and Louis D. Shoenberg, originally the major shareholders.

* * *

Frank P. Rohlman, early employee, by letter, December 28, 1949:

I know I express the sentiments of Mr. Noonan as well as myself in saying that we value very highly the early years of our training and our association with Mr. Henry Ittleson and Mr. Claude Hemphill. We worked hard; we enjoyed our work and we take great pride in knowing that it was the efforts of those eight men under the leadership of Mr. Henry Ittleson which permitted this company to reach the wonderful position that it holds today in the financial development of our great country.

* * *

7

Moving to the
National Stage

In 1913, the important William Barr Dry Goods Company management found itself overextended financially. It had contracted for the huge (in those days) Railway Exchange Building at Sixth and Olive Streets in St. Louis, and the owners and senior executives of the sixty-year-old company let it be known that they would entertain a purchase offer. Again, the May-Shoenberg interests moved promptly to acquire the Barr business. This move was undertaken not only to expand their position in the St. Louis department store market but also to acquire ownership of the Railway Exchange Building. The completion of the purchase in 1913 placed them in a position to combine the stores and solve a facilities problem that had long confronted them because of the timeworn and overcrowded conditions of the Famous store building.

In 1913, Commercial Credit and Investment Company also moved to the Railway Exchange Building, owned by its principal backers. The company's staff had continued to grow along with the volume of business, and the transfer to larger quarters in suite 717–723 of the Sixth and Olive showplace of downtown St. Louis was a welcome one for all concerned.

The character of the company's business had been experiencing momentous changes. The volume of loans made in 1914 crossed the $7 million mark, for a clear gain of $1 million over the 1913 figure. In each of the years 1912 and 1913, similar $1 million increases in loan volume had been achieved. The list of loan clients continued to expand geographically as well as numerically, with a growing list of new contracts covering firms located throughout the Northeast, the South and the Middle West. The Rocky Mountains had not yet been crossed by the company's sales efforts. The parochial nature of the business in the early days, centering around St. Louis, had completely disappeared. Only five firms with St. Louis addresses were placed on the company's books in the entire year of 1914.

To serve its broader markets properly, from time to time the company opened bank accounts in other cities to augment its principal St. Louis banking arrangements. The new institutions included the Chase National Bank, New York; First National Bank, Cleveland; Public National Bank, New York; Fourth Street National Bank, Philadelphia; Corn Exchange National Bank, Chicago, and the Whitney Central National Bank, New Orleans.

The amount of funds required by the company had outgrown the capacity of the Famous Company and the May-Shoenberg interests, which together had been the sole providers of borrowed funds in the early days. Direct lines were established with banks in both St. Louis and elsewhere. These in due time became the main sources of working capital. The first such loan recorded was one of $100,000 in March 1913 with the Mechanics-American National Bank of St. Louis, for one year at 5%. The company's need for funds was also met in part by occasional infusions of paid-in capital by the original founding group.

A subtle but constantly more significant change in the type of products covered by the company's receivables portfolio was also occurring. Most of the early clientele were manufacturers and distributors selling to other businessmen—either to wholesalers, retailers or users of equipment or raw or semi-finished materials. Individual receivables of this kind were relatively large by the very nature of the transactions involved. After several years of this, the company's business began to demonstrate a strong trend toward products that were more consumer-oriented. This shift involved a new clientele of dealers selling individual items directly to consumers, with the obligations of the purchasers being accepted as collateral. However, the merchant was responsible for making collections and for paying the debt itself, or replacing it with "good" collateral if the purchaser failed to meet his payments. The list of such products included buggies and carriages, pianos (a strong item), bicycles, guns, gas ranges, house furnishings, trunks and the like. By and large, the individual invoices created by this business were smaller in amount than the industrial-retailing receivables and may have been more profitable on an item-by-item basis while easing the constant need to seek more borrowed money.

From the beginning, the company's loss experience had been excellent and the expansion of its markets and types of receivables financed had introduced no serious credit problems. This led to an action by the directors at their first 1915 meeting, on January 7. Mr. Ittleson reported to the board that since the inception of the company $26,931 had been paid to four credit insurance and surety companies as premiums for credit-loss insurance. Claims paid by the companies had amounted to $11,051, giving the underwriters a $15,879 gross profit. He recommended that, in view of this experience, the officers be authorized to decide on an account-by-account basis whether surety bonds should be purchased, and that the company self-insure the remaining business by adding in each case the equivalent of a normal premium payment to its loss reserve account. This was approved and the practice of purchasing outside blanket loss protection by the organization soon ended completely and has never been revived.

As the company approached the close of its seventh year, the management realized that for many reasons it had outgrown its original St. Louis base. The ever-intensified need to find new sources for larger amounts of working capital to support its increasing volume of loans, the concentration of more and more of its business in the populous eastern centers and the determination of the officers that the enterprise should become recognized as a truly national rather than a regional company, all dictated a move eastward—to New York City, the nation's financial capital.

Ittleson had been investigating this possibility for some time and at the annual meeting of stockholders held on January 12, 1915, this resolution was unanimously adopted:

> That the board of directors of this Company, acting therein by and through its president, be authorized to establish an office and place of business of this Company in the City of New York, State of New York, to obtain a permit for the present Missouri corporation, Commercial Credit & Investment Company to do business in the State of New York under such name as may be granted by said State, and to make and adopt such changes in the present name of said Company as will conform to the requirements of the State of New York, or, at the option of said president, to incorporate a company under the laws of the State of New York or of such other state as he may determine.

President Ittleson moved rapidly. He reported at the February 11 meeting of the directors that he had signed a three-year lease for 2,630 square feet of office space in the Adams Building at 61 Broadway, in the Manhattan financial district. The space would be available by March 15 and the rent would be $5,000 a year, with a concession of 45 days' free rent and payments beginning on May 1.

He also reported that the firm of Stern & Haberman, working with New York counsel, had determined that the most feasible way to organize the company for doing business in New York State would be to create a "trust estate" under the laws of Massachusetts. He advised that a decision on this action was still pending to allow for further investigation of other possibilities.

The physical movement of the headquarters was the first order of business. This was Claude Hemphill's responsibility. It is well documented that the company's offices in St. Louis closed at the regular hour on Friday, March 12, and opened at 8 A.M. the following Monday morning in New York, with every desk and file in place. With characteristic Hemphill efficiency, a Pullman car and a baggage car were chartered for the move. The twenty-seven transferred employees and their families traveled eastward on the same train with the company's office equipment.

Among those who made the move to New York was Frank W.

Collins, the original office boy of 1908 who had advanced rapidly and of whom more will be heard later. Others among the core group of early employees elected not to leave St. Louis, decisions that may have been costly ones for some of them. The firm of Stern & Haberman continued as the company's legal counsel in St. Louis, and Louis S. Frank, with two part-time aides, kept the company represented in the city of its founding.

The second program to give the company broader national stature involved the "Massachusetts trust" form of organization. In laymen's terms, this meant transferring the capital accounts of all the existing stockholders to the trust, with the directors of the company then becoming trustees of the new entity. Among other factors, this type of organization offered certain tax advantages under the new federal income tax law, when compared with the tax impact borne by a closely held corporation.

The trust came into being on March 29, 1915. The name chosen for it was "Commercial Investment Trust," retaining two elements of the original name. Thus, the initials "C.C. & I." passed out of usage and the now-permanent identifying initials "C.I.T." came into being for the first time.

As a footnote, Commercial Credit and Investment Company, with nominal capitalization of $5,000, remained in existence until August 22, 1918, when it was dissolved.

8

"Paper Taken in Payment of Pleasure Vehicles"

For reasons that the company records do not disclose, in 1915 both business volume and earnings declined from the prior year. This had not happened before. The decreases were not great, 1915 volume being $6,603,918, compared with 1914's $7,016,918, while profits were $150,000 against $187,500. Perhaps the move to New York and the further redirection of the marketing efforts were at least partly responsible.

There were indeed some unusual transactions appearing on the books. In August 1915, a loan of $60,000 was made to the Interboro Brewing Company of New York. The collateral for this loan was forty New York saloon licenses together with notes of the forty saloon-keepers. The licenses, as collateral, were valued at $1,500 each. Various directors of the brewery, "some quite well to do," also endorsed the note for the loan, which was repayable at the rate of $1,200 weekly.

Another loan was made at the same time to the Lutz and Schramm Company of Pittsburgh. This was for $150,000 to purchase pickles, cabbages, tomatoes, etc., for their packing plant. The loan was secured by the inventory of raw crops, any finished products and a bond issue on the entire plant. Lutz and Schramm went into receivership and

C.I.T. eventually acquired, and then disposed of, the firm's entire assets.

Heretofore—and almost uniformly for nearly another decade—the industrial financing business done by the company was on an accounts receivable basis. This meant that the borrower's accounts, owed to him by his customers, were taken as collateral for the loan but the borrower was responsible for collecting these accounts and/or paying off the loan whether his customers paid *him* or not. However, with its new spirit of innovation, in at least one of its 1915 transactions the company entered into a different mode of financing, close to the long-established business of so-called old-line factoring.

This was with the American Auto Press Company, which was manufacturing and selling machine tools to the Selson Engineering Company, Ltd., of London, England. Britain, of course, was at war at the time. C.I.T. was to pay all labor and material costs of the manufacturer, receive a 25% deposit from Selson when the order was placed, retain a factor's lien on the equipment being produced and on all other inventories of the American company, and collect from the buyer its remaining 75% due when the orders were delivered to Selson.

Another point of interest in 1915 was the establishment of a line of credit for $250,000 with the leading investment house of Goldman, Sachs & Company. This was the first of many examples of how the move to the New York financial center resulted in creating new sources of borrowed funds for the company.

The imaginative search for new methods of providing its financial resources and services to the business community had resulted in many highly special kinds of transactions. As 1915 closed, C.I.T. was on the eve of one of the boldest and most successful changes in corporate direction in its history.

It has already been reported that in June 1914 the directors approved a program "to secure business from auto, truck and other manufacturers who sell their product [*sic*] on time payment, securing the indebtedness by lien rights covered by conditional sales contracts and mortgages." The names of a number of such vehicle dealers had appeared on the company's books almost from the earliest days. They included:

Anderson Carriage Manufacturing Co.	Broadway Vehicle Co.
L. B. Tebbetts & Son Carriage Co.	Riefling Carriage Co.
Robinson Fire Apparatus Co.	Universal Motor Truck Co.
Burlington Buggy Co.	Atterbury Motor Car Co.

Dayton Auto Truck Co.

To C.I.T.'s alert management, there were many signs that the financing of motor vehicle sales on a significant scale—both sales from the manufacturer to the dealer and the dealer to the retail customer—was a fast-growing and promising market that was wholly adaptable to the company's experience, business methods and credit-granting philosophy. The volume of vehicle-dealer receivables already on its books suggested this, as did the fast-climbing rate of automobile sales. Passenger car units sold in 1913 numbered 451,500, in 1914, 548,139, and the rate for 1915 promised to approach the 900,000 mark. In addition, it had not escaped the C.I.T. group's attention that in 1915 John North Willys, at the urging of an associate, Edward S. Maddock, had organized the Guaranty Securities Company in Toledo, Ohio, for the express purpose of financing the wholesale and retail sales of Willys-Overland cars. From both the advertising they saw and reports from the press and elsewhere, it was evident that Willys dealers were avidly grasping the opportunity to abandon a cash-only sales policy and offer their prospects instalment credit accommodations.

C.I.T.'s management decided to seek an entry into the business of financing automobiles and realized that this financing must take two forms. The first would be to pay the manufacturer on shipment for cars delivered to his dealers for sale out of inventory. The second would be the financing of the instalment receivables taken by dealers when they made sales on deferred-payment terms to their customers.

Ittleson elected to approach this market along the same lines that the company was using to finance many other products—to make an arrangement with a financially strong manufacturer to provide financing services both for the manufacturer and his dealers and to have the manufacturer's guarantee behind each transaction as a final measure of security.

The Studebaker Corporation, with its factory and headquarters at South Bend, Indiana, was one of the nation's largest and most prestigious car manufacturers, with products that bore an excellent reputation for quality and durability. Its cars were particularly popular in the western states, where hard driving over range roads was the rule and vehicles had to "stand up."

Through New York banking connections, Ittleson arranged an approach to the Studebaker management in the fall of 1915 and within three months an agreement had been reached in approximately the form Ittleson had visualized.

The efficient Hemphill swung into action at once, addressing a letter to the Stern & Haberman firm in St. Louis that reads in part:

IMPORTANT!   QUICK!   January 8, 1916

Gentlemen:

We have closed an arrangement with one of the largest pleasure car manufacturers in the United States, to handle direct from their dealers the paper taken in payment of pleasure vehicles.

The arrangement is that there will be at least one-third paid down in cash, and the balance to be paid by notes of not to exceed eight equal monthly payments, a note for each payment. The note will be negotiable and be secured in every instance by proper lien instrument required by the state in which the sale is made, properly acknowledged, filed or recorded to comply with the laws of the several states.

We have agreed upon a universal form of conditional sales contract, which I am enclosing to you herein. It is my understanding that this sales contract would be good in any state in the United States where a conditional sales contract is good. *If this is not correct,* please advise wherein it is not correct.

All of the advice that we have from you in relation to the requirements on conditional sales contracts is two years or more old, and inasmuch as your original data compiled on this subject differed on some states from the book on conditional sales published by Haring, of Buffalo, we consider it necessary that you compile for us immediately new data.

Our customer advises the following to be the result of his legal investigation, not taken from any book:

In the following states, conditional sales contracts do not need to be recorded or filed in order to retain security on motor cars as against the claims of all parties:

[14 states listed]

Our customer advises in the following states conditional sales contracts must be recorded or filed without delay in order to retain security on motor cars as against claims of third parties, *but that they do not need to be acknowledged or proven:*

[18 states listed]

Our customer advises in the following states conditional sales contracts must be acknowledged by the purchaser in person or be proven by oath by one or more subscribing witnesses and be recorded without delay in order to retain security on motor cars as against claims of all parties:

[6 states listed]

Our customer advises in the following state conditional sales contracts must be acknowledged by the *seller* and be recorded without delay in order to retain security on motor cars as against claims of all parties:

[1 state listed]

Our customer advises in the following states conditional sales contracts must be acknowledged by the purchaser in person and be recorded without delay in order to retain security on motor cars as against the claims of all parties:

[4 states listed]

Our customer advises in the following states conditional sales contracts are not valid as to claims of all parties, even though acknowledged and recorded:

[4 states listed]

I have given you all of the above in detail so that you would know the opinion of the other party and would check each one up, verifying if the same is correct as of today, and advising us in detail any difference of opinion you may have. . . .

In those states which require acknowledgment, please let us have the form necessary, so we may have the same printed on the back of the conditional sales contract, so that all that it is necessary for the dealer to do is to have it signed up and acknowledged. You know that the majority of notaries around the country, particularly in the small towns, do not know the required form to be used, even in their own state. Have as many states use the same form of acknowledgment as possible, in order that we may use the same form of conditional sales contract for as many states as possible.

You understand we will have to print the back of these conditional sales contracts different in each case of where the acknowledging or the recording is different, and in order to have as few forms as possible, we want one form to fit as many states as possible. . . .

I realize that this is some work, but this is a big proposition with us. It means one of the biggest deals we have ever put over and we want to get it launched before anyone else beats us to this method of financing. There are some 4000 dealers that we have to deal with, and, of course, it is impossible for us to get in touch with all of them in one day, so it has been agreed by our customer and ourselves that we will go after the conditional sales states first, or, as a matter of fact, those states that require no filing or recording, and then continue on down the line as fast as we can; so please start in at the top of this list and let us have as many states daily as you possibly can, sending a bunch off on Monday night. . . .

Very truly yours,

C. M. Hemphill

Secretary

Stern & Haberman completed their work of verification and C. C. Hanch, treasurer of the Studebaker Corporation, acknowledged the completion of the agreement in the following excerpted letter:

South Bend, Ind.
Feb. 2, 1916

Commercial Investment Trust:

Desiring to stimulate the sale of automobiles through our retail dealers and agencies by affording them facilities for the negotiation and sale of notes taken by them to evidence deferred payments upon the machines sold by them, we hereby propose that you purchase from our automobile dealers their retail customers' paper acceptable to you, consisting of notes, contracts, mortgages and leases, taken by them in the sale of new Studebaker automobiles and commercial cars, upon the written guaranty hereto attached, and that you will receive and remit for same at your New York or St. Louis offices as may be most convenient for our dealers, provided, however, we reserve the right to hereafter elect upon written notice thereof to you, to approve the credit of the makers and endorsers of the above described motor car paper presented to you for purchase, as a condition precedent to any liability under the guaranty as hereto attached. You shall confine your purchases of motor car paper to Studebaker automobile dealers and will not purchase motor car paper from other automobile dealers without our consent, with the exception of commercial car paper of such motor car dealers as you have been doing business with more than one month prior to this date. It is understood that such paper as is purchased by you hereunder shall not be hypothecated or resold.

The letter then stated that dealers would be required to collect in cash not less than one-third of the list price on each car sold and the balance was to be financed by not more than eight monthly payments. The interest charged would be "at the current rate prevailing in the vicinity where the car was sold" but would not be less than 6%. A dealer would receive 90% of each monthly payment when collected, with 10% of the payment held in reserve. The total reserve would be paid over to him when the customer completed his payments. Customers would be required to purchase fire and theft insurance on their vehicles, with C.I.T. to arrange this coverage.

Studebaker required that C.I.T. not finance the sales of any other dealers besides Studebaker, except for relationships that were already established, and Studebaker agreed not to guarantee the instalment financing of their cars by anyone but C.I.T.

The contract with Studebaker was reported to the C.I.T. board of directors on February 14, together with information that arrangements had been made with the American Automobile Insurance Company to provide the required fire, theft and transportation insurance on the financed automobiles. It was also reported that the St. Louis office would be expanded to handle all Studebaker transactions originating west of the Allegheny Mountains.

Since the western states were the major market for Studebaker cars, by April it was found necessary to have C.I.T. representation on the West Coast. This was accomplished not by opening an office there, but by designating certain Studebaker employees as C.I.T. representatives.

The C.I.T.-Studebaker program was a success from the beginning. Early in 1917, with less than a year of trial, C.I.T. was able to prepare a promotional advertising brochure addressed to all Studebaker dealers that was prefaced by the following letter:

T. Gray Coburn, Pres.

COBURN MOTOR CAR COMPANY, Inc.

Distributors of
STUDEBAKER AUTOMOBILES

Coburn Block
Granby Street Norfolk, Va.

February 8, 1917.

Mr. C. L. Hemphill, Secretary,
Commercial Investment Trust,
61 Broadway,
New York, N.Y.

My dear Sir:

Replying to yours of the 5th instant, asking for my honest opinion of your plan, and service to Studebaker dealers: space will not permit me to say what I would really like, or what your plan and service merit.

Briefly, however, I consider both your plan for financing dealers for Winter* cars, as well as that of purchasing the paper of dealers' customers, and more particularly the latter, to be complete and ideal. It has enabled us to make many sales which we otherwise would have lost, and

---

*This refers to the prevalent practice of permitting dealers to build up inventories of vehicles that would not find purchasers until spring, driving conditions being what they were in the colder months. Often, such cars were stored with the wheels off to protect the tires of the day. This service also helped the manufacturers as it permitted them to stay in production even when sales were slow.

I know that some of our dealers have increased their business on account of some peculiar local conditions, conservatively from two to three hundred per cent. I have never heard a criticism; on the contrary, nothing but praise from all who have used it.

I consider this plan especially adaptable and desirable for Commercial Car business. We know that very few typewriters, adding machines and cash registers would be sold if only for cash; I am sure the same degree of increase in Commercial Car sales can be safely estimated by the adoption of your plan. The sooner all Studebaker dealers try this plan, the sooner they will begin to "cash in" on their possibilities. All of my dealers who are using it consider it one of their biggest and best assets.

Wishing you continued success, I am,

Very truly yours,

COBURN MOTOR CAR COMPANY, INC.

T. Gray Coburn

President & General Manager

The copy in the brochure went on to say:

How many legitimate sales to purchasers who are a good credit risk have gone to your competitors during the last year because your line of credit did not enable you to make the sale and thus add one more satisfied customer-booster to your list of Studebaker owners?

This plan offers you the greatest opportunity you have ever had to meet competition and increase your sales.

Hundreds of the most energetic and far-sighted Studebaker dealers have saved this good credit business for themselves by successfully using our plan for handling customers' notes on deferred payment sales.

Our plan has enabled them to increase their volume of sales and to add to their profit in a greater degree than would have been possible had it been necessary to rely on their own local line of credit.

Read the letter again at the beginning of this booklet. Read what Studebaker dealers who are using our plan have to say about it.

One dealer in a town of 3,000 population made ten sales by our plan in forty-five days.

There was an increase of 150% in the number of dealers who adopted this plan just to handle their Fall business last year.

Are you going to be able to meet the unusual demand for motor cars which is bound to come this Spring and Summer without unlimited credit?

No dealer has ever suffered a loss under this plan. All have profited. The testimony of Studebaker dealers who have used our plan is the greatest endorsement we can offer for it.

You can profit just as much or more in your business by using this plan as these dealers have profited. The plan is not a theory. It has been thoroughly tried and proven.

It is a sound business proposition and conforms to the most conservative banking practice.

It gives you unlimited credit because as fast as you secure notes you can turn them into cash. And it gives you the opportunity for more turnovers per year—*and more profit.*

The program amply fulfilled the promise that Ittleson and Haberman saw in it. In the first three months, $1.3 million in advances was placed on the books. By 1917, the monthly volume of business was exceeding $1 million in the "selling months."

History records that C.I.T.'s contract with the Studebaker Corporation was the first ever entered into by a financial institution and an automotive manufacturer for the nationwide financing of motor cars on either a retail or wholesale basis. The agreement for insurance between C.I.T. and the American Automobile Insurance Company was also a pioneering transaction. It was the first blanket or master contract covering large numbers of motor vehicles whether they were in the possession of dealers or individual purchasers.

9

The First
Decade Ends

As the company's financing of automobiles and other types of consumer products increased, this type of business required reliance on security documents that had not been fully tested legally. The need for increased legal services and on-the-spot counsel was intensified. Mail correspondence between New York and the St. Louis offices of Stern & Haberman, as had occurred in the implementation of the original Studebaker contract, became more and more unworkable. C.I.T. had established certain relations with New York City law firms, but Ittleson preferred to rely on the individuals who had guided him and the company from its inception.

Therefore, he arranged an interview with Gustave Stern, the firm's senior partner, and, as the story is still told in St. Louis, invited him to join the C.I.T. organization in New York, saying, "I'll make you a millionaire if you do." With his family deeply rooted in St. Louis, Stern declined the offer, which Ittleson then tendered to Phillip Haberman. Haberman, in fact, had for some time been the more deeply involved of the two partners in the C.I.T. business.

Haberman accepted and joined the company on August 1, 1916, with the title of fourth vice president and general counsel. He thus entered on a new career, carrying forward his earlier work. He played a major role over many years in first establishing and then broadly perfecting the legal foundation for wholesale and retail financing of automobiles and many other consumer goods.

One of the key developments was that of the "trust receipt," which enabled distributors or dealers to hold automobiles in inventory or seasonal storage, although they were owned by C.I.T. This ownership of the vehicles by the finance company was fully protected by law, since the finance company had paid the manufacturer for the cars on shipment. Speaking of Edward Maddock and the delivery of Willys-Overland autos in 1916, E. R. A. Seligman, in his landmark study, *The Economics of Instalment Selling,* says:

> A trust receipt was worked out at the instigation of Mr. Maddock under which dealers were allowed to receive cars in their own warehouses or showrooms, holding them as the property of the finance companies. . . . Mr. Haberman, vice-president of Commercial Investment Trust, has, however, stated to the writer that he was the first to devise in 1915 a trust receipt applicable to the automobile business. Trust receipts up to that time had been unknown in internal commerce, although familiar in foreign transactions. The probability is that Mr. Maddock and Mr. Haberman each devised his own form; but it seems certain that the form originated by Mr. Haberman was the one generally accepted later on.

Haberman and the legal staff he created around him also were perhaps the leading courtroom defenders and interpreters of the so-called time-price doctrine. The time-price doctrine, which became generally accepted by the states after a series of benchmark cases and legislative enactments, essentially made possible the modern practice of consumer instalment financing. Because of the relatively high handling costs and exposure to credit losses that were necessarily entailed in extending credit to literally millions of consumers, higher rates were required than the usury statutes of most states would permit. Since the outright repeal of the usury laws appeared both unworkable and politically distasteful to the legislators of the states, another solution had to be found to nurture the growing business of consumer financing.

This was accomplished through the validation, by the courts and by special laws, of the time-price doctrine. The doctrine held that the owner and seller of goods was entitled to charge a higher price for an article sold on credit or through deferred payments than he charged for the same article if it was sold for cash. Thus, the total amount of the instalment payments a time buyer might make could exceed what he would have paid on a cash basis. The "differential" between the cash

and time price was held to be not interest, subject to the usury ceilings, but simply a price increase that the credit sale entitled the seller to receive.

The seller of the car or other personal property could then sell or discount the instalment contract to a financing agency, receiving the equivalent of the cash price or more. The financing institution in due course collected the total amount of the contract, which, in return for its services, included the price differential.*

Ittleson and Haberman were believers in and prophets of the instalment-payment principle and, therefore, they made their mark on another aspect of the national way of life that has continued to benefit hundreds of millions of federal taxpayers up to the present day. Revisions to the federal income tax law, first authorized by the Congress in 1913, were under study by the Ways and Means Committee of the House of Representatives in 1916. Ittleson suggested to Haberman that

---

*Over the years, the ability of the seller of goods to charge all that the traffic would bear, or competition would permit, as a time-price differential was increasingly regulated by the states through the passage of instalment financing laws that set limits on the percentage increase over the cash price that could be imposed. These laws were stimulated by the overreaching tactics of some sellers who were found to be victimizing unwary purchasers, retaining for themselves substantially more than the difference between the cash price and the standard finance charge.

he prepare and submit a brief to the committee proposing a change in the income tax law to permit payment of income taxes in four quarterly instalments, instead of the single yearly payment that the law then required. This provision was incorporated in the Revenue Act of 1916 and has remained on the books ever since.

Somewhat stern in appearance, always unfailingly considerate and courtly in manner, ever serious and unremittingly hard-working, Phillip Haberman made many major contributions to the development of the modern C.I.T. Financial Corporation over a period of thirty-two years until his retirement from active service in 1951. He continued as a member of the board of directors until his death in 1953. He brought to his work not only the exercise of a brilliant and learned legal mind but also sound and keen business and administrative talents, on which Henry Ittleson and his other associates relied as much as on his legal counsel.

By the fall of 1916, with the Studebaker retail and wholesale financing business pouring in at an increasing rate, Henry Ittleson gave thought to a looming problem. This was the question of where the trust might turn to raise the additional working funds required to handle the booming automobile business, while still carrying on and expanding its older lines of activity.

What if C.I.T.'s bankers and other established sources of borrowed money would not supply the additional sums the organization might need? Only future developments would provide an answer to this question. But Ittleson thought he saw a solution. It was to borrow the funds from Studebaker itself!

To explore this possibility, he traveled to South Bend, the Studebaker headquarters, and met with the high command there, including A. R. Erskine, the president. Here is his own account of that meeting:

> I outlined to those gentlemen our financial position and told them that the serious problem in this stock car proposition was the uncertainty as to how much business we would have offered to us to take care of. Mr. Erskine said that he understood we had resources to an inexhaustible amount, and the security, being worked out on an 80% advance with the Studebaker recourse accompanying it, was so prime that there ought to be no difficulty in getting all the money needed.

> I told him that that was quite so but we had other commitments outside of Studebaker business, as that was merely one department in our organization and we had to look far enough ahead to take care of our large volume. I said that I would be willing (with the bars to hypothecation and

re-discount removed) to say that under normal conditions we would take between a million and a half to a million and three-quarters total paper from Studebaker dealers, that while I was not at the moment prepared to say we would not handle more, the probabilities are that a congestion would come up at that point, and if and when it did, my idea was that the Studebaker Corporation should come along and in some mutually agreed upon plan, at that time, furnish the additional funds that may be needed.

I suggested that under such an arrangement they should be entitled to a 6% rate on their funds, and in any event, it was a much better arrangement than they had up to the time we did business with them, meaning that they had three and a half to four million in bank deposits, on which they were getting 2 ½% to 3%, and in all probabilities, the way we had worked it out, they would not have to pay up more than a million dollars to swing our excess line.

Mr. Erskine, while not committing himself to any definite plan, made this statement: that he understood the position exactly and that when we got to the end of the line, where the discounts came in so heavy that we could not handle them, that we were not obligated to take these discounts, and that he felt that upon a call from me he would come to New York and work out some mutually satisfactory arrangement, by outside help or otherwise, to handle this additional business.

In my conference, while I indicated that in all reasonable probability we would handle a total volume of from 1-½ to 1-¾ million, I in no wise made any legal commitment, nor would we, and the facts as above stated reflect the expression of opinion at that interview, with which the conferees were all satisfied.

Of course, it is up to us to use every effort to get big enough banking lines to handle this situation, as there are now no restrictions against re-discount or debenturing.

Mr. Hanch gave me the list of the following banks and trust companies in New York City that they are doing business with:

Central Trust Co.
Columbia Trust Co.
Lawyers Trust Co.
Guaranty Trust Co.
New York Life & Trust
Chase National Bank
Chemical National Bank
Corn Exchange
National Bank of Commerce

In Chicago—Continental Commercial, and First National.

In Philadelphia—Philadelphia National.

In St. Louis—Boatmen's.

I specifically put it up to Mr. Erskine, whether it met with his approval, that if we went to any of the banks and arranged for additional lines, that I was at liberty to talk to them freely about the Studebaker arrangement and explain to them just what our deal is. He stated he had no objection at all and felt that that ought to solve any difficulty we might have in a financing line; in fact, he felt that if it came to an emergency, that he, Mr. Goldman and I would work out an arrangement that was satisfactory to everybody.

The upshot of this meeting was that, by virtue of Studebaker's good offices and a strengthening of C.I.T.'s equity capital that was carried out in the following year, C.I.T. established sizable credit lines with the Studebaker banks. There is no evidence that the Studebaker Company itself ever loaned funds to C.I.T.

At about the same time, the tight-money situation was further eased when members of the May-Shoenberg group agreed to form a syndicate to take over up to $600,000 worth of the Studebaker receivables in the coming year, obtaining the same returns that would otherwise accrue to the trust.

A second revision in the Studebaker agreement occurred about this time. The original contract had prohibited C.I.T. from offering similar financing services to other motor car makers, but this restraint was removed with respect to *electric* car manufacturers. C.I.T. then proceeded to sign a contract similar to that with Studebaker with the Anderson Electric Car Company, makers of "Detroit Electric" passenger cars. There was one innovation in this contract. The financing of the sale of used cars was provided for, with dealers to collect 50% of the sale price on units selling for less than $1,000 and the remaining payments to be made in not more than six monthly instalments. On used cars selling for $1,000 or more, the terms were set at 40% down and eight monthly payments. This arrangement marked C.I.T.'s initial venture into the financing of used cars.

As 1916 drew to a close, C.I.T. began doing business in Canada, with the opening of an account with the Canadian Bank of Commerce in Toronto, and the officers were authorized to borrow Canadian funds from that bank. The records do not reflect what types of products were being financed in Canada, but it is a reasonable assumption that the Studebaker business must have been involved, for that company had Canadian dealers at the time.

Of course, the entry of the United States into World War I in April

1917 had its impact on C.I.T.'s activities. The company's direct support of the war effort was typified by a contract authorized on April 16, 1917, ten days after war was declared. This contract, with an individual named E. J. Simon, called for C.I.T. to provide the necessary funds and guarantees so that subcontractors could produce the components of 100-kilowatt wireless sets and wave meters of Simon's invention for use on "U-boat chasers." One hundred and fifty such sets were produced.

In another transaction, C.I.T. sold to Victor R. Browning a machine tool plant at College Point, New York, that it had taken over when a loan to the owners had gone bad. Mr. Browning intended to use the plant for the production of gun mounts for the armed forces. It was indicated that the directors acted favorably on the purchase offer because the plant would be serving the war effort, even though the price they received resulted in some loss to the trust.

As part of the wartime economy, Congress had imposed a corporate income and a corporate excess profits tax. However, when the C.I.T. directors acted at their April 1917 meeting to approve a $15-per-share dividend for 1916, they had before them an opinion from Phillip Haberman that trusts formed under the Massachusetts law were exempt from these taxes, with C.I.T. fully qualified for exemption.

The trust made its first purchase of Liberty Bonds, supporting the financing of the war, before the end of 1917. The amount invested was $100,000. Additional bond purchases followed.

Despite the war's impact on the nation's economy, C.I.T.'s 1917 business volume again set a record, gaining more than $3 million over the 1916 figure to $15,627,000, although profits were down slightly. Automobile unit sales had continued to gain, as did the company's Studebaker financing business.

As previously noted, the pressure on working funds and its capital position generated by the continued growth of bank loans outstanding was considerably relieved before the end of 1917 when C.I.T. sold a $750,000 issue of preference stock to six members of the May-Shoenberg family. This investment raised the invested capital of the trust to $2 million.

As 1918 opened, a contract was signed with Thomas A. Edison, Inc., Orange, New Jersey, for the instalment financing of Edison phonographs sold by the company's dealers. Buyers discharged their obligations in twelve monthly payments.

Henry Ittleson left the organization later in the year to take a post with the Army Quartermaster's Department in Washington as a dollar-a-year man. His C.I.T. salary at the time had been $28,000 a year plus a substantial bonus. He is said to have handled procurement activities and to have assisted government contractors in making the financial arrangements they needed to fulfill their wartime contracts.

Wartime conditions decreased the production of civilian goods, particularly in the machinery, equipment, textile and shoe fields. A decline in C.I.T.'s potential business volume appeared unavoidable but a strong promotional effort was launched to turn the tide. This took two forms. A vigorous direct mail campaign was initiated to dealers in many lines of activity, including Studebaker dealers, and a regular space advertising campaign was conducted in the financial pages of *The New York Times*.

The headlines of the advertisements in this series demanded attention. Among them were these: "MANUFACTURERS AND JOBBERS— MAKE YOUR MONEY WORK," "PUT YOUR BUSINESS ON A 'WIN THE WAR' BASIS," "EIGHTY CENTS TODAY—TWENTY CENTS MORE AT MATURITY," "GET 100% EFFICIENCY OUT OF YOUR INVESTED CAPI- TAL," "INCREASE YOUR RESOURCES WITHOUT ADDITIONAL CAPITAL," "TAKING CARE OF HIGHER INVENTORIES," "WHAT KIND OF COLLECTOR ARE YOU?", "THE KEY TO YOUR FINANCIAL PROBLEM," "INCREASE YOUR WORKING CAPITAL BY DECREASING YOUR LOAFING CAPITAL," "HERE IS A PARTNER WHO ASKS NEITHER SALARY NOR DIVIDENDS," "HOW TO MELT YOUR FROZEN CAPITAL," "TAKE THE HANDCUFFS OFF YOUR MONEY" and "IF YOU DEAL IN MERCHANDISE, BANKING IS OUT OF YOUR LINE."

No doubt the strenuous promotional efforts helped. For the year that brought the return of peace through the Armistice of November 11, 1918, C.I.T.'s business volume registered a moderate decline of less than $1 million and earnings were off $11,000 to $152,000. Nationwide auto sales for the year were nearly halved, dropping to 943,436 units.

IO

" A.O.D. "

To C.I.T.'s executives, as well as business observers generally, the end of the war was seen as an event that would touch off a new era of economic prosperity. There was a general expectation that automobile purchases would regain the momentum that had been moving motor car manufacturing into the forefront of the industrial scene. Roads and streets were being improved, cars were becoming more attractive, more reliable and less expensive, and through the work of Henry Ford and others, the entire American middle class could be considered as prospective car buyers. It was generally known in New York and Detroit business circles that John J. Raskob, chairman of the finance committee of General Motors Corporation, was organizing a subsidiary of General Motors to finance the distribution and sale of GM cars. This was General Motors Acceptance Corporation, which was established in 1919.

There were scores of makers of gasoline-powered autos poised to serve the anticipated market. The names of their lines of cars still ring with historical significance and awaken memories. *A Pictorial History of the Automobile 1903–1953* (Philip Von Stern, Viking Press, New York, 1953, p. 248) lists the following makes of cars being produced in 1919:

Allen	Franklin	Nelson
Anderson	Gardner	Oakland
Apperson	Gearless	Oldsmobile
Auburn	Glide	Overland
Baker	Grant	Owen-Magnetic
Biddle	Halladay	Packard
Bour-Davis	Haynes	Paterson
Brewster	Hollier	Peerless
Briscoe	Holmes	Pierce-Arrow
Buick	Hudson	Pilot
Bush	Hupmobile	Premier
Cadillac	Jackson	R & V Knight
Case	Jordan	Saxon
Chalmers	King	Scripps-Booth
Chandler	Kissel	Singer
Chevrolet	Kline	Standard-8
Cleveland	Lexington	Stanley Steamer
Cole	Liberty	Stearns-Knight
Columbia	Lincoln	Stephens
Crow-Elkhart	Lozier	Stevens-Duryea
Daniels	Marmon	Studebaker
Davis	Maxwell	Stutz
Detroit	McFarlan	Templar
Dixie Flyer	Mercer	Velie
Dodge	Meteor	Waltham
Dorris	Metz	Westcott
Dort	Mitchell	Willys
Elcar	Monroe	Willys-Knight
Elgin	Moon	Winton
Essex	Nash	
Ford	National	

Appearing on the foregoing list are several models of electric-powered or steam-powered vehicles that were still finding a market.

Against this background, and with the experience the organization had acquired in car financing during the previous three years, C.I.T.'s contract to handle Studebaker models exclusively looked less attractive than it had at the time of the initial venture in 1916. The chief advantage that the contract offered was that the Studebaker Company's guarantee was completely behind credit extended to the members of its distribution organization, both on wholesale and retail transactions. If C.I.T. wanted to "play the field," taking on all makes and dealers, this factory protection feature would not be available.

It was at this point that Phillip Haberman proposed a program that proved to be another major milestone in C.I.T.'s history. Captioned "In Re: Automobile Business" and dated January 25, 1919, he prepared a memorandum to Henry Ittleson that read:

> I would suggest a consideration by the Trustees of our policies with respect to automobile paper. Our volume suffered considerable contraction through the diminution of production during the war and we were obliged to make intensive efforts to fill the gap thereby created. This same situation might again arise if a large volume of business is handled for a single factory because of its guaranty, if such factory decided to withdraw its guaranty and thereby again make it necessary to fill up the gap with either other automobile lines or accounts receivable. It would seem to be good policy to go after diversified lines minus factory guaranties, confining ourselves to standard cars. It is apparent that we have lost considerable volume which has gone to other companies of lesser strength than ourselves.
>
> With a view to supply the omission of the factory guaranty, I have been in negotiation with the Fidelity & Deposit Company and I append hereto, their two letters of the 17th instant relating to retail and wholesale automobile paper. The letters are captioned "In Re: Studebaker" as Studebaker cars were the basis of our discussion, but the arrangement can be made with respect to any standard car.
>
> There is going to be a large volume of automobile business during the current year as the factories are all striving to get in quantity production.
>
> I call your attention to the rapidity with which the Studebaker retail department was originally built up with practically no factory cooperation in the business getting. The same thing should be possible of repetition. It will be necessary however to employ a competent and experienced manager for the automobile department who will confine himself entirely thereto.
>
> In this connection, I may suggest that we have recently been approached with a view to financing Pierce Arrow truck paper without the factory guaranty but of course with the endorsement of the retail dealer.
>
> Respectfully yours,
>
> P. W. Haberman

Ittleson wrote across the face of the memo, "Okay on the following conditions: take bonds and select dealers carefully, put a competent man in charge, establish standard cars. H.I."

That the men involved appreciated the significance of this decision is evidenced by the fact that the memorandum was permanently filed as an attachment to the minutes of the January meeting of the board of directors.

The machinery for the new program was swiftly put into motion. The exclusive contract with Studebaker was canceled, although the company continued to provide financing services for a large number of Studebaker dealers, based on the earlier established relationships. Haberman made arrangements with the Fidelity & Deposit Company of Maryland to issue bonds protecting the company against "extensive losses" of a catastrophe nature. The search began for the "competent man" to be in charge of the program, for no one in the C.I.T. organization was considered to have the requisite experience to sell and administer an auto financing program on an all-comers basis.

At the time, the leading independent company in the auto financing business was the Continental Guaranty Company, which had developed from Edward S. Maddock's original Guaranty Securities Company, founded by the Willys-Overland interests in 1915. The company had moved from Toledo to New York City and by 1919 was doing a large business with dealers of a number of makes of cars. Ittleson decided to look there for the man he needed.

He was acquainted with Arthur Watts, the sales manager of Continental Guaranty, and invited him to lunch. Before the luncheon was over, Ittleson had offered Watts the job of heading C.I.T.'s prospective auto financing operations.

Watts declined the offer, saying, according to a reconstruction of their meeting by Ittleson some years later, "I think it's a wonderful opportunity, but I have a wife and family. With a new business like this, one that you've really never tried, I can't afford to take a chance that you may be disappointed."

Ittleson then asked Watts if he could recommend anyone else.

"I know just the man you should have" was the reply. "He's my assistant, a young man named Arthur Dietz. I don't want to lose him, but you are offering someone a tremendous opportunity and I wouldn't want to stand in his way."

Ittleson promptly asked Watts to send his assistant over to be interviewed but Watts again demurred. He said he felt that he would be violating his duty to his employers if he were to send Dietz to a competitor for a position.

Ittleson did not argue with this, but he had, as was his invariable way in any negotiation, an immediate counterproposal.

"I certainly understand your attitude and respect you for it," he replied, "so I have another suggestion to make. Suppose I place an advertisement for a man for the position in *The New York Times*.

Maybe Dietz will see it, but if he does not, would you have any objection to calling it to his attention? That would not be a breach of trust at all and it would be doing your young man a big favor."

Watts agreed to this, and on Sunday, March 23, 1919, the following help-wanted advertisement appeared in the *Times:*

SALES REPRESENTATIVE

We have a position of importance in which a man of absolutely clean record, attractive personality and genuine sales ability may find future opportunities and salary commensurate with his demonstrated ability.

The position is with a financial institution allied with the foremost companies in the automobile industry and consists of educational and sales presentation of a plan for financially assisting the dealers of those companies.

A knowledge of business organization methods, banking, credits, or automobile merchandising experiences or a combination thereof, will be a valuable adjunct.

In your reply please state in addition to qualifications, your age, education, nationality, and if available include photograph.

D 335 Times.

It is not clear whether or not young Dietz actually saw the ad (although he was a great reader of advertising), but Watts called it to his attention in any case. Dietz applied for an interview, as did others. He made a fine impression on Ittleson and his associates and was offered the position of sales representative for the automobile financing department at a $4,500 salary. He was promised the job of sales manager if his early performance was satisfactory.

Arthur Orrie Dietz was born in a humble dwelling on Kentucky Street in St. Paul, Minnesota, on September 17, 1893. His father was a junk dealer and their home stood on a mud flat that was flooded up to three months of the year. He attended the public schools but dropped out of high school before graduating.

He learned stenography from a book, worked at a variety of jobs, and in 1915, at 22, landed a position as an advertising copywriter, despite his limited education. His employer, the Harvey Blodget Advertising Agency, won the assignment to advertise and promote the 100th anniversary of the Savings Bank Division of the American Bankers Association. Dietz was given the job of handling this account, his first major responsibility for his employer.

He traveled to New York City, his first trip away from St. Paul, to take on his new duties. Soon after arriving there and going to work, he happened to be reading a copy of *The Saturday Evening Post*. In a double-page spread, he saw an advertisement by the Continental Guaranty Company offering to finance the retail purchase of all standard makes of automobiles, rather than Willys-Overland cars exclusively.

As Dietz said later, "The idea of getting in on the automobile industry struck me as having a lot more possibilities than writing copy extolling the pleasures of saving money at 3% in savings accounts." He applied for a job with the company and was hired as a sales correspondent. He went into the Army when the United States was drawn into World War I but was discharged before the end of 1918. He immediately returned to Continental Guaranty as a salesman and then responded to Ittleson's advertisement the following March.

In spite of the comparative success that Continental Guaranty had enjoyed, it had always been rather severely restricted with respect to working capital and thus had made only modest inroads into the automobile financing market. Dietz was fully aware of this fact. Backed by the large pool of capital that his new employers commanded and with their promise to provide as much more as he could produce business to employ, he foresaw a future for C.I.T. in automobile financing that was virtually limitless.

He decided to approach the market by two routes. First, he would go directly to successful dealerships anywhere in the country and try to sell C.I.T.'s services to them. Second, he would call on the manufacturers of "standard cars" and seek their sponsorship and willingness to promote the C.I.T. plan with their dealers.

These factory contracts were not expected to include the factory guaranty against losses by C.I.T., as the Studebaker agreement had done. Rather, they would simply be an endorsement of C.I.T. by the manufacturers to their dealers and would usually provide for the assistance of the factory and its field representatives in bringing the C.I.T. plan to their attention. C.I.T. would expect to use the name of each factory in its promotional materials, special rate charts and other documents that were provided to the dealers.

Dietz went right to work on the program he and his associates laid out. "In 1919," he recalled in later years, "I practically lived on the road, visiting hundreds of automobile dealers, distributors and manufacturers to sell them on instalment credit in general and C.I.T.'s services in particular. Most of the dealers were interested, but the manufacturers were polite but cynical."

One of Dietz's first calls was on Charles W. Nash, president and founder of the Nash Motors Company. "I told him that by using deferred payments you will be able to sell cars to people who simply couldn't buy them for cash. Your dealers will get their full price, my company will make a profit on the charges, the customer will be able to use the car while he is paying for it, and everybody will be better off.''

Dietz recalled that Nash replied sternly, "Young man, before I permit one of my automobiles to be sold on instalment credit, I will see this company in receivership!''

Nash cars were popular and the account would be a very good one, so Dietz kept calling on Mr. Nash and showing him what the C.I.T. plan was doing for so many dealers and thus for their manufacturers. Eventually, Nash capitulated in early 1921 and addressed the following letter to his dealers:

> To Nash Distributors and Dealers:
>
> In the past two years The Nash Motors Company has been importuned by many of its distributors and dealers to provide a dependable plan for financing retail time sales and the storage of cars and trucks in the hands of distributors and dealers at reasonable rates.
>
> After months of exhaustive investigation of various financing companies and their plans, we have entered into a contract with the Commercial Investment Trust of New York. This company was selected on account of its financial stability, its years of experience in this field of service, the very attractive rates we were able to procure and the cooperative spirit in which they enter into this undertaking.
>
> It is very gratifying to us to be able to offer you this exclusive Nash financing plan and we believe its use will greatly increase your sales and profits, and we ask for your fullest cooperation.
>
> Yours very truly,
>
> C. W. Nash
> President

He then made a cross-country trip with Dietz, visiting his dealers and extolling the virtues of the C.I.T. program.

Meanwhile, many dealers and other factories were joining the C.I.T. camp. Studebaker continued to give its wholehearted endorsement. President Paul G. Hoffman wrote his dealer body as follows:

> To: Studebaker Distributors & Dealers
>
> This letter to you is part of a most important announcement. C.I.T. in collaboration with Studebaker, have worked out a new financing program which in our opinion is the most comprehensive that has ever been

available to any dealer organization. C.I.T. is doing its full share in its new plan to assist you in securing your full profit potential from your market.

Our dealers have asked for a liberal demonstrator plan. It is being offered them. They have asked for a weekly payment plan on used cars. It is now available. They have asked for short term financing on a basis that would be acceptable to customers. That likewise is provided. In addition, Floor Plan rates are strikingly reduced.

We suggest that you communicate with the C.I.T. representative immediately and obtain from him full details of the "new deal" C.I.T. is offering to assist us in putting over our own "new deal."

Sincerely yours,

Paul G. Hoffman
President

Literature, rate charts and the necessary instalment contracts and other legal documents, prepared by Haberman and his staff, were issued to the dealer bodies of the other manufacturers to whom Dietz directed his company's program. These included Hupmobile, Paige-Jewett, Hudson-Essex, Cleveland, Dodge Brothers, Reo, Franklin, Chandler, Overland, Moon, Willys-Knight and Dort.

The C.I.T. plan was not given endorsement as the "official" factory plan in all cases. Where this was lacking there was no stinting of efforts by the C.I.T. group to sign up as many dealers as possible—that being the second prong of the Dietz plan.

From a strictly legal standpoint, C.I.T. usually had no commitment from the auto manufacturing companies with respect to inventories of unsold new cars that it might be forced to take over in event of a dealer failure. In practice, however, from the earliest days to the present, factories have always cooperated with finance companies and banks by assisting them to "redistribute" such cars to other dealers. In effect, the factory would see that these distressed units were delivered to active dealers in lieu of other direct shipments from the manufacturer, and the financing agency would be paid off. This practice benefited the financing organization, of course, but it also had real advantages for the manufacturer as it removed from the market cars that otherwise would have had to be sold by auction or through independent outlets, at prices that would undercut the standard list prices of the manufacturer and his dealers.

In some cases, however, Dietz arranged factory agreements that, within prescribed limits, did commit the factory to take back repossessed units. An early contract with Dodge Brothers reads:

We agree that if you are obliged to repossess or foreclose upon any such automobiles for non-payment of any instalment or for any other reason, that we will assist you in every possible way to obtain repossession of such automobiles and that we will purchase each such automobile from you at place of repossession (in case of a conversion by purchaser you are to deliver car at our place of business) and pay you the unpaid balance of the note or notes held by you. If any such automobiles shall have suffered material collision damage, you shall cause such damage to be repaired or shall make reasonable allowance to us to repair such damage.

You agree that our net losses, if any, arising out of the resale of cars so repurchased by us, out of the total number financed with you in each complete 12-month period following the date hereof, shall not exceed 5% of the total amount of notes purchased by you from us during the same period. "Net losses" shall mean the difference between the total sales prices of all such cars to retail purchasers and the amounts we paid you therefor plus our actual cost of putting such cars in saleable condition. . . .

Commercial Credit Company had also entered the auto financing business and captured as their "official" factory endorsements those of Packard, Maxwell Motor Company, and after 1925, the latter's successor, Chrysler Corporation.

Commercial Credit's major beachhead in the motor financing business came about in a way that was a bitter disappointment to Henry Ittleson. After Dietz joined C.I.T., Ittleson had maintained cordial relations with Edward Maddock, the president, and Arthur Watts of Continental Guaranty Company. He knew that Continental Guaranty was continually strapped for working funds because of hesitation on the part of the banks to make increased loans to such a lightly financed company engaged in the "dubious" auto-credit business. He therefore had importuned Maddock on several occasions to sell out to C.I.T.

While Ittleson was on a trip to Europe in 1920, matters reached something of a crisis at Continental Guaranty, which was simply unable to accept all of the business its dealer-accounts were offering it. With Ittleson unavailable, Maddock initiated discussions with Alexander Duncan of Commercial Credit concerning the sale of the company. On the day Ittleson returned to the United States, he learned that the purchase of Continental Guaranty by his chief competitor was about to be consummated.

He immediately called Maddock by telephone and insisted that he wanted, and was entitled to, an opportunity to bid for the company. Maddock was actually about to leave his office to go to the meeting where the sale was to be closed, and he explained that it was simply too late for him to back out of his commitment.

Ittleson kept Maddock on the telephone for more than an hour, making him late for his meeting, insisting that C.I.T. would better the price and that C.I.T.'s head start over Commercial Credit in auto financing would make it a much better future partner for Maddock's company. All this was to no avail, as Maddock insisted the hour was too late. The sale went through and C.I.T. found itself with a much more formidable competitor in the automobile field, as Commercial Credit already was in its other lines.

Despite growing competition, by January 1923, Dietz was beginning to receive the rewards earned by his hard work and success. On the first day of the year, his salary (originally $4,500 a year) was increased to $7,500 and he was awarded a future annual bonus of 1% of the company's annual net profits, after payment of dividends. He thus joined Ittleson and Hemphill as the only executives with a bonus arrangement. Later that month, he was also given the opportunity to purchase 25 common shares of stock in the company (out of 30,000 outstanding).

Physically impressive, with piercing eyes, quick movements and a dignified inflexible carriage, softened by a warm and ready wit and smile, Arthur Dietz was a consummate salesman. The mark he was to leave on the C.I.T. enterprise is indelible.

II

Automobiles on
Time Payments?

Commercial Investment Trust and its competitors were establishing the instalment purchase of private motor cars as a national way of life in the years following World War I. They were doing so against the entrenched opposition of many adversaries of the whole idea. These at first included the majority of the automobile manufacturers themselves, many economists, editorial writers and consumer spokesmen. Also numbered among the critics were manufacturers of other products, principally soft goods, who saw in the commitment of future income by consumers to widespread purchase of autos as a threat to their own markets. It is necessary to retrace our story to April 8, 1916, to describe the struggle that was waged (but never completely won for decades) by the proponents of automobile financing.

April 8, 1916, was the publication date of the issue of *The Saturday Evening Post* in which Arthur Dietz had read the two-page advertisement of Guaranty Securities Corporation that was to shape his career. This first national advertisement for time-buying of automobiles said: "YOU CAN NOW GET YOUR FAVORITE CAR ON TIME PAYMENTS. This announces the next great step in the automobile business. From now on you can get almost any car you want—on a monthly payment basis.

The terms are easy and convenient. You simply make the first payment on the delivery of the car. The balance in equal monthly payments. That's virtually all there is to it. . . . No longer is it necessary for you to take a big lump sum from your savings to pay for your car all at once. The Guaranty Plan eliminates that. No longer is it necessary for you to save and save until you have accumulated enough to buy a car. No longer is it necessary for you and your family to be without the pleasure, benefits and advantages of a car."

Twenty-one of the best-known and largest-selling cars, from Buick to Willys-Knight, were listed as being approved for the plan. The ad then went on to paint the joys of automobile ownership: "The day you drive that car home, life will take on a new interest for every member of the family. . . . There will be pleasant short trips on holidays and weekends—and enjoyable long tours when vacation time comes. You will lead a bigger life in a bigger world. . . . Get that car you want now—see the dealer today."

The exact financing terms were not given. On the opposite page was a message addressed to the auto dealer body describing "THE FIRST NATIONAL SERVICE TO HELP DEALERS SELL AUTOMOBILES." This emphasized that the service cost dealers nothing, that hundreds of dealers all over the country were already using the plan and that all details would be handled by mail. The charge to the retail buyer was given as "virtually no added expense beyond ordinary six percent interest of the deferred payments." The plan, it was said, was "backed by a group of capitalists some of whom are among the largest in the country." A list of five banks, three in Chicago and two in New York, was given as references. On both the dealer side and the consumer side of the ad, coupons were provided for those who wished to receive "complete information" on the plan.

Although time-buying of automobiles was presented as a revolutionary concept, the same issue of *The Saturday Evening Post* carried advertisements for the purchase on time-payment plans of the *Encyclopaedia Britannica* (by Sears, Roebuck), billiard tables (by several manufacturers) and vacuum cleaners. For all of these products, instalment payments were obviously well-established and accepted sales methods.

This bold stroke of Guaranty Securities provoked an immediate storm of opposition, particularly within the automobile industry itself. Led by Alvan Macauley, president of the Packard Motor Car Company and of the National Automobile Chamber of Commerce, the chamber on May 3, 1916, voted a strong resolution opposing the time sale of autos and calling the practice "disastrous." This statement read:

Whereas, Certain influences are working and certain efforts are being made for the organization of plans which will have a disastrous undermining effect on the stability of the automobile industry, and

Whereas, it is the opinion of this committee that injurious results will follow the adoption of these methods by any considerable number of automobile manufacturers, and

Whereas, The methods of deferred payments under consideration are very objectionable from the factory standpoint, and are objectionable to a large degree from the dealers' standpoint, and have a disastrous effect on the purchasing public, which will unavoidably react injuriously, now therefore be it

Resolved, That a broad and vigorous campaign of education be conducted by the National Automobile Chamber of Commerce, instructing and enlightening its membership along these lines and calling their attention to the fact that methods which on superficial consideration, seem to have merit, are in reality potent forces for destroying the foundation on which our industry has been built, and that every effort be made to encourage the membership to avoid adopting policies which will undermine the stability of the industry and to encourage them to pursue and develop those policies which can alone maintain and continue permanent success.

In its May 20 issue, *Automobile Topics,* the leading industry trade journal of the time, commented on the manufacturers' action in this way:

Though not mentioned in the resolution, it is known that part of the campaign is being directed against the use of names of competitive cars in the same advertisement. Such advertisements have not appeared for a month, however, in connection with the promotion of credit and finance plans. Also the advertising of credit facilities has been considerably cut down, due to the fact that the early publicity did its work thoroughly, turning up business that the various companies now are most busily engaged in handling.

Macauley did not stop his campaign. He organized a delegation of manufacturers who visited all the banks in New York City and Chicago with which they had working relationships, including the five banks listed in the advertisement. On each of these visits, the car makers described the perils they saw for the entire auto business if every "Tom, Dick or Harry" was allowed to buy a car, with a resulting tidal wave of defaults on their payments. These could be expected to dump enormous numbers of distressed vehicles on the market to be resold in competition with new cars. This would bankrupt most dealers, the car makers claimed, because under the plan the dealers would be forced to reimburse Guaranty Securities for every car buyer who did not complete his payments for any reason whatever.

The bankers were urged, as a matter of sound business principles and public responsibility, to protect a vital and growing industry by withholding credit from Guaranty Securities or any other car-financing organization and by influencing their fellow bankers or other potential lenders to do the same. There were reported threats that the auto manufacturers would withdraw their business from any bank that supported Guaranty Securities.

These actions clearly had some effect, for as we have seen Continental Guaranty (the Guaranty Securities company adopted this name shortly after it "went national" in 1916) had consistent problems in raising sufficient funds to handle its growing business, and C.I.T. also maintained a vigorous campaign of "education" and reassurance to the banking community.

However, the concept of instalment selling of automobiles was an idea whose time had come, and it was unstoppable. One after another, the auto manufacturers capitulated to the demands of their dealers and their own economic self-interest and approved, adopted or grudgingly accepted time payment plans (including Macauley, who signed with Commercial Credit). We have seen that Charles W. Nash, of Nash Motors, was still a hold-out when Arthur Dietz began to call on him as late as 1919–20.

Although the car manufacturers were converted by practical considerations affecting their own pocketbooks, there remained many other critics of the practice of putting people into debt so that they might buy what even Claude Hemphill had described in 1916 as "pleasure cars."

Criticisms came and continued from many quarters. As instalment buying grew in acceptance and volume every year in the early and middle 1920's, the outcries of its critics increased in proportion. A random sampling will illustrate the tenor of these.

In his *The Financing of Instalment Sales* (1927) Harold Emerson Wright quotes these critics:

J. H. Tregoe, executive manager of the National Association of Credit Men:

> When deferred payment schemes encourage extravagance and excessive mortgaging of future income for immediate satisfactions that are neither necessary nor important to proper living, they are a social as well as an economic danger.

Arthur Pound, an economist:

One who brings merely an honest face to the counter and a job to the notice of the credit man, may buy a motor car for $12.60 down and $5 a week, a $200 talking machine for $5 down, a suit of clothes for $3 down and wear it away, jewelry for nothing down and a set of dishes thrown in. Those business men who are busily making debtors through credit sales may well take a few minutes off to ponder the possible social and political results of overselling the consumer on deferred payments.

George F. Johnson, president of the Endicott-Johnson Corporation:

Installment plan buying or urging the poor into debt is the vilest system yet devised to create trouble, discontent, and unhappiness among the poor.

B. E. Geer, president of the Judson Mills, cotton goods manufacturers:

For a long time, I have felt that the buying of automobiles on the installment plan in such volume was one of the outstanding reasons for slow business in many industries. I know that many of our employees at Judson Mills have mortgaged their earnings for anywhere from two to ten months for the purpose of buying machines which were liabilities to them the moment they became possessors. It gives people who are not able the opportunity to "keep up."

Many other alarmed observers of national prominence and reputation were to be heard:

Melvin A. Traylor, president of the First National Bank of Chicago:

If manufacturers and distributors persist in mortgaging future buying power beyond a reasonable point, it is perfectly certain the bankers are going to take care of themselves; and when they do act there will be idle factories and vacant storerooms until the heavy commitments of the community are liquidated, which, with the unemployment that is likely to accompany such adjustment, will not be for merely "just a day or two."

Dominick and Dominick, members of the New York Stock Exchange:

Is it not likely that many families are being lured into believing their spending power is greater because they have only small down-payments to make? In the same way are there not many dealers, the first in their towns to push deferred payments, who have failed to recognize that when all their competitors offer an identical or even more liberal plan, their sales will probably show little change except for distinct falling off in the *good cash business?*

Colonel Leonard P. Ayres, vice president of the Cleveland Trust Company:

The newer finance companies are largely organized by men who are primarily salesmen and promoters. The business calls for the cold, impartial judgment of experienced commercial bankers. These promoter types have been notably successful while prosperity has been general, competition easy and credit cheap. But it is doubtful if they can be equally fortunate when these conditions change. . . . In view of the difficulty already experienced by the ordinary wage earner in scraping together the 10 to 20 percent he is supposed to set aside each year for rainy days, would not credit buying, if, priced at 20 percent, it continues to be so widespread, neatly obliterate all possibility of savings accounts?

George W. Norris, governor of the Federal Reserve Bank of Philadelphia:

There is no doubt about the fact that the enormous growth of instalment selling in the last year or two must have had a very appreciable effect on production and distribution. The latest authoritative estimate puts the total for 1925 at nearly six and a half billion dollars. Most of this huge sum represents goods produced and sold in that year which, under other conditions would either not have been produced at all, or would still be in process of distribution, where they would appear in either manufacturers', wholesalers', or retailers' inventories. Now they are in consumers' inventories—which are not reported. As to approximately two-thirds of their value, they were not paid for on January 1st. This two-thirds was owing by persons from very few of whom any bank had any statement. The very fact that they bought that way is prima facie evidence that they either possessed very limited financial intelligence or very limited responsibility—in many cases both. It is manifest that the whole process is one of borrowing from the future—the manufacturer or dealer borrows from his future business, and the buyer borrows from his future earnings. With such careful and thrifty people as the Scotch or the Dutch, for example, the practice might be safely urged, but with such optimistic and chance-taking people as our own it is fraught with danger.

Who is to apply the brakes? Not the dealer who finds that it increases his sales, and knows that if he refuses to deal in that way he will simply surrender his business to a more alert and obliging competitor. Not the manufacturer, whose god is "quantity production," who knows that the larger his production the less his unit cost. Not the "credit company," whose whole livelihood is dependent upon it. Not the bank, which finds the business profitable and knows that a competitor would be glad to get it. Who then? It seems to me that it must be a process of gradual education in which the schools, the churches, the press, the bankers, the economists, and all other moulders of public opinion must do their part. It cannot be accomplished by misrepresentations or indiscriminate denunciations. It must be done as part of a general process of education in comparative values, in thrift and self-denial, and in sound finance.

However, instalment buying had as many adherents and advocates as it had critics, and in the face of the storm of censure, they were equally vocal. The leaders of the finance companies were in the forefront of this offensive, of course, but they had as allies many bankers, economists, business leaders, editorialists and others who had no personal financial stake in the industry—including the President of the United States, Calvin Coolidge, who epitomized conservatism and thrift to the nation.

James L. Wright, writing in *Nation's Business* in 1926, reported these statements from an interview he had had with "Silent Cal":

As to the individual American family, the President feels that the desire to own a home, to have better surroundings and more comforts in life, even the present tendency to buy commodities on the instalment plan, is entirely sound. He is satisfied that the modern system of extending credit, with its definite obligation to pay fixed amounts on certain days, is infinitely better than the old system of running an open book account at the store, with no plan or purpose of liquidating the obligation.

Mr. Coolidge is convinced that the instalment plan provides credit for those who otherwise could not buy, and gives to the average man and his family luxuries they could not have if they had to pay cash for the entire amount at time of purchase.

While some politicians are inclined to "view with alarm" the present tendency to buy everything from an electric flat-iron to a foreign-built automobile on the part payment plan, the chief executive, who willingly concedes that the new system may be overdone, is convinced that it has not yet reached the danger point in the United States.

Another element of confidence the President has in the instalment plan is his belief that the financing and bonding companies, which have been built up to carry this new system, have anticipated eras of depression that may come from decreases in employment, and an inability to meet obligations on time. He is certain they have cast an anchor to the windward.

President Coolidge found another occasion to express his endorsement of the instalment credit principle. Some months after the Wright interview, *The New York Times* published this account of his confidence in the social morality, the economic value and the soundness of the use of time-buying by the American people:

> Inquiries made at the White House today to ascertain President Coolidge's opinion concerning the widespread prevalence of buying on the instalment plan and spread of credits to persons of modest means, brought out the fact that the President is not in sympathy with the view of some economists that this condition is a bad thing for the country and full of economic danger.
>
> According to the President's way of thinking, there is no cause for alarm in the instalment plan tendency. . . .
>
> It was his recollection that the country's estimated income was $70,000,000,000, and, comparing this with estimated outstanding credits of $2,000,000,000, the disparity was not great enough to cause reason for apprehension. . . .
>
> He looked at it [instalment selling] as a modern method of doing business, beneficial to persons of small incomes, and as presenting a means of obtaining credits that ordinarily would be denied to them. It was, according to the understanding obtained of the President's view, an orderly way of extending credits to those who have fixed regular incomes with whom credit arrangements could be made based on percentages of income to credits desired and length of time within which to pay.

Perhaps the most conclusive as well as exhaustive analysis and defense of time purchasing was Dr. E. R. A. Seligman's monumental *The Economics of Instalment Selling,* published in 1927 as the result of a massive research study sponsored by General Motors Corporation. This two-volume work by the Mc Vickar Professor of Political Economy at Columbia University fully examined all aspects of the extension of instalment credit to the consuming public. Its conclusion was that "instalment credit will be recognized as constituting a significant and valuable contribution to the modern economy." This endorsement by a leading authority, and the massive compilation of facts his research group produced in support of his final judgment gave consumer credit a new status of economic respectability.

C.I.T.'s management, led by Henry Ittleson, also spoke out strongly and frequently in behalf of the soundness and social value of instalment credit. Executives addressed the Babson Statistical Organization, the Philadelphia Chapter of the American Institute of Banking, investment banking groups and similar forums. These addresses usually were reproduced in pamphlet form and given wide distribution.

On one occasion, before a group of national advertisers and advertising agencies, Ittleson declared these to be the basic precepts for the proper administration of instalment credit:

It is a natural evolution of credit.

It can be applied only to products meeting certain qualifications.

As a development of credit it must be conducted on the same principles as all good credit.

It leads people to place money in articles of real value which might otherwise be wasted on articles of transient gratification.

Increased and steady production gives even the time buyer the article at a lower cost.

Individual credit when prudently contracted creates an incentive to work and to produce more.

Experience with consumer credit has proven it to be a sound, healthy thing when properly used and not abused.

"I am convinced," he concluded, "that instalment selling will continue and spread; unsound financing will be eliminated and consumer credit will be accepted as an essential part of our nation's intensified banking system; that families will not wish to relinquish their present high plane of living and will work a little harder to obtain those better things of life that make life worth living."

On one important occasion, Henry Ittleson entered into a direct frontal debate on the issue of the social value and economic impact of instalment credit, his adversary being an economist of high repute. The forum was the 1926 annual convention of the National Retail Dry Goods Association, held in New York on February 11, C.I.T.'s birthday.

Creighton J. Hill of the Babson Institute, Wellesley, Massachusetts, was a speaker at the convention. He called instalment payment plans "the largest red flag on the horizon of American business." He continued:

Eighty per cent of all automobiles manufactured in 1924, approximately 3,000,000, were sold on deferred payments. The volume of credit extended in both new and old car sales last year was not far from $2,500,000,000.

While the automobile is the first charge on the instalment account, it has plenty of company. Pianos perhaps represent the original type of luxury article which was sold on time payments. Today most musical instruments are thus sold, and if we add to the $2,500,000,000 worth of automobile paper contracted in 1925 the commitments for musical instruments, household appliances, furniture and furnishings, radio, clothes, tires, books, furs and scores of other items, the year's total credit must approach and probably will exceed $5,000,000,000. In other words, business has invaded purchasing power, and this insidious undermining of our economic structure is increasing daily.

Hill said that warnings against deferred payments had been issued recently by the International Typographical Union and the National Retail Hardware Association. He continued:

> In order to possess non-essentials, many families are cutting down on essentials, setting a less nourishing table, buying fewer shoes and skimping on living quarters. Statistics of trade increases in instalment lines are clearly not gains for the nation, because part of those gains must be offset by lessened buying power in other lines. The retailer who is doing business on an instalment basis on the same terms as cash is certainly living in a fool's heaven.
>
> . . . the whole situation has resulted in a weakening of the entire credit structure and where formerly credit restrictions were kept pretty tight, now they have been loosened to an almost criminal degree of carelessness.
>
> The expansion of the deferred payment idea has made merchants indifferent to even the most elemental safeguards of credit, and some apparently think that pyramiding could be carried on indefinitely.
>
> My advice to you is to be more careful than you ever were before in granting credit, because a day of reckoning is coming when a lot of retailers are going to be left holding the bag.
>
> We are living in an age which has lost much of its sense of values. It is a gambling age, when quick fortunes are being sought, when the fundamental virtues of thrift are being overthrown. Unearned fortunes in Florida speculation, spectacular clean-ups in the market absorb our interest. One of the results of all this has been to weaken the fibre of our people so that bootleg financing, masquerading under the name of instalment plan buying, has seized us in its grip.

Ittleson met the challenge head-on when it came his turn to speak. He first agreed with his opponent that all responsible businessmen should oppose and avoid "abuses" in the instalment field. Then he continued:

> It has become an integral part of our merchandising system, born of two conditions inherent in our national psychology. The one is the desire of our merchandisers to prosper personally and to benefit the public through

ever-increasing production with attendant lowering of costs. The other is
the irrepressible desire of our people to constantly improve their standard
of living.

He cited the fact that most people purchase insurance on the instalment payment plan, and that corporations transacted business on
time—"a well-organized business even pays its income taxes on time,
creating its reserves month by month." He declared that instalment
selling of such things as pianos and furniture were "economic and
cultural advantages to the masses beyond estimate."

"As I have previously pointed out," Ittleson continued, "the criticisms of instalment selling reveal the significant fact that the unfavora-
ble comment is directed not to the theory of the plan, but to its abuse.
The critic is afraid that we are buying too much and that our purchasing
power will be considerably weakened in the near future. He overlooks
the undeniable fact that where there is purchasing on one side, there
must of course be merchandising and manufacturing on the other." He
concluded with these words:

> Perhaps, the soundness of instalment selling is best indicated by its
> almost universal adoption and its phenomenal development during the
> last five years. Extension of credit to the individual under proper
> safeguards is just as legitimate as extension of credit to a corporation.
>
> The instalment plan has not only taught the American thrift, but has
> given to him a new interest in his personal appearance and in his home.
> He has become, in short, the best customer in the world.
>
> The nation has enjoyed five years of full employment of labor and well-
> distributed national prosperity. No change in fundamental conditions
> seems to be indicated. Hence instalment selling, prudently conducted,
> contains no inherent menace. The constant iteration of a suggested
> menace may, however, create a condition of lack of confidence which
> would be harmful and it is, therefore, important to sound a warning
> against timidity disguised as caution.

At the conclusion of the debate, the convention adopted a two-faced
resolution noting that the rapid expansion of instalment credit was
"occasioning some concern," but that there was much to be said both
in favor and in opposition to the practice. The members were advised
to use "care and caution," to check individual credits carefully, to
require substantial down payments and to reduce the length of
maturities. *The New York Times* gave the Ittleson-Hill debate a news
treatment of over one-and-a-half full columns.

Haberman took a unique view of the soundness and wisdom of

instalment buying over many forms of purchasing for cash. In an address before the Contemporary Club of Philadelphia in 1926, he said:

> Credit may be unwisely extended just as cash may be unwisely expended. However, the ill-advised and harmful incurring of debt is no more frequent than improvident waste in cash outlays; in fact, probably less frequent. The incurring of debt in all instances requires some forethought, but cash in pocket prompts many outlays of an unnecessary character, in the aggregate far more uneconomic than in respect of the incurring of debt. I think there is no doubt that the American people, proportionate to their earnings, expend more money upon trivialities and transitory pleasures than any other people. These expenditures are not necessarily to be condemned. Money so expended is not necessarily wasted merely because it could have been devoted to more tangible economic ends. But what is the result if such money is withdrawn from such uses and devoted to the satisfying of an indebtedness incurred in a purchase for which an advance commitment has been made. The result is that the individual has saved by going into debt in that he has accumulated goods which he would not otherwise have possessed. It would be absurd to suggest that the very best way of saving is to incur debt. The available data as to the increase in savings deposits and number of deposits and as to the increase of the amount of life insurance, proves to the contrary. However, it cannot be successfully denied that the readiness of the American to employ his credit has had an important effect in increasing the national wealth and the national wealth is, of course, merely the sum of the goods and means of the individuals composing the nation.

The storm of criticism was not to be stilled. Even Henry Ford, whose dealers were selling millions of cars on instalment terms, burst forth in June 1926 with this tirade against the practice:

> The thing that is troubling this country most just now is the amount of debt piled up by the credit system and instalment plan of buying. The American people no longer buy. They are backed into a corner and are "sold."

> Credit is the dearest thing we sell in this country. Debt has become a national industry. That is bad business for the debtor and bad business for the creditor also. The debtors are paying for a dead horse and the dead horse is in no man's land, for the goods are no longer in the possession of the manufacturer, who sells to the dealer on credit, and the dealer has lost possession of fresh goods, and the buyers do not yet own them.

> I believe this debt situation will provide the jolt which will bring people back to a cash basis, where they already know they should be.

The Ford business, as far as it affects the Ford Motor Company, has always been on a cash basis. The result is that millions of cars have been sold at a minimum of risk to the makers and dealers and a minimum of outlay to the buyers. We propose to stick to that policy, which is the only sound policy for any business.

Ford was technically accurate in saying the Ford Motor Company sold only for cash—to its dealers. He chose not to recognize that the dealers were selling most of his cars to *their* customers on instalment credit terms, offered by C.I.T. and its competitors! As a matter of fact, it was only two years after this statement was made that the Ford Motor Company organized its own finance company on the model of General Motors Acceptance Corporation.

In fairness to Ford's philosophy, it is historically interesting that his company had tried to develop an alternative to selling its products by creating a debt for the buyer. In 1923, the Ford Company announced a plan through which a prospective buyer could obtain a coupon book from his dealer and make weekly payments of $5, on the Christmas Club model, until he had built up a sufficient balance with his dealer to pay for the car he wanted. With Model T runabouts selling for $265, this process took only a year. More than 300,000 vehicles were sold in the two years before the plan was apparently dropped, for reasons unknown.

Another item from *The New York Times* of this period presents a refreshing view of the growing popularity of "budget buying":

LONDON INSTALMENT BUYERS
CELEBRATE 'PAID-UP PARTIES'

LONDON, Dec. 3—"Paid-up" parties are the latest fads among Londoners. It is not everybody who knows what a "paid-up-party" is, and at least one person was astounded to receive the following invitation:

"Please come to a 'Paid-with-thanks' party at .... on Saturday. Music and dancing."

Ringing up to inquire just what it meant the following explanation was given:

"It's just a little friendly gathering to celebrate the fact that all the instalments have been paid on the furniture and the piano. I'm having another one next January to rejoice over the last payment on the motorcar."

In view of the growing popularity of buying furniture and motor cars on the instalment plan, there will probably be a large increase in paid-with-thanks parties this season.

The New York Times commented on this tongue-in-cheek account in its editorial page in this wry vein:

> Paid-up parties are a London invention, though one might have supposed that the greater prevalence of instalment buying here would have made Americans think of them first. The answer may be that we never reach the happy state of being "paid up." If a party were given to celebrate the final payment on the furniture, the guests would still be jumpy for fear someone would pass the hat to pay off the remaining debt on the automobile or radio.

In 1926, C.I.T. prepared a pocket-sized booklet (written by Ittleson's brother-in-law, L. S. Frank) with the provocative title *What Would Happen If Credit Should Stop?* Ittleson wrote all of the company's dealers, offering them as many copies of the booklet as they could distribute to their customers and others. He asked this, he said, because: "We believe that instalment selling, under proper safeguards, represents a legitimate extension of credit to the individual. We believe that it has aided in raising his standard of living and in stimulating industrial activity."

The booklet answered directly the question posed in its title:

> PICTURE the effect upon American business if credit should stop!
>
> —If railroads, public service institutions, etc., could issue no more stocks or bonds.
>
> —If builders could secure no more mortgages.
>
> —If banks could accept no more notes.
>
> —If farmers could obtain no supplies between harvest times except for cash.
>
> —If manufacturers were required to purchase materials upon a sight draft, bill of lading attached, basis.
>
> —If wholesalers and retailers were denied credit, and
>
> —If ultimate purchasers could buy for cash only.
>
> What *would* be the resultant business condition?
>
> Would everybody be happy, prosperous, content, progressive; or would the entire economic structure crumble as from an earthquake?
>
> Credit is the life-blood of business, and confidence is the inspiration of credit. Without confidence there can be no credit. Without credit there can be no progress. Without progress there can be no prosperity, and without prosperity there can be no contentment.

Throughout the period of this debate between 1920 and 1927, when
the economy was generally expanding and "Coolidge prosperity" prevailed, the critics of instalment buying consistently raised one issue
that its proponents could not directly dispose of. This was the question
"What will happen to the time-buying consumers and those who have
granted them credit when a real depression and widespread unemployment occurs?"

A strike in the winter of 1925–26 in the anthracite coal industry of
Pennsylvania resulted in some rise in defaults and delinquencies on
automobile payments and other consumer debts. This was seized upon
by certain critics as an example of what could be expected from a
stoppage of debtors' paychecks on a nationwide basis. Professor
Seligman's authoritative study of instalment credit showed that this
conclusion was overdrawn. It was pointed out that half the working
force of the area was out of work during the strike (a percentage of
unemployment that was much higher than even a severe depression
would be likely to produce), yet GMAC's accounts 60 days or more
overdue rose only from ½ of 1% to 2.5% of outstanding accounts
during the 6 months of the strike.

Yet the question of the effect of a depression on the nation's new
time-buying economy remained unanswered. In due course, an answer
was to be forthcoming.

12

Leadership in Financing
the Consumer

In spite of the heated debate about its fundamental approach to selling its products on the instalment plan, the automobile business was growing at a sizzling pace, as was the automobile financing business. The year 1923 marked the rise of automobile manufacturing to the lead in dollar volume of sales among all U.S. industries. It achieved sales for the year of $3.16 billion, producing 3,625,000 passenger cars, while the steel industry declined to second position with annual sales of $3.15 billion. Meat packing was in third place.

Through 1923, C.I.T. had continued to handle all details of its direct auto financing transactions by mail. Dealers and distributors were expected to fill out a detailed form and send it to 347 Madison Avenue if they wished to establish their credit with the company. (The company had moved from its "downtown" 61 Broadway offices in 1918.) The requisite supply of forms to use C.I.T. retail services was then mailed back to them. Dealers would then sign up their customers as sales were made and mail the completed forms back to New York, after which their checks would be delivered to them if the credit of the buyer appeared acceptable. It was also the dealer's obligation to file a duplicate of the contract or lien with the proper recording office, according to the laws of his state.

This plan of operation, with the dealer completely responsible to C.I.T. for his customer's repayment performance, also obligated him to repossess and resell at his own risk any vehicles where the purchaser defaulted.

Spurred by the influx of automobile and other consumer receivables, as well as by the recovery of its established industrial financing business when the postwar economy returned to normal, C.I.T. booked $23.5 million in volume in 1919 (against $12.4 million in 1918). The 1920 volume figure rose to $30.5 million. The short-lived 1920–21 recession caused business placed on the books to decline to $25.6 million in 1921, but there was a strong recovery to $42.8 million in 1922. Volume doubled the previous year's figure in 1923, totaling $91.6 million and scored another gain to $95.6 million in 1924. This record put the company far ahead of any competitor among finance companies, except for General Motors Acceptance Corporation, which surpassed C.I.T. in automobile volume from 1919, its first year in business.

While for most of these years no breakdown between classes of business is available, the figures for 1921 are an exception and probably reflect the relative relationships for most of the period. For the year, the business loans-accounts receivable operations brought in $21.5 million in volume, retail automobile financing produced $7.8 million and wholesale auto $4 million.

At the year's end, the portfolio of receivables was almost equally divided between industrial and motor car paper, although retail auto financing was making the sharpest year-to-year gains. Net earnings for the year were a record $512,000, compared with $413,000 for the previous year, the best up to that time.

Early in 1922, the way was prepared for another important forward move when Claude Hemphill reported to the board of directors the results of a survey he had made of the automobile business in Canada. He had visited several of the Canadian provinces and held discussions with distributors, dealers and manufacturers' personnel. He recommended that C.I.T. form a Canadian company, moving as discreetly as possible in order not to offend Canadian nationalistic sensibilities. The function of the company would be to service the Canadian sales of the U.S. motor car manufacturers with which C.I.T. had contractual relationships.

He said he had made tentative arrangements to employ a Mr. John F. McKinnon to manage the new company. His program was approved by the board. Canadian Acceptance Corporation Limited was granted a charter on November 25, 1922.

On December 22, a two-man office was opened at 263 St. James Street West in Montreal, with McKinnon in charge as vice president, Henry Ittleson listed as chairman of the board and Hemphill as president. McKinnon was another alumnus of Continental Guaranty Corporation, having been its Montreal manager.

A Toronto office was opened in 1923 and shortly afterward the C.A.C. headquarters was moved there. By mid-1923, the company not only was purchasing motor car receivables but like its parent was also engaged in financing various other types of equipment such as phonographs and player pianos.

While C.I.T. was attracting increasing amounts of auto business through its special factory plans and endorsements, it nevertheless began to feel a very vigorous form of competition. Hundreds of localized, usually single office, finance companies were springing up across the country. Since they were on the scene, they could offer direct personalized service to dealers and their customers. Even more important, many of them were operating on a non-recourse, or limited recourse, basis with dealers, relieving the latter of the heavy credit responsibility that the with-recourse plans of the national companies entailed. Such non-recourse plans involved greater risks for the finance companies, of course, than did dealer-endorsed receivables. In compensation, the local companies usually imposed higher charges than the with-recourse plans required. They also enjoyed the advantage of being able to investigate and pass on the credit-worthiness of local car buyers with much greater facility and accuracy than was possible for the "national" companies.

By 1922, there were more than one thousand automobile finance companies in business, most of them small and localized. Quite a number had been set up by dealers or distributors themselves. By 1925, the number of companies had increased to between 1,600 and 1,700.

While Ittleson and Dietz continued to build their automobile volume on the original plan in the first postwar years, a tentative step into more localized financing was taken when in 1922 Ittleson bought the Mercantile Acceptance Company of Chicago from his old friend A. D. Nast. It will be recalled that Ittleson had been associated with Nast in a stock brokerage and investment business in 1902 and had initially planned to go into partnership with him in the establishment of the Commercial Credit and Investment venture.

After selling his enterprise, Nast became a member of the C.I.T. organization and continued to manage the Mercantile Acceptance business, which was kept separate from C.I.T.'s operations. By 1924,

Mercantile Acceptance was doing a partial without-recourse ("W.O.R.") business with offices in Chicago, Pittsburgh, Philadelphia and Newark, and C.I.T. had opened its first branch (except for the earlier St. Louis office) in Toledo. The reason for establishing the Toledo office was because the Willys-Cleveland motor car plant was in that city and Willys dealers were a prime source of business for C.I.T., making an on-the-spot liaison arrangement at the factory desirable.

The fierce competition between the many auto finance companies extended beyond the with- or without-recourse issue. Rates came under pressure by 1924, threatening the profits of many companies, and terms were lengthened. The standard down-payment requirement of 40% to 50% was lowered by some companies to 25% and the usual requirement of full repayment in 12 monthly instalments was stretched to 18 months. These departures from tested terms greatly alarmed many conservative finance-company leaders, bankers and most manufacturers.

Spearheaded by leading bankers who were lending to the auto-finance industry, meetings were called throughout the country in 1924 to discuss this apparent threat to the liquidity and safety of automobile instalment paper. More than 300 finance companies were represented at these meetings and resolutions were adopted setting minimum terms of one-third down payments and 12 monthly instalments for both new and used cars, with 40% down required for used cars. Both the manufacturers' trade organization, the National Automobile Chamber of Commerce, and the National Automobile Dealers Association endorsed these standards.

Henry Ittleson was the keynote speaker at the most important of these meetings to establish a set of national credit standards. This was the organization meeting of the National Association of Automobile Finance Companies, held at the La Salle Hotel in Chicago on December 10, 1924.

Introduced by the pro-tem chairman, Arthur J. Morris, founder of the Morris Plan of industrial banking, as "I might say I can think of no man who can better discuss our problem from the finance companies' standpoint," Ittleson told his competitors:

> The problem has been put up to the finance companies by the American Bankers Association meetings with us that there were certain practices creeping into the conduct of this business that in its broadest aspect looked as though they might bring at some future time disappointment and grief to those in the industry, to those interested in the business as a whole and to all credit extending interests.

Gentlemen, I did not have the remotest idea that there were as many individuals and corporations engaged in the finance business in the United States as a preliminary survey prior to sending out the call for this meeting seemed to indicate. I think I am correctly stating it when I say there were approximately 1,400 invitations sent out to various finance companies in the United States.

The method of financing the sale of any commodity, including motor cars, on time, is based upon an old human impulse. We wish to enjoy today what we may not be able to compensate for for some time to come. To put it more concretely, we wish to draw upon our earnings of the future to enjoy the blessings of today. . . .

Now, with the ease and facility with which a businessman could enter into the business of operating a finance company, there came in its wake a group of individuals well intentioned, fairly well financed, some adequately financed but naturally inexperienced in the various ramifications and techniques of operating that type of business, and as the numbers grew competitive phases entered into the situation and as competitive phases enter into any situation there is a possibility of safeguards being gradually liberalized and sometimes entirely forgotten. So I believe I am stating the facts fairly that that is what happened in the motor financing industry.

I suppose there are four or five hundred people in this room and I imagine that each of us when we extend a type of credit feel that we do it a little better than our next-door neighbor, and if there is any money that is going to be lost by anybody it is not going to be by any one of us here but it is going to be by the other fellow. That is rather a plausible but fallacious doctrine.

Competition is the stimulus of all business. We love it and all of us who are ambitious and willing to develop our business are stimulated by the spur of competition, which brings about an anxiety to sell your product, which is your service plus your money, and our service plus our money, on a basis that our misinterpretation of the facts and wrongly drawn out inferences would seem to demand of us, to give types of plans and terms that fundamentally may not be sound.

Now, we come to the question: what is fundamentally sound? In whose mouth does it lie to say that fifteen months is sound, that eighteen months is unsound, or that twelve months is sound and fifteen months is unsound, or that thirty per cent down payment on your time selling price, or thirty-three, whatever the case may be, is sound and twenty-five per cent is unsound? So the individual who has his own particular problem to confront convinces himself first and then seeks to convince his banker that that rule that he is talking about is quite right for the other fellow but you know it does not apply to me. Well, of course, that is a species of argument every man can use, and if every man could successfully use it, then the whole subject matter for discussing sound, conservative business would be thrown in the scrap basket. It is not true. There are certain things that are wise to do and certain things that are unwise to perform, even so the unwise thing suits the pocket book at the moment. If the thing is not based upon the right type of foundation you are bound to come to grief sooner or later.

The important factor in the equation is, where is this going to lead? What is opening the door and unduly liberalizing credit going to lead you to in the future? If twelve months is all right we will drift into fifteen months and then we go into eighteen months and then we go into twenty-four months, just by little three-month steps. If eighteen months is all right twenty-one months cannot be altogether wrong, so it has occurred to the bankers, which is the problem they put up to your organization committee, that there ought to be a limit set that we can all agree on, giving due heed to the importance of the growth of the manufacturing industry itself.

As I understand the program, there are certain fundamental things that if possible we want to come to an agreement on, because it is in the interest of sound business and it is in the interest of the fellows who finally do the credit extending and it is in the interest of your own invested capital, and quite as important as any of the reasons I have stated it is in the interest of the industry at large which it is our business to promote and make grow bigger and better than it ever was.

The convention endorsed the 12-month, one-third down standards. For several years, the "official" terms were reasonably well observed by all important participants in automobile financing, C.I.T. continuing as a staunch supporter. By the late 1920's, however, 18-month terms became the norm for new cars and 15 months for used vehicles. The change, interestingly enough, did nothing to impair the safety of receivables written on these terms.

With its ample resources, C.I.T. had found a way to capitalize on the automobile financing business generated in their immediate areas by its localized competitors. Many of these companies were constantly strapped for working funds because of their limited capital. By 1924 and in a few isolated earlier cases, the company therefore began to enter into contracts with sound and well-managed local companies to rediscount portions of their receivables portfolios. Thus, C.I.T. supplied them with cash so that they could accept the additional business that was flowing in from their dealer accounts, while still retaining a portion of the income from their earlier purchases.

Among the companies for which rediscounting was done were Metropolitan Securities, National Acceptance Corporation and Manufacturers Discount Company, all New York-based; Salem Chattel Mortgage Company, Salem, Ohio; Pacific Finance Company, New York; Industrial Loan & Finance Company, Paris, Tennessee; Fraser-Hoffman & Company, Detroit; Commonwealth Guaranty Corporation, Warren, Pennsylvania; Equitable Credit Company, New Orleans; Underwriters' Finance Company, Hartford, Connecticut; United Finance Company, Gloversville, New York; Service Finance Corporation, New York; Bankers Automobile Finance Corporation, Philadelphia; and National Discount Corporation, South Bend. Some of this rediscounting business continued into the 1930's and there have been occasional renewals of it to the present day.

By the middle of 1924, Arthur Dietz realized that the company's automobile and other consumer-products business could not continue to be handled exclusively by mail and through intensive travel by company representatives working out of New York City. He therefore undertook a painstaking personal study of the problem and a search for a solution. The result was a memorandum of recommendations that he addressed to Henry Ittleson on October 20, 1924. It reads:

> In considering a nation-wide branch office set-up, we believe that it would be expedient to open branches first in those cities of the United States that are general distributing cities for the automobile manufacturers. That will put us in position to co-operate with the distributors in those cities and give us a national representation.
>
> *SURVEY*
>
> Our idea in opening up a branch office would be first to make a survey of the population in a given center to determine what kind of a set-up would be necessary. Rather than looking at the individual city and its population, it would be well to take into consideration the nearby towns which are fed from that city and are within close proximity. Then we can decide on what procedure as follows:
>
> Generally speaking, we believe a center of population of from 100,000 to 250,000 could be handled with a one-man office. The amount of business which we should get out of such a center should approximate $300,000 per annum. A center of population of from 250,000 to 500,000 should be run with a one-man and one-girl office and should produce a volume of $500,000 per annum. A center of population running from 500,000 upwards, should be run with an office of two men and one girl or more and should produce a volume of business upwards of $500,000. Of course, some of these centers of population will produce more business than anticipated while others will produce less and the personnel of the office will naturally have to be governed by the volume of business done.

Before opening up an office, a survey should be made of the field and competitive rate charts should be assembled and analyzed together with the strength of local companies operating there. It is just possible that at some points local competition may be so strong and the rates so low, that it would be foolish for us to open an office.

Our thought is that when a thorough survey has been made, the facts submitted, then we should decide whether it is advisable to open up an office in that center of population and proceed accordingly.

This survey should be made by either Mr. Newald, Mr. Hemphill or Mr. X in the East and in the West this survey should be made by Mr. Dietz, Mr. McGary or Mr. X. The Mr. X will be a high-type salesman whom we will need in this branch office set-up and who can spend practically all of his time circulating among the branch offices and teaching the branch managers how to sell the service and watching the branches to see that they are operating economically.

ESTABLISHING BRANCHES

After a survey has been completed, and we have definitely determined to enter that field, then Mr. Hemphill, Mr. Newald or Mr. X will go to that city in the East or Mr. Dietz or Mr. McGary will go to that city in the West, and after a thorough canvass of applicants, pick the best man to become branch manager. This man will be selected through several sources. He can be found by making application through banks, employment agencies, dealers and newspaper advertisements. A local man is preferable as he knows local conditions.

When the applicant is selected and thoroughly investigated the office will be rented by the man from the home office and the branch manager will be sent to one of the well-running branches, preferably one that is close to him, for a week's intensive training in the passing of credits, handling of collections and general duties which he has to perform. When he has completed this week's training, he will then go to his own branch office and it is suggested that Mr. Newald or Mr. X in the East and Mr. Dietz or Mr. X in the West, spend enough time to cover with him all of the dealers and get some business started. After business starts coming into the office, then it is suggested that Mr. Pardee in the East and Mr. McGary in the West, spend enough time in that branch office to see that the office set-up functions properly and that the branch manager follows through on our credit procedure.

SUPERVISION

It is essential that these offices are properly supervised at all times and that someone from the home office call on the branches regularly to see that they are functioning from all angles. We will need another man in both the Eastern and Western organization and this man, as heretofore advised, we have designated as Mr. X. While this man will spend all of his time in the field and will be essentially a master salesman, the fact remains that in addition to his supervision, these offices will have to be kept in touch with by Mr. Newald or Mr. Hemphill in the East and Mr. Dietz or Mr. McGary in the West.

In addition to personal calls, the telephone will have to be used consistently and constructively to discuss with the branch manager important items which come up in the daily routine of business which affect sales, credit and credit policy. In the East it will be Mr. Link's duties to manage these offices from an office routine stand-point. Mr. Link will watch the credits, collections and repossessions. Any matter of policy or change of rates will be brought to Mr. Hemphill's attention.

The above procedure takes into consideration the handling of automobile distributing centers in the United States east of the Rocky Mountains. We are making no recommendations regarding the Pacific Coast territory as we all feel that that can only be handled by setting up a general office either in Los Angeles or San Francisco.

The Dietz proposals were reported to the board of directors and immediately put into effect. Dietz himself had joined the board six months earlier. One of the first moves was to absorb the "eastern" Mercantile Acceptance offices into C.I.T. within a month. During 1925 and 1926, the company opened twenty additional offices in such cities as Boston, Atlanta, Miami, Cleveland, Syracuse and Wilkes-Barre. Mercantile Acceptance, which continued to serve the Midwest, had twelve offices from Dallas and New Orleans to Omaha and Minneapolis. West of the Rockies, a subsidiary, C.I.T. Corporation, had been established to serve that territory; headquartered in San Francisco, it had seven offices from Los Angeles and Phoenix to Portland and Seattle. Canadian Acceptance had eight offices extending as far westward as Calgary. Including those in existence prior to the Dietz recommendation, the C.I.T. organization thus had fifty-three local offices in operation.

In spite of its move into providing localized financing for its dealers, thus countering the earlier competitive advantage of the small local companies, C.I.T. remained fully committed to the with-recourse system involving dealers' responsibility on retail contracts.

But as C.I.T. and the other "recourse" companies developed local representation through the establishment of branch offices, the system was modified. "Repurchase" plans were offered that required the selling dealer to buy back from the finance company vehicles that the company had repossessed from delinquent purchasers. Earlier, it will be recalled, the with-recourse plans had placed the responsibility for making repossessions on the dealer.

Another program was under way to insure C.I.T.'s continued leadership in financing the consumer purchase of durable goods. Along with the expansion of the automobile department, the company had embarked on a program to handle large volumes of receivables arising from the sale of phonographs, radios, pianos, washing machines, vacuum cleaners, electric cookers, refrigerators and other types of labor-saving household equipment. The terms for financing radios are of interest. They were financed over ten months in 1924 (later extended to one year), with a minimum monthly payment of only $10.

13

The Industrial Side

Paralleling the rapid growth of the company's automobile and other consumer financing operations in the immediate postwar years was the continued expansion of its original business in making loans and acquiring receivables arising from industrial, mercantile and other lines of business activity. Many accounts dating back to the St. Louis days remained on the books together with others that had been added in the period of flourishing economic conditions prior to the interruption of peacetime business activities by the war. These formed a solid bedrock on which Ittleson and Hemphill continued to build this phase of the business.

There seemed to be an almost endless number of businesses and products for which C.I.T.'s innovative financing services could be employed. Just a few of the variety of transactions booked during the early 1920's were those involving:

Adding Machines	Cleaners
Automotive Equipment	Dairy Machines
(Passenger and	Electric Motors
Commercial)	Furniture
Barber Equipment	Hotel Equipment

Incubators	Welding
Kitchen Equipment	Woodworking
Lunch Wagons	Musical Instruments
Machinery—	Office Equipment
Agricultural and	Optical Equipment
Household	Organs
Battery Charging	Physicians' Equipment
Bottling	Pianos
Carbon and Gas	Portable Houses
Canning	Pumps
Contractors'	Radio Receivers
Ice	Refrigerators
Ironing	Ships, Scows, Tugs (inland
Laundry	waterways)
Oil and Gasoline	Store Fixtures
Pattern Machine	Stoves, Ranges, Ovens and
Pressing	Furnaces
Printing	Time Clocks
Steel Punching	Vacuum Cleaners
Textile	Washing Machines

Further evidence of the increasing recognition and acceptance of the company's industrial financing is the number of corporations of national prominence whose names were being placed on the books. These included Emerson Electric Company, Brunswick-Balke-Collander Company, Gulbransen Piano Company, Blaw-Knox Company, American Radiator Company, American Can Company, Hoover Suction Sweeper Company, Savage Arms Corporation and the Easy Washing Machine Company.

The staff continued to expand with the influx of business, and in May 1918, in preparation for the expected end of the war and a return to peacetime economy, the company had made the move from 61 Broadway to a midtown address, 347 Madison Avenue. A number of men of executive stature were being added, and one of the most significant developments in the formation of a broader management team was the continued increase in the responsibilities of Frank W. Collins, the office boy of 1908.

Collins, it will be recalled, was one of the small group who moved with the company from St. Louis to New York. He had already established himself as a reliable aide to Hemphill in the internal office management side of the business and had been given check-signing responsibilities as early as 1913. In New York, he became Hemphill's

Frank W. Collins

alter ego, even adopting many of the mannerisms and working habits of his superior.

He was elected assistant secretary of the trust in January 1918 and secretary a year later. In 1921, he was admitted to the select inner circle of stockholders of the company.

Slightly built, always serious and marked by driving ambition, Collins not only directed the administration of most of the postwar industrial business but also developed into an effective salesman, in spite of his reserved manner. He negotiated many of the important new industrial contracts of the period.

Over these years, he also assumed numerous responsibilities that were previously handled by Haberman and Hemphill in connection with delinquent or "trouble" accounts where the company faced exposure to credit losses. However, the number of such situations was never large. For example, in mid-1922, out of the many hundreds of accounts on the books, only seven were reported to the directors as being in this category.

In 1924, he was elected a director of the company on the same day as Arthur Dietz (March 12). In July, by an action of the directors, he was authorized to take over a number of responsibilities that Hemphill had handled alone since the founding of the organization. These included the power to discharge manufacturers, dealers, distributors, etc., on their endorsements or other obligations to the company when their accounts were fully paid or settled. He was also empowered to execute releases to bonding and insurance companies under similar circumstances and to assign to them collateral held by the company if they had settled C.I.T.'s claims against the owner of the collateral. Still another new duty was to act as representative of the company in suits involving claims against purchasers or dealers.

In the early years, it will be recalled, all of C.I.T.'s financing for manufacturers and distributors had been on a non-notification basis. The buyer of the goods in question made payment as usual to the seller, unaware that C.I.T. was the real extender of the credit accommodation he was enjoying or that his supplier would pay the funds over to C.I.T. By 1918, however, C.I.T. was extending credit on both non-notification and notification bases. The latter form called for the customer to be "notified" that C.I.T. had purchased his account and that payment should be made directly to it. For example, in the first three months of 1920, when twelve new industrial financing accounts went on the books, ten were in the traditional non-notification form and two were on a notification basis. It is of interest that the latter were both in the textile industry where factoring, a form of notification financing, had long been established.

And the combined growth of the traditional "industrial" business and the newer consumer financing operations was being accompanied by marked changes in the structural makeup and form of the organization.

14

Bulwarking the Future

One of the recurring problems with which the trust was faced as its outstanding loans expanded rapidly in the postwar years was the need for increased working funds—both borrowed funds and the additional equity capital to support such borrowings.

It has been noted that, in November 1918, there occurred a timely infusion of $750,000 of additional capital through the sale of preferred shares to the members of the May and Shoenberg families. This had raised the total investment made by stockholders in the trust to $2 million.

While there were regular increases in the annual dividend distributions to the stockholders, retained earnings also helped build a consistently larger equity position. Total resources climbed from $3.5 million at the end of 1918 to $6.8 million two years later. Then, in early 1921, action was initiated to provide a much broader base for the organization's future growth.

At the meeting of the trustees held on January 8, 1921, a resolution was adopted for the purpose of organizing a new corporation under the banking laws of New York State. This involved merging most of the assets of the trust into the new entity and resulted in the eventual liquidation of the trust. The initial capitalization of the new corporation was to be $2 million. The new entity was not then given a name, being referred to in the resolution as "The New Corporation."

Despite the great wealth of the two families backing Henry Ittleson and his own growing fortune resulting from his earnings and dividends from C.I.T. and other shrewd investments, it was obvious that these resources were not without limit. Yet the future capital needs of the C.I.T. organization were without a foreseeable ceiling. The adoption of a corporate structure that would facilitate the marketing of its securities at the appropriate time and provide a means of spreading the ownership beyond the restraints imposed by the Massachusetts trust form of organization, was clearly the course of action indicated to meet the needs of the future. In addition, the federal tax advantages at one time enjoyed by the trust format had been wiped out by successive amendments to the tax law.

Some months passed while preparations went forward to establish "The New Corporation." Finally, at the meeting of the trustees held on October 25, 1921, Ittleson presented a new plan for setting up and financing the corporation and accordingly proposed the rescinding of the resolution of January 8. He then moved the adoption of a substitute resolution to establish the corporation, giving it the name "Commercial Investment Trust Incorporated" and authorizing the acceptance of a stock investment of $400,000 by Edwin C. Vogel, in association with the latter's father-in-law, Henry Goldman. Goldman had been a partner in Goldman, Sachs & Company, C.I.T.'s first private bankers. Edwin Vogel was named senior vice president of the organization, a new title.

Edwin Chester Vogel was a 37-year-old attorney with a broad business and financial background. Born and educated in New York City, he was a graduate of Columbia College and the New York Law School. As a member of a law partnership with his elder brother, he became engaged in corporate organization and reorganization work. In 1910, he played a principal role in converting the privately owned May Department Stores Company into a public corporation and thereafter handled much of the May legal work.

In 1916, his older brother Martin was appointed assistant treasurer of the United States and their firm was dissolved. Edwin joined the Army Ordnance Department as a captain and served until the end of the war. He returned to New York and became associated with a banking and brokerage firm as a partner but after a year and a half decided an investment banking career did not appeal to him. He therefore resigned, and he and his wife went to Europe for a sabbatical tour while he pondered what his future might be.

At St. Moritz in 1920, he by chance met his old client, David May.

While the two were out for a stroll, May asked his younger friend what he planned to do in the future. Vogel replied that he had not made up his mind.

"Well, then, I know what you're going to do," May said. "We have a company, the Commercial Investment Trust, in which we are very interested, and Henry Ittleson runs the company. It is growing by leaps and bounds and we need another top executive to help him and give him some relief. We'd like you to come into the company."

Vogel agreed to think about the offer and when he returned to the United States he studied the affairs of the company, went to St. Louis to talk with other members of the May-Shoenberg group there, and spent many hours with Henry Ittleson. He had known him, but not particularly well, for a number of years, since Ittleson's May Company days.

He made his decision and joined the trust with a substantial salary, a stock interest and options to buy additional stock. He immediately threw himself into two main projects. Because of his previous background in corporate law work, he counseled with Haberman in planning the organization of the new corporation and the absorption of the assets of the trust. He also became the organization's ambassador to the financial community at large, particularly the major money-center banks.

In later years, he recalled, "I think I can say that during those years I developed C.I.T.'s credit nationwide. At that time, instalment selling was not looked on with favor by the banks nor by the public. It was a very hazy, doubtful and questionable type of activity and it had to be sold everywhere. So one of my primary jobs was to sell C.I.T. and its activities and the value and importance of instalment selling to the economy of the country. I made new friends—and I had many friends before I came to C.I.T.—with many important bankers and I worked aggressively, traveling to Chicago, Detroit, St. Louis, San Francisco, visiting the banks wherever I went."

National City Bank of New York was one of the major banks that had never offered C.I.T. a line of credit. It had been an inviolable rule of Ittleson and Vogel that C.I.T. would never request a bank to afford it credit accommodations but would wait to be invited to become a customer. That rule has never been changed. Vogel regularly called on William A. Simonson, who was senior vice president of National City, to discuss C.I.T.'s affairs and the business climate generally. One day, while he was enlarging on the increased use of time buying by the public, Simonson broke in to say: "We here at this bank are totally against it. We have just put in a rule that anybody in our employ who buys on time will be fired."

Vogel quietly replied, "Mr. Simonson, I am absolutely certain you

will not keep that rule very long." Within a year, the bank offered
C.I.T. a $1 million line of credit, which was accepted. As the decades
have passed, First National City Bank (its present name) has become
one of the nation's two leading banks in providing instalment credit to
consumers.

Vogel's wooing of the banking community was continuously fruitful. For example, the number of banks offering C.I.T. lines of credit
was 25 at mid-1922 and 45 a year later. He was also becoming involved in other activities. On November 1, 1922, he addressed a
memorandum to Ittleson recommending that the company aggressively
expand its activities in the market of financing "household equipment
and commodities," particularly electrical products. He stated that he
had made a broad survey among the manufacturers of these labor-
saving devices and found the business of financing their sales would be
"safe and desirable." His recommendation was approved.

The certificate of organization of Commercial Investment Trust Incorporated had been approved by the New York superintendent of
banking on December 5, 1921, and the first meeting of the incorporators and stockholders was held two days later. Colonel Moses
Shoenberg was elected chairman of the board, Henry Ittleson president
and all of the other officers of the trust retained their same titles.

The corporation began business with a balance sheet listing total
assets of $10.7 million, including industrial accounts receivable and
notes aggregating $3.7 million, retail automobile receivables of $4.4
million and wholesale motor obligations of $609,381.

In May 1922, the company offices were moved from 347 Madison
Avenue to the Liggett Building at 41 East 42nd Street, where larger
quarters of 9,300 square feet were leased on the ninth floor.

An addition to the organization of great historical consequence occurred in the summer of 1922. This was the employment of a young
man of 22 in the cashier's cage, operating a Todd Protectograph
machine to enter the face amount on the company's checks as they
were drawn. His name was Henry Ittleson, Jr.

Young Ittleson had attended Colgate University for two years and
then transferred for his junior year to the School of Business Administration at the University of Michigan. In the spring of that year, he told
his father he did not want to continue his education for another year to
get his degree but wanted to go to work for C.I.T. once and for all. A
career with the company had been his intention since childhood.

His father replied flatly that unless he finished college and received
his degree he would never obtain a job with C.I.T. The two strong
wills held their positions until the summer vacation approached and the

father then agreed that his son could take a summer job with the company. He felt sure that when fall came Henry Jr. would decide to return to college.

Before the fall deadline, the younger Ittleson announced to his father he was *not* going back to college and, if he could not have a permanent job with C.I.T., he would go to work somewhere else. After a few days, the father capitulated and Henry Jr. went on the regular payroll, earning his first raise from $20 to $25 a week as of October 1.

Here is Henry Jr.'s recollection of the father-son relationship in the business:

"Before I went to work at C.I.T., my father made it perfectly clear to me—and he was a man who didn't beat around the bush—that I was not going to get any concessions because I was the son of the head of the organization. And as a matter of fact, I probably would be penalized by being in that position because he would lean over backwards to see that I only progressed because I was entitled to progress and not because of any relationship with him. And this policy was carried out about 99% or 100% during the time that I was with C.I.T. and my father was active in C.I.T., this policy of not favoring me. I felt it was not only good for me but was the right thing to do for the other executives and employees of C.I.T."

The policy of providing no special treatment for the founder's son was reflected even in the processing of his employment application. As his company personnel file shows, the personnel department conducted a regular personal investigation of Henry Ittleson, Jr., and also obtained a credit report on him before he was permitted to go to work!

Actually, the elder Ittleson gave the faithful Hemphill the assignment of supervising and guiding Henry Jr.'s indoctrination and progress, and Hemphill did so for several years.

Henry Jr. soon was transferred to the collection department and after two years was given responsibility for all collection problems west of the Mississippi. As was the practice in that period, these were handled by correspondence, including dunning letters and eventual assignment of bad accounts to local attorneys for collection. He was named a vice president and director of Commercial Investment Trust Corporation in 1924, not long after it became a publicly owned enterprise.

This was the beginning of the C.I.T. career of Henry Ittleson, Jr., which was to span 51 years. For the final 12 of these years he was to be chairman and later honorary chairman of the board.

On December 6, 1922, the capitalization of the corporation was increased from $4 million to $6 million, partly through a declaration of a dividend out of surplus, but primarily through increased investments by the existing stockholder group, plus purchases by a limited number of employees who were given the privilege of buying a few shares apiece. The company had not yet "gone public."

For the year 1922, receivables purchased passed the $42 million mark, against $25 million in the previous year. Retail auto outstandings at the year-end were $8 million, doubling the year-earlier figure, and all other receivables outstanding stood at $5.4 million, compared with $4.2 million at the close of 1921. Total year-end outstandings were $15 million, against $9.2 million a year earlier.

The first reference to C.I.T. that appears in *The New York Times* Index was on January 23, 1923, reporting that Henry Goldman had been elected a director of the corporation. In a sense, he was the company's first "outside" director, all of his predecessors having been either members of the original investor group or active officers.

Less than a year after the capital stock of the corporation had been increased to $6 million, action was taken at a stockholders' meeting on October 19, 1923 to raise the capitalization to $9 million. Once again, the existing stockholders agreed to subscribe their proportionate shares of the total new issue.

The year closed with outstanding receivables crossing the $24 million mark, for a 12-month increase of nearly $8 million.

The year 1924 opened with the crystallizing of the decision to make a stock offer to the investing public. It was clear that the original backers and their families could no longer continue to meet the equity capital requirements of the fast-growing business. At the first directors' meeting of the year, held on January 21, the board approved in principle the draft of an agreement calling for the organization of a new corporation that would acquire all of the stock of Commercial Investment Trust Incorporated in exchange for its own securities. The program also called for the sale of an additional $3 million of preferred stock and 50,000 shares of common stock to Dillon, Read & Company, as underwriters. Dillon Read also would receive an option to buy 5,000 shares for its own account.* The officers were authorized to complete such an agreement with the proposed underwriters.

Action was swift. The new entity, Commercial Investment Trust Corporation, was incorporated under the laws of the State of Delaware on January 28 and the first meeting of the incorporators and stockholders was held later that same day. Messrs. Ittleson, Vogel, Harmon August, Haberman and Hemphill were elected as the first board of

---

*Dillon Read did not exercise this option within the required four months and was paid a fee of $50,000 in lieu thereof.

directors. The latter, in turn, elected the officers of the corporation to the same positions they had occupied in the trust.

Dillon Read & Company was to pay $4 million for the preferred and common stock sold to it and C.I.T. agreed to make application within six months for listing both classes of its securities on the New York Stock Exchange. Dillon Read also was given the privilege of naming two additional members to the board of directors. The agreement was consummated on February 11, the date of C.I.T.'s sixteenth birthday.

The offering price for the 30,000 shares of 7% cumulative preferred stock was $98 per share plus accrued dividends. The common stock was offered at $30 a share, with the intention stated that it would initially be placed on a $2.50 per share annual dividend basis.

Among the interesting facts stated in the offering circular for the public issue were these:

●Following their original investment of $100,000 the founders and their families and associates had paid in an additional $6.5 million of capital over the years.

●Total net earnings during the 16 years had amounted to $5.3 million, of which $2.5 million had been retained in the business and $2.8 million paid in dividends.

●Obligations purchased had increased from $738,000 in 1909 to $91 million in 1923.

●During 1923, the company earned $16 million for a 28.7% return on capital employed in the business.

●In the eight-year period prior to December 31, 1923, the company had acquired $256 million of purchased receivables with total credit losses only amounting to $250,000, less than 1/10 of 1%.

●The company had more than 600 employees.

At a meeting of the original five directors on February 28, the board was enlarged to include all of the previous directors plus Arthur O. Dietz, Frank W. Collins and, as the two Dillon Read representatives, William A. Phillips and E. G. Wilmer.

Application for listing both classes of stock on the New York Stock Exchange was made on February 29, showing total capital of $13 million and total assets of $34.7 million. The application was approved by the governing committee of the Exchange on April 9.

Actually, the gaining of a listing on the New York Stock Exchange was hardly a routine matter for a company such as C.I.T. Edwin Vogel explained this to Ittleson in a letter written on March 28:

Replying to your inquiry, the Commercial Investment Trust Corporation stock is not yet listed on the New York Stock Exchange. Several matters came up in this connection that require considerable time and careful handling. As a matter of fact, I had intended to go West about a week ago, but have remained here mainly on this account. I now have things pretty well in hand, however. I appeared before the Stock List Committee informally last Monday in order to give them a real picture of the workings of our company. As you know, there is no other company of our kind listed on the Exchange, and it was necessary to get before them to acquaint them with the way in which we operate and what our business really means. They were most courteous and in fact let me talk to them for about an hour and a half without interruption. As a result we have now been advised that the formal listing application will be received for consideration on Monday next, when I shall appear before them again to answer any formal questions, and I believe everything will run along very nicely and smoothly and expect to see the stock listed in short order.

In the first several trading days following the formal listing, the common stock sold at $33 a share, or 10% above the offering price. (It closed the year 1924 at $52 a share.) The preferred stock fluctuated in a range slightly below or above $95 a share, against the offering price of $98 a share. From time to time during the following months the corporation bought up and retired some of these shares.

The year 1924 drew to a close with action by the board of directors to authorize the organization or acquisition of an operating subsidiary located on the Pacific Coast. This decision was implemented within two months through the purchase of the San Francisco Securities Corporation for cash. Identified in the company's announcement of the transaction as a "trust company," San Francisco Securities had been engaged in automobile and other forms of financing for seven years.

As a listed company, C.I.T. complied with Stock Exchange rules by issuing for the year 1924 its first printed annual report. The entire president's letter read as follows:

To the Stockholders of Commercial
Investment Trust Corporation:

I take pleasure in submitting herewith, the Consolidated Balance Sheets as of December 31, 1924, together with the Consolidated Surplus and Income Account of your company for the year ended December 31, 1924.

The total volume of bills and accounts purchased during the year 1924 was $95,509,475, compared with $91,518,525 for the year 1923. The new profit for the year 1924, as shown on the income statement submitted herewith (after deducting dividends paid on the 10,000 shares of

Mercantile Acceptance Company Preferred Stock not owned by your Company) was $2,275,146, compared with $1,858,506 for the year 1923.

The net profit shown on the income statement is arrived at after charging off all known losses and setting up adequate reserve for contingencies, taxes and unearned discounts collected in advance.

In pursuance of the policy of developing an efficient nationwide service for the industries which your companies serve the number of branch offices was increased to twenty-nine during the year. These branch offices, in the main, are small units giving local service and are located at important centers in the United States and Canada.

The current business of your companies shows a satisfactory increase.

Respectfully submitted,

Henry Ittleson, President

Assets were given as $44.2 million, with notes and accounts receivable outstanding aggregating $36.5 million.

A new source of short-term working funds was established in January 1925 when an agreement was reached with the investment firm of A. G. Becker & Company for that firm to sell C.I.T.'s commercial paper to investors on the open market. The Becker firm received a commission of ½ of 1% of the amount sold. The amounts involved were minor for some years.

Continuing their program of developing new and larger sources of working funds, on March 27, 1925, the directors authorized an agreement with the Dillon Read firm to sell $10 million of serial gold notes. When these were marketed on May 1, they were to mature at the rate of $2 million every two years for a period of ten years. Interest rates varied from 4½% for the shortest maturity to 5¾% for the longest.

The purpose of the issue, the management stated in the offering circular, was "to replace short time obligations with longer maturities at a fixed reasonable interest rate, unaffected by fluctuations in the money rates and to enable the corporation to increase its business by having at its command larger unused bank lines of credit."

On July 19, 1925, there occurred the first death among the founding group of the corporation. Colonel Moses Shoenberg, who had served as chairman of the board since 1914, died, and a memorial resolution by his fellow directors read in part:

> The difficult period of an institution is normally the early portion of its existence and it was during this period that the benefit of Colonel Shoenberg's personal contact was the more largely experienced. To his

younger associates he was an unfailing inspiration, grasping the significance and advantage of their enthusiasm, yet counseling the practice of conservatism in the making of decisions. He was a man who could and did foster sanity of decision. His influence was at all times constructive. With courage he evidenced his confidence in the corporation and its management by increasing at every opportunity his investment in the corporation's capital.

At the same meeting, Henry Ittleson, Jr., was elected a director of the corporation to fill the vacancy created by Colonel Shoenberg's death. The office of chairman of the board was not filled until 1939, when Henry Ittleson assumed that title on the election of Arthur Dietz as president.

A further infusion of capital took place before the end of 1925. At a stockholders' meeting on December 26, it was voted to offer the present stockholders 72,000 common shares at a price of $60 a share and to sell to Dillon Read, as underwriters, 10,000 additional common shares and 75,000 shares of new preference stock at $100 a share ($7.5 million par value). The latter carried five-year warrants entitling the holders to subscribe to one share of common stock for each two shares of preference stock held. The prices of the common shares would be $80 a share in 1926–27, $90 a share in 1928–29 and $100 a share in 1930. Dillon Read also received warrants to purchase 10,000 additional shares at the same prices.

In announcing the offering, the directors also raised the annual dividend rate on the common stock from the initial $2.50 a share to $3.60.

15

The New Era Unfolds

Firmly financed to handle the vast inflow of business from their multiple lines of activity, C.I.T.'s management continued to plan and work aggressively to build their enterprise to new dimensions of profitability and importance.

In December 1925, a project developed that, had it been carried through, would have had far-reaching historical results. The press carried reports that discussions were being held in New York City on the possible merger of Commercial Investment Trust Corporation and its chief competitor, Commercial Credit Company. In Baltimore, William H. Grimes, president of Commercial Credit, confirmed the story. But he said, "The Commercial Credit Company is a Baltimore institution and here it will remain."

Ten days later, the companies issued a joint announcement that the proposal had been dropped. Their terse statement said, "The discussions were purely tentative and have been terminated. The conclusion was reached that at the present time the best interests of the two companies might best be served by continuing to operate independently."

In later days, C.I.T. executives ascribed the failure of the merger

107

plan to the complete inability of the two parties to agree on which company and which chief executive would assume the primary position in the combination. C.I.T. would have been the larger partner by a considerable margin, but as Grimes's earlier statement indicated, the Commercial Credit group was insistent on maintaining its complete autonomy. Therefore, Ittleson and Dietz and their opposite numbers at Commercial Credit, Duncan and Grimes, with their respective associates, continued as friendly rivals down through the years.

At about the same time, *The New York Times* reported another potential expansion move:

> The Commercial Investment Trust Corporation is considering the extension of its operations into Europe to facilitate distribution of products of the American industries that it serves, it was learned yesterday. A survey of the European field is being made by the corporation, which this year will do $140,000,000 of business in the United States and Canada, and conditions are now believed to be favorable for expansion overseas. It is expected that the company will open its first European office in London and will later enter countries on the continent.
>
> The foreign expansion was brought up for consideration in response to a request by American automobile manufacturers, who decided that the American system of instalment buying, now almost unknown in Europe, would be an advantage and would stimulate European business in general. Henry Ittleson, President, and Edwin C. Vogel, Vice President of the Commercial Investment Trust Corporation, recently returned from their study of the foreign field, and C. L. Hemphill, another Vice President, is now abroad. The corporation finances manufacturers and merchandisers through purchases of evidences of indebtedness arising from the sale of a diversified line of products, including automobiles, machinery and household or electrical appliances.

Although all his company's affairs appeared to be in a highly flourishing condition, Henry Ittleson nevertheless expressed his usual hard-headed sense of caution and preparedness in a letter written from London to Edwin Vogel, dated March 5, 1926:

> Keep well and happy and educate our staff to keep digging for facts and get on top of their problems. You know Wall Street has a flair for discounting prosperity—also reverses—some six months or so ahead. Let's prepare for easing off in industrial conditions and get and keep our house in order. So we can say later on Oh expense where is thy sting. Hardtimes where is thy victory. Otherwise I am cheerful—and optimistic for eternity. But prepare for 1926–1927.
>
> Do the business but do it our way.
>
> Your friend—Henry Ittleson

Ittleson was in England at the time to negotiate for the purchase of United Dominions Trust Limited, a leading British finance company. The various automobile manufacturers with which the company had contracts or other working relationships were rapidly expanding their export business. They expected C.I.T. to provide the same financing services for their dealers in foreign markets as the company did in the United States and Canada. The acquisition of United Dominions Trust was the first important step in this direction.

Ittleson closed the deal before the end of April for a cash price of £315,000. The British management was retained and plans were put into effect to increase the capitalization. In reporting to the C.I.T. directors on the transaction, Ittleson commented, "This will immediately give us an important European position and we can probably do Berlin and other European financing through London. We have a good organization here and will develop a branch organization."

Phillip Haberman spent two months later in the year surveying the potentialities for expanding instalment credit operations in Europe. Returning to the United States in October, he told *The New York Times* that he had identified an "intense interest in American merchandising methods" among European businessmen. He said that instalment selling was the main point of their interest. The interview continued: "Leaders of European industry have been particularly impressed by the part that the deferred payment method of merchandising has played in increasing the purchasing power of the American public and widening the market for a great many types of articles. Instalment selling along American lines is gaining in volume in England and Germany."

C.I.T.'s full ownership of United Dominions Trust continued for two years. In April 1928, 90% of the company's stock was sold to British interests, including some of the original owners and other individuals already associated with the management. A substantial profit was realized from the sale and it was reported to the directors that in consideration of these profits, the 10% interest C.I.T. had retained "represented no actual investment in the corporation."

In the 1928 mid-year report, stockholders were told that the management had decided that to have the control of the company in British hands was in the "best interests of all concerned." In connection with the sale, C.I.T. entered into a long-term exclusive agreement with United Dominions Trust for the latter to handle the business of C.I.T.'s clients in the British Isles and in other areas to which U.D.T. intended to expand. Thus, the original purpose of owning the company, to provide financing facilities for C.I.T.'s factory accounts' export sales, continued to be served.

The plan to handle German or other business on the European continent from London was soon abandoned. Later in 1926, Commercial Investment Trust Aktien-Gesellschaft ("CITAG") was established in Berlin. During the year 1926, the two foreign subsidiaries handled a business volume of $8.5 million, or about 4% of the company's total. President Ittleson commented in his annual report for the year that the two foreign units were showing "satisfactory profits."

In early 1927, small operations which were conducted by a newly organized subsidiary, Commercial Investment Trust Company Limited, were opened in Mexico and Denmark. To round out the story of the development of the company's foreign operations, a substantial interest in a French company, the Société Pour Le Developpement de la Vente A Crédit, was purchased in 1928, with headquarters in Paris. The sellers were the Citroen motor car interests. In the next two years, offices or agent-representatives were operating in Cuba, Puerto Rico, Chile, Argentina, Paraguay, Brazil, Uruguay, the Canal Zone, all European countries, the Union of South Africa, India, Australia and New Zealand. All of the offices except those in Puerto Rico and Cuba were acquired in 1928 through the purchase of Motor Dealers Credit Corporation from the Studebaker Corporation for $5 million. Concerning the Motor Dealers addition, the C.I.T. mid-year report in 1929 commented that "The acquisition . . . was advantageous not only in respect to domestic operations but also because the company thereby acquired the organization and facilities of this company for extensive financing in other countries. This organization, added to that which your corporation has been developing, gives it a comprehensive world-wide organization, enabling it to extend and improve its services to American manufacturers in financing their distribution abroad."

The foreign operations produced many new problems and complexities for what had been essentially a domestically oriented business organization. One of the most amusing arose in connection with the Indian organization. In 1929, the home office controller's department received an invoice for $2.00 for "cotton bed sheets." An inquiry was immediately fired off to determine the reason for this expenditure.

The formal answer came back from Herbert Huestis Dawson, the Motor Dealers manager in India, that the messenger boys he had to employ were accustomed to going naked and owned no clothing. He felt it was essential for the maintenance of the corporate dignity of such a company as C.I.T. that its messengers be appropriately attired and he thus had bought sheets for the boys to wear while on duty!

While the company had found it necessary, because of the demands of its valued domestic accounts in the automobile and appliance industries, to take the plunge into a far-flung international operation, both

One Park Avenue Building

Ittleson and Vogel had misgivings about the program As early as August 1927, Ittleson was instructing Vogel to see that C.I.T.'s permanent investment in the German company be minimized. The selling off in 1928 of the principal share of United Dominions Trust was at least in part another expression of this cautious approach. During a European inspection trip in 1928, Vogel wrote the following to Ittleson: "I need not tell you I am very half-hearted about this foreign development of ours but I suppose there is nothing else to do but go ahead with it and as long as we must do it, let us do it as nearly right as possible."

Dropping back chronologically to cover domestic developments during the years when expansion on the international scene took place, one of the significant events of the year 1926 was the moving of the corporate headquarters to the seventeenth and eighteenth floors of a new and imposing building at One Park Avenue, at 32nd Street. This occurred on May 1. C.I.T. was to occupy these same quarters for the next 31 years.

In many respects the year was a difficult one. This is the way Henry Ittleson early in 1927 summarized to the board of directors the trying nature of the conditions his company had encountered in the previous year:

In the year 1926 the company went through a period of test. There had developed in the latter part of 1925 and through the greater part of 1926 a serious competitive situation. Many companies had joined the finance field during the preceding years that were not experienced. Men from all walks of life, retired merchants, bankers, insurance men and others had formed finance and credit companies believing that it was an easy way to make money quickly and without any knowledge of the proper methods of operation or the management problems involved. In their eagerness for business, and due to the desire of manufacturers and dealers to sell as many automobiles as possible, a great deal of business was taken through the country without proper credit checking and upon terms with respect to down payments and the duration of the notes that should not have been purchased.

Our company adhered as strictly as possible to its standards of business and in order to meet competition we reduced our rates substantially in the latter part of 1925. It is doubtful whether we could have secured the volume of business in 1926 that we did secure if we had not made this reduction in rates, but if we had been able to do that volume on our former rates our return would have been far greater than shown for 1926.

Furthermore, our cost of money in 1926 was on an average of a half percent more than it was in 1925 and, with an average outstanding liability of approximately $55,000,000, this meant a difference of about $275,000. Notwithstanding these factors, we were able to show a considerable increase in profits over the profits of 1925. [Note: $1.59 million vs. $1.03 million]

We have reason to believe that a tendency has developed toward a sounder basis of financing. The industry has been going through that period of test and re-adjustment that is usually met with in all new industries at some stage. We are happy to say that while our performance during the year was not up to our entire satisfaction, it was very much better than that of most of our large competitors. In the last four months of 1926 we charged off items amounting to $354,000 in the State of Florida in addition to writing down the value of repossessed cars on hand in the State of Florida by the sum of $67,700, making an aggregate of $422,000.

We enter the year 1927 with the affairs of our company in good condition and taken on a conservative basis. It will be our policy, however, not to expand our volume at the expense of safety, and we are insisting upon conservatism in the passing of credits.

The losses sustained by the company in Florida, which were the largest C.I.T. had experienced in one situation in its history to that time, were caused by the collapse of the land boom in that state in 1925–26. Henry Ittleson, Jr., recalled in later years that he was dispatched there to help with collections and that a corps of men from all of the company's other offices also were pulled into Florida to try to cut the losses. Both automobile and electrical appliance transactions were involved in a wave of delinquencies from all over the state.

Concerning the Florida difficulties, in May 1926 Vogel wrote this report to Ittleson, who was in England:

> I am satisfied that the Florida situation is now well in hand but it has taken quite some handling. We have had sixty adjusters in the State of Florida, and, of course, that kind of operation cannot be handled without heavy expense. The great lesson from this is that volume of business is of no value to us unless that volume is of the kind that can be handled profitably and with little expense.

A committee management structure had been introduced, replacing the unilateral Ittleson, Hemphill, Collins or Dietz decision-making process of the past. The following typical examples from the committee's 1926 files illustrate this system:

> It was decided to definitely limit the amount of new car paper which we would take from any one dealer running over 12 months, to an amount not exceeding 10% of the total number of transactions which we finance for a given dealer. [April 26, 1926]

> Owing to the accumulation of the following credit files due to our policy of having the Committee pass on amounts of $100,000. or over, nothing was discussed at this meeting with the exception of the approval of and the placing of commitments on the following accounts:
>
> James Manufacturing Company, Fort Atkinson, Wis. $150,000. line subject to increase when it gets to that point, divided as follows: $100,000. for the purchase of barn equipment paper and $50,000. for incubator paper.
>
> H. G. Fischer & Company, Chicago, Detroit, San Francisco and New York. $125,000. for our New York Office (their Chicago, Detroit, and New York Offices) and $25,000. for our San Francisco Office (their San Francisco Office).
>
> Henry Pels & Company, New York City and Germany—$50,000.
>
> Alfred Hoffman & Company, West New York, N.J.—$175,000.
>
> Wood Newspaper Machinery Company, New York City—$200,000. subject to increase.
>
> Pittsburgh Water Heater Company, Pittsburgh, Pa.—$150,000.
>
> Peppas & Alex Company, Cleveland, Ohio—$100,000. Dealer should be advised immediately that this is as far as we will go with him, so that he will have a chance to make other arrangements if necessary. [October 28, 1926]

Two important acquisitions were made in the summer of 1927, only a week apart. The Chicago Acceptance Corporation, operating in Illinois, Indiana, Wisconsin and Minnesota and with assets of $4 million, was bought for cash. The company had been organized by Hudson Motor Company distributors in the Midwest and financed Hudson and Essex car sales exclusively. *The New York Times* noted, "Its absorption by Commercial Investment Trust follows closely the announcement made recently by the Hudson Motor Car Company of Detroit of a nationwide contract with Commercial Investment Trust to extend low finance rates to Hudson and Essex dealers throughout the United States."

The second purchase, also for cash, was the L. F. Weaver Company. This San Francisco-based company had pioneered in automobile dealer financing, its activities antedating those of C.I.T., although it operated only in its immediate local area. Total assets at the time of the acquisition were $2 million. The Weaver operations were merged with C.I.T.'s newly organized Pacific Coast operations. Two members of the Weaver family, the company's principal officers, joined the C.I.T. organization.

An interesting incident occurred in the fall of 1927 when the City of St. Louis was devastated by a hurricane on September 29. Total damage exceeded $50 million. C.I.T. had more than $400,000 outstanding in retail automobile contracts in the city of its birth, but its total losses were under $500. An account written at the time said:

> One of the main reasons why this loss was so small throws an interesting sidelight on the company's operating policies in view of the popular conception that large finance companies are cold financial institutions with but one aim—to get their money. When the hurricane occurred and a great part of the city was laid waste, the company, instead of rushing in and repossessing automobiles and other goods, followed not only good business judgment but also a most humane policy by advising its clients that it would extend their notes until such time as business had readjusted itself, and in some instances where automobiles had been damaged, and the owner was unable to pay for the repairs, the company arranged for the necessary repairs. This method of handling the situation is the principal reason why losses attributable to the catastrophe were negligible.

The New York Times published a somewhat similar account:

> To show the stability of instalment credit in periods of strain or depression, the Commercial Investment Trust Corporation reported yesterday that its losses resulting from the St. Louis hurricane in September totaled less than $500, although it had credits of $400,000 outstanding in the city at the time.

This experience was similar to that met in the area affected by the Pennsylvania anthracite strike of 1925. The losses of the company in this area, while abnormal, were not serious. The company reports that in the past twelve years its credit losses, which were covered by reserves created out of income and based on total obligations purchased of $894,813,000, were less than one-fourth of 1 per cent.

The general standard in automobile financing is to require a down payment of one-third of the cash price, according to the company. On this basis, it estimates that repossessions of automobiles for which sales were financed by credit companies amounted to about 2 per cent of sales financed in 1927.

Although 1926 had been characterized by Ittleson as a testing year for C.I.T., business conditions in 1927 proved to be even more exacting. The volume of business purchased, which had scored an 800% gain during the six previous years, actually showed a decline from $206 million in 1926 to $188 million. Earnings were also off, from $3.57 million to $3.02 million.

The reasons for this reduced showing were several. All of the competitive problems of 1926 did not diminish as much as Ittleson had hoped, money costs remained high, and there was a sharp drop in retail auto sales and related financing volume. In 1926, 3.69 million passenger vehicles were sold in the U.S., but the 1927 sales reached only 2.93 million. C.I.T.'s automotive portfolio dropped from $34.71 million at the end of 1926 to $20.73 million at the close of 1927, while truck and motor bus receivables declined from $5 million to $3.5 million.

The decline in motor vehicle sales was caused by a so-called pause or slight recession in the U.S. domestic economy during the latter half of 1926 and all of 1927. This was really only a "minor interruption of the great onrush of economic activity from 1921 to 1929," as the National Bureau of Economic Research has described it.

The more conservative credit stance that Ittleson had established as 1927 began had its effect on the delinquency record. At the end of 1926, accounts 60 days or more past due were 0.77% of total outstandings, with auto receivables at 0.91%. On the following June 30, overall delinquencies had dropped to 0.59%, with auto paper at 0.75%. By the year-end, total delinquencies were 0.33% ($154,000) of the total portfolio of $46.4 million, while auto delinquencies were only 0.36% of the amount outstanding.

In a formal report to its lender banks at the time, the company listed the principal makes of cars it was financing at wholesale as Chandler, Dodge Brothers, Hudson, Essex, Hupmobile, Overland, Nash and

Reo. These were all the leading "independent" makes except Studebaker, which, as we have seen, had its own finance company, Motor Dealers Credit Corporation. This company, of course, was bought by C.I.T. in 1928, increasing the company's dominant position in the "independent" market.

The industrial division's business, under the leadership of Frank Collins and a young right-hand man, Roman J. Greil, stood up very well. Receivables outstanding in this category gained $7.47 million—from $12.27 million at the 1926 year-end to $19.74 million. Young Greil had been a college-years friend of Henry Ittleson, Jr., attended Cornell, and had joined C.I.T. shortly after his graduation. He had made his mark from the beginning and was rising rapidly in the company. Older members of management expected his brilliance and industry to win him a top position in C.I.T.'s affairs in time. Unfortunately, he was fatally stricken by poliomyelitis in 1930.

In August 1927, David May died. Second only to Henry Ittleson in his contributions to the creation of C.I.T. and to its success up to that time, he was memorialized by his fellow directors in a lengthy resolution of tribute, which read in part:

> David May was the pioneer type. He knew the meaning of personal labor, the significance of sustained endeavor and the value of human contacts. Simple in his nature, in his tastes and in his habits of life, he was approachable by all men. He was fundamentally tolerant when seemingly combative. No man need ever to have refrained from the expression of an opposing point of view, so long as it was honestly entertained. But he was intolerant of sham and possessed a rare faculty for its detection. By indefatigable labor, by the force of example, and by the exercise of a clear natural intelligence, he succeeded signally in enterprise. His capacity for surrounding himself with able men, his ability to vest them with responsibility which they were able to carry, and the example of application which he afforded contributed to the successful up-building of the structure associated with his name. Notwithstanding the greatness of the institution which he created, he never failed to have comprehensive knowledge of its status. He was a builder who built the quality of his character into the structure that he reared. And he continued to build though he well knew that posterity, not he, would be the user. The fullness of his years in no wise lessened the respect of those who were associated with him for his judgment.

Economic conditions rallied sharply in 1928. The organization's financial resources, local office expansion program and operating controls were prepared to handle any increases in business that might occur and the reversal in volume and earnings of 1927 was followed by impressive gains in 1928. Business volume rose nearly $100 million over the previous year to $282 million and earnings were 57% higher at $5.28 million. At the year-end, the retail automobile portfolio showed an increase from $49.5 million to $75.8 million and the industrial portfolio kept pace by increasing from $22 million to $37.8 million. Earnings per common share were $9.71 against $4.92 for 1927.

Financial developments in 1928 included the sale of $15 million of convertible 20-year debentures in March and the sale of an additional 127,429 shares of common stock to stockholders in November at a price of $95 a share. Coincident with the sale of the common stock, the annual dividend rate was raised to $4 a share in cash plus a 4% stock dividend.

Early in the year, the operating subsidiary, "C.I.T.I.," had entered into a contract to supply management and supervision for the Westinghouse Electric Acceptance Corporation. The offices of that organization were moved from Pittsburgh to One Park Avenue, as a tenant of C.I.T.

Another interesting transaction involved the purchasing of retail and wholesale collateral notes of the Refrigeration Discount Corporation, Detroit, as a joint venture of C.I.T. and Commercial Credit Company.

There was one significant acquisition during the year. The Carolina Credit Company, operating five offices in North Carolina, was purchased from interests associated with the Richardson-Merrill pharmaceutical company. At the end of the year, through the execution of the Dietz plan to develop a localized service network, the company was operating 99 offices in the United States and Canada. They functioned under four virtually autonomous "companies" or profit centers, located in New York, Chicago, San Francisco and Toronto.

16

On to New Heights

For C.I.T., the surging momentum of 1928 carried over into 1929 and was intensified. In fact, an entirely new and ultimately most important field of financing activity had been opened for the company in the latter half of 1928. This was a direct entry into old-line, non-notification factoring.

As has been noted, the company had long engaged in discounting accounts receivable on a non-notification basis (payment to be made to the seller, who would remit to C.I.T.) as well as on a notification one (direct collection by C.I.T. from the debtor but with the seller responsible for non-payment). Factoring, however, involved the not-so-subtle difference that the factor would *purchase* the buyer's obligations outright from the seller and would not only handle their collection but would assume all credit risks.

Chance may have played a part in taking C.I.T. into the factoring business. In 1926, the company was carrying a large amount of accounts receivable for a large textile firm. The firm had a very dynamic and reputedly successful sales manager who one day committed suicide in a hotel room in St. Louis.

This development caused great concern among the C.I.T. executive group and one of its key accountants was detailed to investigate the situation and the condition of the firm's accounts. He could find nothing wrong, but his assurance did not seem enough, in view of the exposure involved. Sigfried Peierls, the principal partner of Peierls, Buhler & Company, Inc., a leading factoring firm, was a close friend of Henry Ittleson. Because of his firm's experience in textile financing, he was asked to have his organization undertake the collection task, which was successfully accomplished.

This association appears to have quickened the interest of C.I.T. in factoring as a logical extension of its existing lines of business. Over a period of months, Ittleson and then Vogel held discussions with the principals of Peierls, Buhler, several of whom were at or over retirement age. Estate problems loomed for them, and their company, despite its excellent reputation, was encountering tight money conditions.

The upshot of these talks was that on August 20, 1928, C.I.T. purchased all of the preferred and common stock of the factoring firm. Cash was paid for the $2 million (par value) preferred stock, and 16,500 shares of C.I.T. common, with a market value of approximately $70 a share, or $1.15 million, were exchanged for the common stock. In addition to employment contracts signed with certain of the older Peierls, Buhler officers, Robert G. Blumenthal, a youthful vice president of the firm, received an agreement appointing him president of that firm and a vice president of Commercial Investment Trust Corporation. He also received a four-year option for 4,000 C.I.T. common shares at the attractive price of $55 a share. Shortly afterward, he was elected to the C.I.T. board of directors.

Backed by Vogel, the aggressive and imaginative Blumenthal soon began to urge C.I.T.'s managers to make a major invasion of the factoring field by acquiring others among the many family-held concerns that comprised it. He offered to spearhead such an effort and told the C.I.T. board soon after he joined it, "Some day you can do a $300 million business a year in factoring."

Whether the particular action preceded or arose from Blumenthal's strong advocacy of expansion into factoring, C.I.T. made a second important acquisition in the field only six months after buying Peierls, Buhler. On February 1, 1929, the directors approved the purchase of another of the largest and most prestigious firms in the factoring business. This was Fredk. Vietor & Achelis, Inc., which had been founded in 1828 and had just observed its centenary.

The consideration was a large one—nearly $6.5 million in common stock, plus a cash payment of $315,000. There are conflicting interpretations in the records of exactly what influences motivated the Vietor and Achelis families to sell their company. Certain members of the families were said to be heavily committed in the stock market and eager to raise cash. The firm itself was encountering the same tight money conditions that plagued other financing organizations with limited capital during the period.

Two of the younger, active officers of the Vietor firm were given opportunities and options to buy C.I.T. stock in order to retain their services. They were Johnfritz Achelis and Thomas Smidt. Thomas F. Vietor was elected to the board of directors.

A month later in early March, the Peierls, Buhler and Vietor & Achelis firms were merged into a single company, which was given the name "Commercial Factors Corporation." Blumenthal was named president to head the new organization. The merger caused much pain and many heartaches for staff members of the two proud and long-time competitive companies. There were some departures, but the C.I.T. high command maintained a "hands off" policy, and in due course Blumenthal, Achelis and their associates welded the two acquisitions into a strong and effective combination, which was the world's largest factoring organization.

For the stated purposes of "providing additional working capital necessary for the large volume of business resulting from the acquisition of Fredk. Vietor & Achelis, Inc., the contracts for taking over the financing companies of the Studebaker Corporation and the Pierce-Arrow Company and for other developments of the Corporation's business," the directors authorized the sale of $35 million of 5½% convertible 20-year debentures to the public on February 4, 1928. The issue was underwritten by Dillon Read & Co. and Lehman Brothers. This was the first underwriting relationship between the latter firm and C.I.T.

The debentures were to be convertible into common stock at a price of $200 a share during the first two years, $220 a share in the next two years and $240 in the next two years to February 1, 1935. They would not be convertible after that date. Call privileges, at the option of the corporation, also were established.

The business of Equipment Finance Corporation, primarily engaged in financing industrial and household equipment and furniture, was purchased in May for a price of $2 million. This Chicago-based company had been in existence for fifteen years and was handling an annual business volume of $10 million. It was merged into the C.I.T. operating company.

The first half of 1929 was resoundingly successful for C.I.T. Earnings were $4 million, compared with $2.2 million in the first half of 1928. Total new business booked reached $265 million against $130 million for the '28 period. At June 30, the portfolio of receivables outstanding had scored a solid $100 million gain over the preceding mid-year date, rising from $90 million to $190 million. Automobile and industrial financing operations made nearly equal contributions to the increases in new business and the portfolio of receivables held.

President Ittleson, who had been consistently brief in his comments to his stockholders in earlier reports, was moved to a more sweeping comment on general economic conditions in the June 30 report. He wrote:

> We have been witnessing an extraordinary increase in industry and commerce in this country and it is my belief that we are now in an era of world-wide industrial and financial development. The reparations settlement and the establishment of the Bank for International Settlements will undoubtedly result in further stabilization among the nations of Europe that should give additional stimulus to industry and increase our overseas trade. American financial services must keep pace with the growing demands of a peaceful and prosperous world. Recent important bank mergers are indicative of intelligent preparation for new and enlarged financial requirements. In these anticipated developments, it is our purpose that C.I.T. shall be prepared to take its necessary part. I earnestly believe that as our country continues its progress, C.I.T. will constantly enlarge its fields of activity, its usefulness and the diversity of its operations.

The next forward step in the development of the factoring operations took place shortly after the mid-year when Ridley, Watts & Company, a factoring concern doing a $25 million annual business in the cotton goods industry, was acquired. Its operations were merged into those of Commercial Factors Corporation.

At the July directors' meeting when this transaction was approved, allotments also were made to seven employees for the purchase of common stock at $100 a share. Four of these individuals were destined to assume increasing prominence in the affairs of the company. They were (with the number of shares allotted to each): Ottar Nerby (75), Joseph G. Myerson (20), L. Walter Lundell (15) and Alan G. Rude (15). The market price of the stock at the time was in the $170-per-share range.

Noting the high market price of the stock, which seemingly put its purchase beyond the financial reach of many investors, in August, Ittleson proposed to his fellow directors that the common stock be split on a 2½-for-1 basis and that a stockholders' meeting be called to authorize this. It was believed that this would broaden the market for the stock and increase the number of shareholders. He also recommended that the existing $4 annual cash dividend policy be continued after the split ($1.60 annually on the split shares) but that the stock dividend after the split be raised from 4% to 6%.

He also recommended that the stockholders be asked to approve the sale to the public of 50,000 new common shares at $182 a share through an underwriting by Dillon Read and the granting of a one-year option to them for the purchase of 25,000 additional shares at (pre-split) prices ranging from $190 a share to $218 a share.

The stockholders approved this program on September 10 and the split became effective on October 8.

With the economy flourishing, the stock market booming and C.I.T.'s own operations picking up increasing momentum on the heels of the excellent showing of the first half of the year, further financing developments followed closely after the stock-split program. On October 2, an agreement was completed with Dillon Read and Lehman Brothers, as principal underwriters, for the sale of 400,000 shares of a new issue of convertible preference stock at $94.50 a share and 125,000 split shares of common stock at $70 a share. The contract was approved by the stockholders at another special meeting held on October 9.

No doubt because of the size of the offering, for the first time in C.I.T.'s history the two original underwriters formed a syndicate of investment houses to market it. The members were, in addition to the principal firms, A. G. Becker & Company, E. H. Rollins and Sons, Shields & Company, Inc. and the Chemical National Company.

The management had stated to the stockholders in the proxy solicitation for the October 9 meeting that the increase in the company's permanent capital (in excess of $56 million) would raise its capital and surplus "not subject to withdrawal or fluctuating interest costs" to more than $108 million. "With business and receivables at record high levels," the statement continued, "and current bank indebtedness reduced more than fifty percent (by the infusion of new capital) the corporation will be enabled, at a more stabilized money cost, to continue the vital services rendered by it to manufacturers and merchants throughout the world."

17

. . . And the Crash of '29

Following the offering of the 400,000 shares of preference stock and 125,000 shares of common stock at $70 per share on October 14, the market price of C.I.T. common rose as high as $76. Beginning with October 18, however, the price eased into the 60's, below the recent offering price. At the beginning of the week of October 21, it was at 65½.

The general market was weak through Monday, Tuesday and Wednesday. Then came "Bloody Thursday," the day of the most catastrophic market break in the history of the New York Stock Exchange and the nation's other securities markets. On that day, with the ticker running hours late, a record of nearly 13 million shares changed hands and the Dow-Jones industrial average crashed from 312 to a low of 229. Tens of thousands of margin calls were issued and thousands of margin accounts were sold out by the brokers holding them. Commercial Investment Trust Corporation common opened that morning at 60½, dropped to a low of 46½ and rallied (as did many stocks) to close the day at 56⅞.

The rally was touched off at 1:30 when Richard Whitney, vice president of the Exchange—acting for J. P. Morgan & Company, for which he was the regular floor broker, and a group of the major New York City banks—stemmed the receding tide of prices with his dramatic bid to buy a large block of U.S. Steel at 205, although the previous sale had been 12 points lower. Often called the most celebrated trade in stock market history, this bid was followed by others as Whitney went from trading post to trading post to make other purchases for the supporters of the market whom he represented. He bid 57⅜ for General Electric when it had last sold at 49, 74 for Montgomery Ward against a prior price of 50. Block after block of other blue chip stocks were bought at confidence-restoring prices until he had invested a total of $20 million for his group.

On Friday the 25th, C.I.T. sold at 55. On Monday the 28th, a further decline was registered to a low of 45½, and in the holocaust of Tuesday the 29th, the price dropped to a low of 31⅞ and closed at 38, cutting the value of the stock in half in two weeks. The Exchange traded a record 16.4 million shares as prices collapsed. The average broke through the low of the previous Thursday to 212. On the following two days, C.I.T. common rallied to a high of 48¾ and then fluctuated between that price and a low of 28 during the rest of the year, closing 1929 on a final sale of 39¼.

C.I.T.'s management reacted promptly and sharply to the market break. A special meeting of the executive committee was assembled on the morning of October 30. Ittleson reviewed the conditions in the securities markets. He then proposed that in the event of a further decline in the prices of the company's preferred and common stocks and debentures, it might be possible to buy in "at favorable prices" such securities, either for investment or retirement. The officers were given a blanket authorization to take this action.

The president also reported that the company had made substantial investments in the stocks of May Department Stores, Lehman Corporation and Commercial Credit Company. The May Stores purchases, at an average price of 82¾ for 20,000 shares, appear to have been made during the week of the 21st, as the stock ranged between 81 and 76 in that period, after previously selling at higher prices. The Lehman purchase of 1,600 shares at 102 also fell within the price range for that week. The Commercial Credit purchase of 9,900 shares apparently was made earlier in the month when the price was in the 48 range. (The earlier high for the year was 60.) In the October 21st week, Commercial Credit fluctuated between 32 and 29. Against the general market performance, the investments looked favorable, as Ittleson commented.

In another action of the executive committee at the October 30 meeting, the officers were authorized to make loans to employees who had purchased company stock on the open market, using the stock as collateral for purchase-money loans. If these loans were called, the company stood ready to repay them and would accept the employee's stock as collateral for the funds advanced. The reason given for this action was to "prevent the forced sale of such stock in order to avoid disturbance on the part of such employees so that their interest in their duties would not be distracted."

As the C.I.T. officers met, the nation was in a state of financial daze. It had been decided to close the Exchange to trading on that Friday and Saturday and to open Monday, but another closing was scheduled for Tuesday, Election Day. While the stunned stock traders caught their breath, a rallying chorus of reassurance and support for the fundamental soundness of the general economy and the securities markets was being raised.

John D. Rockefeller, Sr., made his historic announcement on the 30th that "my son and I have for some days been purchasing common stocks." Similarly, John J. Raskob, Democratic national chairman and the financial power for both Du Pont and General Motors, said stocks were selling at bargain prices and he and his friends were buying stocks. William Wrigley, Jr., also declared the market offered many bargains. Julius Rosenwald, chairman of Sears, Roebuck, announced that he was confident of the economy's health and that Sears would make loans to any employees who needed funds to cover their margin accounts. Many other business leaders voiced similar statements of faith and optimism. American Can Company raised its common dividend and voted an extra dividend on the 30th, and the board of U.S. Steel voted a $1 extra payment on the common stock on the same day.

Henry Ittleson also was heard from. On Friday, he joined the other business spokesmen by issuing a statement saying C.I.T.'s collections from its borrowers had not been affected by the market break. While he foresaw a "moderate recession," he said, "automobiles are purchased on the instalment plan by high-grade artisans and middle-class businessmen and executives rather than by stock market speculators. Besides, automobiles are now regarded as necessities rather than luxuries in this country."

He followed this with an interview for *The New York Times* that appeared on December 1. This was a forthright call for confidence and a testament to the soundness of the instalment credit mechanism.

> In the stock decline, ownership of securities changed hands, but management of American industry is unchanged, its record of earnings still

stands, the physical value of its properties is unaffected and inventories are generally low in volume and cost.

Only a small percentage of the people actually lost cash or savings and the majority of those who did lose have not lost their earning power or credit. Money is plentiful and will be cheap. Labor in general is employed at wages well above actual living necessities. The very acuteness and speed of the deflation of security values is in itself a good factor. In previous deflations, besides inventories inflated in price and volume and tight money, the people of the country faced a continuing decline of long duration.

Mr. Hoover's prompt action in asking industry to cooperate to prevent a decrease in the earning power of the American public should result in quick restoration of confidence.

Diagnosis of a nation-wide condition and a survey of the operations of the corporation show no effect to date in the current volume of consumer credit and the current payment of consumer credit instalments. This, in my opinion, is a confirmation of the general belief that the percentage of people who were directly and seriously involved in stock market operations were small and that the percentage was still smaller among people of moderate income, who buy on the instalment plan.

We believe that this is a time of opportunity. We have instructed our organization to go more vigorously than ever after new and sound business, granting both production and consumer credits wherever they are deserved. If there is a recession in business many people who have heretofore purchased for cash will use the facilities of instalment credit. Furthermore, in such periods our corporation has had, and will have, increasing opportunities for extending credit to industrial activities of all kinds that in times of greater prosperity do not require our credit facilities.

Our organization has absolute confidence in the soundness of so-called instalment paper. This confidence is an expression of faith in the responsibility and integrity of the average American consumer.

A few days earlier, C.I.T. announced that it had entered into a major contract with the Radio Corporation of America through which it would lease talking motion picture equipment to theatre exhibitors on a ten-year basis, with all lease payments to be completed within three years. RCA was playing the leading part in manufacturing the sound equipment for the talkie boom that was sweeping the nation. The agreement complemented C.I.T.'s earlier contract for the financing of RCA radio sets.

During the early days of November, the officers also acted on the authorization given them by the executive committee to repurchase shares of the corporation's preferred and common stocks and debentures. It was reported at the directors' meeting of November 18 that blocks of the 7% and 6½% first preferred stock, the common stock and the gold notes and 6% and 5½% convertible debentures had been acquired at what Ittleson described as "favorable prices." Prices paid for the common stock were in the low and middle 30's and in the $80–$96 range for the preferred stock, notes and debentures, against their issuing price in the previous year of $100. The board voted to continue such purchases under favorable circumstances.

C.I.T. again set across-the-board records in its 1929 operations. New business volume reached $490 million, surpassing the record 1928 performance by more than $200 million. Net earnings nearly doubled to $9.1 million from 1928's $5.3 million, and earnings per common share were $4.47 against $3.88 in the preceding year.

Based on this showing, President Ittleson seemed to have ample support for his comments to the stockholders in the annual report for the year that:

> The business recession through which the country is passing, in my opinion, should not be of long duration and is only a pause in the country's industrial progress. The Corporation's commodity—Credit— is in demand and will continue in demand. Its exceptionally strong capital and credit position, plus a trained, loyal organization will enable it to continue its growth and development along sound conservative lines.
>
> The Corporation's services are used during periods of business recession as well as in periods of business activity. They are also services that by their very nature are instrumental in stimulating production. We look forward with a firm faith in the country's industrial future and in our ability to serve it.

18

The Depression Years

The very unusual nature of C.I.T.'s business allows a greater rate of safe expansion (or contraction) than is inherent in almost any other type of business. If a store, a manufacturing enterprise, public utility or any such business engages in expansion, this necessarily requires a substantial increase in fixed investment. At a later time, if the expanded facilities are not required, it is most difficult to contract or safeguard the investment that has been made in fixed assets. This being the case, such managements must always proceed with relative caution and wait carefully on their commitments before permitting further growth.

In the case of C.I.T., however, since our capital remains in the form of cash or receivables, no fixed assets were required by growth and it was relatively easy to put all new resources immediately to work in transactions offering good possibilities for profit. The management did not need to weigh elements of caution in the same degree that is necessary in other lines of business. This in itself contributed greatly to the essential *conservatism* of C.I.T.'s growth.

The truth of this statement was borne out in the period about 1931–32 when the business of the company actually did contract materially from the levels obtained in the late 1920's. When this occurred, C.I.T. called a number of issues of preferred stock, which carried high dividend rates. C.I.T. thus contracted almost as readily and as flexibly as it had expanded. The net result of this was that there was at least one period in the early 1930's when C.I.T. actually owed no debt at all and was operating purely with its own capital.

—Edwin C. Vogel
from an interview, August 10, 1951

In a nutshell, in the years 1930 through 1932 C.I.T.'s volume of new business booked, total assets and net income declined each year but remained comfortably above the levels of 1928, the all-time record prior to 1929. Only the assets figure was an exception, decreasing slightly below the 1928 year-end figure in 1933. As for total dividends paid on the common stock, these topped both the 1928 and 1929 distributions in every year of the period, although earnings per share were lower than in '28 and '29.

The following table gives these yardsticks of corporate operations for the years while the nation was in the depths of its worst depression:

	Volume of Business Purchased (Millions)	Total Assets at End of Year (Millions)	Net Income (Millions)	Earned per Common Share*
1928	$282,164,000	$142,591,000	$5,294,000	$3.88
1929	489,544,000	209,130,000	9,166,000	4.47
1930	392,044,000	166,877,000	8,319,000	2.75
1931	374,094,000	159,462,000	7,555,000	2.54
1932	317,398,000	119,160,000	5,720,000	2.04

*Adjusted for 2½-for-1 split October 8, 1929.

Another forward move of consequence was completed in implementing the Vogel-Blumenthal plan to expand the factoring operations. In April 1930, the 102-year-old, highly respected firm of Schefer, Schramm & Vogel was acquired by Commercial Factors Corporation for cash. Later in the year, another factoring firm, L. Erstein & Bros., Inc., was similarly purchased.

An industrial finance company, Manufacturers Finance Company, of Baltimore, sold most of its portfolio and active accounts to C.I.T. at the year's end.

In the year 1930, the automobile department was hardest hit by the effects of the depression. The retail motor portfolio dropped to $68.3 million at December 31, compared with $102.8 million a year earlier. Industrial receivables (including factored obligations) were down only a slight amount, to $67.6 million from $71.5 million.

At the annual meeting of stockholders held on March 20, 1931, action was taken to retire 20,800 shares of the 7% first preferred stock, 25,000 shares of the 6½% first preferred stock, 73,497 shares of the 1929 convertible preference stock and 125,000 shares of the common stock. All of these securities had been purchased in the market by use of the company's surplus cash. The total reduction in capital (with accompanying savings in future dividend requirements) totaled $12.9 million at the time of the meeting. Some of the common stock was purchased at a price as low as 24½ a share.

The stockholders were told that the reduction in capital was being made because of the corporation's reduced need for funds as financing volume declined and that the capital position of the enterprise would not be impaired in any way by the action. The repurchase of the company's various classes of securities was to continue.

Effective with the common stock dividend paid on April 1, 1931, the annual rate was changed from a payment of $1.60 a share plus a 6% stock dividend to a cash payment of $2.00 a share, discontinuing the stock dividends. C.I.T. thus became one of the few listed companies to increase its cash payout to its stockholders in the difficult year of 1931.

Recognizing the financial difficulties that C.I.T. employees and their families could experience especially in times of worsening economic conditions, Commodore Louis D. Beaumont established the Louis D. Beaumont Foundation on June 27, 1930. Commodore Beaumont, as Louis D. Shoenberg, had been one of Henry Ittleson's closest friends and associates and was one of the founding directors of the corporation. In 1930, he was still an active member of the board. He adopted the Gallic form of his family name during World War I at the height of the antipathy in the United States to all things German.

Commodore Beaumont endowed the foundation for the purpose of "rendering charitable assistance to whomsoever shall be in need thereof and more especially the employees of Commercial Investment Trust Corporation and their families." It was directed that "the trustees shall apply the net income in assisting financially those who because of illness or for any cause whatsoever shall be in need of charitable aid, or in their discretion shall pay over said net income to such incorporated charitable institutions, engaged in a similar charitable endeavor, as they may select provided, however, that the Trustees shall first give preference to faithful and loyal employees, and to their families and dependents, if said employees be dead or disabled, who now are or who have been or may at any time hereafter be or have been in the employ of the said Commercial Investment Trust Corporation, or any of the companies which both at the date of this Indenture and during the period of such service shall be owned or controlled by it."

Messrs. Ittleson, Haberman, Dietz, Ittleson, Jr. and the corporate treasurer, Frederick A. Franklin, were named as trustees. The Beaumont Foundation has continued to render great benefits to the employees of C.I.T. and others to the present day. As most of its funds were invested in C.I.T. securities, the value of its assets has increased considerably over the years despite the distributions from both capital and investment income that have been made.

Commodore Beaumont's generosity was duly and gratefully acknowledged by his C.I.T. associates. No doubt motivated by the earlier action of his friend Beaumont as well as the evident financial straits that C.I.T. families were experiencing even when one member was still employed, Henry Ittleson in the following March (1931) established the Ittleson Beneficial Fund for use as the officers might see fit "to render charitable assistance to employees of the corporation and their families." This gift was acknowledged with warm thanks by the directors. In total, the two funds had an original endowment of $120,000, which was increased by later gifts.

At the July 1931 board meeting, President Ittleson observed that the corporation's name had been criticized on the grounds that the words "investment trust" were misleading. It was agreed that it would be desirable to adopt a more accurately descriptive name. Vogel was appointed chairman of a committee of five directors to study the matter and perhaps propose a new name. The committee was directed to make a report at the October meeting, but no meeting was held in that month and the matter apparently was dropped since no further references to it appear in the records of the time.

While the assets of several small local automobile and general instalment financing organizations were purchased during the year, the next major stride forward in the acquisition program took place on November 12 when another leading factoring firm, Morton H. Meinhard & Company, was purchased. The founder, whose name the organization bore, had recently died and the major seller was his estate. Concurrently, most of the accounts of Greeff & Company, Inc., another century-old factor, were acquired. The Meinhard organization and the Greeff business were then merged to establish a second C.I.T.-owned factoring company under the name Meinhard-Greeff & Co., Inc. The former Meinhard company had been doing a $30-

million-a-year business and the Greeff organization also had many
loyal clients with long-standing personal ties to its management, so it
was thought wise to preserve the identity of the two firms, rather than
merge them into Commercial Factors Corporation.

Throughout the year, the company continued to make repurchases of
its various classes of securities. By the year-end, 90,000 shares of the
common stock had been purchased at an average cost of $23.11 a
share. In addition, $11 million of the 5½% convertible debentures,
7,900 shares of the 6½% preferred stock, 115,000 shares of the 6%
preferred stock and 1,000 shares of the 7% preferred stock had been
reacquired. Most of the securities were retired but some of the common
stock was retained in the treasury (and subsequently used) for acquisitions, particularly in the factoring field.

Soon after the 1932 New Year, a still more important factoring acquisition was completed. This was William Iselin & Co., Inc., the old-
est factoring firm in the nation and second only in size to Commercial
Factors. Its annual business volume was in the $60-million range.

The Iselin business had been established in 1808 by Isaac Iselin, a
youthful emigrant from Switzerland who began his career in the New
World as a counting house clerk and maritime supercargo. He then
struck out on his own by forming a partnership to sell European-made
textiles on commission to the U.S. market. This involved receiving the
goods on consignment, selling them on credit, assuming the collection
risks and keeping separate sets of books for each European source.

He passed the business on to his descendants and their various
partners who were taken into the firm. By the middle of the century, the
firm was known as Iselin, Neeser & Company. With the passing years,
the domestic textile business had come of age in the United States,
greatly reducing the need for European imports. The Iselin firm took
on many domestic mills as clients, but in due course most of them built
up their own sales staffs, so they no longer required the primary
commission-selling services of the firm. However, the functions of
extending credit to purchasers, accepting the credit responsibility and
maintaining the underlying ledger records was of vital importance to
these manufacturers, who, like Henry Ittleson's first clients in other
lines, did not have the resources to offer credit to their customers.
Thus, while almost all the factoring firms continued their selling function on a limited basis, by the opening of the twentieth century they
were primarily engaged in the same activities they were pursuing at the
time of C.I.T.'s entry into the field—a financing function involving
the purchasing of trade receivables.

Each acquisition of a factoring enterprise by C.I.T. involved somewhat different reasons why the sellers elected to dispose of their interests. However, the background of the Iselin purchase, the largest in the series, is very typical of the entire program.

In the 1920's, Henry Ittleson served on an informal advisory committee of the Central Union National Bank, a New York City institution. He had often been invited to join boards of directors of banks and other business organizations but had consistently declined to do so. The "advisory board" affiliation was as much of a commitment of this sort as he would permit himself.

Jarvis Cromwell, one of the younger partners of the Iselin firm, was also a member of this advisory board. His grandfather, James W. Cromwell, had succeeded Neeser in the Iselin partnership when the latter died in 1890. When C.I.T. began to acquire factoring companies, Ittleson on several occasions proposed to Cromwell that the Iselin partners entertain an offer from C.I.T. Cromwell politely declined these overtures, but Ittleson, as he did to others on similar occasions, regularly replied, "Some day you'll be coming to me!"

In 1930, after experiencing some reverses because of credit losses that in no way impaired the solvency of the firm, the Iselin partners, through Jarvis Cromwell, held discussions with one of their principal bankers to evaluate the financial structure of their business. The banker's principal concern proved to be the vulnerability of the partnership because of the fact that 70% of the stock was held by four men, all over 70 years of age. One of these was the senior partner, William Iselin, the grandson of the original Isaac. He alone held a 40% interest. There were ten partners in the firm.

Cromwell did not immediately see this situation as a problem, pointing out that all the partners had made wills directing that their interests be sold back to the firm. "That may be all right," the banker replied, "but the older men are the only partners with any substantial personal wealth. You younger men simply will be unable to provide the credit backing for the business that you must have if you are to continue."

When this conversation was reported to the other partners, William Iselin immediately recognized the validity of the banker's point. He at once agreed that the partnership should be converted into a corporation and committed his stock to that plan, "locking in" his investment conclusively. Investment bankers were consulted to implement that project and a plan was drawn up to carry it out by marketing four million preferred shares at an expected price of $100 to give the new corporation an adequate capital base to assure its bank credit lines.

However, this was 1931 and the market for new preferred stock suddenly collapsed, following the earlier common stock debacle. The best price the underwriters could offer was completely uninviting to the Iselin group. At this juncture, another banker suggested that Henry Ittleson's C.I.T. company might buy the stock, and such an offer to C.I.T. was made.

Ittleson and Vogel immediately rejected it. They said they were not interested in preferred stock or buying a partial interest in anything but would only be interested in buying the whole Iselin company. After much discussion, the Iselin partners concluded they had no alternative, in view of their bankers' reservations, but to go through with a total sale. They received an initial payment of 25,000 shares of C.I.T. common stock for their interests, with an additional 10,000 shares to be delivered to them if the Iselin organization's annual earnings for the years 1932–34 averaged $500,000 or better.

In the first year of C.I.T.'s ownership, the Iselin firm—it was not merged with either of the other two factoring subsidiaries but continued under the name William Iselin & Co., Inc.—fell below the target projection and the partners' $100,000 escrow fund was taken up by C.I.T. In the next two years, however, the earnings objective was amply exceeded, the fund money was returned and the withheld stock delivered. As the market price of the stock had increased appreciably during the three-year period, the partners ultimately received a far better price than they had originally bargained for.

With three independently operating factoring companies, some centralized supervision of C.I.T.'s activities in this field was necessary. Therefore, Robert G. Blumenthal, who had spearheaded the factoring program with Edwin Vogel, was selected for this responsibility and elected to the executive committee. He was succeeded as president of Commercial Factors by Francis T. Lyons in January 1932. Unfortunately, the brilliant young Blumenthal, whose future role in the company's management seemed to hold so much promise, met his death on January 14, 1933. Supposedly in excellent health, at the age of 37 he suffered a fatal heart attack at the end of an indoor polo game in which he had played a starring part.

When Lyons became a vice president of the parent company and overseer of all factoring operations, he was succeeded in the presidency of Commercial Factors by Johnfritz Achelis, a member of the family that had sold Fredk. Vietor & Achelis to C.I.T. The latter continued to head the company until his retirement as chairman of the board in 1958.

Jarvis Cromwell was made president of William Iselin & Co. in 1932 and continued as the principal officer of that subsidiary until his retirement in 1951. Edward F. Addiss was the first president of Meinhard, Greeff & Company when that company, combining several of the C.I.T. factoring units, was established. He was succeeded in 1935 by Fred Meissner, another longtime employee of the old Meinhard organization. Meissner continued to head the company until his retirement as chairman of the board in 1955.

The impact of stock market conditions on the corporation's affairs was further reflected in an action taken in the final directors' meeting of 1931. It was noted that in 1929, 1930 and 1931 contracts had been made with selected officers and employees (but not including most of the senior management members) allowing them to subscribe to allotments of common stock at $30 a share or more, with payments to be made in instalments. In the latter part of 1930, all allotment prices higher than $30 a share were reduced to $30.

When the market price fell into the low 20's in the latter months of 1931, the holders of the contracts were making payments on stock purchased at a price well above the market. To ease their plight, the directors voted to postpone the collection of any further payments from the purchasers "for the present" and to fix December 31, 1932, as the date for final payment.

Another new venture, dubbed "pay as you fly," had been launched early in 1930 when C.I.T. signed a contract to finance the wholesale and retail sales of the many types of airplanes manufactured by the Detroit Aircraft Corporation. Among these were the Ryan monoplane of which Charles A. Lindbergh's *Spirit of St. Louis* was the prototype. The Lockheed Company was another Detroit Aircraft subsidiary. An aviation department was organized and the contract was said to be the first between an aircraft manufacturer and a nonaffiliated "independent" financing source. As time passed, the aircraft program was given the support of an ambitious advertising campaign in *The Saturday Evening Post, Nation's Business* and *The New York Times* and *Chicago Tribune*. However, economic conditions of the thirties and limitations on the utility of the designs then available brought this venture to an unsatisfactory conclusion.

Another development arising from the economic decline was an opportunity offered to C.I.T. to buy the entire One Park Avenue building, of which it occupied two of nineteen floors, for the equivalent of two years' rental payments. Despite the attractiveness of the offer from the distressed owners, Ittleson rejected it summarily. He did so because of a lifelong belief that C.I.T. should remain in a wholly liquid financial condition and not invest in real estate or other fixed assets. All such investments to come in the future were made years after his death.

As 1932 opened, the company embarked on a program to liquidate all of its overseas instalment financing operations except those in Puerto Rico and Germany, plus the contractual arrangements in Great Britain. By the end of June, foreign outstandings of $4 million at the beginning of the year had been halved, with $1.4 million coming from countries where operations were to continue. (At the year-end, this figure was $910,000.) Funds were recovered from the discontinued operations, the largest amount brought back from any one country being $933,000 from Australia.

There were several reasons for the action taken. Because of the world-wide depression, U.S. automobile export sales had fallen off drastically. Thus, pressure by the manufacturers for overseas financing service was relaxed or could be largely ignored because of economic conditions, while many of the overseas branches had been only marginally profitable or were operating at a loss.

As for the countries where operations were continuing, the directors were told at their June 27, 1932, meeting that collection experience was excellent, with the record in Germany "better than it has ever been."

At that same meeting, the board was informed that since the inception in 1929 of the program to repurchase C.I.T.'s own securities, $24 million in capital stock and $27 million of debentures had been acquired and retired, reducing total capital to $85 million as compared with $105 million at the end of 1929.

During the summer of 1933, representatives from the C.I.T. management group spent much time in Washington, working with a commission that had been established to develop a government-insured credit plan for financing home improvements. The result of this effort was the creation of the historic Federal Housing Administration ("FHA") program. As another response to depression conditions, in 1932 the corporation initiated its first formal program of corporate philanthropy, making contributions to emergency relief funds in a number of cities.

It will be recalled that in the swirling controversy over the social and economic validity of consumer instalment credit in the mid-1920's, many critics prophesied disaster for creditors and debtors alike when an inevitable business recession would occur and serious unemployment would result.

Of course, the post-'29 period was not an easy time for the consumer instalment credit business, but the record entirely refuted the dire predictions of its detractors. According to Dr. Clyde William Phelps, of the University of Southern California:

> The lesson of the Great Depression with regard to sales finance companies is summed up in the statement that the remarkable stability of such companies in periods of depression attests to the soundness of their methods in general. The record made by the companies established and enhanced their standing in the eyes of bankers and all students of financial institutions.

Milan V. Ayres, in his history of the sales finance industry, wrote:

> It has been said that during the depression many finance companies lost money through bank failures but no bank lost money through finance company failures. The saying is almost literally true. Finance company failures were confined to a very few small institutions, and most of those paid their creditors in full, only their own shareholders suffering any loss.
>
> In fact, from the beginning of finance company existence, there have been hardly any failures of such companies resulting in serious loss to their bank creditors. This is true in spite of the fact that banks habitually loan to sales finance companies much larger sums of money than they would to practically any other kind of business enterprise with the same net worth.

The year-by-year record of the nationwide percentage of cars repossessed to cars sold on time payments is as follows:

1928	4.1	1931	8.5
1929	4.2	1932	10.4
1930	5.4	1933	5.7

C.I.T.'s experience in the depression was clearly better than that of the industry as a whole. At one point, in his reserved way, Ittleson wrote to his stockholders: " . . . [our] experience confirms our faith in the fundamental soundness and safety of instalment paper. While repossessions and charge-off items arising out of instalment paper acquired by us have been somewhat greater than usual in proportion to the volume of business, they have not been disturbing at any time. . . . Our outstandings . . . are in excellent condition."

The C.I.T. statistical record for the period bears out his statement:

Percentage of Instalment Accounts
30 Days or More Past Due

	Auto	Other
June 30, 1929	.23%	.59%
December 31, 1929	.18	.81
June 30, 1930	.19	1.64
December 31, 1930	.19	2.17
June 30, 1931	NA	NA
December 31, 1931	.15	1.59
June 30, 1932	.17	1.23
December 31, 1932	.11	1.22

Dollar Value of Repossessed Vehicles on Hand
vs. Total Motor Instalment Receivables Outstanding

	Value Repossessed Vehicles	Total Motor Receivables Held (Millions)
June 30, 1929	$294,000	$54,500,000
December 31, 1929	371,000	50,600,000
June 30, 1930	188,000	40,500,000
December 31, 1930	294,000	33,200,000
June 30, 1931	NA	NA
December 31, 1931	238,000	31,300,000
June 30, 1932	196,000	27,600,000
December 31, 1932	211,000	23,900,000

In a study of the loss records of sales finance companies, published in the *Harvard Business Review* in July 1956, Dr. Sidney E. Rolfe, an economist, reported that these companies estimated their credit losses "over a 20-year span of depressions, war and prosperity" at less than ½ of 1% of receivables outstanding and never to have been as high as 1% in any year.

He also made the point that combined figures of C.I.T., General Motors Acceptance Corporation and Commercial Credit show that on the $941 million of retail automobile instalment contracts purchased in 1929, the ultimate net loss, including repossession and liquidation expenses and insurance losses on repossessed vehicles, totaled less than $6 million, or less than ⅔ of 1% of the value of their combined portfolios. Their percentage of credit losses on other types of consumer instalment contracts acquired in 1929 was even less.

Fortune magazine, in January 1933, published its first study of the

C.I.T. organization. It encapsulated the company's depression experience as follows:

> In 1931, on its $374,000,000 turnover, C.I.T. made a net profit of $7,554,998; the net being almost precisely 2 per cent of the volume. In the first half of 1932, on a $171,000,000 turnover, C.I.T. made $2,900,000. For these six months its earnings were about 72 per cent of the corresponding earnings in 1929. In a business which many observers thought would be the first to feel the results of bad times, C.I.T. has shown far greater depression resistance than corporations engaged in apparently more stable enterprises. Nearly every motor-car manufacturer operated in 1932 at a large deficit, yet—although the motor car itself supplies one of the most basic and probably by far the most profitable item in C.I.T.'s operations—the company continues to collect an excellent return (7.05 per cent) on its investment. Few companies listed on the New York Stock Exchange share with C.I.T. the distinction of having raised the common cash dividend since October, 1929, and having maintained the increase. C.I.T. stock was not a conspicuous Blue Chip during the Bull Market, but few securities have better withstood the more searching test of the depression. . . .
>
> C.I.T.'s chief asset is the banking judgment of its executives. Thus far the results of that judgment have been an excellent testimonial to its soundness and its flexibility. Finding that the old accounts receivable business had a little bit outgrown its day, the company shifted smoothly and promptly into auto instalments. Fearing that an auto accessory was too much dependent upon auto prosperity, the company built up its industrial equipment business as an anchor to windward. Believing that further diversification was desirable and given an opportunity to enter the factoring field, the company went into factoring so whole-heartedly that, starting from scratch in 1928, it has become in four years' time the largest unit in a closely-held business dominated largely by family groups dating back to the middle or early 1800's. And finally, faced with the depression slackening of the demand for its capital, the company employed its surplus cash in a most successful market operation, which has materially increased the equity of every common stockholder and kept the earnings per share most respectably in the vicinity of their boom-time standard. Many an economist (and especially many a banker) shrugged his shoulders at the type of financing represented by Commercial Investment Trust. But the depression proof has made the pudding a great deal more appetizing than the economists or the banker ever imagined that it could be.

One of the staunchest defenses against the many charges that excessive growth of instalment buying had "caused" the depression and that both the grantors and users of consumer credit were exposed to

heavy losses was made by Edwin Vogel. He delivered this in a major address before the annual meeting of the United States Chamber of Commerce in Atlantic City, New Jersey, on April 30, 1931:

Although in recent years opinion of economists, bankers and business men has definitely tended toward a recognition of the soundness of instalment selling, yet it has been maintained by some that when a severe depression in business should come, with consequent unemployment, a collapse of outstanding instalment credits might ensue, that finance companies might sustain heavy losses and that instalment credits might become a financial burden. It has also been said that instalment selling has caused an undue expansion of purchasing which would cease in a period of business depression, thereby making the depression more severe. . . .

Prior to the stock market crash in October, 1929, many men of business suffered from what was near mass insanity, an unreasoning faith in the unending forward march of business, a reckless disregard of warning signals, a belief that I heard often expressed by men who are usually normal, sound and conservative, that we were in a new era in which the old tried and tested economic laws would not apply. Men were carried away by mounting, though fanciful, prosperity. Judgments were warped. It was this frame of mind, leading as it did to undue factory and business expansion, to frenzied speculation in land and securities without regard to values and with a guideless belief that prices should be based on what values would be a decade hence—it was this frame of mind, this unbelievable optimism, that was the direct cause of the reaction.

If I am correct, only in part, in my analysis of the causes of our economic disturbances, does it not seem unbelievable that any should seek to place the blame even in small part upon instalment selling? Those who do so are closing their eyes to the truth and are searching for an excuse, not for a logical reason. This must be particularly apparent when we realize that the depression is worldwide, affecting countries where instalment selling is practically unknown. . . .

Speaking for our own company, I can say unhesitatingly that the experience of the past year and a half has confirmed our faith in the fundamental soundness and safety of instalment paper. While repossessions and uncollectible accounts have been somewhat greater than in normal times they have at no time been disturbing. We did not need this test to be sure. We have been in business since 1908 and have weathered a number of depressions and business and financial disturbances, both local and nationwide.

I very much dislike to constantly refer to the experience of our own company, but its facts and figures are most readily available to me and I must, therefore, ask you to pardon me if I again refer to its experience. The crash in Wall Street came at the end of October, 1929. Of the instalment obligations outstanding on the books of our company on October 31, 1929, 69% were completely paid and liquidated by April 30, 1930, that is within six months, and 95% were liquidated by October 31, 1930, that is within one year thereafter.

It does seem to me that these facts and figures completely and conclusively answer the claim that instalment purchasing anticipates purchasing power for a long period ahead. . . .

I am firmly of the conviction that the present generation will see America in its era of greatest development, power and prosperity. To attain this end, we must employ all the proven tools that we have available, and among those that will be most helpful in restoring business to its normal condition will be the system of instalment selling. This system will not be a panacea. It will not, of itself, bring back prosperity, but when business starts to recover, it will be of substantial aid in this recovery. Merchants and manufacturers who will require new and additional machinery and equipment for more efficient and more profitable operation, will be enabled to more quickly purchase such machinery and equipment upon instalment credit, paying for it out of savings and additional profits, and the consumer, with courage restored and employment more certain, will again purchase more readily with the aid of the instalment credit that will be available to him.

We want no more booms. In our country, with its great natural wealth, its sturdy hard-working and growing population, its inventive genius, its ability to employ new methods—what we seek is not a boom, but a restoration of a reasonable balance of production and consumption. This is the true "normal," which is a condition of sound prosperity.

Phillip Haberman was the author of another comprehensive defense of his company's primary business, during which he presented a definitive analysis of the instalment credit industry's record in the depression. He did this in a challenge to one of the nation's most illustrious economists, Dean Wallace B. Donham of the Harvard Graduate School of Business Administration. *The New York Times* treated his views at length, in part saying:

> Instalment purchases have proved to be basically sound during the eighteen months of the current depression and will continue to follow the movement of cash sales in the same ratio that has prevailed for several years, in the opinion of Phillip W. Haberman, vice president and general counsel of the Commercial Investment Trust, Inc. in commenting yesterday on the assertion during the week by Wallace B. Donham, dean of Business Administration of Harvard University, that instalment selling had run its course.
>
> "There is a misconception in many quarters," Mr. Haberman continued, "that in times of depression instalment buying increases, when consumers have less money. This is not true. Experience has proved that the volume of instalment purchases during a period of depression declines in the same ratio to cash sales. Buying on time amounts to about 5 per cent of the total volume of sales in all lines of industries, and this percentage seems to be maintained from year to year.
>
> "That instalment sales are sound and will endure is proved by the fact that since the stock market crash instalment obligations have been liquidated better than many other types of credit. Percentage losses have been only a small fraction greater than those prevailing before the depression. The volume of past-due items is less than in the period before the crash.
>
> "Buying on time is not applicable to all types of products," Mr. Haberman continued. "Articles sold under such terms must be useful and durable, where obsolescence is not in inverse ratio to the declining balance. Where a purchaser has to budget his earnings to cover such items, he really makes commitments more prudently than many who are prepared to pay with cash. Buyers are also investigated thoroughly before being permitted to enter contracts."

Henry Ittleson, Jr., through the perspective of time, recalled his father's reaction to the depression years with these words:

My first recollection was that, while there was panic all over the country, there wasn't much as far as C.I.T. and its business was concerned. As I recall, the very fact that there was a panic around helped C.I.T. rather than hindered it. They had access to more business because the banks were tightening up. We had at that time built up a very strong relationship with the banks, who had a great deal of confidence in the company and in my father. Incidentally, at that time, it was really known as the Ittleson Company—not like C.I.T. today with its in-depth management.

My father never had any show of panic. He felt that he was on solid ground and the company was being built up and that the situation would resolve itself ultimately and that we would go ahead. There were three years when our income went down, then it started to go back, and this bore out my father's feeling about not only C.I.T.'s future but also the general economy of the country. He felt that the depression was a temporary thing, that things had been overdone and that the stock market crash was caused by speculation, that stocks had been bid too high and there had been too much gambling in the market.

19

Broadening the
Management Team

Henry Ittleson, Claude Hemphill, Edwin Vogel, Phillip Haberman, Frank Collins and Arthur Dietz continued to fill their primary leadership roles during C.I.T.'s spectacular growth of the mid-twenties and the period of consolidation and testing during the depression years. However, it would be a mistake to leave the impression that this small team of managers, who had served the company so well in its earlier years, had not brought in and built around them a cohesive and talented group of other executives. The contributions of these men were to help shape the fortunes of C.I.T. for decades to come.

It is appropriate at this point to move away from a strictly chronological narrative and introduce some of those who had joined the organization and begun to make their marks starting in the early 1920's.

An early addition was British-born Frederick A. Franklin, who came to the United States as a young accountant in 1910. After working as a bookkeeper prior to World War I, he joined Continental Guaranty Corporation, the pioneering auto financing organization, and rose to the office of treasurer and director. He came to C.I.T. as comptroller in November 1922, taking over many of the general internal management duties that had been Hemphill's. At the formation of Commercial

Investment Trust Corporation in 1924, he was elected treasurer and a director, working with Vogel on financial matters and relinquishing the accounting function. He also became responsible for overseeing the New York end of the European operations. He resigned his offices at the end of 1934 for reasons of health, having been an influence on many aspects of the corporation's affairs.

Joseph G. Myerson, a young Brooklyn attorney, became the second member of the in-house legal staff in March 1925. Up to that time Phillip Haberman had been the only staff counsel, using outside firms for the work he could not handle himself. Myerson had read for the law as a clerk in a Manhattan law office from 1915 to 1919 while attending the New York Law School. After passing his bar examinations, he went into practice for himself.

One of his early clients was the Thayer Mercantile Company, a predecessor of Continental Guaranty in automobile financing in the New York City area. Thayer had clients among the used car dealers along Broadway and Myerson took over their collection problems where legal action or the threat of it was involved. (C.I.T. was rediscounting Thayer's auto receivables.)

As a result of this experience, by 1922 or 1923 he began to provide similar services for the collection department of C.I.T. in the Liggett Building. Early in 1925, Haberman felt the need for another attorney to assist him and the C.I.T. men with whom Myerson was working recommended him.

Haberman interviewed Myerson and offered him the position, but Myerson replied that he would prefer to keep his independent practice. To this, Haberman responded, "Well, I am going to employ someone anyway, and if it is somebody else, you are going to lose the business you are getting from us now."

As Thayer's business had declined, another client had gone out of business and C.I.T. had become his principal source of income. Myerson had second thoughts and agreed to cast his lot with the C.I.T. organization.

At first, he handled collection and repossession problems and worked as general assistant to Haberman but he soon became involved with the federal and state regulation of consumer instalment credit, a rapidly expanding and fast-changing field.

Coincident with the emergence of the new body of law affecting the company's business was the rapid increase in the number of the company's regional and branch offices, as envisioned by Arthur Dietz in 1924. It was essential that the employees in these new offices, as well as the home office personnel, be carefully educated and guided in the constantly more complex legal requirements they had to observe. This task occupied Myerson's close attention.

During the 1920's, C.I.T. and the other organizations financing retail automobile sales had to contend not only with the hazards to their collateral position in transactions involving delinquency and default by purchasers but also with the exposures to loss introduced by the Eighteenth Amendment to the Constitution and the National Prohibition Act of 1919. The Internal Revenue Code enacted in 1866 had held that a vehicle was subject to confiscation if it was found to have been used in violation of the code—namely for the *concealment* of untaxed liquor.

The forfeitures were absolute and did not recognize creditors' liens, whether or not they had been entered into in good faith. This had been upheld by the United States Supreme Court to the effect that in a violation of the code, the car itself and not the driver was "the guilty thing" and therefore was subject to the penalty of forfeiture.

On the other hand, the later National Prohibition Act had provided that in the event a vehicle was seized while *transporting* (as distinguished from *concealing*) contraband liquor, the good-faith holder of a lien had full protection. The federal authorities uniformly acted to seize and retain cars and trucks involved in liquor violations under the Revenue Code rather than the more lenient Prohibition Act.

It should be noted that all bootleggers and rum-runners sought to finance their vehicle purchases so that their losses would be limited in case of confiscation. Moreover, in such circumstances the finance company and not the selling dealer normally took the loss.

Individual automobile dealers simply had not been able to contend with the legal complexities of this situation. Therefore, C.I.T. and other financing agencies were forced to assume the full responsibility. As was stated in a C.I.T. agreement with Nash dealers (1925) and subsequently extended to all dealers, "If a car is confiscated by authorities because of violation of the liquor laws, C.I.T. will protect the dealer provided he had no knowledge of a liquor hazard when he sold the car."

In an effort to obtain meaningful relief from this costly situation, Myerson put forward the theory that the wording of the Prohibition Act prevented proceedings against a seized car under the Revenue Act of 1866 and made the Prohibition Act, which recognized liens, the only means of confiscation available to the enforcement agencies.

In two cases, Appellate Courts in North Carolina and California had found that the Richbourg Motor Company, in the former state, and Davies Motors, Inc., in the latter, had no protection for their liens on cars that had been involved in rum-running violations and were held forfeit under the Internal Revenue Act. C.I.T. had not been concerned in these cases, but in order to bring his theory to an early and conclusive test, Myerson offered to represent the Richbourg Motor Company in an appeal to the United States Supreme Court with C.I.T. meeting the costs of the action.

This offer was accepted and the cases were joined and tried by the high court in 1928. Myerson presented the brief and argument for the dealers. The result was a finding by the court that the provisions of the Prohibition Act were binding on the federal authorities and that the Revenue Act penalties were no longer available to them. Accordingly, in subsequent seizures of cars, proper liens were recognized. Thus ended a decade of serious losses to C.I.T. and the other finance companies.

Myerson became C.I.T.'s representative and spokesman before regulatory bodies and legislative committees throughout the country, often being recognized as the advocate not only for his company but for the entire consumer credit industry. As assistant general counsel of the corporation, he continued in this important role until his retirement at the end of 1961.

There were three additions to the company's central staff in 1926 that were to have great future significance. The first was Stanley Brady Ecker, a young lawyer with a degree from Harvard. He had practiced law with a New York City firm for three years, and while vacationing at Lake Placid, he learned that C.I.T. wished to enlarge its in-house legal staff by the addition (preferably) of a Harvard law graduate.

Ecker decided to apply for the position. He had been given Haberman's name but found the latter was out of town, so Arthur Dietz agreed to see him. After only a ten-minute interview, Dietz, who often made quick, intuitive decisions, particularly about people, said, "You're hired." Ecker was not prepared to act that precipitously and took three months to study the company and meet Haberman and other of its executives, including Henry Ittleson. In the end, it was Ittleson who repeated the offer of employment and Ecker went to work for the company on April 1, 1926, the day of the move into the new headquarters at One Park Avenue.

Ecker took over an increasing share of the general corporate work that Haberman had previously handled, concerning the company's adherence to federal and state laws and its stockholder and securities exchange relationships. He was elected assistant secretary of the corporation in February 1927 and succeeded Haberman as secretary in March 1929, continuing to hold this title until 1963. He joined the board of directors in 1931.

It was about this same time that his career abruptly took off on a new tack. Sears, Roebuck and Company, which was strapped for ready cash because of depression conditions, asked C.I.T. to consider the advance of approximately $15 million collateralized by instalment receivables taken for the sale of Coldspot home refrigerators, with this portfolio to be replaced by new receivables as older ones matured. Dietz and Ecker were hurriedly assigned to go to the Sears offices in Chicago to negotiate this transaction. En route, Ecker drew up a two-page contract and dictated it to the train stenographer as they traveled overnight to Chicago on the Twentieth Century Limited. The next day, he assisted Dietz in the actual negotiations with General Robert Wood, the Sears chairman, and other executives, and the deal was brought off successfully.

A few days later, Dietz called Ecker to his office and said he had been impressed with the part Ecker took in the negotiations. He asked if Ecker would like to consider giving up most of his legal work and becoming a member of the central management group, handling general executive responsibilities in addition to those of corporate secretary. He offered Ecker this or the option of being designated acting general counsel, as Haberman's health was failing. The latter would lead, he was told, to his becoming general counsel whenever Haberman retired, as he was then expected to do over the near term. (Haberman actually continued to hold the general counsel title into 1944. He retired from active service as a vice president in 1951 and as a director in 1952. He was 77 at the time of his death in 1953.)

Without hesitation, Ecker said he would prefer to move to the general management side. He recommended another young attorney he had brought into the company, Alphonse A. Laporte, as acting general counsel. One of Ecker's first executive duties after Robert Blumenthal's death was to serve with Frank T. Lyons (until the latter's death in 1936) as liaison between the parent company and the factoring units and to handle this assignment alone thereafter. He also assumed all sorts of troubleshooting and negotiating responsibilities. As corporate secretary, he was responsible for investor relations, including the company's contacts with the securities analyst fraternity, for several decades. After functioning as a vice president of various operating subsidiaries for several years, he became a vice president of the parent company in 1941. In many respects, he served as the third member of a senior management triumvirate with Dietz and Henry Ittleson, Jr. after the original leaders relinquished their roles.

Leo H. Spanyol was employed by a public accounting firm before he joined C.I.T. in August 1925 as assistant to the comptroller. He was 30 years old. He had also worked for Western Union and in the textile

Leo H Spanyol.

business. He recalled that on his first day at work he went to the
personnel department and asked for a key to a locker. The personnel
man refused to give him one and Spanyol indignantly asked why.

"Your boss has worked here since April and do you know how many
assistants he has had in that time?" the personnel man asked. "Well,
you're the seventeenth, and three or four of them went out to lunch the
first day and never came back. Others never showed up for the second
day. I'm not going to lose any more locker keys giving them to fellows
in your job!"

Spanyol assured the man he was going to stay in C.I.T.'s
employ—and he did, until his retirement as a vice president at the end
of 1963. When his first superior left the company after about two
years, Spanyol was named to the position of auditor. In February 1930,
he was appointed comptroller. He was elected to the board of directors
in 1948 and became a vice president in 1952. Throughout his career,
he made important contributions to the corporation's success not only
in his fields of special expertise, namely accounting and taxation, but
also in general areas of business, particularly the company's insurance
operations in the thirties, forties and fifties.

John I. Snyder was another 1926 addition to the staff. With experience as the treasurer of a textile firm, he, like Arthur Dietz and Frederick Franklin, had also worked for the old Continental Guaranty Corpo-

ration. Later, with General Motors Corporation he was associated with the formation of General Motors Acceptance Corporation and organized the first General Motors program for financing electrical household appliances such as the Frigidaire refrigerator. He came to C.I.T. as assistant treasurer, working with Franklin until the latter's retirement because of illness at the end of 1934, when he was elected Franklin's successor. He took an important part in conducting the company's banking relationships and, in association with Vogel, Franklin, Haberman and the corporation's directors from the financial community, in executing the various financing and refinancing programs of both the twenties and thirties. He retired in 1946.

Another addition to the staff in September 1929 introduces a name that has already appeared in this narrative at several points—that of Maddock. The newcomer was Sydney D. Maddock, the younger brother of Edward S. Maddock, who had played a pioneering role in the development of passenger automobile financing. Sydney Maddock had worked, mainly in sales, for another of his brother's companies, New Amsterdam Credit Corporation, for several years beginning in 1926. This organization was engaged not in consumer instalment financing but in the financing of industrial accounts, primarily selling "big ticket" machinery and equipment. In 1928, the elder Maddock sold the company and Sydney agreed to work for the purchasers for at least a year.

At the end of that period, he felt he did not want to continue with the new group and decided he would apply for a position with C.I.T. After being interviewed by Ittleson and then Dietz, Maddock was hired as assistant to the rapidly rising Roman J. Greil, the college contemporary of Ittleson, Jr. Maddock worked closely with Greil, whom he admired greatly.

Maddock had based his employment approach to Ittleson and Dietz on the fact that C.I.T.'s so-called industrial department at that time was almost exclusively engaged in financing small appliances and a miscellaneous list of relatively low-cost fixtures and other products used in service businesses and light industry. He said he would bring them his experience in obtaining financing business involving heavy industrial, income-producing machinery and equipment. When Greil passed away at the end of 1930, he was placed in charge of the eastern industrial division as an assistant vice president and was elected a vice president of the division two years later with a green light to put his plans into effect. It was Maddock and the corps of men he organized around him who developed the heavy industrial financing programs that C.I.T. has administered with outstanding success through good times and bad since the early thirties.

Maddock undertook special responsibilities with the company's wartime manufacturing activities in the forties. These will be discussed later. He returned as a vice president of the newly organized industrial financing subsidiary, C.I.T. Corporation, in April 1945. He was elected a vice president of C.I.T. Financial at that time and joined the board of directors in February 1946. On January 1, 1949, he became executive vice president of C.I.T. Corporation, with Henry Ittleson, Jr., serving as president. Ten months later, Maddock became president of that unit, holding the position until he retired in 1957.

As management realignments developed, the invaluable Hemphill assumed new duties. In 1926, he had taken his first vacation since the company was founded, visiting European countries and combining this with a survey of the corporation's operations and prospects there. On his return, he assumed the executive vice presidency and later the presidency of the "Chicago company," which handled all Midwest instalment financing operations. He rapidly built up this business during the prosperous years of 1927–29. Late in 1929, he took over the supervision of all European operations, with headquarters in Berlin. He then presided over the liquidation of this business, when that program was initiated in 1932.

Thereafter, in failing health, he became less active in day-to-day affairs but continued as a director until February 10, 1959, thus completing to the day 51 years of association with the organization. He died in 1961 at 85.

20

The Bank Holiday

As the year 1933 opened, the inflow of new business was still seriously affected by the depression doldrums. In his annual report for 1932, President Ittleson did not venture any statement whatsoever as to his expectations for the new year.

No doubt his uncertainty was a reflection of the obvious instability of the banking system that had become apparent by the middle of 1932. Worsening economic conditions, the uncertainties of a presidential election year, an unbalanced budget, fears that the gold standard would be abandoned and the obvious mismanagement and illiquidity of many weaker institutions were shaking the public's confidence in the entire banking system. One bank after another experienced mass withdrawals of depositor's funds, so that in 1932, 1,453 institutions were forced to close their doors. In the fall of the year, so many Nevada banks were in difficulty that the lieutenant governor proclaimed a twelve-day bank holiday in the state. This alarmed depositors and bankers everywhere.

When 242 more banks closed in January 1933, Louisiana declared a bank holiday of several days' duration for the purported purpose of "commemorating the severance of diplomatic relations with Germany" before World War I.

An even more stunning event was the closing of all banks in the State of Michigan on February 14. Everywhere, more and more holders of currency or deposits were demanding gold payments, with the outflow topping $200 million in the week ending March 1. On the early morning of March 4, Governor Lehman closed the banks in New York State. Later on that day, immediately following his inauguration, President Roosevelt declared the national bank holiday.

As the overnight news of the emergency closing of the New York banks reached C.I.T.'s apprehensive executives, Edwin Vogel in particular expressed the concern at a very early morning meeting that the closing order might also be applicable to C.I.T., forcing it to halt all operations. As the sun was rising, a young attorney was dispatched to Albany to investigate this possibility with state officials.

The same reaction attended the nationwide closing of the banks later in the day. C.I.T. asked one of its outside attorneys to telephone Washington at once and raise the question with the officials of the Treasury Department who were charged with administering the President's closing proclamation. He managed to reach Arthur A. Ballantine, Secretary of the Treasury. The C.I.T. attorney's first question was: "Does the bank closing proclamation apply to Commercial Investment Trust Corporation—C.I.T.?"

"What's C.I.T.?" was Secretary Ballantine's rejoinder.

"It's a finance company" was the reply.

"What's a finance company?" Ballantine asked.

The C.I.T. representative gave a brief description of C.I.T.'s business in financing autos, industrial equipment and factoring.

"You don't accept deposits?" the Secretary asked. He was assured C.I.T. did not.

"Well then, go back to clients and tell them to go about their business, if they have any money to do it with," Ballantine answered. With New York and all other state jurisdictions ruling that their respective bank-closing orders were not applicable to C.I.T.'s operations, these were never suspended for a moment during the bank holiday.

No banks were permitted to reopen until their sound condition had been established. In accomplishing this, many institutions were assisted by loans from the Reconstruction Finance Corporation or help from other federal agencies. Public confidence in the system rallied as a result of this program and more than 75% of the banks that were members of the Federal Reserve System, including more than 5,000 national banks, were reopened in less than two weeks.

These events had great impact on C.I.T.'s operations, of course. The local situations in Nevada, Louisiana and elsewhere were dealt with on an extemporaneous basis, but the first major move was made after the Michigan closing, which was quickly followed by closings of many Ohio banks and others in the Midwest. At this juncture, Sydney Maddock realized that many of his division's manufacturing clients and prospects were certain to be without available funds to meet their payrolls because they had no access to their deposits in closed institutions. He therefore issued instructions to all his field men to offer C.I.T. cash to any clients or desirable prospects who found themselves in this situation.

Although a number—and eventually all—of C.I.T.'s own accounts were frozen, the company always had large amounts of funds at its command. The reason for this was that its *consumer* customers continued to pour in their payments when due, not by check but in *currency*. With their local banks closed, the company's field offices began to accumulate uncomfortably large sums of money, so instructions went out to deliver these funds by hand to One Park Avenue and the other headquarters points. At One Park Avenue, an office vault was pressed into service and so much money was stored there that two armed guards were posted over it on a round-the-clock basis.

Thus, Maddock had ample available funds to assist his clients and these were delivered in each case by a company representative. From this action C.I.T. derived much good will that lasted for years. A number of companies wrote letters of appreciation to Ittleson, including some that had not actually taken advantage of the offer.

In later years, Maddock recalled, "Mr. Ittleson called me in afterwards and asked how we happened to do it and I told him it was a perfectly normal thing for us to do because we were running long on cash and they should not be frightening people by missing payrolls. He thanked me for what I had done."

Clearly, C.I.T.'s experience during the bank closings, which was similar to that of other well-managed finance companies, once again proved the unqualified soundness of consumer instalment credit. This was in the face of a total suspension of the nation's banking system, which none of the earlier detractors of time purchasing could possibly have envisioned.

C.I.T.'s directors met on March 23 to appraise the effect of the bank closings on their company's operations. Various executives reported in summary:

> Past-due factored accounts were approximately 40% above normal but were being reduced on a daily basis. . . . In the motor and industrial divisions, there had been a general tightening of credit standards. . . . There had been some increase in delin-

quencies because debtors' bank accounts were frozen, but where purchasers showed "evidence of a willingness to pay, the policy is to play along with them, ascertaining the facts in each case. . . ." Efforts were being made to impress on all purchasers to whom extensions were granted that a courtesy was being accorded them, thus building purchaser good will through the consideration being shown. . . . While a national bank holiday was a new experience, the operating companies had already experienced banking moratoriums in several states. In Nevada, where bank deposits bore the same proportionate relationship to the company's outstandings as the national average, there had been an increase in delinquencies immediately following the state bank holiday but collections were back to normal within thirty days.

The reports continued that the same was true in other areas where there had been wholesale bank closings prior to the national holiday. These included St. Louis, Philadelphia, Pittsburgh and South Carolina, where one bank with sixty branches was forced to suspend operations. While in these situations there had been a temporary increase in delinquencies, the operating companies had been able to bring collections back to normal in a reasonable time. . . . The operating companies had not attempted to force collections or make repossessions but arrangements had been set up to throw emergency collection forces into any areas where special problems might develop.

As for the company's own bank deposits, as of the date of the meeting it had a total of 203 bank accounts, involving $11.6 million in cash plus $2 million of U.S. Treasury bills due at the end of the month. Of these banks, five remained closed, four were operating on a restricted basis and the total amount of funds frozen was $145,000.

The company's domestic Canadian operations had not been significantly affected during the period because there had been no bank holiday there. In *Chartered Banking in Canada*, A. B. Jamieson gives this description of the impact on the Canadian financial community of the U.S. bank closings:

> It would be too much to expect that such an upsetting event could happen as the closing of every bank in the United States, without its effects being felt in Canada. However, the fact that Canada had already gone through so much travail and overcome so many difficulties since the onset of the depression, doubtless made her less vulnerable than she would have been earlier. There were repercussions on the stock markets and breaks in prices of leading commodities, but nothing of a serious nature. The

banks and the various exchanges functioned as usual. On the day that all the banks in the United States were ordered to close, Canada's Minister of Finance, Hon. E.N. Rhodes, issued a reassuring message in which he said, "The Canadian banks are in a very strong and exceptionally liquid position, and wholly capable of meeting any demands made upon them." Naturally, normal banking relations between the two countries were completely disrupted for some time. Cheques and drafts drawn on United States banks could only be accepted on a collection basis and many other difficulties arose.

By the May meeting of the directors on the fifth of the month, it was reported that past-due percentages in automobile, industrial and factoring operations had returned to normal and there had been no increase in repossessions. Automobile sales were rising rapidly. The bank holiday had come and gone.

21

Universal Credit Corporation

In another way, the national bank holiday resulted in the year 1933 becoming one of the most important milestones in the history of C.I.T. Financial Corporation.

As noted previously, despite Henry Ford's earlier antagonism to instalment buying, the Ford Motor Company organized its own financing subsidiary, on the model of General Motors Acceptance Corporation, in 1928. The name selected was Universal Credit Corporation, and it rapidly took over the lion's share of the financing business of the Ford dealer body.

Two executives were chosen to operate Universal Credit Corporation. The organization was built around an individual of unusual versatility, Ernest Kanzler, who became president. Kanzler, a graduate of the University of Michigan and Harvard Law School, had practiced law briefly in Detroit in 1915–16. He joined the original Ford manufacturing company, Henry Ford & Son, in 1916 as production manager on the Fordson tractor. He assumed the same duties for the automobile production division of the Ford Motor Company in 1920. In the interim, he and Edsel Ford, Henry Ford's son, became brothers-in-law by marrying sisters.

In 1926, Kanzler embarked on a new career after leaving the Ford manufacturing organization to organize the Guardian Detroit Bank and the Guardian Detroit Union Group in association with executives of the leading Detroit business institutions. In 1928, Edsel Ford asked him to organize a new finance company to assist in the sale of the new Model A cars that were just coming off the production line. Kanzler became president after its organization in 1928.

George Herbert Zimmerman was another of those who received his indoctrination in the automobile financing business from the Continental Guaranty Company in the pre-World War I period. He went off to war, but when he returned the only job he could find was as a collection man for a funeral director. While doing this work, he ran into an old friend who asked him to come down to see A. L. Deane, who was a former vice president of Continental Guaranty Company. Deane was doing organization work for what was to become General Motors Acceptance Corporation and invited Zimmerman to join him in setting up the Collection Department for the new company.

Zimmerman worked for GMAC for five years and was responsible for the development of credit and collection manuals for the expanding branch organization. He then was transferred to general supervisory responsibilities.

Then Alexander E. Duncan, chairman of Commercial Credit Corporation, asked him to come with that company as a vice president. Commercial Credit had made a number of acquisitions of smaller and weaker companies and was encountering collection difficulties that needed expert handling. In addition, there was a need to integrate the operations of these various companies with those of the established Commercial Credit branches. This required a complete reorganization of the accounting and reporting procedures. Zimmerman at first demurred but then was offered what was for the time the excellent annual salary of $17,500. He made the move to Baltimore.

Zimmerman supervised Commercial Credit's eastern division until 1928. That winter, while in New York for the National Automobile Show, he made a courtesy telephone call to his old boss, John J. Schumann, president of GMAC. Schumann told him he had someone sitting in his office who would like to meet him on a very important matter. This was Ernest Kanzler, who was seeking Schumann's counsel to help him establish the Ford credit arm.

Zimmerman had several engagements but finally agreed to cancel them and meet with Schumann and Kanzler. Kanzler stated he wanted Zimmerman as operating head of his new company. Zimmerman expressed his disbelief that Henry Ford, an outspoken foe of banks, credit and debt, would really back a Ford financing company. To counter his reservations, he was invited to Detroit, met with Edsel Ford, received face-to-face assurances that they meant business and would never give up the credit business as long as General Motors had the General Motors Acceptance Corporation to assist dealers in the sale of cars. Zimmerman then accepted their offer and took over operations of Universal Credit Corporation, as vice president, with Kanzler handling bank relations and relations with the Ford dealer body and factory.

All went well until the Michigan bank holiday of 1933.

Henry Ford obviously had never entirely lost his distrust of the banking system and became very alarmed when he found millions of dollars of his company's money were tied up in closed banks. He was also alarmed by the realization that the company was deeply in debt for the operating funds it had borrowed from banks across the nation. He did not realize that, as the depression deepened, Universal Credit had been collecting its receivables and reducing its debts so that it had excess funds that had been marshaled in the two largest Detroit banking institutions. Even after the bank holiday, Universal Credit was able to carry on and meet every payroll by making its collections in cash and retaining the cash in the safe deposit boxes in each of its branch cities. It was also able to use those collections to help finance Ford dealers who were continuing to make some sales with this additional help. However, Mr. Ford sent his male secretary to Zimmerman with instructions to liquidate Universal Credit Company forthwith.

Kanzler was not immediately available because he was tied up in Washington with congressional hearings by the Pecora Committee investigating the securities business. Zimmerman took it upon himself to refuse to obey the order. This "mutiny" so shocked Ford's messenger that he did not dare return to the elder Ford with word of it. Instead, he got his hands on some idle funds and disappeared. He was found days later, wandering in the wilderness of upper Michigan.

In the meantime, Zimmerman had reached Kanzler, who had been struggling with bank-closing problems and convinced him it would be in the best interests of the Ford Motor Company, the Ford dealers and all concerned if Universal Credit should be sold rather than liquidated. He pointed out that this would maintain the existence of an exclusive financing agency for Ford dealers and would doubtless result in the Ford company not only getting back its investment in Universal Credit more promptly than through the liquidation route but also would enable it to obtain a probable profit rather than suffer a possible loss.

Kanzler convinced the Fords, father and son, of the wisdom of this course and was given authority to try to sell the credit company. He and Zimmerman went at once to Baltimore and offered the enterprise to Duncan and his associates at Commercial Credit. A series of secret meetings was held at Duncan's home over a weekend and a deal was hammered out. An acceptable price was agreed to, Kanzler and Zimmerman were offered tenure in their positions and it was also agreed that Universal Credit would remain a separate enterprise and not be merged into Commercial Credit.

A few days later, Duncan called Zimmerman in Detroit to inform him that his board of directors had accepted all provisions of the agreement of sale except for the stipulation that the two companies would be operated separately. Duncan said his directors could not see why or how Commercial Credit should have "two offices in Amarillo, Texas—one for Commercial Credit and one for Universal Credit." "Two offices in Amarillo, Texas," became a much-quoted phrase in later years, for it was on this consideration that the acquisition of Universal Credit by Commercial Credit foundered.

Kanzler and Zimmerman refused to back down on the separateness issue. They proceeded to get in touch with the investment house of Kuhn, Loeb & Company to see if the latter firm could interest British interests in buying the company. The chaotic conditions of the U.S. money markets because of the bank holiday seemed to rule out an American buyer. Kuhn, Loeb was unable to excite any immediate British interest in the offer, but Lewis Strauss, a senior Kuhn, Loeb partner, suggested that C.I.T. might consider the purchase.

Because of Henry Ford's foray into anti-Semitism in the 1920's, Kanzler and Zimmerman doubted that the C.I.T. group would be interested in Universal Credit, but they agreed to a meeting with Ittleson and Dietz. Ittleson exhibited a lively immediate response and offered to match the Commercial Credit deal and guarantee independence for Universal Credit for at least five years. He also offered Kanzler and Zimmerman attractive options on C.I.T. stock and the retention of their offices in Universal Credit.

The Universal Credit representatives replied that they felt the transaction should be renegotiated from the beginning rather than to adopt Commercial Credit's supposedly confidential offer, and this was agreed to. New but not very different terms were worked out, and Kanzler and Zimmerman also were given the opportunity to buy a block of the Universal Credit stock at the same price C.I.T. was paying, plus the options to buy C.I.T. stock at favorable prices over a period of time.

The C.I.T. board of directors on May 5, 1933, approved the purchase of Universal Credit Corporation for $15.5 million, the com-

pany's book value. Thirty percent of the Universal Credit common
stock was then sold to Kanzler and Zimmerman, at the same book
value.

Representing Zimmerman in the negotiations was Donald M. Swat-
land, of the New York law firm of Cravath, deGersdorf, Swaine and
Wood. His handling of his client's interests so impressed the C.I.T.
executives that he and his firm were subsequently retained as C.I.T.'s
outside corporate counsel, a relationship that was to continue for more
than four decades without interruption.

When Universal Credit Corporation was thus acquired, it had a
branch network of more than thirty offices and had purchased more
than $1 billion of time sales contracts in five years of operations,
involving more than two million retail contracts. In the first six months
of 1933, including its first two months as a C.I.T. subsidiary, Universal Credit acquired $16 million of retail receivables and $20.6 million
of wholesale paper. For the year 1933, retail volume was $58.2 million
and wholesale $64.6 million.

Attached to the agreement of sale was a list of the legal actions
pending against Universal Credit, concerning the outcome of which the
sellers agreed to protect C.I.T. A sampling of the alleged grounds for
some of these suits casts a sidelight on the operating problems that
arose with regularity during the formative period of the automobile

financing business. They included: The purchaser of a repossessed car at public auction claimed misrepresentation. . . . An unbalanced individual claimed he had bought a car although he never completed the purchase formalities with the dealer. . . . A collector was charged with physically assaulting a delinquent purchaser. . . . A purchaser's wife jumped on the running board of a company car that was pursuing her husband, a delinquent purchaser who was trying to escape with his car. She was injured. . . . A purchaser's wife was in a car when it was repossessed by a towing company. . . . A purchaser claimed he was slandered and his reputation damaged by having his car repossessed. . . . Another claimed his hand was injured during repossession of his auto. . . . A purchaser claimed personal property in the glove compartment disappeared during repossession of the car. . . . An author claimed a valuable manuscript, notes and a scenario disappeared under similar circumstances. . . . A car was repossessed after a purchaser made his payments to another branch but was not credited for them. . . . Universal Credit repossessed a truck, but a Morris Plan bank claimed ownership of the attached dump body . . . and so forth.

Despite such down-to-earth and by no means unusual problems, the acquisition of Universal Credit Corporation was to prove to be a masterstroke for the management of C.I.T. Against the purchase price of $15.5 million, the company had net earnings in only the first four years of C.I.T.'s ownership of $32.5 million—$5 million in 1934; $6.8 million in 1935; $10.2 million in 1936 and $10.5 million in 1937.

In their authoritative history of the Ford Company entitled *Ford: Decline and Rebirth,* Allan Nevins and Frank Ernest Hill quote Kanzler concerning the Universal Credit transaction: "It was a terrible mistake on Ford's part to sell the finance company." To which the authors add: "Actually it was a triumph of Ford's prejudice over his business interest."

22

The Years of
Resurgence

In the annual report for 1932, President Ittleson for the first time reported to his stockholders not only the volume of business acquired in the various classifications of C.I.T.'s financing operations but also the amount of receivables outstanding by classifications at the year-end. In explanation of this innovation, he wrote, "Inasmuch as certain classes of receivables remain outstanding for longer periods of time than others and therefore income is related more directly to funds employed and outstanding than to the volume of business during the year, it will be more informative to show the classifications of dollar outstandings, as well as the division of volume."

The importance of this change in reporting practice was promptly demonstrated in the way it reflected the growth of the corporation's business in 1933. A tabulation will illustrate this:

Class of Receivables	Dollars Outstanding Dec. 31, 1933 (Millions)	Dollars Outstanding June 30, 1933 (Millions)	Dollars Outstanding Dec. 31, 1932 (Millions)
Retail Auto	$ 79.4	$ 62.0	$38.0
Wholesale Auto	10.9	12.9	3.9
Factoring	28.3	25.7	19.5
Other Industrial	27.2	27.6	36.1
All Foreign	1.3	1.0	.9
Total	$147.1	$129.2	$98.4

Thus, investors were able to note that C.I.T.'s earning assets had increased by 50% during the year, with the important retail automobile portfolio more than doubling. President Ittleson noted that all of the gain in receivables had occurred in the last nine months, the first quarter having been behind the previous year. Total volume of business for the year was $476 million, an increase of 51% over 1932's $317 million. Net earnings were $7.5 million, or $3.42 a common share, compared with $5.7 million, or $2.04 a share, in 1932.

As 1934 opened, business conditions throughout the nation were rallying strongly. With the economic skies brightening and aided by the Universal Credit purchase, the total volume of financing booked by C.I.T. in the first half of the year was $438 million, nearly equal to the volume acquired in the whole previous year. Retail auto volume, at $117 million, actually was $2 million higher than for the full year of 1933.

Two significant corporate events occurred about mid-1934. Midland Acceptance Corporation of Ohio, operating in the midwestern states in automobile and other forms of consumer instalment financing, was purchased mainly for cash. The issuance of a limited amount of treasury stock also was involved. The company had been founded in 1924 and had compiled an excellent record during the depression years. Its business volume in 1933 was $7.9 million.

As the result of negotiations begun in the latter half of 1933, the sale of C.I.T.'s remaining non-U.S. subsidiaries (with the exception of Canadian Acceptance Corporation) was completed by mid-1934. The French and Danish companies were disposed of to local interests. In the case of "CITAG," the German company, the political situation in that country under the Hitler regime, with its violent anti-Semitism, made a continuation of a C.I.T. investment there out of the question.

Claude Hemphill had devoted some fourteen months to on-the-spot negotiations with German banking interests before a transaction could be worked out in the spring of 1934 that would permit C.I.T. to recapture its investment of some $1.2 million from Germany. As the C.I.T. money was withdrawn, the CITAG general manager for C.I.T. and his secretary, both of whom were Jewish, fled the country overnight. C.I.T. executives arranged havens for them in England.

C.I.T.'s Canadian operations in this period felt the impact of the depression even more severely than those in the United States. A fiftieth anniversary history of Canadian Acceptance Corporation gives this account of the period:

> Through the lean depression years of the early thirties Canadian Acceptance continued to serve the needs of the Canadian consumer, although for the first half of the decade the use of credit was seriously curtailed. The economy was slow to recover from the crash of '29 and our growth was considerably hampered.
>
> The automobile industry as well as the finance industry was hit extremely hard. Repossessions grew to alarming proportions, auto dealers went broke almost daily and suicides among them were not uncommon. The period was one of severe stress.
>
> During these difficult times the company's attitude was one of complete co-operation in extending terms, rearranging payments and, if at all possible, avoiding taking possession of a customer's automobile.
>
> In 1933, the country started to come out of the depression and in January of 1934 we opened our first new branch in five years. . . .
>
> The forerunner of our Equipment Financing Division was the establishment of the National Accounts Department. Its function was to handle contracts from manufacturers of machinery and other products, the purchasers of which could be located anywhere in Canada. . . . Throughout 1934 and in subsequent years, with the general improvement in economic conditions, our business once again prospered.

In all respects, 1934 proved to be a banner year for the corporation. Total business booked totaled $780 million for a year-to-year gain of 65%. Retail motor volume fell just short of doubling the 1933 figures and total outstandings at December 31 reached $194 million from $147 million 12 months earlier. Net profits were $11.6 million, or $5.50 a common share, against the $7.5 million, or $3.42 per common share, in the prior year. A 25% stock dividend was declared on the common stock payable on October 1 and an extra cash dividend of $0.50 per share was paid at the year-end.

The upsurge continued in the next two years. With the volume of receivables purchased reaching $966 million in 1935 and crossing the $1 billion mark to $1.17 billion in the following year, year-end outstandings climbed from $256 million to $398 million. Earnings for the two years were $15.8 million—$6.25 per common share (1935) and $21.2 million—$6.07 per common share (1936). The decline in per-share earnings in 1936 was attributable to a 20% stock dividend distributed in May 1936 and the conversion of preference stock to create an additional 437,000 common shares during the year.

The regular common dividend of $0.50 quarterly was increased to a $0.70 rate on October 1, 1935, and an extra dividend of $0.40 per share was paid on that date. The regular rate on the common was lifted to $0.75 per quarter on January 1, 1936, and a $0.25 extra was paid. In the next twelve months, in addition to the 20% stock dividend at mid-year, the quarterly cash dividend was raised to $0.90 on July 1 and to $1.00 on October 1. In addition, a $1.25 extra was paid for the final quarter.

Between January 1, 1933, and December 31, 1936, the market price of C.I.T. common, with two stock dividends of 25% and 20% occurring during the period, rose from 18½ to 77. The high for the period was 91½ on November 18, 1936.

The repurchase and redemption of outstanding common and preferred shares during the post-1929 years had reduced the corporation's capital and surplus position so that the 1929 year-end figure of $105 million stood as a record until the end of 1935. Retention of earnings over the year plus the sale of $25 million of convertible preferred stock in July lifted the stockholders' equity position to $109 million at December 31, 1935.

There were a number of significant organizational developments in the 1935–36 period. In 1935, Congress amended the Federal Housing Administration Act so that government insurance would be extended to instalment contracts involving machinery and equipment of all kinds, in addition to household equipment transactions that earlier had been covered by F.H.A. insurance as a depression-fighting device. C.I.T. decided to enter this line of business aggressively, and about the middle of 1935 organized a new subsidiary, Equipment Acceptance Corporation, for that purpose.

This program enjoyed a flying start. The minutes of the October directors' meeting contain this report:

> Mr. Dietz then outlined the proposed operations of Equipment Acceptance Corporation, the recently organized subsidiary of Commercial Investment Trust Incorporated, as follows: Up to this time none of the subsidiaries of this Corporation has participated in the Government

F.H.A. Plan—to the extent that this plan applied to the instalment sales of small units. Equipment Acceptance Corporation has, however, recently announced a financing plan pursuant to which it will purchase instalment paper covering larger units on which the unpaid balance will run from $800 to $50,000. The rate of return to E.A.C. on this type of business is satisfactory and the type of business which will be purchased will be excellent. A great many contracts have been signed with outstanding manufacturers.

The introduction of this plan has given entree to manufacturers who had never before been interested in instalment financing plans. He then described the plan, pointing out that there is no recourse against the manufacturer, Equipment Acceptance Corporation, relying on the 20% government guarantee for its recourse. Mr. Dietz explained, however, that E.A.C. is passing credits in the same way as if there were no guarantee from the government.

The annual report for 1935 stated that by the year-end more than three hundred manufacturers, "including many firms of national importance," had signed contracts with Equipment Acceptance after it was launched in October. The progress of this division of the business was further reflected in the record for the full year of 1936. Total industrial financing volume was $79 million, compared with $48 million in 1935, and the portfolio of outstanding industrial receivables increased during the year from $34 million to $63 million.

The federal government issued monthly reports of the volume of this so-called Title I F.H.A. industrial financing by states and holders. At one time, C.I.T. was doing at least 25% of the business in every state in the union, running to a high mark of 87% in West Virginia. Nationally, C.I.T. was handling 50% of all the business being written.

C.I.T.'s dominance of the F.H.A.-insured market continued until the end of the decade. At that point, however, federal regulations had grown so burdensome and imposed so many administrative difficulties that it was decided to abandon the F.H.A. affiliation. C.I.T. continued to offer the same financing services under its "P.I.P." (property improvement plan) as a self-insurer.

It was during this period that the Sears, Roebuck revolving credit arrangement that Dietz and Ecker had consummated several years earlier also came under review. One day, the elder Ittleson called Sydney Maddock into his office. By this time, Maddock was responsible for all industrial financing operations, including the Sears account.

"Syd," Ittleson said, "you know the banks are required to observe a regulation that they may not have more than 10% of their capital and surplus invested with a single borrower. We are under no obligation to

maintain any such ratio, but I think we should observe the same general principle. We now have $130 million of capital and surplus and more than $13 million outstanding in the Sears account. I know they are good for it and our money is perfectly safe, but I still think we should cut back to the bank loan ratio.

"What you ought to do is get on the train tonight and go out to Chicago and tell Sears we would like them to make arrangements for somebody else to handle a part of their business. You don't need to cut them off overnight. They can take their time working out other accommodations and we'll handle all the business they offer until they do so. But let's get on it right away."

Maddock said in later years that he found the decision to reduce the excellent Sears business a very hard one to take but that he agreed with the soundness of Ittleson's position. He followed instructions and met with the top executive echelon at Sears to explain the matter.

"I assured them that we would carry on and meet all their requirements until they could make additional arrangements," he said. "Actually, we continued in that and our outstandings went to more than $16 million before we heard from them again.

"Unhappily, the rub came then, when Mr. Joseph of Sears, Roebuck came to me and said, 'Look, you've been most helpful. We would like to continue to do some business with you, so we have arranged to bring some other people into the picture on the same terms as we are dealing with you. Won't you permit me to take a copy of our contract with you to the National City Bank here in New York and show it to them, as they are offering to take over some part of the business?'

"I told him of course to do it (he really didn't need our permission) and that we would be happy to have the National City Bank working with us on his business. The upshot was the bank copied our contract and that put them into the indirect financing of receivables. Inside of two years' time we were completely out of the deal and the bank had all the business because they offered a rate differential that we would not meet.

"The lesson here is something I have always preached to our men across the country. The success of our business is and always will be our ability to keep two steps ahead of the banks. They can copy anything we do and their money costs them a fraction of what it costs us. Thus, they would put us out of business if we were not everlastingly innovative, developing new ideas and plans and promoting them. That has been the secret of the success of our industrial division for the past forty years and more."

Another prophetic incident occurred about this time. It foretold the competition that C.I.T. and all the other established finance companies were to encounter in the years to come as commercial banks vigorously invaded the consumer credit field, offering both direct loans and dealer financing services. This is the first reference to bank competition to appear in the minutes of a C.I.T. directors' meeting:

> Mr. Dietz reported regarding his trip to the Coast, stating that the operations of the Coast subsidiary have been very satisfactory; that the volume of this company has increased more rapidly than the volume of any of the other subsidiaries—despite increased competition from certain of the banks on the Coast which have been purchasing instalment paper and also extending loans to prospective purchasers on the instalment plan. Mr. Dietz reported that among the banks there is a decided difference of opinion as to the wisdom of the banks' extending their operations into this field.

The year 1936 also was marked by the purchase of National Surety Corporation, one of the nation's largest bonding and surety companies. The company, a writer of fidelity, burglary, plate glass and other types of bonds and insurance, had been taken over by the New York State Insurance Department because of financial difficulties and was offered for sale through competitive sealed bidding. C.I.T.'s price of $10,031,000 was the highest received and the ownership of the company was awarded to C.I.T. The C.I.T. executives involved in the transaction had decided to make their bid an even $10 million. They went to Ittleson for approval and he immediately told them to bid a higher amount. "Make it $31,000 more," he said. There was another bid of exactly $10 million, so C.I.T. came out ahead because of its president's intuitive foresight.

The sale was challenged in the state courts, but the C.I.T. case, which was handled by the great trial lawyer, Max Steuer, working with Ecker, prevailed on appeal and the purchase was consummated before the end of the year.

National Surety's executive organization, staff and branch organization were continued, as well as its business-producing plant of more than 6,000 agencies throughout the country. Vincent Cullen, a veteran executive in the surety bonding business and president of National Surety since 1933, continued in that office as chief executive. He was elected to the C.I.T. board of directors in 1938 and continued to direct National Surety operations with marked success until his retirement in 1949. C.I.T. also contributed additional capital to bulwark the financial strength and underwriting capacity of its new subsidiary.

Another 1936 acquisition was Bachmann, Emmerich & Company, Inc., an important factoring organization. C.I.T. had been rediscounting its receivables since 1930 and moved promptly to buy the company for some $2.6 million in common stock when the principals indicated a desire to retire. The Bachmann, Emmerich business was merged into that of Commercial Factors Corporation.

23

Legal
Entanglements

As their day-to-day business activities expanded and flourished in the middle years of the 1930's, C.I.T.'s managers were brought face-to-face with two external issues that were to assume great magnitude. Both involved legal, governmental and public relations considerations of a sweeping nature.

The first was the so-called dealer packing controversy. This problem had its roots in the earliest days of the financing of retail automobile sales through dealers and reached serious proportions by the mid-1920's. As we have seen, the early "repurchase" or "with recourse" financing plans of C.I.T., General Motors Acceptance and the other "standard" companies of that period required that the dealer assume liability to the finance company for the unpaid balance owed on a vehicle that was repossessed from a defaulting purchaser. The finance company was only required to return the car within a stipulated period of time after the default occurred. The dealer could then sell the car at a profit or loss and was required to pay off the original buyer's account with the finance company.

At an early date, GMAC, C.I.T. and Commercial Credit began to incorporate in their schedule of charges to customers a so-called dealer reserve. This was an amount, averaging about 1% of the face amount of the instalment contract on new cars and a "flat" charge in the $10 to $15 range on used cars, that they put aside in a fund held to the dealer's credit to protect the finance company if the dealer should be forced to default on his repurchase obligations.

When this fund reached a certain maximum, based on the amount of each dealer's total repurchase exposures, any excess reserve credits would be paid over to him, so long as an adequate balance in his reserve fund was maintained.

The automobile business was so good in the pre-depression period and used cars normally brought such satisfactory prices that dealers quite regularly covered their full repurchase liability out of the resale of each repossessed vehicle. As a GMAC bulletin to its dealers put it in the winter of 1930:

> Up until 1930, little dependence was placed upon the reserve by the average dealer, because he rarely needed it. So usual was it to resell repossessions at a profit offsetting those sold at a loss that the reserve came to be regarded *as a source of additional profit*. [author's italics] AND THAT IS WHAT IT SHOULD BE, in good years.
>
> So goods properly sold should IN THEMSELVES offer adequate protection against the possibility and cost of resale. But every so often things happen to disturb the orderly course of events. A sudden drop in retail values would wipe out an equity which was previously well protected. Forced liquidation of inventories produces the same result. Reduced purchasing power of a considerable part of the buying public lessens demand and reduces values. These periodical and irregular happenings break the usual rules and create the need for RESERVES. They happened in the Winter of 1930–1 and the reserve payments which GMAC had been steadily making since 1925 provided the funds for just such contingencies.

In other words, in normal times many dealers found the dealer reserve factor to be a source of income in addition to the commission or mark-up netted from the sale of the auto itself.

All of this business was being carried on against the background of the time-price doctrine. "Time-price" transactions were not subject to the restraints of laws limiting interest charges since they were defined not as loans but as expressions of the dealer's right to sell his property for whatever price the purchaser was willing to pay.

Thus, with many dealers finding that they could enhance their profits through their dealer reserves, many of them began to add into the time price a "reserve" amount higher than the financing agency required.

Even dealers on without-recourse plans, which relieved them of repurchase liability, began to charge a "reserve." It will also be recalled
that the national finance companies at first mounted strong opposition
to the without-recourse approach but eventually were forced to capitu-
late to it in part.

In the competitive heat of the depression period, when the automobile market virtually collapsed and dealer profits were at the vanishing point, many dealers began to look to their part of the finance
charge as a vital source of income. Whether they were assuming
liabilities that required a reserve or not, the "dealer participation" in
the finance charge was defended as recompense for handling the
paperwork or other details of the time-purchase transaction. Dealers
also considered their part of the finance charge to be justifiable compensation for their securing the time-purchase transaction on behalf of
the finance company, just as they were compensated by their sales
commission for making the sale of the car for the manufacturer.

In the depression years, finance charges fixed by many dealers
spiraled higher and higher as they sought to increase their profits or to
advertise and offer highly attractive trade-in allowances or discounts to
bait prospects. They relied on the added finance profit to replace the
reduced margin from the car sale itself. The result of these practices
was that the entire dealer reserve practice fell under a torrent of criticism. The disparaging label "dealer's pack" was placed on it.

The more responsible finance companies were greatly alarmed by
this trend, which they viewed as both economically unhealthy for the
auto industry and a serious public relations problem for the dealers and
for them. However, there was a great deal of uncertainty as to what
course of action was open to them. In the first place, the courts had
regularly held that the dealer could price his product as he saw fit.
Those who did not want to handle "packed" contracts, which the
companies defined as those bearing a dealer time-price mark-up higher
than the respective company's standard "reserve," were free to do so,
but there were local or regional competitors in almost every territory
who were always ready to buy such transactions with no questions
asked.

GMAC was the first company to take positive action against the
"pack." In October 1935, it initiated a series of newspaper advertisements on the "General Motors 6% Plan." Car buyers were urged to
apply this percentage factor to the balance owed in order to determine
the dollar finance charge they were paying. In small type, and not
necessarily very illuminating to the average buyer, this 6% charge was
defined as "a multiplier—not interest." In other words, the finance
charge was the original balance owed, including the insurance costs

involved, *multiplied* by 6% for each twelve months. Since regular monthly payments reduced the *average* balance owed over the full term of the contract to approximately one-half the original balance, the simple interest rate that actually would result from a 6% multiplier would be approximately 11% per annum, depending on the length of contract.

The principal reason the 6% multiplier approach was adopted is plain. There simply appeared to be no workable formula based on a simple-interest approach that could be expected to be made reasonably understandable to the general public. Payment dates, varying maturities and the very complexity of the arithmetical computation involved appeared likely to confound anyone but a student of advanced mathematics. Also, it is fair to say that, although the public had been paying without question simple interest rates that were well above the 11% to 12% range the 6% multiplier invoked, there was an apparent hesitation to advertise any interest charge above 6% in a period when any rate above 6% was regarded in many quarters as usurious.

C.I.T. and Commercial Credit, with some other smaller companies, promptly adopted the new stance in their desire to eliminate the "pack." As the *Automotive Daily News* at the time reported, "The 6% finance plan was adopted almost simultaneously by the national sales finance companies, in effect serving notice that they intended to combat 'packing' vigorously in an equal bid for fair play with the public in connection with finance rates."

The record shows that the 6% plan had a dual effect by bringing down average financing rates paid by all car buyers and by making it more difficult for overreaching dealers to conceal a "pack." A study by Robert P. Shay of the National Bureau of Economic Research (1963) showed that average new-car rates for *all* finance companies dropped from an equivalent simple interest rate of 15.5% in 1935 to 12.1% by 1938, while the equivalent rates for the four largest companies declined from 14.9% in 1935 to 11.8% in 1936, where they leveled off at that figure for two decades.

The other salutary effect of the advertised 6% plan on the packing problem lasted for only thirteen months. On December 3, 1936, the Federal Trade Commission issued a complaint stating that the 6% plans of the major automobile financing and manufacturing companies "have the capacity and tendency to mislead and deceive, and have misled and deceived, a substantial part of the purchasing public into the erroneous and mistaken belief that the said '6%' contemplates a simple interest charge of 6% per annum upon the deferred and unpaid balance." Advertising or use of 6% identification was subsequently ordered stopped forthwith. The ruling was appealed but was finally upheld by the United States Supreme Court in 1941.

There was chaos in the wake of the F.T.C. ruling and the prohibition of "6% plan" advertising. Only a relatively small number of dealers apparently exploited the "packing" practice, but the whole issue of dealer finance charges had become an issue of national interest and concern. Newspapers, magazines and legislators competed in making headlines through exposures or criticisms of the practice. "PACKING OF FINANCE CHARGE GYPS BUYER MORE THAN HE KNOWS," the *Cleveland Press* proclaimed. "DO YOU KNOW THE 'TIME SELLING PRICE' OF THE NEW CAR YOU ARE BUYING?????" a local dealer replied in a full-page advertisement. Another boasted, "OUR SKIRTS ARE CLEAN! We are happy the unfair practice of packing or padding finance charges is being exposed."

A Better Business Bureau program told the public:

> Automobile dealers are in the business to make a fair profit, therefore the dealer who takes a loss on your car may have to make it up in overcharging you for financing.
>
> Your best protection is to trade with a legitimate dealer who will inform you as to the complete charges for financing, insurance, etc. BEFORE the transaction is signed for by you.

The New York State legislature ordered an investigation because "Automobile finance companies have charged exorbitant rates of interest . . . [and] many persons have suffered unnecessary losses and have been subject to most unfair treatment." The Massachusetts legislature took similar action.

C.I.T.'s management realized an aggressive response was necessary to support the conscientious majority of the dealer body and the public's confidence in instalment buying and also to counteract the outpouring of criticism in the press. On February 19, 1937, Dietz wrote to Ittleson, who was vacationing in Florida, as follows:

> Dear Mr. Ittleson*:
>
> I am enclosing copy of the *Automotive Daily News* dated February 13th, which has some interesting stories on the subject of "packs."
>
> For your confidential information, these stories, including the editorial, were all written by John Darr. A copy of this publication has been mailed to every dealer in the United States and our men are carrying this copy in their portfolio when they call on dealers. We have been working on this campaign now for the last three weeks and by March 1st we will be on a "no pack" basis. . . .

---

*Dietz never addressed his superior any less formally.

Of course, what might be considered an untenable position on our part is the fact that we are telling dealers and the world that a "pack" on new cars is anything that the customer pays over 6% flat on a twelve months transaction, plus manual fire, theft and collision insurance. Many finance companies combat this by saying that they were never on the so-called 6% plan, that the plan is unsound to begin with, and that if they have a rate chart which is not built on this particular formula who are we to say that their rate chart is not a proper one to use. . . .

There is a great deal of merit in that contention but, on the other hand, there is no way, in my opinion, to correct the "pack" evil unless you do have a definite yardstick, and that yardstick, at the moment, happens to be the 6% plan. If the rate chart becomes elastic and the 6% plan is thrown into the discard, then there will be no way of controlling the "pack" situation.

John Darr was C.I.T.'s first professional public relations executive. He had joined the company as vice president in January 1936 after operating his own successful public relations firm. *Automotive Daily News* was the recognized press authority of the motor vehicle industry, and through Darr's efforts, it placed itself strongly behind the anti-pack campaign.

"INDUSTRY UNITED TO END PACKING OF FINANCE CHARGES ON CARS," its front-page headline read. The paper said it (or perhaps Darr) had collected statements showing reputable dealers had joined in a united front in opposition to packing by the "comparatively few dealers which bring disrepute to the whole field."

The story went on to say:

State legislatures are growing impatient with the slowness of some dealers to see the light. . . . The 6% plan was an effort to eliminate the packing practice by giving the retail buyer a method of figuring for himself what should be his finance charge. Unfortunately, the Federal Trade Commission disagreed with the methods used in advertising the 6% plan. The curtailment of the advertising of the 6% plan was a signal for some short-sighted dealers and finance companies to start again the systematic practice of loading on charges which the customer would have to pay for retail financing.

The article then quoted many dealers from coast to coast who deplored the packing practice and stated they would not countenance it. Similar statements were obtained from most car manufacturers. The article continued:

Full credit should be given the leading finance companies for adopting the 6% Plan. . . . [It] should result in a very material reduction in cost to the consumer. . . . C.I.T. Corporation has instructed its local offices and advised dealers that it intends to safeguard the interest of purchasers, honest dealers and manufacturers without compromise. That applies to its non-factory account dealers as well as to paper purchased from dealers on the official sales finance plans which C.I.T. operates.

Finally, the publication editorialized as follows:

WHAT PROFIT PACKING?

Following the ban of "rate plan" advertising by finance companies, dealers and manufacturers, *Automotive Daily News* has received numerous reports of a growing tendency among short-sighted or unscrupulous dealers to pack their finance charges. . . .

Now that the bars are down and the purchaser has no definite means of computing his cost, it is charged that some charges are being packed unmercifully. This gives the packing dealer a sharp advantage over his more ethical neighbor in the matter of over allowance on used cars which he hopes to make up in the hidden pack in the finance charges. . . .

Few customers have the crust to question the finance charge at the time of the sale. In numerous instances, however, where packing has been resorted to instalment automobile purchasers have suspected it afterwards and written to the manufacturer or finance company for an explanation. The result is that dealers, manufacturers and finance companies as a whole reap a harvest of ill will.

The "budget car purchaser" is the dealer's best customer. There is more of him than of the cash variety. To antagonize him therefore is to destroy the dealer's best source of potential sales volume. Finance rates have been reduced along with automobile costs; charges have been simplified and made uniform. This without taking away an ample dealer reserve against losses. . . .

The national finance companies are entirely within their right in refusing any longer to condone the practice of "packing" even though they are not directly responsible for it. We will go further and say that they should refuse even more forcibly than the manufacturers to be a part of it. The public naturally assumes that whatever charge is quoted by the dealer has been set by the finance company. . . .

With no packing anywhere, competition will be on a lot cleaner basis. Trade-in quotations and charges for extra service will have to stand on their own feet. And with packing put into the museum with the relics of a bygone age, the automobile industry will have further earned the position of leadership which it holds among American industries. . . .

Undoubtedly, the efforts of finance companies, dealers and manufacturers had the effect of inhibiting the packing practice but they could not eliminate it. It was only through legislative action by the several states, beginning with Indiana in 1935 and followed by Wisconsin in the same year (but most of which occurred after World War II), that laws were put on the books to establish maximum rates and otherwise regulate the instalment credit business. These brought an effective end to the evil of charging the time buyer whatever the traffic would bear.

Another program initiated by Darr in 1936 may have had at least a limited connection with the atmosphere of public criticism and controversy in which the automobile financing business found itself embroiled. This was the organization of the C.I.T. Safety Foundation.

The establishment of the foundation was announced, receiving considerable attention from the press, on May 25, 1936. The foundation received a grant of $250,000 from C.I.T., payable over five years in equal instalments of $50,000. The senior Ittleson, Dietz and Darr were named its trustees. In a message to employees, Dietz defined the foundation's objectives as follows:

> I need not rehearse to you the appalling statistics of traffic accidents. You are all too familiar with them. However, when we realize that deaths from motor car accidents in the United States in ten years have exceeded our country's total loss of life in the world war, we cannot longer ignore these facts. Last year alone more than 40,000 persons died as a result of traffic accidents. More than a million persons were injured in the same kind of accidents. To say nothing of the suffering involved, if these injuries and loss of time were converted into dollars, adding on hospital bills, doctors' fees and property damage, the total would exceed a billion dollars.
>
> After studying and analyzing the different phases of the situation, we came to the conclusion about a year ago, that the individual driver is the key to all accidents and that in proportion to the individual's sense of responsibility toward his fellow drivers, his individual fitness for driving and his care and skill, together with the condition of his vehicle, are the things on which any sound safety program must be based.
>
> Our company has branch offices in more than 150 cities throughout the country and Canada. Out of these offices our own company cars operate with our own field employees as drivers. Of course, in a fleet of cars such as this we had our share of traffic accidents, perhaps more than our share. So we decided to begin at the beginning and see if by education and the encouragement of care and safe driving, we could cut down our own

accident figures. Without going into the details of this program, I can tell you that in the first eight months our accident figure had been reduced more than 50%.

The *second step* which this organization took in the interest of safety was a substantial contribution toward the campaign which the American Automobile Manufacturers Association is conducting.

We are now prepared to take our *third step* which is the establishment of the C.I.T. Safety Foundation. We are setting up a fund of $50,000 per year for a period of five years, hoping by the proper expenditure of this fund to reach a large segment of the driving public in a way which will impress upon the individual driver his own social responsibility. A part of this fund will be devoted each year to the making of awards to individuals who enlist themselves in the cause of safety. They are being made to those persons who in their normal capacities have great contacts with the public. Frankly, we are hoping that in offering awards to news-paper men, that they will write about safety; in offering awards to car-toonists we are hoping that more impressive cartoons will be drawn and used; in the awards to high school students, we are hoping to stimulate the interest of this important group, so many of whom are just beginning to drive. In the awards to teachers we are hoping to interest them in teaching pedestrian safety to the children in the lower grades. In regard to the *grand award*, it may be made to anyone from any of the other groups outlined, or to some individual or organization entirely apart.

The C.I.T. Safety Foundation has been created out of our desire to stimulate greater interest in this subject and to make safe driving the smart thing to do. Our principal concern will be with the education of the individual and all activities of the Foundation will be directed to this end.

The awards to those Dietz defined as having "contacts with the public" were fixed at either $1,000 or $500 a year. The "grand award" was to be $5,000.

One of the foundation's first programs was to select a representative "safe driver" from each state and the District of Columbia, based upon years of accident-free and law-abiding driving, with the American Automobile Association serving as the selecting organization. A "motorcade" of these forty-nine drivers converged on New York City on August 31. They met in a two-day safety seminar with a group of recognized experts and leaders in the highway safety movement. While some of the latter delivered prepared talks, the emphasis of the meeting was on the safe drivers' own recommendations for reducing accidents. These were duly publicized and circulated in many ways. The safe drivers had their expenses paid, were amply entertained and received much local recognition in their home communities.

Lieutenant Franklin M. Kriml, a pioneer in developing police department traffic bureaus and founder of the Northwestern University Traffic Safety Institute, was the recipient of the first "grand award." Recipients in later years were Paul G. Hoffman, president of the Studebaker Corporation and president of the Automotive Safety Foundation, and Sidney J. Williams, director of the Public Safety Division of the National Safety Council.

A Safe Drivers League was organized, involving the enrollment of several hundred thousand individuals through C.I.T. local offices and by other means. The members signed pledges to drive safely and work for highway safety and from time to time received considerable supporting material on these subjects from the Foundation.

Annual "C.I.T. Seminars for Safety" also were held in New York City, beginning in 1937. These were attended by editorial representatives from newspapers throughout the country, forty to fifty papers being represented on each occasion. Regional seminars also were organized on a similar pattern.

Over the years, the Foundation and its activities were hailed or endorsed by most of the governors of the several states. In addition, President Franklin D. Roosevelt, in a letter to Darr dated November 6, 1937, said in part:

> We must redouble our efforts to achieve traffic safety. The newspapers of the country have given generously of their space in the campaign to arouse individual responsibility which alone will solve the problem which, with the increased use of motor vehicles, every year becomes more urgent. It is fortunate, therefore, that your Seminar has for its object the bringing together of newspapermen from all parts of the country. The efforts of the newspapers in behalf of traffic safety have been continuous and unremitting.
>
> May I, in sending my greetings to the Seminar, express the hope that their interest will be given new stimulation as a result of the forthcoming conference.

The outbreak of World War II and Darr's change of status from a full-time officer of the corporation to a consultant's role brought an end to the Foundation's activities in 1941 at the conclusion of the five-year period for which it was originally established. C.I.T.'s management, however, continued to commit both funds and the time and effort of executives to the cause of highway safety. This was primarily through support of the Automotive Safety Foundation, which had been established (with C.I.T. as a leader) in 1937. Through this organization, the automobile manufacturing industry matched dollar-for-dollar all contributions received from other business interests involved with highway travel and construction, such as the petroleum, cement, construction equipment, insurance and similarly placed industry groups. These funds then were disbursed to agencies engaged in making travel by automobile safer by whatever means.

C.I.T. was a substantial annual contributor to the program. President Dietz served as its vice chairman and treasurer for many years and in later years, Walter Lundell represented the company in the Foundation's affairs.

Dietz also served as chairman of the nationwide Highways for Survival Committee in 1953–54, which played an important role in mobilizing the support of business and the public on behalf of the $33 billion National Highway Act of 1954. This legislation created the Interstate Highways System.

A second major legal-regulatory situation demanded the maximum attention and concern of C.I.T.'s management team in the latter years of the 1930's. This was a suit filed in the federal courts by the U.S. Department of Justice and the so-called independent finance companies, organized as the American Finance Conference. It attacked alleged antitrust practices in the relationships of C.I.T. and Universal Credit with the Ford Motor Company, Commercial Credit with the Chrysler Corporation and GMAC with General Motors Corporation.

Each of these relationships had a different basis. General Motors owned GMAC outright. Chrysler had an investment interest in Commercial Credit and a "factory contract" with the latter that included designating the Commercial Credit financing plan as its "official" one. C.I.T. was operating Universal Credit as a financing organization that served Ford Motor dealers exclusively and Universal Credit was designated by the manufacturer as the "authorized" Ford financing plan.

In 1936, as the result of complaints by competitors of the three major finance companies and some automobile dealers allied with them, the Department of Justice launched an investigation of what were claimed to be "monopolistic, restrictive and coercive practices in the handling of instalment sales practices, particularly automobile paper."

The result of this investigation was a presentation of evidence before a federal grand jury at South Bend, Indiana (headquarters city of Associates Investment Company, the largest member of the American Finance Conference). On May 27, 1938, the grand jury returned criminal indictments against all three car manufacturers and the three major finance companies. Certain corporate officers of the defendants also were indicted.

Eleven separate charges were contained in each indictment. These boiled down to the allegations that the manufacturers had used their power to grant or terminate dealer franchises, to control the shipment of cars to dealers, to spy on dealers through inspection of their books, to advertise and endorse their "official" finance plans, to require dealers to do the same and to refuse assistance, endorsement or other privileges to the independent companies—all for the benefit of their favored financing organizations. The finance companies, in turn, were charged with conspiring with the manufacturers to maintain these coercive practices.

The indictments were set down for trial in the U.S. District Court at South Bend, but before they could be heard, Ford and C.I.T. and Chrysler and Commercial Credit entered into consent decrees with the government on November 15, 1938, and the indictments against them were dismissed.

In the consent decrees, without acknowledging that there had been any violations of the antitrust statutes, the companies agreed in effect to eliminate or not enter into any of the practices that allegedly favored the major finance companies over their independent competitors. Chrysler's stock interest in Commercial Credit also was terminated. General Motors refused to sign a consent decree and prepared to go to trial. One provision of the consent decree was to have great future consequence. This was the condition that if the government did not succeed in forcing the permanent divorcement of GMAC from General Motors by January 1, 1941, the other manufacturers were to be free to establish their own financing subsidiaries or to deal with any finance company and their dealers without being restrained by the provisions of the consent decrees.

When the consent decrees were signed, Edsel Ford, as president of Ford Motor Company, wrote all his branch managers and dealers as follows:

> At the inception of the Universal Credit Corporation, I wrote a letter to each branch manager, outlining the attitude of the Ford Motor Company as it related to the time sales of Ford products. In this letter it was stated that we realized there were a great many finance companies anxious to secure Ford business, and from our standpoint they were in every way entitled to such Ford business on a fair competitive basis. I also stated as clearly as possible that there was to be no coercion, either direct or indirect, of Ford dealers, to get them to use the facilities of Universal Credit Corporation.
>
> No change was made in the policy set forth in that letter at the time the Ford Motor Company sold its interest in the Universal Credit Corpora-

tion. Neither has there been any change in our attitude regarding such matters since that time.

We have always endeavored to make our cars available to the public at the lowest possible price. For this reason, we are vitally interested in the time delivered price of Ford products. We will continue to maintain this interest because we want to avoid, as far as possible, having the manufacturing economies which we have effected for the benefit of the purchaser, offset by excessive time sales charges. . . .

It is not of any particular interest to the Ford Motor Company what finance company a dealer does business with, as long as the public obtains the benefit of the lowest possible time sales delivered price and the most complete protection.

We believe our position has always been clear to you, but to avoid the possibility of any misunderstanding arising out of the above mentioned proceedings, we are writing this letter.

After a lengthy trial, on November 17, 1939, General Motors and GMAC were found guilty in the U.S. District Court of violating the Sherman Anti-Trust Law, as charged in the indictments. Each defendant was fined $5,000. It was implicit in the decision that the defendants cease any of the actions found to be collusive in the indictments and in the jury's verdict.

The conviction had no bearing on the possible divorcement of GMAC. Therefore, on October 1, 1940, the government filed a civil suit in U.S. District Court at Chicago asking that the divesting of GMAC by its parent be ordered. Wartime conditions and legal delays prevented this action from being brought to trial for a number of years. Therefore, the other manufacturers and C.I.T. and Commercial Credit agreed to several extensions in the original January 1, 1941, deadline for the General Motors-GMAC divorcement.

24

A Recession . . . and
Gathering War Clouds

In spite of the distraction of outside events and problems that demanded so much of the time and attention of the C.I.T. senior management group, business had to be—and was—carried on as usual.
The four-year period from 1937 to 1940 was not marked by any outstanding corporate advances or developments such as had become the
modus operandi of the prior years since the company's founding. It
might be a mistake, however, to attribute this solely to the impact of
the regulatory and public relations difficulties of the period. Clearly, a
time for consolidation and digestion of the fast-moving events of the
past was in order. Also, the sudden and severe economic depression of
1937–38, which affected the automobile industry as much or even
more than any other, obviously had a restraining influence on corporate
gains and growth.

There were only a limited number of potentially significant acquisitions or shifts in management direction during the four years. One
acquisition would have resulted in a complete change in the character
of the company, but the opportunity was rejected. This was a proposal
that C.I.T. purchase Eastern Air Lines, then a major link in the nation's air transport system as it remains today.

Lewis Strauss, of Kuhn, Loeb & Company, who had brought the Universal Credit purchase opportunity to the attention of the C.I.T. management and had subsequently joined C.I.T.'s board of directors, originated this new transaction. Eastern was a division of North American Aviation Corporation, which in turn was controlled by General Motors. General Motors had developed and was soon to announce the production of the famous Allison engine of World War II. Under federal law, if it engaged in aircraft engine manufacturing it could not also operate a transportation company carrying the mails, as Eastern was doing. Thus, General Motors was preparing to put the airline on the market.

Colonel Edward Rickenbacker was managing the line and was seeking a buyer who would allow him to continue as its chief executive. Strauss proposed to Dietz on February 14, 1937 that C.I.T. become the buyer, adding to the investment of the purchase price an infusion of an additional $3.5 or $3.75 million in needed working capital.

He suggested that when the property had passed into C.I.T.'s hands, it could then be retained as an investment (a net profit of $550,000 was forecast for the year) or, in time, part or all of it could be profitably sold to the public through a stock issue. He also told Dietz that if C.I.T. was not interested, perhaps Henry Ittleson would like to join or head up a group of individual investors to swing the deal.

Dietz duly passed the Strauss proposition along to his superior, who was in Florida. He noted, however, that "he did not think that this was anything for C.I.T. to go into as a corporate matter." Ittleson agreed with that opinion and also had no personal interest in the proposal.

Rickenbacker succeeded in getting the backing of the Rockefeller interests and carried through the purchase of the airline from General Motors before the end of 1938.

One change that would prove to be of very considerable importance in building the corporation's earning power in the years after World War II was initiated in March of 1938. Up to that time, all physical damage insurance written on automobiles financed in the United States and Canada, and in which C.I.T. thereby held a collateral interest, had been placed through brokers with various established insurance carriers. Since the car buyer as well as C.I.T. derived protection from the insurance, the cost of it was paid by the purchaser as a separate charge under his contract.

It was evident that, on an overall basis, this insurance business was very profitable for the brokers who placed it and the companies that underwrote it. After due study, C.I.T.'s managers decided to organize or acquire their own insurance carrier in order to keep this profitable business for their own. The purchase of a sizable, qualified carrier seemed unattractive, so it was agreed that a suitable vehicle to handle the insurance business would be built up virtually from scratch.

A very small company, Service Fire Insurance Company of New York, was selected for this purpose and acquired through a subsidiary in early 1938. The following year was devoted to having it admitted and qualified to do business in all the forty-eight states and later in Canada. In February 1939, Service Fire became the recognized principal carrier of all automotive physical damage insurance generated by C.I.T.'s financing operations.

Another acquisition was the purchase for cash in late 1939 of the Michigan Bank. This step, to bring into the enterprise a small but growing "industrial," or consumer-oriented, banking institution, was directed at probing and possibly finding some answers to two of the vexing problems that C.I.T.'s managers realized they were facing as they looked into the future.

The first was the recurring proposal that the company, with its broad consumer financing franchise and experience, begin making direct personal loans to consumers by entering the "small loan" business. This recommendation had been repeatedly brought up to the top management during the 1930's and perhaps earlier. To executives on the firing line and seeking new avenues for expansion, it seemed a natural move to put the company in a position to make direct loans to the same people (or others just like them) for whom it was financing autos and household equipment. Even the very same equipment, when a given number of purchase payments had been made, could serve as collateral for such loans.

There were in existence, of course, hundreds of successful so-called consumer finance companies, including some giants, operating under state small loan laws. On more than one occasion, the possibility even arose that entry into the business might be gained by purchasing one of the larger companies.

However, all such proposals met with the fixed opposition of Arthur Dietz and Edwin Vogel. The senior Ittleson's personal views are not known, but he apparently never took issue with the attitude of his immediate associates.

A series of reasons were given why the personal loan business was not for C.I.T. However, the argument running through all discussions of the subject was that to begin making direct personal loans would in some way be damaging to the company's hard-won reputation and standing in the financial community.

The second disquieting development that clearly could be foreseen was the growing interest and participation of commercial banks in the overall field of consumer financing. The horror with which many bankers viewed instalment buying and personal lending to wage and salary earners in the 1910–30 period had all but vanished. As we have seen, more and more banks were organizing "retail" credit departments, and their aggressiveness and advertising had become a matter of real concern to Dietz.

The latter had countered some of the proposals for opening small loan offices by saying it might be acceptable for C.I.T. to adopt the so-called Morris Plan or industrial banking approach. This primarily involved the making of loans to the bank's own depositors who repaid their obligations through future deposits to their accounts. This was a somewhat legalistic but sanctioned exception to the state regulations governing licensed small loan companies.

It was decided that the purchase of one or more of these banks would not only give the organization an opportunity to evaluate the small loan business per se but would also help in developing competitive responses to the rising level of bank competition.

The Michigan Bank was a small institution headquartered in Detroit. Soon after it was purchased and C.I.T. management installed, the capital was increased from $100,000 to $300,000, and it is probable that only the intensification of the war situation deterred a more active expansion program in the following years.

As for the course of the company's regular business, 1937 proved to be the most successful in its history; net income for the year was not to be exceeded again for more than a decade. The net rose to $21.5 million from 1936's $21.1 million, resulting in earnings per common share of $6.36 from the 1936 figure of $6.07. The total volume of business acquired rose to $1.29 billion from $1.17 billion, and the portfolio of outstanding receivables scored a $68 million gain during the year, to $466 million.

A $1 extra dividend on the common stock was declared at the year-end, bringing to $5 a share the payout on the stock against $4.90 in the prior year.

President Ittleson, however, sounded a warning note in his report to stockholders, saying that because of a recession in the automobile and textile industries that had become apparent about mid-year, the monthly volume of new business placed on the books "declined progressively from August through December."

Bank competition in automobile financing also was becoming an increasingly troublesome matter. This is clearly evident from a letter Dietz wrote to Ittleson on March 16, 1937:

Dear Mr. Ittleson:

From recent developments I have come to the conclusion that we have made a mistake in handling banks who have gone into the finance business. As you know, our usual action has been to withdraw our account from that bank, in some instances taking out our operating account and in others taking away our borrowing account. In some places we have taken both accounts away from the bank in question.

The other day Charles P. Partridge, Vice President of Bank of America, spent considerable time with me. It seems that C.I.T. is the only finance company to have taken this action, in so far as Bank of America is concerned. He pointed out that GMAC continues as it has in the past and so does Commercial Credit. He also pointed out that the General Motors Corporation's big account on the Pacific Coast remains with his bank.

In presenting his story to me he mentioned the fact that since C.I.T. has withdrawn its account from Bank of America and its numerous branches a spirit of ill will has grown up toward C.I.T. on the part of the personnel of his main bank and branch banks. This has gone to the extent of where the local branch managers refuse to cooperate with us in inter-change of credit information and, in some instances, they are beginning to charge us with exchange on floats because there is no other way that they can receive an income from C.I.T. His view is that nothing that we can do, or will do, will prevent the Bank of America from continuing to handle instalment paper and there is nothing that they can do to drive us out of business. So with that situation it is his opinion that we would be much better off to retain a friendly relationship and put a stop to recriminations.

Upon thoughtful consideration I am inclined to believe that there is a great deal in what he says. For instance, we withdrew our account from the Lincoln Alliance Bank of Rochester, New York because they went into the instalment business. That bank is probably the best bank in Rochester and by taking our account away they have adopted an offended attitude which does us no particular good.

I am wondering whether the same situation doesn't exist with every bank that we treat in like manner. I doubt very much whether the withdrawal of our account is going to stop these banks in their efforts to build up a time payment business of their own and my own conclusion is that we would be much better off to continue our account with the bank so at least we can, from time to time, discuss with them the progress that they are making on their own instalment business and, in a measure, hold them in line from going overboard on terms and so forth.

I am passing this on to you for your consideration and my own recommendation at the moment is that we reverse ourselves and see if we wouldn't be better off in handling this problem by "boring from within" rather than remaining on the outside deliberately antagonizing the banks who have lost our account.

Ittleson promptly concurred in the recommendation of his right-hand man. C.I.T. restored the accounts it had withdrawn, mended its fences and did not attempt again to use its account relationships to deter banks from going into auto financing. However, for the next thirty years it continued to contend against the financing of car buyers through banks with every sales and service weapon at its command.

Because of tight money conditions, rising unemployment and general concern over the unsettling diplomatic conditions in Europe, automobile sales virtually collapsed in 1938, dropping from the record 3.93 million units in 1937 to 2.02 million for the year. C.I.T.'s retail auto paper acquired fell to $190 million, less than half the $392 million in the previous year. The volume of industrial receivables declined from $125 million to $70 million and factoring receivables showed a drop from $295 to $218 million. The result was a total volume figure for the year of $696 million, compared with bookings in 1937 of $1.29 billion.

With the portfolio of earnings assets running off steadily during the year, total net profit was $16.2 million, a decline of nearly 25% from the 1937 return on the business. Earnings per common share were $4.75 against $6.36.

While the $4 regular common dividend rate was maintained, no extra dividend was declared for the year. Thus, with stockholders receiving a total of $4 per share compared with $5 in 1937, 1938 became the first year since the company was founded when there was a reduction in the cash dividend payout from the previous year.

Although the 1938 results were a disappointment, the management evidenced an unshaken confidence in the company's future. This statement appeared in the annual report for the year:

> The experience of the past year has provided another convincing demonstration of the underlying strength and liquidity of our companies.
>
> Collections throughout the year have been highly satisfactory, past due accounts continue to be small and the receivables are in excellent condition. Instalments thirty days or more past due at December 31 were 35/100 of 1% of the total instalment receivables, compared with 25/100 of 1% on the same basis at the end of 1937.

At the final board meeting of the year, A. O. Dietz told his fellow directors that an upward trend in auto sales and financing was beginning to evidence itself and that he was optimistic about 1938 car sales. He thus began a series of accurate predictions about future automobile markets that he issued publicly in the years to follow and which earned him nationwide recognition as a reliable seer in this area of paramount economic importance. For the record, retail sales of new cars were up 870,000 units to 2.8 million in 1939 and reached 3.7 million in 1940.

At the very close of 1938, C.I.T. bought the remaining 30% minority interest in Universal Credit Corporation that it had not acquired in the original purchase from Ford Motor Company. The consideration was $1.5 million in cash plus 200,000 shares of C.I.T. common stock, selling at the time at $60 a share. The sellers also were granted five-year options on an additional 50,000 C.I.T. shares at $32 a share. Thus, the price paid for the 30% interest at least equaled that of the original 70% purchase. The sellers were Ernest Kanzler and George Zimmerman and members of their families.

Recognition came to Arthur Dietz for his outstanding contributions and the leadership he had assumed in the broad range of corporate affairs, as Henry Ittleson and Edwin Vogel reduced their involvement in day-to-day operations, when he was elected president of the corporation on April 27, 1939. Henry Ittleson relinquished this title and assumed that of chairman of the board. He remained the final authority on all important corporate matters.

There was a steady pickup in all aspects of the business during the year and the portfolio of receivables increased to $362 million at December 31 against the $290 million figure a year earlier. Nevertheless, *average* receivables outstanding for 1939 were $43 million under the 1938 average because of the high point at which they stood at the beginning of the latter year and the low level at which 1939 began. Thus, another decline in net earnings, to $15.7 million, or $4.34 a common share, was registered, compared with the 1938 earnings of $16.2 million, or $4.75 per share.

During the year, the corporation retired a substantial amount of its funded debt bearing interest rates of 3% or higher. These were replaced in part with two new borrowings from the Metropolitan Life Insurance Company and the Prudential Insurance Company. These took the form of 3-year notes for $5 million each from the two companies at an interest rate of 1 ½% and 5-year notes of $10 million each carrying an interest rate of 2%!

With the recession now a thing of the past, it was noted that 30-day delinquencies on consumer retail obligations never rose higher than 35/100 of 1% during the downturn and had dropped to 18/100 of 1% by the end of 1939.

With Europe at war and the involvement of the United States looming, the following year was marked with several developments of historic importance. A companion company to National Surety Corporation, National Surety Marine Insurance Company, was organized to

Arthur O. Dietz

handle inland casualty risks of a nature foreclosed to surety companies. It was emphatically stated in the announcement of this action to the stockholders that "the new company will not cover ocean transportation, perils of the sea or war risks."

Frank W. Collins, who had been associated with the company since it opened for business, died on June 27. After spending the years from 1931 to 1934 as president of the "Chicago Company," he had been forced by ill health to retire from any further active participation in the corporation's affairs, but he continued as a director. His fellow directors memorialized him in part with these words: "Frank W. Collins had no business career other than with this Corporation. As a boy he began his service thirty years ago in a humble capacity. His career evidenced the success which can be attained by men possessing initiative and industry. Through his ability and integrity he rose to one of the senior executives of the Corporation. His loss will be keenly felt."

With the passage of the Selective Service Act on September 16, 1940, the C.I.T. directors acted ten days later to adopt a program of benefits for employees who might enter military service. These included a bonus of one month's pay on leaving the company, the continuation at company expense of their group life insurance protection for the duration and a commitment to offer reemployment to them when they were discharged from service. Still another concern for the welfare of employees was evidenced when the board also authorized a management study leading to the development of a formal retirement plan, which the company had not offered up to that time. The plan was adopted on February 28, 1941, and was partially contributory on the part of employees. It provided for the retirement of women at 60 and men at 65.

The founder's and his associates' concern for the well-being of the general employee group was also evidenced when Henry Ittleson observed his seventieth birthday on January 27, 1941. He increased his contribution to the Ittleson Beneficial Fund, established to make grants and loans to employees who experienced personal misfortunes, by $10,000 to $35,000. His fellow board members authorized a corporate contribution of an additional $15,000 to the fund in his honor.

Symbolic of this increased concern for the welfare of employees was the appearance for the first time of a section devoted to this subject, captioned "Employee Relationships," in the 1940 annual report. This summarized all of the company's programs, including those instituted during the year.

Net profits for the year were slightly ahead of 1939 at $15.8 million against $15.7, with an extra $2 million of higher federal income taxes, generated by the nation's military preparedness commitments, being absorbed. Volume again crossed the $1 billion mark to $1.29 billion and the portfolio of receivables showed a $143 million increase to $506 million.

Messrs. Ittleson and Dietz closed the report with these words of cautious confidence:

> Whether the production of consumer goods will continue at the 1940 rate, and thereby enable instalment buying to continue at the recent levels, cannot be forecast. If the National Defense needs require deflection of plant facilities which will reduce the production of peace-time durable goods, the satisfaction of consumer demands must necessarily be curtailed as the successful consummation of the Defense Program is paramount to all other considerations. However, increased employment and income will apparently sustain a demand which could readily absorb production at the 1940 rate.

> The foregoing reference to the Corporation's financing operations in the field of consumers' goods does not comprehend the total of its diversified activities. Its factoring subsidiaries render financial and credit service to more than 650 manufacturers and wholesale distributors of textiles, shoes and other commodities, and its subsidiary National Surety Corpo-

ration is one of the leading surety companies. The varied services of the Corporation's subsidiaries are available to business and industry through 512 branch offices in the United States and Canada. As has been our practice, we are constantly exploring new avenues in which to develop demand for our facilities.

25

The Nation
Takes to Arms

As 1941 opened, a military holocaust of successive Axis invasion strikes and battlefield victories was engulfing Western Europe and Russia. All phases of life in the United States were affected by a Presidential Declaration of National Emergency. As a result, both a profound uncertainty and a determination to conduct business as usual to the maximum extent possible were the watchwords of C.I.T.'s management.

Business in the first quarter was excellent. The volume of new receivables acquired was up almost 50% over the opening quarter of 1940, at $157 million versus $109 million. Arthur Dietz attributed part of this gain to the favorable reception by the public and dealers of the company's introduction of a "Purchaser's Protective Plan." This was a pioneering step to offer automobile time buyers a cluster of additional benefits, in addition to the basic credit and vehicle insurance services that had been standard. The new benefits included a personal accident insurance policy, travel and accident bail bond insurance, insured towing and road service cost reimbursement and a travel emergency and repair plan entitling car buyers to additional credit for such expenses if needed.

194

Dietz told his fellow directors at their February 28, 1940, meeting that this program was "an example of the advancing standards of public service on the part of C.I.T. and Universal Credit. . . . such comprehensive protection for the time buyer's convenience and pocketbook never before having been combined in a national financing plan."

At the 1941 stockholders' meeting, Ernest Kanzler and George Zimmerman were elected to the board of directors for the first time. Despite the close association and leadership roles they had assumed in the company's affairs ever since the Universal Credit purchase, their substantial minority interest in Universal had been seen as a bar to their joining the C.I.T. board. The elimination of this interest thus cleared the way for them to become C.I.T. directors.

The remainder of the year was marked by a series of fast-breaking and sweeping developments. Before the start of the 1942 model year in August, the automobile manufacturing industry agreed to cut back production by at least 20% from their output of 1941 cars. There was much discussion of the possibility that the federal government would impose selective controls on instalment credit in order to dampen the demand for consumer durable goods, channeling available industrial capacity into military production, and to reduce consumer indebtedness so that more of the public's money would become available to the government and the war effort.

The June 30 report to C.I.T.'s stockholders contained these comments concerning this possibility:

> There has been considerable discussion regarding the desirability of and the economic results which may accrue from the regulation of consumer credit terms through shortening the maximum running time for payments and increasing the required percentage of down payment. If the Government should decide that such regulation is necessary in aid of the Defense Program, your management will cooperate to the best of its ability. We assume that any regulation imposed will be so designed as to avoid dislocating business unnecessarily, and, that it will be made applicable, without discrimination, to all commercial and financial agencies which service consumer credits either directly or indirectly.

Regulation W, to establish minimum down payments and maximum maturities for the instalment purchase of a lengthy list of consumer durables, was imposed effective September 1 by Executive Order of the President under general authority granted him by the Trading with the Enemy Act. The Federal Reserve Board, named administrator of the program, established original terms for new and used automobiles at a minimum of one-third of the cash price as a down payment and a maximum contract maturity of eighteen months. These terms were not unduly restrictive as compared with those in general use prior to the issuance of the regulation, although down payments as low as 25% had not been uncommon and some new car contracts were being written for as long as 24 or 36 months.

For electrical and other household appliances, the regulation established terms of 20% down and maximum maturities of 18 months. These were rather more stringent, based on preregulation trade practices, than were the automobile terms. Instalment loans greater than $1,000, if secured by any of the listed durables, were also subject to regulation, the terms being the same as those applicable to a purchase of the article involved.

C.I.T. began to cut back its employment rolls in late September as business volume eroded. Stockholders felt the pinch too when the directors in November voted to reduce the common stock dividend, effective with the January 1, 1942, payment, from the prevailing $1.00 a share rate to $0.75.

After the December 7 attack on Pearl Harbor and the Japanese declaration of war on that date, the U.S. Congress declared war against Japan on December 8. Germany and Italy announced a state of war against the United States on December 10, and war against these powers was declared on December 11.

At the turn of the year, all production of motor vehicles for civilian use was stopped and inventories of cars and trucks in dealers' hands were frozen, pending the introduction of a rationing program.

Ernest Kanzler told his fellow directors by letter at the December meeting that, after resisting previous overtures, he had accepted the invitation of William S. Knudsen, the General Motors production genius who was the director of the Office of Production Management, to become head of the organization's Automotive Branch. His duties would be to direct the mobilization and conversion of the production capacities of the automotive industry to military production. He would serve on a dollar-a-year basis.

"This was a call that I felt I could not refuse," his letter read. "Now that we are in the war, I know there is complete agreement that all of us get behind the war effort with all the ability we possess. As businessmen, we know that the sooner it is over, the more will be left of what is now worthwhile."

His fellow directors released him from his contractual employment obligations at once and he served with distinction in the O.P.M. and the War Production Board that succeeded it. Zimmerman assumed full responsibility for the affairs of Universal Credit in his absence.

Another 1942 departure from the executive group was that of Henry

Ittleson, Jr., who had been elected executive vice president of the Commercial Investment Trust Incorporated subsidiary in April 1941. He joined the Air Force, attained the rank of lieutenant colonel and served in various management branches of the air arm until the conclusion of hostilities. He promptly returned to C.I.T. after his discharge.

Although earnings for the year and the volume of business handled showed significant gains over 1940, the impact of the military crisis was reflected in the results for the final quarter, which fell well below those of the previous year. For the full year, however, net profit was $17.3 million, compared with $15.8 million, or $4.78 against $4.35 on a per-common-share basis. Higher federal income taxes raised this impost to $11.5 million from 1940's $7.3 million. Volume of receivables acquired was $1.64 billion, compared with $1.28 billion. (In the following war years, 1942 through 1945, earnings declined successively—to $14.4 million, $10.7 million, $7.5 million and $5.8 million. With the record volumes of business being received by the factoring companies from manufacturers and distributors delivering goods directly or indirectly related to the war effort, the annual volume of business purchased remained in the range of $673–$786 million for the period.)

The industrial division of the company poured tens of millions of dollars into loans and other advances to enterprises supporting the war effort either through sales to the military services or as subcontractors to others engaged in making the United States the "arsenal of democracy." Later in the war period, surplus funds freed up by the decline in general financing operations were diverted to the mortgage financing of construction projects or the outright purchase of mortgages on existing buildings. The largest mortgage on a construction project was a $5.2 million investment in two apartment buildings at Middle River, Maryland, to house employees of the Glenn L. Martin bomber plant.

Two other novel financing plans were initiated in the early days of the war in an all-out effort to replace in some part the eroding auto and appliance financing operations. One was a plan intended to help retain dealer account relationships and to build a backlog of assured postwar auto financing business. Under the plan, car owners who wished to dispose of their vehicles because of their entry into military service or because of gasoline rationing restrictions that otherwise would force them to lay up their cars could sell them at high wartime prices and have the proceeds held toward the purchase of new autos when the war was over. The dealer would purchase the car and the proceeds would be deposited to the credit of the former owner in an escrow account with the nearest C.I.T. office to be used as the down payment on a postwar purchase.

A second, "Funeral Directors' Budget Plan," was modeled on automobile financing procedures. Morticians could offer credit terms and monthly repayment arrangements to bereaved families, discount these receivables with C.I.T., and be relieved of future collection responsibilities.

Neither plan enjoyed any notable success.

When dealers' stocks of motor vehicles were abruptly taken off the market by the freeze order at the end of 1941, C.I.T. had $79 million invested in these so-called floor-planned cars and light trucks. Accordingly, these sums similarly were tied up. The Reconstruction Finance Corporation entered the picture through a program to guarantee to pay off the advances as the vehicles were sold. This underwriting protected C.I.T. and the other financing institutions against loss, but the freeze order created a somewhat uncomfortable situation that lasted for many months.

The terms permitted by Regulation W received a further tightening in March 1942. The standard maximum maturities were reduced from eighteen to fifteen months, except for advances for home improvement or modernization purposes and for pianos. Down payments on household electric appliances were raised from 20% to 33%. The stated purpose of the more stringent restrictions was to achieve "further dampening of consumer demand . . . to facilitate the transfer of materials and resources to the war effort."

In later amendments, the list of consumer products subject to the regulation was greatly expanded to include such items as bicycles, lawn mowers, silverware, bedding, draperies, binoculars, jewelry and many other durables, as well as charge accounts and single-payment loans. There were no other significant changes in the terms of the regulation until after hostilities were ended.

At the mid-year, Ittleson and Dietz told their stockholders that "opportunities have developed for acquiring ownership of certain manufacturing enterprises. We are carefully examining these businesses and propose to study others that may be presented for consideration, so that we may devote some of our resources to participating in the war effort and at the same time further diversify our activities by making acquisitions which seem consistent with the successful development of the Corporation."

To implement this program, Ittleson had placed Sydney Maddock in charge of it. This choice was no doubt premised on Maddock's World War I experience with the War Trade Board, and more particularly, on his extensive familiarity with all phases of industrial production through the key role he had played in developing C.I.T.'s industrial financing division for more than ten years.

To quote Maddock: "Mr. I. laid down a very exacting specification: namely, that any company we bought must not be bought simply for the profit we could make out of it. Rather, we must buy only companies whereby our adding additional financial strength would further the war effort, be there a profit or otherwise for us. He said he wanted no part of anybody ever being able to point to C.I.T. and say we were out to make a profit out of the war."

Maddock recalled that more than four hundred companies were considered in the course of the project but only two purchases were closed. Perhaps the largest single company that was involved in serious negotiations was the Doehler Die Casting Company, but a mutually acceptable agreement was not reached. The first purchase was the Holtzer-Cabot Electric Company, with headquarters and a plant in Boston and a smaller factory in the Chicago area. Employing 1,300 workers at the time of the purchase for $1.3 million, the company produced custom-made fractional horsepower motors and generators, paging and call systems and fire and intruder alarms. It was a 67-year old organization with an established management group that it was planned would continue to run the business. After the purchase, C.I.T.

Sydney B. Maddock

provided additional capital of $550,000 for plant expansion to lift the production capacity of its new property.

The second addition came just before the year-end. This was the Micro Switch Corporation, the purchase price being $526,000. Micro Switch produced snap-action switches of great precision and reliability. Its output was totally devoted to the war effort, the products going into aircraft and other forms of armament. In announcing the purchase, C.I.T. said it was providing funds for the immediate expansion of the company's production facilities at Freeport, Ill.

Maddock's third possible transaction was a small machine tool company, the V. and O. Press Company, Inc., located at Hudson, N.Y. An option was taken to purchase this company. Ittleson informed Maddock that Marshall Field, the publisher of the Chicago *Sun* and possessor of the large retailing fortune, was seeking some investments associated with the war effort. Ittleson asked Maddock to "keep his eye out for something for Field." Maddock's reply was that the V. and O. Company was a rather small venture for C.I.T. It was agreed to offer the option to Field and an associate at C.I.T.'s purchase price, with C.I.T. retaining 10% of future profits. The offer was accepted.

This gesture bore fruit in the postwar period. Maddock was seeking a contract to finance instalment sales of the *World Book* encyclopedia, published by Field Enterprises. Field was most helpful to C.I.T. in obtaining the contract.

After the C.I.T. purchase, Micro Switch operated efficiently and profitably and made a very substantial contribution to the war effort. The Army-Navy "E" Award for "high achievement in producing materials needed for the war effort" was presented to the company and its employees on four occasions, the first on August 21, 1943, and the last on April 14, 1945.

The durability of the company's products was vividly demonstrated through a chance discovery of a group of English choir boys who were hiking through a bog near Cheviot, Northumberland, in the summer of 1968. They came upon the wreck of a U.S. B-17 bomber and removed from the fuselage two control switches that bore the Micro Switch name and the Freeport address.

One of the boys sent the switches to the Micro Switch factory, where it was noted that, despite being buried in the muck of a bog for more than 20 years, one functioned perfectly and the other still conducted electricity. However, the switches soon ended up in a desk drawer.

It happened that the firm's public relations man spotted the switches and learned of their origin. To him, they represented an excellent opportunity to tell in graphic terms of the quality and trustworthiness of his client's products. The upshot was a major ceremony on two sides of the Atlantic on the following Memorial Day.

The seven surviving members of the B-17 crew had been located. They were brought together for a reunion by Micro Switch and were guests of the City of New York for the annual Memorial Day parade. Through a transatlantic telephone hook-up, they then participated in another ceremony at the crash site. There, the school the boys attended had erected a modest memorial to all American airmen who had died in World War II. This was dedicated by using the still-functioning switch, pressed in New York, to unveil the monument. On both sides of the ocean many of the most distinguished military airmen of the war were present at the two ceremonies.

The switch—still in working order—was placed on permanent display at the Wings Club, in New York City.

Holtzer-Cabot encountered troublesome production difficulties, and Maddock eventually was detailed to go to Boston and become president of the company. He did so, and in due course Holtzer-Cabot met its delivery schedules and achieved a 50% increase in production in 1943 over the 1942 output. Leo Spanyol had also applied his exceptional financial and accounting skills to the tangled affairs of the company, which helped accomplish the company's turnaround in a period of less than a year. On November 27, 1944, the company and its employees also were awarded the Army-Navy "E."

Another war-influenced development of historic significance was the merger of the consumer financing operations of Commercial Investment Trust Corporation with those of Universal Credit Corporation to form a new subsidiary, Universal C.I.T. Credit Corporation. This put an end to the exclusive financing for Ford dealers that had been the function of Universal Credit. No longer was it necessary to have "two offices in Amarillo, Texas," and such separate offices in the same geographical area were discontinued wherever they existed. The number of consumer financing offices was reduced from 507 to approximately 300 during 1942, both as a result of the combining of the two companies and a complete withdrawal from some areas that could not support continuing localized operations.

The announcement of the merger by Dietz and Zimmerman to their respective organizations contained these words of explanation and reassurance.

> Because of changed conditions growing out of the war effort, much consideration has been given to steps which would most effectively make use of the combined facilities of U.C.C. and C.I.T. in maintaining a national organization to serve the best interests of our customers and dealers, as well as the welfare of our employees.
>
> It has been decided to have an orderly, systematic combination of the operations of both companies. During August, the operations of the New York Region of U.C.C. and C.I.T. will be combined, and this will also take place in additional territories as rapidly as practicable. It may be that a joint Corporate name will be used. These moves will necessarily take some time to accomplish. Meanwhile, each organization will continue to function and report as it has in the past. . . .
>
> Every possible consideration will be given to past performance seniority in period of employment and position, and other personnel factors in preserving the strongest possible organization to carry on our nationwide business. No employee need have undue concern over termination of employment. While adjustments must be made as outstandings are reduced, our present policy of liberal separation allowances gives each one ample time to secure another position if it becomes necessary.

There were indeed some terminations as a result of this cutback, but the employment problem was eased by the entry of more than 1,400 employees into the military services during the year. Still others took civilian posts connected with the war effort. In all, operating expenses for the year, exclusive of the cost of borrowed money, were reduced by more than $7.3 million, or 30%, compared with the 1941 figure.

National Surety Corporation was the one subsidiary that showed a marked increase in profits. This resulted from the large amount of business written in the form of performance bonds on war contracts and from the growth of the "inland marine" underwriting of the new National Surety Marine Insurance Company, principally covering furs, jewelry and other personal effects.

Several financial programs were carried through by Treasurer John Snyder in 1943. All outstanding preferred stock was redeemed, leaving the common stockholders as the sole owners of the enterprise. The $20 million of 2% notes held by the Metropolitan and Prudential insurance companies were paid off from the proceeds of a loan for the same amount arranged with four banks at a rate of 1½%. Short-term commercial paper, normally comprising about 60% of the company's borrowings for less than one year, was being placed at an interest rate of ½ of 1% per annum. The remaining 40% was kept in bank loans.

A second move into the industrial banking field was taken in the fall of the year. The Miami Industrial Bank, in Florida, was acquired, no doubt with the intention of using it to augment the exploratory program begun when the Michigan Bank was purchased. Claude Hemphill, who had retired to South Florida, assumed the chairmanship and oversight of the affairs of the Miami Bank, the last responsibility he undertook for the enterprise he helped to found.

The annual report for the year contained an excellent summary of the achievements and hopes of the management:

> The current year marks the twentieth anniversary of your Corporation as a publicly owned company, and the thirty-sixth anniversary of the founding of the enterprise in 1908. The intervening years have witnessed an ever-broadening diversification of activities, as evidenced first by the pioneering operations of subsidiaries in the financing of instalment sales of automobiles, the granting of wholesale accommodation to automobile dealers, and the financing of credit sales of machinery, home appliances and other consumer durable goods; then, by entering the field of textile factoring; next, by the acquisition of National Surety Corporation and Service Fire Insurance Company of New York; and, finally, by the purchase in 1942 of the two manufacturing companies. . . .
>
> After the war it is expected that instalment financing will again become the largest division of the activities of the enterprise, and that volume of business in this field will expand rapidly in view of the accumulated demand for durable goods.

With earnings for the first quarter of 1944 falling to $0.51 a share, the directors reduced the common stock dividend payable on April 1 to $0.60 from the prior $0.75 rate. The corporation subscribed $30.6

million to the Fourth War Loan campaign, bringing its holding of
government obligations supporting the war effort to $73 million. Also,
90% of the employees were purchasing war bonds under payroll deduc-
tion arrangements. Active support also was being given to the Red
Cross, National War Fund and other war relief agencies. The 1944
subscription to the Red Cross was $57,500.

About the mid-year, National Surety Corporation announced its
entry into the casualty insurance field, primarily the writing of work-
men's compensation and auto liability insurance. This program was
designed to establish National Surety as a "full-line" insurer, except
for the life and accident fields. Vincent Cullen, the company's president, assured his fellow C.I.T. directors that the entry into this untried
area (for National Surety) would be on a "very conservative" basis.

When the time came for the declaration of the July 1 dividend,
members of the management group raised the question with the full
board as to whether the current $0.60 per share payment should be
continued or a reduction to $0.50 be voted. They stated that their best
estimates were that earnings for the year would approximate $2.00 per
share and that this would not cover a $2.40 payout that would result
from continuation of the $0.60 quarterly rate.

Board members from the financial community put forth the view that
C.I.T. was regarded as an "investment" stock, with a large majority of
the stockholders owning their shares because they believed they would
receive a steady rate of return. They felt that a dividend policy that
fluctuated frequently would have the effect of weakening the confidence of investors, and thus would be harmful to the ability of the
corporation to market its securities if this should become desirable in
the future.

It was pointed out that the $0.60 payment had prevailed for only two
quarters and that the corporation had ample funds in its earned surplus
account to cover any shortfall between earnings and dividend payments
for the year. At the beginning of the year, that account amounted to
$35.8 million, so that this would be reduced by only $1.4 million if the
dividend pay-out was $2.40 a share and earnings only $2.00. The
directors voted unanimously to continue the $0.60 quarterly disburse-
ment.

Earnings for the year actually came to $2.10 a share. The board had
voted to reduce the dividend rate payable January 1, 1945, to $0.50 a
share. Management said it believed 1945 earnings would be close to
those of 1944.

26

In Time of War,
Prepare for Peace

Even though a conclusion of the worldwide hostilities was not then in sight, the C.I.T. directors had established a special reserve fund of $2 million from earnings in 1942 and 1943 to be used during the war period to prepare for reconversion to peacetime operations and thereafter for their rapid expansion when the fighting was over. Future events proved this decision to be among the most farsighted and productive actions in the company's history.

The plan was the concept of Arthur Dietz, and he backed it with complete confidence and utmost devotion of his time and efforts. Even at the height of the war, he was impatiently waiting for the automobile pipelines from Detroit to begin flowing again and he was determined that C.I.T. would be ready for that day.

The reductions in the number of local offices and employees during the retrenchment period had been severe. In the first year, the office count for the C.I.T. company and Universal Credit combined had dropped from the prewar high point of 512 to 272. The number of employees fell from more than 7,000 to 5,000. The cuts continued until the beginning of 1944 when a low point of 103 offices and 1,327 employees was reached.

A slight turn in the tide began at the opening of 1943. In February, Dietz reported to the directors that twenty-five men had been detailed to call on automobile dealers for the purpose of "rehabilitating the C.I.T. good will in the field." He detected an immediate improvement in the volume of business secured.

The program continued under the day-to-day supervision of Marcus Link, as operating head of Universal C.I.T. In September 1944, Dietz was able to give the board the following report on its progress:

> Mr. Dietz reviewed at length the history of operations of instalment financing subsidiaries since Pearl Harbor, with particular reference to branch operations, the program to build up dealer good will, which started in January of 1943, and the results of this program as shown by the substantial increase in volume of retail and wholesale automobile business. In connection with this review Mr. Dietz gave the figures showing the increase in number of branch and regional offices since January 1, 1943, and the expansion of the sales force, and also reported regarding the work that had been done in preparing for expansion of instalment financing operations after the war.

It was also noted that in the first six months of the year, $510,000 of the $2 million "reconversion" reserve had been spent.

The program bore fruit immediately, as Dietz expected. At the end of 1944, the automotive receivables portfolio had grown to $20.5 million from $14.1 million a year earlier, despite the wartime dislocations and the continuing heavy liquidation of "prewar" contracts.

Marcus Link (he was called "Mike" and preferred "M. Link" when formally addressed) was another C.I.T. executive who began his business career as an office boy. He joined the company in the New York office on July 14, 1915, four months after the company moved from St. Louis. Claude Hemphill hired him.

He became an accounting clerk in 1917 and worked in the discount, wholesale and insurance departments. In 1925, he was named manager of one of the first branch offices the company opened to handle automobile financing, at Charleston, West Virginia. He became manager of the newly created southern region, with headquarters in Atlanta, in 1927 and was brought back to New York in 1929 as supervisor of all consumer financing branches in the eastern United States.

His next assignment took him to Chicago in 1935, as assistant vice president in charge of the operating department for the company handling operations in the Midwest. In 1937, he became responsible for all branch operations in the United States and Canada.

One of those who worked with and under him for years, L. Walter

Lundell, a qualified judge if ever there was one, has said that he regarded Link as the "best finance man," in an operating sense, who ever worked for the company.

Link was hard-driving and openly ambitious throughout his career. In the fall of 1946 he gave the equally strong-willed Dietz one ultimatum too many and left the company.

Two individuals who were to have major parts in both the development of the company's postwar operations and the shaping of its future through more than two decades were drawn into the planning and rebuilding programs of the war and immediate postwar period. Their recruitment for the effort was clearly part of Dietz's program to build an executive organization for the years ahead.

The first was L. (for Lawrence) Walter Lundell. He had entered the consumer financing business in 1924 through employment by the Chicago Acceptance Corporation—the newly formed financing arm of the Hudson Motor Company of Illinois, then called the world's largest distributor of Hudson-Essex motor cars. Three years later, he became a member of the C.I.T. organization when C.I.T. purchased Chicago Acceptance and made it a part of its "Chicago company."

His business career had begun in 1918, when, at 14 years of age, he had gone to work for Swift and Company, first as a messenger-office boy at a salary of $6.50 a week, then as a clerk in the office of the president, Louis F. Swift. Guided and encouraged by William B. Traynor, the assistant to President Swift, Lundell completed high school through an arrangement that permitted him to attend school while working part-time. Becoming interested in accounting as a career, he next joined Swift's accounting department, where he continued until leaving in 1924 to go with Chicago Acceptance Corporation. This change came about through an answer to a blind help-wanted ad offering a ground-floor opportunity. And so, as the first employee of Chicago Acceptance, he began a career in financing of almost half a century.

One final note—his association with Swift and Company did not completely end in 1924, because in 1925 he married Jewell B. Hussey, who had been secretary to Mr. Traynor in the president's office. They celebrated their golden wedding anniversary with their children and grandchildren in 1975.

During this period and in subsequent years with C.I.T., he continued his studies in accounting, business and finance at Northwestern University and ultimately received his degree as a certified public accountant in the 1930's. He became controller of the Chicago company in 1928 and continued in that position until the summer of 1934, when he was sent to San Francisco to clear up some problems that had arisen at the western California headquarters. He completed this assignment successfully in about six months and so impressed Arthur Dietz with his handling of it that in early 1935 he was asked to join the New York headquarters organization as an assistant treasurer under John I. Snyder.

Within two years, he was posted back to Chicago as vice president supervising branch operations there. The midwestern company was headed by Claude C. Paxton, who had succeeded Frank Collins in the position in 1934. Paxton had been a successful sales executive in the automobile industry before he joined C.I.T. With his excellent contacts and standing in that industry, he was instrumental in building the Chicago organization into one of the company's major operating units. Contraction of the company's operations after the nation entered World War II forced the closing of the office.

The nation's entry into World War II and the enforced contraction of C.I.T.'s operations as automobile production and sales came to a standstill brought an end to the company's policy of decentralized operations. All management functions were brought back to the New York headquarters. The Chicago office was closed in June 1942.

Lundell was still in the Chicago office when Paxton stood on a desk to announce the closing to the assembled staff. Paxton was so moved, however, that he broke down before he could speak more than a few words. Lundell finished the announcement and then shouldered the details of winding up the "Chicago company's" affairs. He moved on to San Francisco to do the same for the western operation. He then returned to the New York headquarters to administer some phases of the corporation's further cutbacks and eventually took a major role in the postwar building effort.

Throughout his C.I.T. career, Lundell was always poised, keenly analytical and an ever-courteous, considerate perfectionist. His courage and integrity were unassailable. He had been marked as an employee with special promise as far back as 1929 when he was one of seven individuals who received the rare recognition of being offered an allotment of company stock. When "Mike" Link resigned in 1946, he was designated Link's successor, in charge of all operations of Universal C.I.T. Credit Corporation. He was selected for that position over the heads of several executives who had previously outranked him. Much more will be read of Walter Lundell in this narrative.

The second individual chosen from the field force to help shape the future of the automobile financing operations was Alan G. Rude, a native of New Jersey. He had worked in a variety of sales and sales

correspondent jobs from 1921 to 1925, after graduating from the Dover
(New Jersey) Business College. He joined C.I.T. in 1925 as a sales
correspondent in the industrial division, but was soon transferred to the
automobile operations, handling credit and collection work. Impressive and articulate, and a forceful public speaker, he was a natural
salesman who perfected his personal sales skills and leadership
abilities by hard work and an unquenchable determination. He studied
business management courses at New York University at night. He
moved into sales work first on Long Island, then in Cleveland, the New
York metropolitan division and northern New Jersey. He headed the
so-called central division in the early war years until October 1944,
when he was called to New York to become vice president in charge of
sales of Universal C.I.T. His assignment was to spearhead the sales
side of the Dietz plan to prepare for vast postwar expansion.

In his own words, as he looked back on those years from retirement:
"I was brought into headquarters for the purpose of rebuilding. Over
the next twenty-three years I traveled almost constantly, opening division offices, acquiring and training company personnel, calling on
various factories and addressing state, regional and national meetings
of all kinds—not to mention countless company personnel meetings.
To put it mildly, there was a lot of blood and sweat that went into
building the base which was indispensable to the company's growth
and future potential."

Ever in demand as a speaker, Rude was evangelical in the messages
he delivered before scores of automobile dealers' meetings in virtually
every state in the nation. He primarily preached from four texts—the
essentiality of sound managerial policies and practices, the dignity of
selling as a profession, and the importance in American life of the automobile business and the pride those involved in it should derive from
this.

Titles of his speeches describe what he told his listeners. They speak
with implied optimism and inspiration: "Keys to Survival and Success," "Let's Be Realistic," "Building New Castles from Old
Stones," "Management Standards for Your Business," "The
Future—Through a Rear-view Mirror," "How Good Is the Automobile Business?" "The Five M's of Management," "A Look
Ahead at Your Market and Your Future," "Getting Ready for Tomor-
row's Markets Today."

His advocacy of pride in themselves and in their industry was often
expressed to his dealer audiences in such words as these:

I firmly believe, as I have believed for many years, that the career of

owning and operating an automobile dealership is one of the finest, most
rewarding business opportunities a man can have.

I have seen hundreds of exceptional personal successes achieved by automobile dealers. I have seen many fortunes made and retained. I have
seen able, honorable, hard-working men live lives of great accomplishment as automobile dealers.

Many of you are the outstanding businessmen in your communities. You
give employment, security and well-being to large numbers of people.
You offer opportunities for young men to rise in business. You contribute
to the economic resources of your community.

Gentlemen, you are in a great business. It has contributed more to the
progress and even the happiness of mankind than any other single industry. Be proud of it and be certain that all of those associated with you and
those with whom you come in contact understand and appreciate the jus-
tification for this pride.

The future was to take Rude into the senior management group of the
whole C.I.T. enterprise in the fifties and sixties.

Although the industrial division, bulwarked by war-related financing
opportunities, had not suffered as greatly as the consumer financing
operations during the war years, it too faced the necessity of a rebuilding effort to be ready for normal peacetime industrial conditions. When
Maddock returned from his assignment at Holzter-Cabot, for a time he
assisted Dietz in the overall supervision of the company's financing
operations. Once Lundell was given the executive responsibilities for
the consumer financing arm, however, Maddock concentrated on the
so-called heavy industrial side, his first love. He continued to direct
these operations until his retirement in 1957.

The company's Canadian operations had been even harder hit than
those in the United States, in part because Canada was involved in the
war for a longer time. The number of branches was reduced to four and
only a token force was maintained. To get a bit ahead of our story, in
1946 with the war over and peacetime opportunities looming ahead,
the company won a special charter from the Canadian Parliament under
the Small Loan Act. In that same year, Ottar Nerby was elected president of Canadian Acceptance Corporation. Previously, members of
the C.I.T. home office group had held the presidential title since the
company was established.

Ottar Nerby, who had worked with several early sales finance companies in both the United States and Canada, was employed by the

Studebaker Motor Dealers Credit Corporation at the time it was acquired by C.I.T. in 1929. He was named a vice president of Canadian
Acceptance Corporation and held that position, serving also as general
manager of Canadian operations, until he was promoted to the presidency. He retired from active service in 1962.

The anticipation of peace brought another change—in the company's corporate name itself. Although the plan to adopt a new name in
1931 had been an abortive one, the officers had continued to be uncom-
fortable with the "Commercial Investment Trust Corporation" name
because it was a misnomer. The term "investment trust" had come to
mean a mutual fund or investment-holding company, and this definitely was *not* C.I.T.'s business. Moreover, the inclusion of the word
"trust" in the name had precluded the parent company from being
admitted to do business in the State of New York, although its subsidiaries were so qualified. Under New York regulations, the word
"trust" was reserved for banking institutions.

In planning for the postwar period, management decided the parent
company should be qualified to do business itself in New York. This
decision finally triggered a change in name.

In 1942, the industrial financing division had been incorporated
under the name "C.I.T. Financial Corporation" by New York State.
When it was decided to adopt a new name for the parent, this name,
already available, was descriptive of the nature of the entire enterprise
and appealed to Ittleson, Vogel and Dietz. Moreover, it made use of
the "C.I.T." initials, which was the way the organization commonly
was referred to throughout the business world and among its customers. It was also the symbol for the corporation's stock used in market
trading. Therefore, it was preempted and adopted for the parent company at the stockholders' meeting on April 24, 1945.

The industrial financing unit assumed the name "C.I.T. Corporation." The underlying "parent" of the financing subsidiaries alone
continued as "Commercial Investment Trust Incorporated."

27

Peace . . . and Striving for Plenty

V-E Day came on May 8, 1945, bringing the final capitulation of the Axis powers and peace to the Western world. Three months later, Japan surrendered on August 14, ending the Pacific hostilities.

The business, industrial and financial capacities of the United States, enormously expanded by the pressures of achieving, with our Allies, military victories on two fronts, faced another massive task. This involved not only reconversion to the pursuits of peacetime but the maintenance, with the participation of the federal government, of a high level of employment and economic prosperity. In this, the production task required to meet war-created shortages of all manner of civilian products assumed paramount importance.

The automobile industry swung into this effort with its leaders voicing the highest hopes that an early return to prewar production rates—and even higher ones—could be achieved. So did most other industries, particularly electrical and home appliances, construction equipment, producers of the tools and machines to reequip industry, textile and clothing manufacturers and many others served either by C.I.T.'s consumer or industrial financing-factoring subsidiaries. In Canada, the challenge of moving from war to peace was the same.

Prepared by eighteen months of careful planning and a substantial investment of manpower and money, the C.I.T. organization was ready to seize the opportunities of a peacetime economy. At June 30, 1945, it was reported to stockholders that the number of branch offices to serve consumer instalment buyers had increased from the low point of 103 at the beginning of 1944 to 150 at the end of that year; another 27 had been opened in 1945. By the end of September, the field organization had been increased to more than 200 branches and 23 divisional offices had been established to supervise them. Another 50 branches were opened in the fourth quarter. This national network completely blanketed all the territories that C.I.T. and Universal Credit had served through their separate organizations in the prewar era. To accomplish this, another $980,000 was spent in 1945 from the $2 million reconversion reserve, exhausting that fund.

Despite high hopes on all sides, the nation's reconversion effort was plagued for more than a year by shortages. Essential raw materials, parts and components had to be produced and poured dependably into the pipelines of production before the projected output levels of finished products from autos to toasters could be attained.

Labor troubles swept the nation, and in addition to the work stoppages, there were complaints of low rates of productivity in many industries. The strikes included a 114-day strike of 200,000 workers at General Motors and others in such key industries as steel, coal, public utilities, electrical manufacturing, iron castings and the railroads. In the last four and a half months of 1945, 28 million man-days were lost from production because of strikes, without measuring the effect of the strikes on other industries dependent on supplies from the struck industries. In 1946, 4½ million workers went out on strike and the loss of man-days was 113 million.

While the auto manufacturers other than General Motors experienced only sporadic work stoppages, both Ford and Chrysler and the others were repeatedly forced to halt their production lines in both 1945 and 1946 because of parts shortages. In May of 1946, General Motors reported that 331 of its supplier firms were being struck. Some suspensions by the auto builders were for as long as five weeks.

Despite the waiting market of insistent and impatient consumers who wanted to buy new cars, and the all-out effort of the auto makers to meet the demand, only 70,000 passenger cars were produced in 1945.

In the first six months of 1946, passenger car production was 639,000 units against a planned output of 2.3 million cars. In all, output for the year was 2.1 million, compared with prewar production rates of nearly 4 million per year.

All of this held back the flow of new financing business that C.I.T.'s managers and staff were prepared for and eagerly awaiting.

C.I.T. rehired all of its former employees who had served in the armed forces or worked in the war effort if they wished to return, whether there was an immediate need for their full-time services or not. This was done for solid business reasons—the experience and skills they brought with them would clearly be needed as business picked up. Moreover, hundreds of commercial banks were plunging into the consumer financing business and were bidding freely for people who could offer finance-company experience.

In all, more than 2,000 C.I.T.-C.A.C. people had entered the United States or Canadian armed forces during World War II. Fifty-two gave their lives for their country.

Henry Ittleson, Jr., returned from his Air Force service in September and was elected executive vice president of C.I.T. Financial Corporation, the parent company. In this position, he promptly assumed a major share of the responsibility for all of the organization's financing operations.

One event just before the end of 1945 dispelled a cloud that had troubled the company's directors and principal officers since 1939. This involved a suit filed by stockholders owning only a small number of common shares seeking an award of $7 million from the directors as individuals. It was alleged that the acquisition of Universal Credit Corporation in 1933 and the subsequent purchase of the Kanzler-Zimmerman minority interest in 1938 were fraudulent actions.

After war-induced delays, the case went to trial in December 1945 before Judge Ferdinand Pecora in the federal district court in New York. The judge dismissed the suit as groundless when the plaintiffs had presented their case and before the defense was heard. His decision included these comments:

> No loss whatever has attached to the interests of C.I.T. because of the transaction. By that I mean that the net result has been one that, up to the present time, has proven profitable to the C.I.T. and its stockholders. The net result has proven profitable, according to the evidence, even in the face of the abnormal effect of the war exigencies upon business—the business in which Universal was engaged.
>
> Nobody can be outraged more quickly than I can, let me say, and I have

been, by evidences of breach of trust by the directors and managers of corporations whose stock is held by thousands and thousands of persons scattered all over the country, if not all over the world, in small and large holdings, and who, especially those who have small holdings, are not in a position, under ordinary circumstances, to keep a close watch and scrutiny upon the acts currently of those upon whom the law places the responsibility of trusteeship. But in this case—and I have given the evidence much consideration, and I have studied the trial briefs on both sides with much care—I am frank to say that there is an utter absence of any proof upon which anybody could justifiably stigmatize the acts of these defendants as fraudulent or as having been committed in bad faith, or as having been motivated by desire of personal gain or enrichment, or as representing anything other than a judgment honestly believed in and carried out by men who, in so doing, were motivated solely by the purpose of serving the best interests of their company. And that I say even if I were to consider making a finding upon the evidence that their judgment was bad, intrinsically bad. I do not make such a finding. I do not think the evidence even warrants the making of a finding that their judgment was bad though honest.

The board of directors paid a special tribute to Phillip Haberman for the guidance and years of effort he had devoted to the case, which was tried by distinguished outside counsel.

At the final board meeting of the year, George R. Urquhart was elected to the board of directors. Urquhart, as a C.I.T. Financial vice president, had assumed overall executive supervision of the factoring companies, through their chief executives. These were, at the time, Johnfritz Achelis (Commercial Factors), Fred Meissner (Meinhard, Greef) and Jarvis Cromwell (William Iselin).

Urquhart had joined the organization in February 1944, his addition in that important position being part of the postwar planning program. Previously, he had been president for ten years of an important textile manufacturing company, Manville Jenckes Corporation. He had extensive personal connections in both the textile industry and banking circles, as he had also been an officer of Bankers Trust Company in New York. He continued to hold the principal position in the factoring operations until his retirement in 1957.

With the disappointing output of consumer durables and industrial equipment, C.I.T.'s operating results for the year also were a disappointment. The total volume of business put on the books reached $786.4 million, compared with 1944's $693.2 million. The portfolio of receivables gained only $18 million during the year, from $99.4 million to $117.7 million. Retail motor receivables purchased amounted to $90 million, a $23 million gain over the previous war year, and wholesale motor financing more than doubled to $64 million from $31.4 million. With the greatly increased expenses from the enlargement of the staff and the increased number of both consumer and industrial local offices, earnings fell to $5.8 million, or $1.61 a share, from $7.5 million, or $2.10 a share, for 1944.

Although earnings were no longer covering the $2 annual dividend on the common stock, this rate was continued through the period of reconversion and rebuilding difficulties.

As a whole, the year 1946 was even more frustrating for C.I.T.'s managers than the previous one. Automobile production did make sharp gains in the latter half of the year but the slow recovery overall, combined with low production rates in other industries served by the company, was not sufficient to generate volume at a pace to build adequate profit margins in the face of a constantly growing expense account. Another negative factor was the dominant place in the market that was occupied by two groups of buyers for whatever vehicles that were available. One was comprised of large business and other fleet buyers, who were given priorities by both the manufacturers and dealers, and the other was made up of individuals of means or influence, who were willing to pay cash, often including an extra premium, to obtain the cars they wanted so desperately. The fulfillment of their orders kept many less favored time buyers out of the market.

Another negative factor was the steady erosion that had taken place, before and during the war, in the ranks of the independent passenger car manufacturers who had provided the bread-and-butter market for Commercial Investment Trust since its entry into the automobile financing business. This had greatly increased the dominance in the market of the "Big Three" companies—General Motors, Ford and Chrysler.

At the opening of 1946, only seven "independent" manufacturers remained of the scores who were competing for the public's favor in 1919 (as listed on page 59). They were Crosley, Kaiser-Frazer, Hudson, Nash, Packard, Studebaker and Willys. Including those produced by the major manufacturers, a total of 18 makes of domestic autos were made available, compared with 91 on the 1919 list.

Of course, the position of Universal C.I.T. Credit Corporation was fortified by its still-predominant role in handling the business of the Ford and Lincoln-Mercury dealer body. In addition, it could compete aggressively with Commercial Credit and the many smaller finance companies for Chrysler business and a small amount of General

Motors business could be won away from GMAC. But the narrowing of the market by the elimination of literally thousands of dealers selling the independent makes was a serious handicap that was to grow heavier as the "Big Three" took over virtually the entire new-car market in the next two decades.

Another serious threat loomed as C.I.T.'s managers launched the effort to regain their prewar place in the all-important auto financing market. This was the invasion by commercial banks throughout the country, who were offering to make direct loans to car buyers to cover their purchases or to handle the business as it originated from dealers, in the manner of C.I.T. and its competitors. *Fortune* magazine in September 1947 summarized the situation accurately in this way:

> The prospect [for a comeback of C.I.T.'s auto business] would be even more pleasing were it not for 10,000 ugly heads [ugly, that is, from the finance companies' standpoint] that have reared themselves on the expanding horizon of instalment credit. The heads belong to as many commercial banks, ranging in size from the gigantic Bank of America down to the Kanabec State Bank of Mora, Minnesota. Once upon a time bankers regarded instalment buying as only slightly more venial than speculation—even though they loaned money to finance companies that underwrote the unthrifty practice. But around the mid-thirties the banks, on the basis of the finance companies' record and their own idle funds, decided that the business was a good thing to get into. By the end of 1941 commercial banks held 32 per cent of the $2.3 billion in outstanding retail automobile paper along. . . . Today they have around 60 per cent.

The threat was there and it was serious, but C.I.T.'s auto-financing arm successfully met bank competition head-on for the next two decades.

Earnings for the year at $4.5 million, or $1.27 per common share, were the lowest since the pre-depression year of 1927. Moreover, only $700,000 of this came from operations; the remainder was derived from interest and capital gains from security investments. GMAC, with its complete dependence on automobile and appliance financing business, lost $4.4 million for the year. This showing, however, did mark the nadir of the postwar period. Entering 1947 with the momentum built up in the final months of the prior year, C.I.T.'s earning power again reached new record heights within two years. Graphically, this is the story:

(1947–1950)

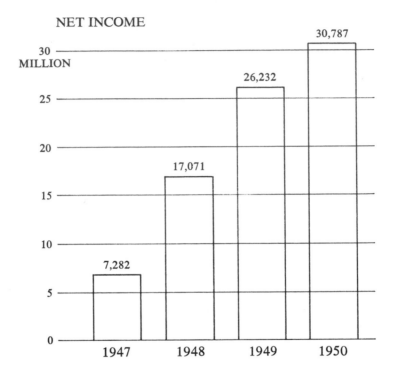

NET INCOME

In addition to the years of planning and preparation and the resurgence of consumer goods production, another factor contributed greatly to the soaring business volume and earnings results of 1948, 1949 and 1950. This was the hard-driving marketing promotion and sales efforts of the veteran and completely rebuilt Universal C.I.T. and C.I.T. Corporation organizations. Directed by the strong home office staffs developed by Lundell, Rude and Maddock, promotion and sales efforts were led in the field by a seasoned corps of division heads, almost without exception men who had learned the business completely in the prewar years. The factoring companies, which had been able to maintain their organizations to a very considerable extent throughout the war, also did their part.

In the case of Universal C.I.T., the chief sales weapon was the "package plan" of consumer insurance protections and services, in addition to the financing accommodation per se, that had been introduced in 1940–41. This cluster of extra features was particularly useful in persuading car buyers to arrange their financing through their dealers at the time of purchase, rather than to choose a direct bank loan that would not offer such benefits.

In those years, a continuing parade of significant internal and external events and influences were being recorded. One of the first was the purchase, in equal partnership with Kuhn, Loeb and Company, C.I.T.'s investment bankers, of the important title insurance company, Lawyers Title Company. This was consummated in June 1946, with each partner investing $1.7 million. It was the intention of the purchasers to groom the acquisition for a future sale to the public. However, uninviting market conditions discouraged this plan and the investment was disposed of to another title company after two years.

There were a number of personnel changes at the top in 1946. In July, Edwin C. Vogel relinquished all of his operating or management duties except the chairmanship of the investment committees that managed the portfolios of the insurance subsidiaries. Otherwise, he continued only as a director of C.I.T. Financial Corporation and a limited number of subsidiaries. However, he filled an invaluable role as an elder statesman until the day of his death in 1973.

In October, John I. Snyder retired as vice president and treasurer and was succeeded in those positions by Fred W. Hautau. At the same meeting, Melbourne Bergerman was elected vice president and general counsel, succeeding Phillip Haberman, and joined the board.

Before joining the C.I.T. organization in 1938, Fred Hautau had been employed in the Wall Street investment community for 35 years. After only one year in high school, he began his career as an office boy and worked for several firms and a bank before becoming sales manager for a well-known house specializing in the placement of commercial paper, or the short-term promissory notes of creditworthy companies. C.I.T. had decided to expand its direct placement of commercial paper and, after a considerable search, employed Hautau for the position as an assistant vice president of Commercial Investment Trust Incorporated. In 1948, after two years as vice president and treasurer, he was elected to the C.I.T. Financial board of directors.

He served as vice president and treasurer of the corporation and as a director until his death from illness in 1953.

Bergerman, a graduate of Harvard Law School, had been a partner in a Manhattan law firm prior to accepting an offer from C.I.T. to head its law department. He continued in this position until 1961 but maintained his association with the company until 1965.

Finally, Lewis L. Strauss, who had made so many valuable contributions as a director, resigned from the board to accept a presidential appointment to the original Atomic Energy Commission. His Kuhn, Loeb partner, John M. Schiff, was elected his successor.

C.I.T. also experimented with the underwriting of public securities issues in the immediate postwar years. Commercial Investment Trust

Incorporated, the "first-tier" underlying subsidiary that was the corporate parent of all the operating and insurance companies engaged in consumer and industrial financing, was permitted by its charter to engage in this business. During 1945–46, several ventures were undertaken. One of the better-known names involved in these transactions was Reeves Brothers, Inc., a large textile firm. All of the companies from which underwriting business originated were similar companies, clients of the factoring subsidiaries. C.I.T. ceased its underwriting operation when it was learned from bitter experience that the practice of assisting such companies to become publicly owned only resulted in their gaining access to other sources for operating funds, costing the factors their business clients.

By the end of 1947, the number of U.S. branches of Universal C.I.T. Credit Corporation had reached 374 and the count of its employees totaled 4,673 against the wartime low of just over 1,300.

In mid-1946, Henry Ittleson, Jr., had urged on Dietz that the so-called small appliance financing business be dropped, including the sizable Westinghouse factory relationship. He reasoned that this small-balance business, requiring nearly as much handling as automobile financing on a payment-by-payment basis, was unlikely to yield a sufficient return, considering the mounting expense factors involved. With overall volume in the branches still at a low point and Regulation W still in effect, a decision on this proposal was deferred.

By the fall of 1947, however, with automobile volume building at a rate that was not only certain to return handsome profits but also gave promise of requiring vast amounts of additional working capital, the time came to act. Dietz announced to the organization a five-pronged program stressing profits and curtailment of low-margin lines. This called for 1) withdrawal from low-balance appliance financing; 2) elimination of F.H.A.-insured home improvement financing because of the low yields it offered and the substitution for it of non-insured, higher-balance home improvement business only; 3) all-but-total elimination of personal loans; 4) a dealer-by-dealer review in the automobile financing area with the elimination of unprofitable or low-profit accounts unless they could be made acceptably profitable by upward rate adjustments; 5) other rate increases on a broad basis.

The reference to personal loans requires some explanation. As will be recalled, the management had firmly resisted entry into the direct consumer loan area in the 1930's. However, during the war years, when business volume was so desperately needed to keep even a minimum network of branches operating, direct lending licenses were obtained under state small loan laws for a number of offices and others already had such licenses that had been retained from previous ownerships.

The first mention of these operations appears in the 1944 stockholders' report, when the existence of a $5.7 million portfolio of such loans was listed. The amount increased to $7.9 million in 1945, $8.6 million in 1946 and was beginning to take off in 1947, with a portfolio totaling $24.4 million as the curtailment order was laid down. By the end of 1948, the portfolio stood at $19 million and rapidly declined thereafter to a purely nominal amount.

While many of the wartime restraints and regulatory influences on the civilian economy were eliminated within a few months after V-J Day, this was not the case with the regulation of the terms for granting consumer instalment credit—Regulation W.

When the war ended, the March 1942 terms for financing new and used automobiles were still in effect, although there had been modifications in the terms of other types of transactions from time to time. The automobile terms required down payments of at least one-third of the purchase price and established the maximum period for paying the balance at fifteen months.

During the war, C.I.T.'s management had supported the regulation without question, but with the return of peace and with automobiles and other durables beginning to flow again from the factories, C.I.T. opposed the continuation of restraints on normal financing patterns. In the report to stockholders for 1946, Dietz asserted:

Federal Reserve Board Regulation W, which originated as a wartime economic measure, limits the number of months within which the unpaid balance of purchase price of automobiles and other durable goods may be paid, thereby necessitating excessively large monthly instalments. Since Regulation W was enacted, the prices of automobiles and other durable goods have increased substantially. Because of these price increases, the amounts needed for the payment of monthly instalments would be greater at the present time—even if Regulation W were not in effect—than they were before the war. As a result of the still larger monthly amounts required under the Regulation, it has become increasingly difficult for those in the lower-income brackets to make instalment purchases.

High production levels cannot be maintained without wide distribution, which in turn depends upon the free flow of consumer credit. It is the conviction of your management that Regulation W should be eliminated promptly if mass markets are to be made available to support the high level of production which is projected for the period ahead.

The drumfire of opposition to the regulation of "The People's Credit" was continued in the 1951 annual report:

> In the United States, as well as in Canada, the present instalment credit controls are adversely affecting employment, production and sales in the automotive industry and discriminate unnecessarily against the vast number of families who use the time-payment method to purchase needed automotive transportation. We believe that there should be a prompt liberalization of these restrictions.

The continuation of Regulation W was supported by many economists and federal government officials as a device to dampen potential postwar economic inflation, which many feared. The board of governors of the Federal Reserve System in mid-1946 recommended to Congress that its authority to control time-buying terms be made permanent. The opponents of controls were equally numerous and outspoken. Thus, the debate raged in the 78th Congress until a joint resolution was approved by both houses on June 30, 1947, terminating instalment credit controls as of November 1.

Instalment credit remained free of controls for nearly a year until September 20, 1948. Regulation W was reinstated on that date as a result of congressional action in August. In the decontrolled period, terms had generally been eased somewhat as a result of the increased production of durables of all kinds and the pressures that arose because of competition among sellers. In addition, the decontrol of wages and prices on June 30, 1946, was forcing prices up. Again, the control of instalment credit was viewed as a useful weapon to combat the growing inflationary trend.

The new terms were somewhat less stringent than those in effect when the regulation was ended the year before. Down payments for automobiles were set at one-third with maximum maturities at 18 months. Other products had down payments fixed at 20%, with maturities of 15 or 18 months, depending on the amount of the purchase price.

The following March, with the inflationary pressures vanishing and a business recession developing, the Federal Reserve governors increased the maximum maturity for automobiles and other controlled items to 21 months, and cut down payments for all durables and loans, except those involving autos, to 15%. Scarcely a month later, on April 27, all maximum maturities were lengthened to 24 months and nonautomotive down payments were reduced to 10%. The renewed Regulation W was due to expire, under the act of Congress, on June 30, 1949. It was allowed to do so.

The off-again, on-again nature of the selective controls on instalment credit was burdensome to C.I.T. and all other credit granters. In addition, the more restrictive terms on maturities, fixing them in the 15-to-21-month range, penalized earnings as compared with the standard 24-month terms that prevailed in automobile financing in the absence of regulation. This was so because the typical transaction became more profitable if the funds in question were advanced for a longer term. In addition, car sales themselves, with resulting financing business, were being intentionally discouraged in the periods of tighter credit terms. There were other criticisms. Dr. Robert P. Shay in his *Regulation W: Experiment in Credit Control* (1953) observed:

> There are many valid criticisms levied against Regulation W. For example, businesses are burdened with costs involved in complying with the regulation's terms. Special forms must be filled, reports made, and records kept. There is the possibility that minimum down payments and maximum maturities tend to standardize credit terms at the limits. It may be argued that certain income groups are penalized by consumer credit regulation while others are not.

With the outbreak of the Korean War, Regulation W was again reinstated on September 18, 1950. At first, C.I.T. approved the action. Dietz, in the June 30, 1950, stockholders' report said:

> It is anticipated that Federal regulation of consumer credit will become effective shortly. A flexible program of regulation which will assure sound credit standards and help to limit upward pressures on prices is in the interest of the general economy. We favor such a program under today's conditions.

By the year-end letter to stockholders, Deitz's patience with the policy of making instalment credit the whipping boy for other economic problems and excesses was exhausted. He wrote as follows:

> Under current federal regulation of instalment credit, known as Regulation W, maximum maturities in passenger automobile financing transactions are limited to fifteen months, and down payments may not be less than one-third of the purchase price. Prior to the Regulation, it had been our normal practice to require down payments of approximately one-third in financing both new and used automobiles, and most of our new car financing transactions were written on twenty-four-month terms, with shorter maturities on used cars. While the fifteen-month limitation is quite severe, its effect on our business should be offset in large measure by the demand for automobiles which we believe will continue to be very

strong. We have reserved for discussion at the end of this Letter our views on the influence which consumer instalment credit has had in the development of the current economy.

* * * * *

Earlier in this Letter we referred to the impact of federal instalment credit controls on the business of your Corporation. Entirely apart from the question of the effect of these controls, however, we take issue with the assertions, usually emanating from government sources, that undue expansion of consumer instalment credit has been one of the primary causes of the present inflationary situation.

In determining if there has been an overextension of instalment credit to consumers, consideration must be given to the present levels of personal income and the accumulation of personal liquid savings. According to the latest available federal estimates, the American public on September 30, 1950, owed, in the form of instalment debt, 6.5% of their annual disposable personal income. This represents a large increase over comparable figures in the period immediately following World War II, but this increase has little significance because the amount of consumer instalment debt was abnormally low at that time due to the fact that automobiles and other durable goods ordinarily sold on instalment terms were just coming into the market.

It is also significant that while the amount of instalment credit was increasing after World War II, liquid personal savings were increasing at an even greater rate. In the third quarter of 1950, when consumer spending for durable goods was at its height, the rate of increase in personal savings was more than two dollars for every one dollar of increase in consumer instalment debt.

It is apparent from this analysis that the use of instalment credit has been conservatively managed. Furthermore, the history of consumer instalment credit makes it clear that this method of distribution has made important contributions to our economy. Time-buying has developed mass markets for durable goods and thus has been a major factor in creating the facilities and techniques of the American production system. But for this system of quantity production, consumer prices would be much higher. Mass production has made possible progressively broadening markets and a higher standard of living and has equipped the nation with a vast industrial capacity which is the principal safeguard of our security today.

Regulation W finally had its demise on June 30, 1952, a full year before the conclusion of the Pacific hostilities. At this writing, it has never been revived, but as we shall see, the issue was by no means a dead one.

In May 1948, the Holtzer-Cabot company had been sold. Both it and Micro Switch had encountered the typical postwar problems involving immediate cancellation of their government contracts and severe parts and material shortages as they sought to regain their peacetime businesses. Holtzer-Cabot had the greater difficulties once again. All employees were laid off and the plant was closed for three months in 1947. Neither of the manufacturing units had attained a profitable level of operations for the year after their contract cancellations.

In announcing the sale, Dietz said it was made at a loss but that, with the write-down of C.I.T.'s investment from profits during the war years, the corporation had fully recovered its investment in the property.

Micro Switch had a better reconversion record, earning more than $2 million in 1949, but it too was sold in March 1950 to the Honeywell Corporation. C.I.T. was well repaid for this investment. Under the aegis of the technically oriented Honeywell company, Micro Switch has turned in an excellent record in the following years.

Of C.I.T.'s wartime manufacturing experience, it can be said that the original condition laid down by Ittleson in initiating the program was fulfilled. Through its investment, the corporation assisted the war effort but it did not make any significant money out of its war work.

During the period under review, financing operations on a massive scale had to be undertaken to provide the working funds to support the rising volume of business. Debenture and note issues were sold repeatedly, private term loan placements were arranged with insurance companies, pension trusts, foundations, educational institutions and other sources of large amounts of money. An issue of 400,000 shares of cumulative preference stock was sold to the Prudential Insurance Company of America, adding $40 million to the equity capital. Another $200 million issue of cumulative preference stock was sold to the Prudential and Metropolitan Life Insurance companies in March 1949. Between January 1, 1946, and the close of 1950, the combination of term borrowings and capital stock and surplus increased from $104.9 million to $486 million. In the same period, short-term debt rose from $44.5 million to $562 million, bringing total working capital to $1.048 billion.

The Miami Industrial Bank was sold in June 1948, since it apparently offered little of value in the corporation's long-range scheme of things. The Michigan Bank was retained for some time, but it too was sold in 1950.

A momentous development on the legal front occurred on November 15, 1948. In May 1946, Ford Motor Company and C.I.T. had filed a suit against the U.S. government in the federal District Court in South Bend, Indiana, where the original 1938 antitrust actions against Ford-Universal Credit, Chrysler-Commercial Credit and General Motors-GMAC had resulted in the first two sets of defendants entering into consent decrees with the Department of Justice. It will be recalled that General Motors had chosen to contest the action and was found guilty of violating the Sherman Anti-Trust Law and fined. In October 1940, the government initiated an additional suit in the Chicago District Court to force the divestiture of GMAC by General Motors.

It also will be recalled that one of the provisions of the consent decrees was that their restraints on the companies would be lifted if the government failed to bring about the permanent divorcement of GMAC from its parent by January 1, 1941. The Chicago action was in response to that stipulation. Legal maneuvers and the disruption of the war period prevented the divestiture action from going to trial by the 1941 date, but the other parties had voluntarily agreed from time to time to allow the government more time to bring the case to trial.

Time ran out on these extensions when the 1946 action to end the consent decrees was begun. However, the District Court in due course ruled for the government and an appeal was taken directly to the U.S. Supreme Court.

In November 1946, the high court agreed to hear the case. Two years later, in November 1948, it found in favor of Ford and C.I.T. by a five-to-two vote, with two justices not participating. The opinion was written by Justice Felix Frankfurter. Charles Evans Hughes, Jr., son of the great U.S. Chief Justice, pleaded the C.I.T. case before the court. However, the ageless Haberman, although now retired from active service, played an important part in masterminding the preparation of the successful effort.

The decision restored to the plaintiffs the specific rights they had waived in the consent decrees. The most important of these were that Ford could "recommend, endorse or advertise" the services of a given finance company to its dealers and the public, that Ford and finance company representatives could visit dealers together, and that Ford was permitted to own or have an interest in a finance company.

All of these rights continued to be dependent on the outcome, if any, of the General Motors divestiture action, then still pending, or any showing in the courts by the Justice Department that Ford and C.I.T. had violated the antitrust laws by exercising them.

With earnings showing strong improvement, C.I.T.'s patient common stockholders who held on to their investments were rewarded by an increase in the quarterly dividend from $0.50 a share to $0.75 with the payment made on January 1, 1949. A year later, the rate was lifted to $1.00 quarterly and an extra dividend of $1.00 was paid, bringing the 1950 disbursement to $5.00. In the war and postwar period to that time, the market price of the common stock had fluctuated from a low of 19⅛ on December 17, 1941 to a high of 68½ on March 22, 1950.

At the midpoint in this chapter of the story of C.I.T. Financial Corporation, Henry Ittleson, the Founder, died on October 27, 1948. He was in his seventy-seventh year and death came from the burdens of age.

28

Eulogy

Henry Ittleson was a man of remarkable contradictions. He put millions of his fellow Americans at the wheels of their own automobiles, but he never learned to drive a motor car himself.

He welded together a loyal and devoted team of close business associates, but he was characteristically austere and impersonal in his relationships with them. Arthur Dietz was not the only member of the C.I.T. executive group to address him consistently as "Mr. Ittleson." The others with whom he worked intimately for decades—such as Haberman, Hemphill, Collins and Ecker—did the same. Edwin Vogel was the only exception. They were "Henry" or "H.I." and "Edwin" to each other. In addressing his subordinates, Ittleson alternated between using their first names and their full set of initials.

It is impossible to pierce the veil of secrecy with which he cloaked his countless charitable activities. He preferred to give from his wealth without fanfare. However, when it would be likely to help the cause, he would back his personal fund-raising efforts and gifts by permitting the use of his name, and he encouraged his associates to do the same. He served as chairman of the board of trustees of the Federation of Jewish Charities of New York, honorary chairman of the United Jewish

Lobby plaque, 650 Madison Avenue

Appeal and an executive committee member for the American Jewish Committee. He derived substantial satisfaction from the service of Arthur Dietz in heading a British war fund drive before the United States entered World War II. He supported this generously as he did the manifold charitable interests and activities of his wife, Blanche.

Henry Ittleson's benefactions often were singularly astute or imaginative. In one instance, he was visited in 1938 by Dr. Hudson Hoagland, who then was chairman of the Department of Biology of Clark University. Dr. Hoagland asked Ittleson to provide the funds to make it possible for Dr. Gregory Pincus, a brilliant young biologist, to join the Clark faculty and continue his research studies in the field of animal reproduction. Dr. Pincus had not had his appointment renewed as an assistant professor at Harvard for reasons that, Dr. Hoagland said, "seemed to me unjust."

Dr. Pincus had been the first to produce a mammal that had a mother but no father. He succeeded in stimulating by an electrical current the ova of female rabbits so that they conceived and delivered normal offspring even though they had not been impregnated with sperm.

Although Ittleson was constantly besieged for financial assistance by pleas from many sources, he promptly agreed to underwrite most of the cost of bringing Dr. Pincus and his work to Clark.

Subsequently, Dr. Pincus played a leading part in research involving the use of steroid hormones in the treatment of cancer and in the discovery and development of the first effective birth control pill.

In 1932, to better organize and perpetuate his charitable endeavors he established, with Mrs. Ittleson and Henry Ittleson, Jr., the Ittleson Foundation. In 1940, the name became the Ittleson Family Foundation and its principal philanthropic direction became the support of programs focused on the fields of health, welfare, public education for mental health and intercultural relations. The trustees of the foundation in 1953 established and endowed the Henry Ittleson Center for Child Research, devoted to studies in the areas of mental health and retardation in children. It is located at Riverdale, New York.

In its first thirty years, total grants by the Ittleson Family Foundation exceeded $10 million.

Ittleson was ever-generous to members of his family. This had an early beginning. Even as an up-and-coming but still struggling young businessman in his teens and early twenties, he lavished gifts on the children of his sister Emma—dollhouse furniture, clothing and such. When the novel *Little Lord Fauntleroy* swept the nation with its popularity after publication in 1888, he sent Emma's five-year-old son, Henry, his namesake, an authentic Lord Fauntleroy costume, complete with lace collar and cuffs and a "gold-headed" cane—hardly appropriate for Carbondale, Colorado!

This concern for others also carried over to his other "family"—the individual employees of C.I.T. In contradiction to the often brusque and totally businesslike exterior he displayed to his subordinates, there are many stories of quick and kindly acts that he performed for them. As just one example, there is the incident recalled by John Cooney, who represented C.I.T.'s auto financing operations in St. Louis in the World War II years and for many years thereafter. As he tells it:

"In early 1945, Mr. Ittleson, while visiting St. Louis, dropped in to see our little office. We talked about the company's postwar plans and prospects and then he asked about my personal situation—health, family, things like that. I told him I had a problem. We were renting a house from an army officer who was soon going to be discharged and had served notice that he was coming to take his house back, as the law permitted. With two sons, six and eight, we had been unable to find anything to rent or buy except at prices we couldn't afford. I told him I didn't know what we were going to do.

"It was only a few weeks later that I got a telephone call from a Mr. Cohn, who said he was Mr. Ittleson's brother-in-law and that he had a nice six-room apartment in a building he owned that he could let Mr.

Ittleson have at a good price, if he said so right away. He said Mr. I. had told him to phone me when he had a place for him.

"I couldn't figure why Mr. Ittleson wanted to rent an apartment in St. Louis but I immediately called New York, reached one of the executives there and asked him to get the word to Mr. Ittleson, if possible—he only came to the office part-time, I knew.

"That evening I got a return call from New York. When Mr. Ittleson was told Cohn had the apartment for him, he said, 'Lord, I don't want the apartment! I asked him to get it for Cooney and his family. We can't have our St. Louis representative out on the street!'

"Well, I had bought a house in the meantime, but the experience was an insight to the character and humaneness of Mr. Ittleson. He had made a mental note of my personal problems and, without making any comments or promises of assistance, he had taken the time and trouble to be helpful and to get a place for an employee of minor corporate stature.

"It was my memory of this and also other instances where company policies (which no doubt Mr. Ittleson played a major part in establishing) were so much for my benefit that in later years caused me to reject a number of outside opportunities offering bigger pay and so on."

Henry Ittleson was a brilliant speaker, philosopher and prophet in areas of social and economic concern. During his active business career in New York he was ever in demand to address audiences of fellow businessmen, and he wrote his own speeches. Hear him before the Association of National Advertisers in October 1927:

Although a very substantial number of motor driven vehicles are used for commercial purposes, some have said that automobiles, and also washing machines, radios, etc., are not income-producing goods—not capital equipment in the sense that land and buildings are—and therefore are not valid bases of credit. With this contention I take issue.

Just as essential as capital in production is labor; and the worker has his capital which is health, intelligence, and contentment of mind. The automobile which brings the farmer into stimulating contact with the city, which takes the city dweller to the healthful suburbs and in touch with the great outdoors; the washing machine which lightens the burden of Blue Monday; the radio which brings art and great men and great events to the hearthside—these things, whether we choose to call them capital or not, are surely instruments of greater power.

They all tend to enrich the life of the individual, to free him from the monotony of routine. They generate new desires, new standards, provide new incentives to work and initiative. There is no reason why I need elaborate on this point. It carries us into a field of speculation which is too broad to be charted, but which a moment's thought will convince you is none the less because it may be too large to grasp easily.

Nor is the distinction between necessities and luxuries, in my opinion, a valid one to be set up as a criterion for judging the appropriateness of the instalment method of merchandising. The term "luxury" is purely relative. Caesar's greatest luxury was a 25 B.C. model chariot in which no self-respecting American working man of today would be seen riding. It is useless for you or me to assert that some things are necessities and others are luxuries. That question is settled by the circumstances of the buyer and by the concept of the times.

He had a caustic sense of humor, often aimed at the foibles that he found in the doings of others. He was frequently consulted for investment advice. His invariable answer was, "Do you want to try to eat well or sleep well?" His meaning was that the speculator might be fortunate enough to end up in the lap of luxury, but the conservative investor could expect to live a more peaceful life.

At one time, Mrs. Ittleson, who at all times was notably independent of her strong-willed husband, purchased for the family a handsome suburban estate on Manursing Island in Long Island Sound, off Rye, New York. Her husband never saw the place until the day they moved in to the completely furnished mansion. Yet this was a man who for many years insisted on reviewing virtually every detail and decision affecting the operations of the business enterprise he headed!

One of her first projects was to develop an extensive vegetable garden. One day a visitor from England was having luncheon with the Ittlesons when fresh peas from the garden were served. The guest politely declined any when the servant offered them.

"Don't you want any peas?" the master of the house asked. "Don't you like them? Well, then we will fetch you a bottle of Piper Heidsick champagne!"

The puzzled visitor said he thought he was being well fed without the peas, but he inquired, "Might I ask what the champagne has to do with my not taking any peas?"

"Well," Ittleson replied, "I'm just suggesting a substitute. The bottle of champagne hasn't cost me a cent more than that dish of peas!"

Another time, the elder Ittleson returned from a business trip and checked his baggage at Grand Central Station, as he had some matters to attend to. His son, Henry, Jr., and a young bachelor friend were going out to the Westchester house, as they had dates with two very special young ladies from the vicinity that evening. Ittleson asked them to pick up his luggage and bring it along with them.

In their eager anticipation of the evening's engagement, the young men forgot to do as they were bidden. At the last moment, as they entered the house, they remembered their oversight. The elder Ittleson's temper was legendary and they feared the worst when they confessed their misdemeanor. He heard them out calmly and then simply said, pulling out his watch: "That's perfectly all right, boys. There's a seven-fifteen train back to town and another that will get you back here with the luggage by ten-fifteen. You can just make the trip if you leave now, without any dinner—and you'd better call off your dates!"

Another of his axioms has survived in the annals of C.I.T. It is that "risk and rate have nothing to do with each other." His meaning was that no matter how attractive a rate of interest might be, this could never be an excuse for making a bad loan. It was his way of doing business that every transaction into which his company entered had to afford convincing evidence that it was a sound one. He recognized and forgave bad luck and human error; he never forgave stupidity.

As the number of his years passed 75, Henry Ittleson's health, which had not been good for a decade, began to fail rapidly. He had always held the chief executive's position in virtually all the C.I.T. companies as each company developed, in addition to his chairmanship of the parent C.I.T. Financial Corporation. On the last day of 1947, he resigned all his offices except the latter one. Death followed within three months.

The board of directors of Commercial Credit Company graciously memorialized their competitor for 35 years in these words:

> Mr. Ittleson was a pioneer in the field of finance companies, a leader blazing the way and showing the path by which others, who came into the field later, could strive to emulate his accomplishment. From small beginnings and of local activity, through his vision, courage and ability, the Corporation grew until it became a leader in that domain and an institution of inestimable usefulness and benefit in the business world. By his death, that Corporation has been deprived of an outstanding leader and his associates of a friend, whom they will greatly miss.

His fellow directors of C.I.T. Financial Corporation expressed their sense of consummate regard and loss in this way:

> Mr. Dietz advised the Board of the passing of Mr. Henry Ittleson on the previous day. He expressed his deep sense of personal loss and his admiration of the outstanding character and ability of the man who more

than forty years ago founded the institution which today stands as a symbol of his achievement. Mr. Dietz then called upon Mr. Haberman, whose association with Mr. Ittleson dates back to the founding of C.I.T., and Mr. Haberman thereupon responded by making a statement in which he referred to outstanding events which had transpired during his long period of friendship with Mr. Ittleson and in which he traced, in outline, the history of the enterprise.

Thereupon, by rising vote, the following minute was unanimously adopted by the Board of Directors:

> We have convened today in the shadow of a great loss occasioned by the death on October 27th of Henry Ittleson, Founder and Chairman of the Board of Directors of this Corporation.
>
> Henry Ittleson laid the foundation of this institution four decades ago and its growth to the proportions of a national institution reflects the consummate ability which he manifested in its administration. The accumulated wisdom that was his was an influence of immeasurable value in the deliberations of this Board. His advice was always consonant with high business ideals; he commanded admiration for the forthrightness of his character, the wide horizon of his understanding, the brilliance of his intellect and, above all, the exceptional quality of foresight and prevision which was his.
>
> It has been a high privilege for each of us to have had contact with the inspiring leadership of Henry Ittleson. In him there was greatness arising from moral integrity, broad human sympathies and understanding and creative imagination. We shall gratefully cherish our memories of him.

Henry Ittleson's funeral service was held on October 29, 1948, at the Central Synagogue in New York City. The list of honorary pallbearers included many names of the most distinguished leaders in the nation's life. All were his devoted friends—Bernard Baruch, long a trusted counselor to Presidents of the United States and a revered elder statesman of the investment community; James Forrestal, Secretary of National Defense of the United States; ex-Governor Herbert H. Lehman, of New York, among others.

The address in tribute was delivered by Herbert Bayard Swope, distinguished newspaperman, author and Pulitzer Prize-winning executive editor of the *New York World* in its days of journalistic greatness. He said:

> Dear Friends of Henry Ittleson:
>
> In this coffin lies a part of me—lies a part of each of us.

Into the life of Henry Ittleson has gone some of the good and some of the bad of all who knew him. And he, in turn, entered into and merged with our lives.

None of us can know know another well without being affected by the impact of such knowledge. Each of us has a jury from whom we seek approval—whose good opinion we want, second only to our inner sanction. Henry was one of my panel. He was an honest, searching, understanding judge.

I knew him for many years. I knew him when I was a boy. As an older man, he had a pronounced influence upon my development. I am grateful for the example he set; I am regretful for my failure to have profited more than I did.

He had gaiety, charm, good looks, a sense of humor, an infinite capacity for hard work and great integrity.

In nothing did he create a finer impression than in the effect of his home life. It is given to few men and women to hold together for fifty years of wedded happiness, an anniversary he celebrated just a few weeks ago.

And it is given to even fewer men to have such a wife as Henry had to share his life. Part of me lies dead with him, for he was the friend of my family and of my youth for many years. But those years that have gone and the years yet to be, were and will be better because of Blanche, his widow, whose life is a warmth and a benediction to all who know her.

Death becomes more real as we grow older. Some fear it and some, more fortunate, are indifferent to its approach. In Henry's case, death was welcome. It came on friendly feet, for his former activity and strength had been dissipated, and he had gently tired. At best, our life is all too brief. It ends with so much to do and so little done. But we cannot gain a reprieve because our tasks are incomplete. It is at such moments that we feel how swift and bitterly short our shrift is.

Henry Ittleson represented the true American romance. He was born poor and became rich. He grew with his responsibilities. He met each challenge with courage and understanding. Love was in his life, and to that he owed much. He grew in stature with his years. He had a deep sense of justice. He practiced a generous charity and, as his lot grew easier, he gave himself more and more to guiding younger men. He had deeply implanted within him that curiously Hebraic love of culture and learning.

He had a zest for living. He warmed his hands at the fire of life and found it good. He gave back to those who knew him what they gave him in affection and respect.

This man had a rare faculty for friendship. He could make each of us feel that he was a devoted friend, the one, above all, most wanted at the moment. He revelled in the warmth of his relations with those about him. At the end, his burning energy sapped, he faced his destiny without flinching. I could wish none more than that.

Henry is now at rest. Regardless of the eloquence of Dr. Wise; regardless of what I may say; regardless of what mementoes may be set up in his name, now nothing remains but Character.

In that Henry Ittleson will live. His monument lies in the hearts of those who loved him and felt his spirit; not in the eyes of those who merely saw his success.

Goodbye, Henry. And when we say goodbye, each of us dies a little.

29

The Flourishing Fifties

With the years of planning and patience of the mid-forties bearing fruit at last, C.I.T. had entered the decade of the fifties with large increases being booked in the amounts of business handled in its financing operations and with earnings at record heights. But again, warfare caused a temporary setback.

As a prelude to this, there had been a business recession of moderate intensity lasting for about twelve months, which began before the 1948 Christmas holiday season. The postwar boom had simply overextended itself. Industrial production fell 8½%, orders for durable goods declined a sizable 16½%, and business failures during the period increased nearly 14% over the prior twelve months. While the slowdown in business activity obviously restrained the overall growth of the company's business volume for 1949, automobile sales were much less affected than many other areas of the economy. Aided by this fact and by the large portfolio of earning assets that had been built up during the previous three years, earnings for the year had continued to move ahead strongly, to a record of $26.2 million ($6.81 per common share).

A vigorous business recovery began to evidence itself in the spring and early summer of 1950. It was then, on June 25, 1950, that the communist military forces of the People's Republic of North Korea invaded South Korea, which was regarded as the free world's bastion in the Western Pacific area. It required only three days for the United Nations (which the Russian delegation was then boycotting) to demand that the invaders withdraw and on that same day, June 28, U.S. troops, under the U.N. flag, entered the war.

The combat lasted just over two years, until the truce of July 27, 1953. During this period, with something like half the nation's resources and efforts devoted to military requirements, and with 350,000 men and women involved in the Korean engagement, C.I.T.'s business volume was well maintained. However, earnings in 1951 and 1952 fell below the record figure of $30.8 million ($8.04 per common share) that was attained in 1950. For 1951, the profit figure was $28.2 million ($7.31 per common share) and this was increased to $29.6 million ($7.71 per common share) in 1952. Part of the reason for the decline in earnings during these two years was the impact of the heavy federal income taxes imposed to help finance the costs of the Korean involvement and to dampen inflationary pressures that were stimulated by the war.

Of the $2.6 million decline from the 1950 earnings figure that occurred in the following year, $2 million was due to the higher tax impost. A year-end extra dividend payment on the common stock of $1.00 per share in 1950, for a total disbursement of $5.00 for the year, was reduced to $4.50 per share in 1951 and 1952 through a cut in the "extra" to $0.50.

The increase of $1.4 million in the earnings for 1952 over the 1951 results has special historical significance. It was the first in an unbroken series of year-to-year gains in net income that C.I.T. Financial Corporation maintained for the next twenty-two years.

With "business as usual" as the watchword in the C.I.T. organization in spite of the war conditions, certain developments in 1951 and 1952 were notable. The good showing in automobile financing in 1951 in part reflected a gain of $50 million in the amount of used car financing. At the year-end, stockholders were told that there had been a substantial increase in the number of vehicles financed, in the number of dealers doing business with Universal C.I.T. and Canadian Acceptance Corporation, and in the number of local offices the companies were operating. This network was described as "the largest in the field of motor vehicle financing." Earnings of Service Fire Insurance Company from its auto financing policy writings were under pressure because of increased claim settlement expense, but it was anticipated that recent premium rate increases would improve the picture.

The board of directors had not passed on specific industrial financing contractual arrangements for many years, as they had regularly done in earlier days. However, new contracts with American Can Company and Continental Can Company, Inc., for the financing on a nationwide basis of the sales of can-closing and other manufacturing equipment were regarded as being of such major importance that they were brought before the board in early 1951 and approval action was taken. These transactions with the two companies were the result of an adverse antitrust decision against American Can, requiring it to offer can-closing and auxiliary equipment for sale. Such equipment had previously been made available to canners only on a lease basis. Continental fell into line because it had agreed prior to the trial to be bound by the result of any action against American.

At a special meeting of stockholders on June 26, 1951, a "Stock Option Plan for Key Employees" was adopted. A total of 150,000 shares of common stock was set aside for allocation through options to officers and employees to be selected by a committee of the board of directors. The option price was fixed at 85% of the price on the date the option was granted. This plan has been regularly renewed and extended, with revisions, since that time.

Among the organizational changes of the period was the retirement of Jarvis Cromwell as president of William Iselin & Co. and the election of Morton Goodspeed, a veteran Iselin executive, to succeed him on January 1, 1952, both as president of the subsidiary and a member of the parent company's board of directors. On the same date, Walter Lundell became president of Universal C.I.T. and a vice president of C.I.T. Financial Corporation. Sydney Maddock, president of C.I.T. Corporation, was also named a vice president of the parent company. One year later, they were elected to the C.I.T. board of directors.

On November 25, 1952, the stockholders approved a 2½-for-1 split in the company's common stock. Apparently discounting the difficulties imposed by the half-war, half-peace economy, the market had pushed the price of C.I.T. shares in the summer and fall of the year from the low $60 range to the high $70's. The action was recommended by the board in the expectation that the split would "result in a market price suited to a wider circle of investors, which should produce a broader distribution of the corporation's common stock." The split became effective on February 4, 1953.

Some of the expectations of the market were recognized by the board's action with respect to the January 1, 1953, dividend. While the $0.50 year-end extra was continued, the regular quarterly rate was increased to $1.12½ per share, or $0.45 a share after the split.

A consumer financing office was opened in Hawaii for the first time in early 1953. This unit has been consistently successful over the years.

With the end of the nation's Korean involvement, the national economy followed a comparatively even course. C.I.T. resumed its record of steady earnings growth during the remainder of the decade of the 1950's. This was the overall showing:

Year	Volume of Financing Business Purchased (Billions)	Outstanding Receivables at Year-end (Billions)	Net Income (Millions)	Earned per Common Share
1953	$4,578	$1,486	$34.8	$3.62
1954	3,958	1,352	35.6	3.85
1955	5,393	1,932	36.9	4.03
1956	4,782	1,949	37.8	4.12
1957	5,257	2,151	39.1	4.27
1958	3,754	1,766	40.7	4.31
1959	4,777	2,048	42.5	4.57

As will be noted, the portfolio of outstanding receivables, the business already on the books from which earnings flowed, made greater gains than the volume of business acquired from year to year. This was the result of a definite program to change and improve the "mix" of the business being handled. The consistent increase in net income was a reflection of this program of refinement and betterment of the return on funds invested.

As this record was compiled, the march of new events and circumstances continued within the ever-changing organization.

As 1953 opened, a new subsidiary was organized. This was Patriot Life Insurance Company, which initially was capitalized at $1 million. As we have seen, life insurance for its consumer creditors, particularly automobile purchasers whose original obligations were relatively sizable, had been a principal feature of the C.I.T. "package plan" from its inception. The insurance coverage wiped out any remaining indebtedness if the creditor died before completing payment of his debt. This insurance had always been placed with a major life carrier, some income accruing to C.I.T. from the transaction.

It was evident that underwriting this insurance was excellent business for the outside carriers, who also received certain preferential treatment under federal income tax laws. The organization of Patriot

Life was an action taken to retain all of the benefits of writing creditors' life insurance within the C.I.T. family.

The task of qualifying the new company in all states was a considerable and expensive one, requiring years of effort. However, this was accomplished and Patriot Life flourished virtually from its inception. In due course, it also entered the business of selling "ordinary" life insurance to individual purchasers, through agents or by direct mail, competing directly with all carriers in the established life insurance industry.

Industrial financing operations were making great strides. At June 30, 1953, this portfolio stood at a record $187.2 million, for a gain of $60.5 million, or nearly 50%, during the previous twelve months. This increase was sparked by an excellent market in the capital-goods industries and a strong build-up in highway construction, creating a need for contractors' equipment of many kinds. Earnings kept pace with the growth in industrial financing volume.

In August, the corporation adopted its first hospital, surgical and major medical expense program for employees. This plan has undergone a number of liberalizing amendments over the years.

January 1, 1954, saw the common dividend increased to $0.50 from $0.45. This action restored to stockholders the same record rate of return they had enjoyed when the "old" (pre-split) shares were paying $5.00 in 1949. The annual payout to common shareholders moved to a new high of $2.25 per share in 1954 when a year-end extra of $0.25 was distributed. The regular quarterly dividend was then raised to $0.60 per share with the October 1, 1955, payment, and a year-end extra of $0.25 was again declared.

The casualty insurance industry encountered serious underwriting difficulties in the late forties and early fifties. The causes of this included, among a number of factors, postwar inflationary pressures on replacement costs and the "lag" or relative inadequacy of state-regulated premium rates to keep up with mounting claim losses. C.I.T.'s National Surety subsidiary shared the industry experience. In 1949, higher investment portfolio profits offset lower underwriting income and earnings were about the same as in 1948. In the following years, portfolio income was insufficient to make up for "poor" underwriting results and only a "small" net profit was earned, as stockholders were told. Some recovery was made in 1952 and 1953, but for the three years 1951 to 1953 the company had an average annual underwriting loss of $679,000.

Adding to the problems of managing the subsidiary was the constant pressure from National Surety's executives for permission to broaden the company's line of coverages and raise the size of the risks they could undertake. They emphasized that only as a "full line" company, with relative ability to assume major risks, could they recruit many additional brokers and agents. They insisted that continuous growth of their agency force was essential to increased premium volume. The latter, they claimed, would in the long run solve their underwriting problems. In the face of poor results from current operations and the inescapable cost of developing new lines, Dietz, Ittleson, Jr., Vogel and the other C.I.T. Financial executives found this thesis unacceptable.

They decided to dispose of their National Surety property. This took several years. The story of how it was done is told in engaging fashion in *Still Flying and Nailed to the Mast* (Doubleday, New York, 1963), the official history of the purchaser, Fireman's Fund Insurance Company. It is reprinted here with the permission of the author, William Bronson:

> The biggest step of all [during the year] was taken on January 12, 1954, when [James F.] Crafts [president of Fireman's Fund] and Arthur O. Dietz, president of the powerful C.I.T. Financial Corporation, announced that the Fireman's Fund had purchased National Surety Corporation from C.I.T.
>
> The news hit the street like a thunderclap. Although the purchase price was not given at the time, it was obviously one of the largest transactions of its kind ever made. A few industry leaders privately felt that the purchase might have been a bit ambitious, but in general, the reaction was one of respect with a touch of awe in face of the company's appetite.
>
> Although the possibility of acquisition had been discussed by the companies back in 1951, the asking price was too high and the talks were dropped. But the industry was in a period of transition. As a result of the "multiple lines" legislation of the 1940's, the day of the specialty company was on the wane. By the end of 1953, Dietz decided that it would be better to sell the National Surety, which wrote a tremendous book of surety and fidelity business, rather than to tie up the additional millions necessary to expand in the other fields. Crafts wanted the National Surety in order to capture a much larger share of the then profitable surety/fidelity business and to strengthen Eastern operations generally.
>
> Most of the negotiations were handled through an intermediary, Dudley Cates, who in earlier years had been very active in the affairs of the Nation Surety. [Cates had been a director from 1935 to 1941.] Dietz and Crafts admired him personally, not only for his business acumen but

for his courage in meeting a great handicap. Twelve years before, surgeons had removed his cancer-ridden larynx, and from that time he had spoken only with the aid of a clarinet-like reed.

Shortly after he approached Crafts with National Surety's proposal, Cates discovered a malignancy in his hip. Advised by his doctors that this time there would be no cure, Cates entered the Presbyterian Hospital in upper Manhattan, and with the help of round-the-clock nursing and strong sedation carried on negotiations from his bed.

Crafts and Dietz found themselves a million dollars apart. Dietz had transferred $10,000,000 from the National Surety to another corporation within the C.I.T. complex and wanted $20,000,000 for what remained. Crafts was not willing to pay more than $19,000,000.

In a personal recollection, Crafts later wrote, ". . . every question that was put forth by Fireman's Fund or C.I.T. was answered without hesitation by Cates for he had studied the facts and figures and he could support the contention of either side. His problem was how to bring them together. He realized that time was not on his side and that something must be done quickly if his family were to benefit from his efforts."

Knowing that he had but days to live, Cates called Crafts to the hospital to again review National Surety's value to Fireman's Fund. Cates talked of many things—of business and family and eternity—and when Crafts said good-by, he felt he would never see his friend again.

The following morning, Dietz called him to say that if the Fireman's Fund would pay Cates' fee as intermediary, he would reduce his price $1,000,000. Crafts immediately agreed and then called Cates to determine if a reasonable fee could be negotiated. Before he could say more than "Hello, Dudley," Cates announced, "Whether you have reached agreement or not, I have decided to reduce my fee." It was obvious that Dietz had told Cates of his decision on price.

In the conversation that followed, all important details of the transaction were resolved. Fireman's Fund bought the National Surety for $19,200,000.

Crafts closed his story of the purchase with these words, "Who got the best of the transaction? What difference does it make?

"Dudley Cates passed away not long thereafter."

Before his death, the last $200,000 of the "compromise" price was paid to Cates by C.I.T. as his broker's fee from the transaction. C.I.T. realized a $5 million profit from the sale.

Perhaps, at least from a short-run view, the Fireman's Fund history provides an answer to its president's question:

> In 1956, the Company suffered underwriting losses equal to almost twice what it lost in the 1906 fire. The industry as a whole was hit so badly that Crafts was prompted to say at a meeting of insurance brokers, "If this be a lesson in experience, let us rejoice that perhaps it will be the year 2006 before similar misfortune strikes again."

> The reasons for the disastrous results were many, but high on the list was the fact that inflation had finally caught up with the industry with a vengeance. Both auto and fire losses were appalling, and most of the blame could be laid at the door of higher labor and material costs. Premium rates were based on past experience, not on current costs, and when one is forced to sell a product for less than it costs to produce, it is somewhat difficult to show a profit. Marine losses were likewise extraordinary. When the *Andrea Doria* went down off Nantucket, the world's underwriters suffered one of the greatest losses in marine history. That was also the year when two airliners collided over the Grand Canyon in the worst air disaster up to that time. Jury awards in liability cases continued to increase, as did the incidence of burglary and theft.

> The only thing 1956 lacked was a storm to match those sweethearts of other years—Diane, Audrey, Donna and Carla.

> The Fireman's Fund was hit harder than most of the companies for several reasons. First, the company has through all the years of its existence, followed a conservative approach in the matter of reserves. In 1956, large increases in both the loss and unearned premium reserves made the underwriting losses considerably bigger than they might have been under a less conservative policy.

> To what extent the Company's troubles were complicated by the pains attending integration of operations with the National Surety will never be calculated, but there is no doubt that they had their effect. It should be noted that while combined premium income rose twenty per cent between 1956 and 1960, the number of employees dropped about twelve per cent over the same period.

> *Business Week* turned its attention to the Fireman's Fund in July, 1957, on the occasion of the opening of the new home office at 3333 California Street, twenty-nine blocks west of the corner Staples had purchased ninety-one years earlier. The editors commented on the Company's 1956 misfortunes, then went on to say:

> "There was some head wagging in the trade when the 1956 results were known. Insurance men remembered that the [Fireman's Fund] acquisition of National Surety Corporation in 1954 stirred talk—particularly in

the East's traditional insurance centers—that the company was getting too big for its britches.

"But as 1957 went along, Fireman's Fund began to look better. In the first quarter of the year, it chalked up a net underwriting loss of $1.4 million. That was 74% less than it lost in first-quarter of 1956.

"At the same time, 20 other large companies recorded a 57% increase in first-quarter losses."

30

The Flourishing Fifties
(continued)

The thriving condition of his company's business was reflected in a comment made by President Dietz at the 1954 stockholders' meeting. He noted that a compilation by "a business magazine" showed that C.I.T.'s 1953 earnings were higher, with but one exception, than those reported by any bank or financial institution in the United States.

At the July 1954 meeting of the directors, approval was voted of a proposal by the officers that the corporation purchase the entire block-front on the west side of Madison Avenue between 59th and 60th streets in New York for $3.1 million. The plot also covered part of the adjoining 59th and 60th street fronts. The purpose of the purchase was to obtain a site on which to erect the first headquarters building to be owned by the corporation, after forty-six years in rented space.

Dietz pointed out to his fellow directors that the four floors and basement space occupied at One Park Avenue (where the company had been housed since 1926) had grown increasingly inadequate, over-crowded and "costly in manpower and dollars." The original concept was to build a skyscraper providing 450,000 square feet of floor space, with C.I.T. utilizing approximately one-third and tenants the remainder. The transaction was closed in the summer of 1955 and financial,

The 650 Madison Avenue Building

architectural and engineering studies for the building were initiated.
They were to result in a radical revision of the first plan. By early
1956, it was decided to reduce the height and floor space of the building to provide a maximum of 335,000 square feet of space. C.I.T.
would use the entire building except for two ground-floor areas. The
resulting C.I.T. Building, which has been recognized as one of New
York City's most impressive office structures, was occupied on October 28, 1957.

In the tradition of the 1915 move from St. Louis to New York City,
the complete headquarters operation was transferred from One Park
Avenue to the new address, 650 Madison Avenue, over the weekend.
A staff of 770 persons were at their new desks in the new building that
Monday morning.

The building was hailed as an architectural landmark because it was
the first commercial structure in the nation to be completely faced with
black granite. This sheathing was set in a grid of stainless steel. Recognized for its handsomeness and other excellent qualities, black granite nevertheless had been regarded as one of the most expensive of all
building materials and had been considered practical only for entrances
or in lobbies. However, a new method of cutting and polishing the

stone had been developed at just about the time planning began for the C.I.T. structure, and this innovation reduced the cost of the material to a practical level. While the choice of granite was still a relatively expensive decision, as C.I.T.'s executives conceded, it was regarded as a sound investment because it would require "a minimum of maintenance and is virtually indestructible." As this is written, nearly two decades of exposure amply support that prediction.

As to the other decision to reduce the size of the building and forgo rental income from tenants, Henry Ittleson, Jr., who had conceived and overseen every aspect of the architectural, construction and interior design details of the project, had this explanation: "It is true that the provision of rentable space would produce income but such a program would require that we get deeply involved as real estate investors and operators, which we do not consider ourselves to be."

Echoing this, *Architectural Forum* commented that "the building achieves its elegance mainly through its height, which has been held to a seemingly uneconomical eight stories. The decision to keep the building low came partly from C.I.T.'s reluctance to get involved in renting and running an office tower. C.I.T.'s business is lending money; the company's management saw nothing to be gained by going outside their field."

The first meeting of the board of directors was held in the new building on October 31, three days after the opening. The board saluted Henry Ittleson, Jr., for his "tremendous expenditure of time and effort" that had brought the building into being.

The first annual meeting of stockholders in the building occurred on April 22, 1959. While the structure housed a sizable auditorium, the size of the overflow crowd in attendance required that both the adjoining employees' cafeteria and lounge be pressed into use, with the proceedings being broadcast to and from these areas.

Throughout the decade, the financial resources to support the company's receivables outstanding, as they climbed to and then went over the $2 billion level, were obtained through a continuing series of term borrowings. These were in addition to its shorter-term commercial paper sales that produced available funds normally maintained in the $750 million range. The repeated term loans, several of which were arranged each year to meet prior obligations as they matured or to provide additional funds, were placed with insurance companies, banks and the investing public. They took the form of notes or debentures, various placements being in amounts from $25 million to $100 million.

Events of 1955 included the launching in the spring of that year of a national advertising campaign, with a seven-figure annual budget, to promote the company's automobile financing services. These advertisements featured scenes at national and state parks, emphasizing their attractions and the pleasures of traveling to them by automobile with C.I.T.'s "package plan" to protect the travelers. The series appeared in full color in *Life* and *The Saturday Evening Post*, the two most widely read general magazines of the day. Special promotional ceremonies were staged at each park to which an advertisement was devoted.

In April, The C.I.T. Foundation, Inc., was incorporated under the laws of New York. Capitalized at $1 million, it was organized for "religious, charitable, scientific, literary and educational purposes." Since that time, it has been the principal philanthropic arm of the corporation, although various subsidiaries have also conducted charitable contribution programs in their own names. The resources of the foundation have been maintained through millions of dollars of funds provided by C.I.T. Financial Corporation, and its affairs have been managed by C.I.T. executives.

In the same month, The Tuition Plan, Inc., was acquired for 4,000 C.I.T. common shares, having a market value at the time of approximately $200,000. C.I.T. had for many years provided the working funds for this organization through advances against its receivables. It was engaged in extending instalment financing arrangements to parents for payment of the educational expenses of their children attending secondary schools and institutions of higher learning. The Tuition Plan usually purchased the parent's obligation from the school and handled collections.

With only limited resources at its command, the organization had nevertheless enjoyed considerable success and filled an important function for the educational world. The purchase was made from Rudolf Neuberger, the founder, with the intention that C.I.T. would provide new capital and backing that would materially build up the business. This objective has been realized over the years, although many of the operating methods of the plan underwent revision from time to time. In recent years, the Tuition Plan often has dealt directly with parents, rather than through the educational institutions.

A special stockholders' meeting in November 1955 approved a proposal by management to make the corporation's employee retirement plan noncontributory on the part of the employee participants. Further liberalizations of the plan have occurred at regular intervals since that time.

C.I.T. Financial Corporation completed its fiftieth year in business on February 11, 1958. All significant indicators of corporate success and growth reached record levels as the Golden Anniversary was observed. In the calendar year 1957, profit, earnings per common share, receivables purchased (which surpassed $5 billion for the first time), receivables outstanding (which crossed the $2 billion mark), deferred income (over $200 million for the first time) and total resources were at new highs.

As 1957 drew to a close, however, the economic skies were darkening, as the annual report to stockholders pointed out. A nationwide steel strike that began in July 1957 and lasted until November hurt business badly, augmenting a cyclical downturn that was already under way. The result was a recession of medium severity from which recovery did not begin until the 1958 mid-year. Automobile sales tumbled from 6.1 million in 1957 to 4.2 million in 1958. A partial recovery to 5.6 million was recorded for 1959. Thus, while the company's diversified sources of earnings made possible a small income gain in the earlier year, a sharp drop in financing volume and receivables occurred. A strong comeback was registered on all fronts in 1959, however.

The improved outlook and the consistent increase in earnings resulted in the directors increasing the quarterly dividend on the common stock from $0.60 to $0.65 with the payment on July 1, 1959. It was pointed out that $150 million had been added to the corporation's earned surplus account in the previous ten years.

Management developments during the decade of the fifties included the premature death of Fred W. Hautau on January 10, 1953, and the subsequent election of C. John Kuhn to replace him as vice president and treasurer. The latter had joined the C.I.T. organization in 1943 after being associated with several insurance companies in their investment portfolio administration operations. His first assignment was to manage these activities for the C.I.T. insurance companies. He moved into broader financial management responsibilities until he was selected as Hautau's successor.

Later in the year, he and Emil C. Chervenak were elected to the board of directors. Chervenak had joined the Service Insurance Companies organization (Service Fire Insurance Company and Service Casualty Company, which was organized in the postwar period to provide for the placement of Service's auto coverages through general agents) in 1947 as executive vice president. He was elected their president in the following year. From 1965 until his retirement in 1967, he was chairman of the Service subsidiaries.

Phillip Haberman, who had remained a director of C.I.T., died in April 1953 at the age of 77. This was the tribute paid him by his fellow directors:

> With deep sorrow, the Board of Directors of C.I.T. Financial Corporation records the death of our beloved associate, Phillip W. Haberman, whose service and good counsel have supplied an irreplaceable link between the present and the earliest days in the life of this Corporation.
>
> Phillip W. Haberman had a responsible part in the founding of C.I.T. and continued to give this company essential legal guidance during the difficult formative years. As Vice President, General Counsel and Director, he accepted broader responsibilities over the years, pioneered with brilliance in new fields of law, and vigorously and successfully advocated the best interests of this Corporation for more than four decades.
>
> Wise, learned and of practical mind, he added distinction to his career through kindly understanding and love of his fellow beings. Both his achievements for this Corporation and the affectionate remembrance of his friends will be living memorials to him.

Charles L. Harding, Jr., had succeeded Fred Meissner as president of the Meinhard factoring organization (by then known as "Meinhard and Company, Inc."). When Meissner retired, he became a C.I.T. director early in 1956. After broad experience in the textile industry, he had joined Meinhard in 1936 as a new business representative, earning successive promotions thereafter. He was chairman of Meinhard when he retired at the end of 1969.

Sydney Maddock's retirement as chief executive of C.I.T. Corporation and a vice president of C.I.T. Financial Corporation occurred on December 27, 1956. He remained a member of the C.I.T. board. He was succeeded by Thomas E. Lenihan as president of the industrial financing subsidiary that he had virtually created. At the time, Lenihan was 44. Lenihan's first job, at 16, had been with the C.I.T. company as a messenger. He had a brilliant career, filled with promise, but died tragically of an illness in 1962.

Another signal event in the careers of Walter Lundell and Alan Rude came at the close of 1956. Lundell, who had taken on broader responsibilities through his election two years before as executive vice president of Commercial Investment Trust Incorporated and a member of the C.I.T. Financial executive committee, was named chairman of Universal C.I.T. Credit Corporation, continuing as its chief executive. Rude succeeded him in the Universal C.I.T. presidency. Lundell then became president of "C.I.T.I." in June 1958 and executive vice president of the parent company six months later.

As Rude advanced to ever-greater responsibilities in the company, he no doubt was reminded of the time in the 1920's when his C.I.T. career hung by the proverbial thread. In July 1927, while still in the field force at the Pittsburgh office, he wrote to a Chicago finance company applying for a job and citing his fine training in C.I.T. This company was Mercantile Acceptance Corporation, which C.I.T. had just recently purchased, a fact that was unknown to the job applicant. Rude's letter was duly forwarded to New York, to the attention of Henry Ittleson, Jr. Reminded of this a number of years later, Ittleson said he was incensed by Rude's action and "if I had him right there, I might have fired him on the spot!" However, he realized this was a matter best left to Rude's immediate superiors. He checked with the Pittsburgh manager and was told Rude was a valued employee. Rude was unavailable because he had been forced to return East by the sudden death of his mother. The manager hazarded a guess that perhaps Rude had been motivated by the fact that the business conditions in the Pittsburgh area were poor and he might have been afraid that his job would be eliminated as others had been.

Ittleson told the manager to discuss the matter with Rude on his return and make his own decision as to what should be done. In spite of the awkwardness of the situation and perhaps because of Rude's undeniable ability to make a sale even under the worst of conditions, the

Alan G. Byde

manager decided to retain him and so informed Ittleson, closing the matter.

At this same 1956 directors' meeting, Walter M. Kelly, who had replaced Johnfritz Achelis as president of Commercial Factors a year earlier, also was elected to the latter's seat on the C.I.T. board. Kelly, with a management engineering background, had been brought into the Commercial Factors organization several years earlier. He continued to head that subsidiary until it was merged with Meinhard and Company in 1965 and became a vice president of C.I.T. Financial, serving in that capacity until the end of 1966.

A most important addition to the senior management group occurred in March 1957. Charles W. Dow, who had been president of Equitable Life Assurance Society and had earlier been involved in investment analysis, was elected chairman of a newly created finance committee and a C.I.T. director. He soon assumed responsibility for the corporation's entire insurance operations and subsequently became financial vice president, overseeing all functions of the treasurer's department and other financially-oriented activities. He retired in July 1971.

At the July 1, 1958, board meeting, Thomas Lenihan was elected to the seat on the board of directors held by retiring Sydney D. Maddock. Joseph H. Fechteler, who had been closely associated with George

Urquhart in the supervision of the factoring division and who was a C.I.T. Financial vice president, also joined the C.I.T. board, succeeding Urquhart.

On February 26, 1958, C.I.T. Financial Corporation issued the annual report for its fiftieth year in business. To epitomize that first half century of its corporate existence, the report said:

> For those fifty years, C.I.T. has been an organization dedicated to the principle that the administration of credit requires the same high order of imagination, judgment and courage that has spurred the progress of science, production and distribution in America during this century. The report that follows describes in some detail the achievements of C.I.T. in its fiftieth year. It tells how C.I.T. employs its resources, which exceed two billion dollars, and its capital funds of nearly two hundred fifty million dollars. It portrays as well the significance and usefulness of the company's services to the American economy and the life of the American community. . . .
>
> A corporation, like a person, does not build for the future by exalting the past. Nevertheless, there is much to be gained by seeking inspiration and

instruction from the pages of history. In looking back over the first half century of C.I.T.'s existence, it is possible to discern some of the forces which have made this story possible and which will help write the future.

First, vigor and adaptability are characteristics that have always been encouraged within the organization. As new opportunities to develop or expand the usefulness of credit or related insurance services were seen, the corporation has moved quickly and flexibly to fill these needs.

In addition, there has been a basic conviction concerning the integrity and validity of the institution of instalment selling, dating from early days when the economic and social soundness of the people's credit had to be defended from prejudiced attack.

There has also existed great confidence both in the national economy and in the ability of the C.I.T. organization to forge ahead within that economy. C.I.T. was born during the financial panic of 1908. It grew stronger in spite of two world wars and the repeated recessions of the past half century.

Finally, there is the fact that C.I.T. grew up during the period of history's greatest economic expansion. The resources and institutions of our free American economy have provided the ideal environment for the growth of instalment credit and, in turn, the broadening use of credit has contributed substantially to this expansion.

These are among the major influences that have accounted for C.I.T.'s progress in its first fifty years. And they are important today in giving promise for the second half century, because the pattern of C.I.T.'s future, like that of any business entity, inevitably will be molded by its environment, history and traditions.

31

On the National Scene

Public and governmental relations problems of serious proportions were receiving concentrated attention from the C.I.T. management group during the early years of the fifties. As we have seen, Regulation W had expired in mid-1952, but many influential voices still called for its reinstatement on a permanent basis.

The case for federal intervention into the area of consumer instalment buying had first been advanced as early as 1938, in a doctoral dissertation entitled "Consumer Credit Dynamics," by Dr. Rolf Nugent, of the respected Russell Sage Foundation economic research group. This received considerable attention in Washington and over a period of years gained adherents at the White House, among congressional staff personnel and in the Federal Reserve System. The Nugent paper presented three lines of argument for permanent controls:

1. The need to protect the public from over-buying because of high-pressure advertising and salesmanship and the higher cost of credit buying as compared with buying for cash.

2. The alleged lack of wisdom of having merchants engaged in extending credit, the alternative being for those who must buy on credit to take out direct personal loans and then buy for cash, at presumably lower overall cost.

3. The hypothesis that controls could be used to dampen or manage fluctuations in aggregate credit buying, thus theoretically lessening the intensities of the business cycle, both up and down.

The World War II and Korean conflicts had each provided the necessary background for "emergency" imposition of consumer credit controls. With the nation no longer mobilized for war, the proponents of controls, particularly certain governors and staff personnel of the Federal Reserve, shifted their arguments back to the original Nugent theses—that the time buyer needed protection from himself and from those with whom he did business and that the changing levels of consumer debt outstanding had an unstabilizing effect on the economy.

Many financial writers, economists and business leaders picked up these themes, and the peacetime reimposition of controls on a permanent basis moved to the forefront among national economic issues. Much emphasis was placed upon the fact that consumer instalment debt, with the burst of postwar buying activity at the beginning of 1953, had reached record heights in excess of $21 billion. The governors of the Federal Reserve System asked Congress to give them authority to reimpose controls.

Dietz and his associates, like other leaders in the credit field including most bankers, were adamant in their opposition to such an action. They saw it as an unjustifiable intrusion by the federal government that would be seriously damaging to the public interest and national economic well-being and growth. To mount a campaign of public communication on the issue, Dietz assigned the author of this volume to develop an anti-regulation program that would place C.I.T. in a position of leadership on the issue. The writer, with a background in newspaper work and as a public and industrial relations executive, had joined C.I.T. in late 1946 to head up its public relations and advertising activities and subsequently was elected vice president–public relations. His active service with the company ended with retirement in 1975.

The in-house public relations staff was a small one and lacked the depth of manpower, specialization and geographical coverage that a broad national communications effort would demand. Thus, it was decided to engage a public relations counseling organization to augment the company's own resources. Presentations were invited from several of the major public relations firms based in New York City. As a result of this evaluation process, Carl Byoir & Associates, Inc., was retained in March 1953, inaugurating what was to be a long-standing relationship. Robert J. Wood, a vice president of the Byoir firm, was assigned to the C.I.T. account. He concentrated primarily on C.I.T.'s interests for a number of years until he was elected president of the Byoir organization in 1965.

The program adopted was an affirmative one. It was to create increased public and official confidence in and understanding of the institution of instalment credit as it had developed without government intervention in either the matters of terms offered or the volume of credit extended. At the 1953 meeting of C.I.T. stockholders, President Dietz enunciated what was to become the credo of the program. This stated in part:

> Instalment credit—mass financing—is the fundamental support of the American system of mass production and mass distribution. However, the fulfillment of the needs of the public, which is made possible through instalment buying, is not the full measure of the benefit of mass financing. If markets were restricted only to customers who could pay cash for goods, the economies of mass production would largely disappear. Prices for automobiles, refrigerators, kitchen ranges, and the like, would be out of reach for most American families.

> Instalment buying has made our American standard of living the envy of the world. But we do not fully realize how much it contributes to the nation's total employment. Mass financing makes customers of people who do not have the full cash price to buy the articles they want and need.

> Mass financing, therefore, helps to create and assure jobs for those who provide these articles, whether they produce the raw materials, whether they work in the factories which process them, or take part in their wholesale and retail distribution. Thus, mass financing makes jobs, as well as articles for use by the whole community.

> Consumer debt can be "too high" only to the extent that it includes debt which should never have been incurred in the first place. We in C.I.T., with more than forty years' experience in administering instalment credit, firmly believe that the vast majority of American consumers are capable of budgeting their instalment purchases on a sound basis. We have confidence in their integrity and common sense.

> We are also convinced that those who have extended the credit have done so on a basis of the consumer's ability to pay and on terms which will insure the repayment of the debt without harm to the economy.

The Survey Research Center at the University of Michigan was commissioned to conduct a study of the public's attitude toward instalment buying. This produced the disturbing findings that 34% of the respondents were opposed to any use of instalment credit, describing it as irresponsible or immoral; more than 50% believed its use should be controlled by government, and only 10% gave the institution their outright approval. And this after buying and selling on time payments had been a principal support of the U.S. economy for almost two generations!

As spokesman for the C.I.T. program to build confidence in "the people's credit," Arthur Dietz crisscrossed the nation, speaking before audiences of many kinds and being interviewed by newspaper and magazine writers on dozens of occasions. As he told the American Bankers Association members in Chicago in 1954:

> We owe it to our customers and to the economy to bring about the widest possible public understanding of what consumer instalment financing is, how it operates and the important contributions it makes to the public welfare. It is our job to teach the public how to use instalment credit to the best advantage and how to value it. In the past, in times of economic uncertainty or difficulty, there have been many people who tried, with some success, to blame consumer credit for all of the nation's economic ills, no matter where they came from.

> We owe it to the economy to work in good times and bad to educate every American to the true facts of consumer credit. We must try to make them understand that consumer credit is of tremendous service to the economy, and that there is no evidence that consumer credit is a significant contributor to deflation, nor is it an unstabilizing force. Consumer credit has provided—year after year—a vital prop to the economy. It is the boon which has raised the comfort of the American home and the living standards of the American family to levels which are higher than those enjoyed by any other class, in any other nation, at any other time in history. We must supply facts which will offset widely-held prejudices and misconceptions.

> I believe the principal responsibility of financing institutions during 1954 is to continue to have faith in the American consumer. We have learned from experience that the average instalment buyer is a person of integrity and sound judgment. We can prove our faith by recognizing that we must follow a firm, middle-of-the-road course in all of our operations. We must maintain practical credit standards, sensible collection policies and realistic rates. We must also provide the necessary services to protect our customers and ourselves against unexpected loss. And we must all use every available method to create a clearer understanding by the general public of the functions and principles of instalment credit.

His efforts were augmented by those of other C.I.T. spokesmen, particularly executives of Universal C.I.T. Credit Corporation and the public relations group. A standard address, entitled "The Pocketbook Democracy," was prepared for use by field representatives. Over the years it has been delivered, with appropriate revisions to make it timely, to thousands of businessmen's clubs, school groups, women's and civic club audiences, in radio interviews and through other means of reaching the public. The conclusion was brief and clear.

> The American standard of living had been erected on the availability of credit, and the willingness of the American people to use it wisely. Buying capital goods on the instalment plan has helped millions of young people to establish their homes. It has enabled them to obtain possession of real wealth. It has provided a background of security and respectability for everyday living. It has helped expand capital goods production and created jobs for millions in the capital goods area. Financing is not something of which you should be afraid. It is something you should use wisely.

As the months and years went by, Dietz received hundreds of letters from manufacturers, members of the financial community, economists, individuals in government and others expressing approval and congratulating him on his and his company's efforts.

Discussion of what came to be designated as "standby," rather than mandatory, consumer credit controls continued on the Washington scene for a number of years. For example, in his 1956 Economic Message, President Eisenhower recommended a congressional study of the desirability of enacting legislation to permit standby controls.

When federal credit control authority was enacted on December 23, 1969, consumer credit was not singled out in the measure. The law gave the President the power to authorize the Federal Reserve Board to impose a broad spectrum of controls on the extension of credit of all kinds wherever he determines that "such action is necessary or appropriate for the purpose of presenting or controlling inflation generated by the extension of credit in an excessive volume." Despite continuing concern over the inflationary spiral during the first half of the decade of the 1970's, no action was taken under this statute in those years. Moreover, no responsible sources have attributed serious blame for any of the economic recessions of the sixties or seventies to the public's excessive use of instalment credit.

With the passage of time, concern at the federal level, and among economists, consumer advocates, editorialists and others on the subject of instalment buying shifted to another issue. This was the *cost* of such credit to the public—and, more particularly, the alleged ignorance on the part of the users of credit as to what they actually were paying for it.

By 1960, well over half the states had enacted specific statutes fixing the maximum charges that could be imposed in various classes of sales financing transactions, especially motor vehicle financing. These enactments not only limited charges but required various forms of disclosure, generally in dollar amounts. By 1965, more then a dozen additional states had enacted such laws.

There was some apprehension in the sales finance industry that to state the charge in terms of a simple interest rate—so much per annum on the amount owed—might destroy the time-price concept and subject sales finance transactions to general usury limitations. There was also much concern expressed in the same quarters that in many types of transactions, sellers of goods or the credit granters themselves would find it mathematically most difficult, if not impossible, to convert the add-on charge into simple interest terms.

To these concerns of the banking and credit groups, the simple-interest proponents had one rejoinder: the public is being misled because virtually all other money costs are stated in terms of simple annual interest and some buyers or borrowers are likely to confuse quoted add-on percentages with simple interest. This was the finding of the Federal Trade Commission in 1936 when advertising of the "6% Plan" was enjoined. As explained earlier, when an add-on or discount finance rate is recomputed in terms of simple annual interest, the simple interest figure will be almost double the other rates. For example, a 6% add-on charge for a twelve-month transaction is equivalent to a simple annual interest rate of 10.90%.

In a speech in the Senate in 1963, Senator Paul H. Douglas gave this interpretation of the conflict between simple interest and other forms by which finance charges might be expressed:

"The borrower is told that the finance charge will be $6 on a $100 loan. The lender represents this to the borrower as being a 6% rate. . . . The actual rate is almost 12%, or nearly double the stated rate, because a borrower over the period of the year has the use of approximately $50 credit rather than the $100 face amount. . . .

"In the case of the add-on, the borrower receives $100 in cash or goods and must pay back $106. In the case of the discount technique, the borrower receives $94 but repays $100. The finance charge again is represented as being 6%. Again, the actual rate is almost 12%, or twice the quoted rate because the borrower is periodically repaying the loan."

Senator Douglas had first introduced a bill in 1960 to require the expression of financing charges in terms of both simple interest and the total dollar amount. The Production and Stabilization Subcommittee, which he headed, of the Senate Banking and Currency Committee held more than three years of hearings in Washington and in various principal cities. Extensive testimony was taken from both opponents and proponents of the legislation, which had been given the popular designation of the "Truth-in-Lending" bill.

C.I.T.'s management, along with many others engaged in the day-to-day administration of providing instalment credit services to the public, found the bill unnecessarily complex and in some respects redundant.

As early as 1961, C.I.T. filed with the subcommittee a statement in opposition. In part, this read:

> We are obliged to oppose this Bill in its application to sales of consumer goods on credit.
>
> A major program of Universal C.I.T. Credit Corporation and C.I.T. Corporation for many years has been the advocating of legislation to eliminate abuses in the field of instalment selling through effective state laws. In this endeavor they have not stood alone. The finance industry and especially the larger companies in that field have acted together in this program and have pursued it forcefully and with marked success.
>
> The history of regulatory legislation, as sponsored by the finance companies, was fully related to your Subcommittee in 1960 by Dr. Albert Haring, appearing on behalf of the National Retail Furniture Association. Attorney General Louis J. Lefkowitz of New York told this Committee at its last session how effective legislative regulatory controls at the state level had been in New York. We shall accordingly not burden the Committee's Record with a recital of the full story. We note, however, that at the present time some 35 states or more have regulatory laws that go much farther in protecting the consumer than does the Bill now before your Committee. We are continuing to urge the enactment of similar regulatory statutes in those states which do not have them now.
>
> The legislation which we favor and which has been enacted in most of the states affords effective protection against abuses in credit sales. For example:
>
> a provision for the licensing of finance companies. In the absence of such licensing, a consumer with a legitimate complaint of abuse, but who does not want to hire a lawyer and take his case to court, is without a forum at which his grievances may be heard. This is one of the most important regulations for curbing and controlling abuses. . . .
>
> the inclusion in the contract of a notice to the purchaser advising him of his rights under the law. . . .

the inclusion of a statement of any expenses such as those for filing or recording or other matters incidental to the transaction which the purchaser may have agreed to pay. . . .

a provision which limits delinquency charges for defaulted instalments. . . .

the disclosure in the contract of a statement of insurance coverages and of the cost of such coverages. . . .

the inclusion of a provision giving the purchaser a fair and proper refund upon anticipation of payment. . . .

a provision in the law prohibiting the inclusion of wage assignments or confessions of judgments in the contract. . . .

the inclusion of limitations on the seller or finance company's right of repossession. . . .

and perhaps the most important regulation of all, a statutory limitation of the amount of the credit charge, and we favor a requirement that the contract separately state the dollar amount of such credit charge. We believe that the purchaser is interested in knowing the dollar amount he has agreed to pay. He thinks in terms of dollars and not of percentages. "How much will the article cost me? How much will the credit cost me? How much do I have to pay? How much do I have to pay a month?" These are the questions which the purchaser wants answered. The percentage does not have any great meaning to him. To the purchaser, a statement of the dollar amount of the credit charge represents a full disclosure of that item. This disclosure is now required to be given the purchaser in 35 states, and where the law does not require it, disclosure of the dollar amount of the credit charge is given to him in most other states as a voluntary act of business policy on the part of the sellers and finance companies.

In this connection note the testimony before your committee last year of the president of The National Association of Better Business Bureaus:

"I have a great deal of doubt in my own mind from talking to thousands of customers over the years that they are particularly interested in what the so-called interest rate is in the instalment contract. They are interested in what the dollar cost is and how much it is going to cost them per month to pay the balance which they have obligated themselves for."

The Bill before the Committee does not begin to cover this long list of corrective recommendations that we make to the state legislatures. It is such tested, all-inclusive legislation, enacted at the state level, that will do a complete job—not the type of experimental, incomplete legislation such as that before you. . . .

The proposed legislation unnecessarily and unwisely invades an area of commerce that heretofore has been reserved for regulation by the several states. Moreover, as compared with the laws now on the books in a large majority of the states, it inadequately and imperfectly protects the consuming public, while introducing confusion and complexity that the public and business will find burdensome and objectionable.

The company's position on the truth-in-lending issue was forthrightly incorporated in its national public relations and consumer education programs emphasizing the contribution of consumer instalment credit to the nation's economy and social fabric. Walter Lundell, having succeeded to the presidency in 1960, became the company's chief spokesman. Throughout the 1960's, he delivered many addresses, as did other members of the management group, to audiences across the country. Their central theme was this, as stated in a 1961 speech:

1. The foundation of the consumer finance business is confidence, based on fair dealing.

2. Our business should be a constructive force in community life, affording considerate and responsible sources of credit.

3. Our funds shall be employed solely for the purpose of improving the financial circumstances of our customers.

4. This business shall be adequately regulated by law, at the state level.

5. Members shall assist and cooperate with authorities for the effective enforcement of all laws governing the business.

6. We shall support and cooperate with all agencies striving to better the economic and social condition of the American people.

Although the first truth-in-lending bill was introduced in Congress in 1960 and reintroduced with certain revisions in each new session, the legislation made no progress out of committees of the Senate or House until 1967. Senator Douglas had been defeated for reelection in 1966. Senator William E. Proxmire had taken over leadership for the bill in the Senate and Representative Leonor K. Sullivan in the House. The Senate passed a newly drawn bill by a unanimous vote on July 11, 1967; the House approved it on February 1, 1968. After certain changes in conference to conform the two versions, both houses approved the bill on May 22, 1968. President Johnson signed it into law on the following day.

The original Douglas bill of 1960, which contained many provisions that Lundell and other industry members had found objectionable and unworkable, had been substantially revised in the version that became law. Through the lengthy period of hearings and consideration by the two houses, the industry's views and counsel had been effectively set forth. Language of the law had been clarified and interest rate tables and schedules were developed that greatly simplified the task of making simple interest rate disclosures. The Federal Reserve Board, which was given enforcement authority under the act, was authorized to exempt transactions from federal regulation in any state where the state laws were substantially similar to the federal law and were adequately enforced. That section of the law made it clear: "the Congress does not intend to pre-empt consistent state laws but merely to build upon them."

In addition to requiring the full disclosure of charges for credit, the other principal provisions of the law regulated credit advertising, garnishment of wages and extortionate credit and collection practices.

C.I.T. was prepared to comply fully with the new regulations, which became effective on July 1, 1969, one year after the law was enacted. Thr financing industry soon found that it could operate efficiently and comfortably under the federal truth-in-lending statute and continues to do so. It is undeniable that the law has reinforced public confidence in the institution of consumer credit and has eliminated abuses by marginal operators that had tended to discredit it.

32

The Lundell Decade

At the time L. Walter Lundell retired as chairman and chief executive officer of C.I.T. Financial Corporation of June 30, 1970, his close associates were calling the C.I.T. years between 1960 and 1970, "The Lundell Decade."

On May 3, 1960, Walter Lundell was promoted to the presidency of the corporation from the position of executive vice president that he had held for two years. As president, he assumed complete operating responsibility for the company's affairs. Arthur Dietz became chairman of the board, assuming a title that had been unused since the death of Henry Ittleson in 1948.

The Swift and Company office boy of 1918 had traveled far. For the twenty years of his C.I.T. career prior to taking the president's chair, Lundell had been a man marked with promise by Arthur Dietz and Henry Ittleson, Jr. However, what Dietz in later years identified as the event that lifted Lundell's career from the relatively narrow channel of accountancy and subsidiary operating responsibilities was one that took place in early March of 1946.

It will be recalled that C.I.T. had handled household appliance financing for the Westinghouse Electric Company prior to World War

L. Walter Lundell

11. In the period of preparing for the peacetime production of consumer goods, a meeting of C.I.T. and Westinghouse executives and sales supervisors was held at C.I.T.'s New York headquarters to mobilize for the joint marketing opportunities that lay ahead. Lundell was one of three speakers, his assigned subject being "How To Approach Sound Consumer Credit." These were some of his words:

> I have outlined many factors that enter into this problem of approaching consumer credit on a sound basis. It is seldom very difficult to pass good credits or to determine bad credits. The consumer credit field unfortunately does not, however, establish itself with certainty into classifications which are either wholly black or wholly white. There is a wide marginal area where the weighing of compensating factors enters into the final judgment exercised, and it is these areas, the black, the white and the marginal, that the job of administering consumer credit meets its real test, for to be successful it must be dynamic. It must facilitate the making of sound sales. It must eliminate the unsound sales. It must be able to weigh all of the various compensating factors so that its credit appraisal in the final analysis will result in the fulfillment of its economic function—the job of moving the goods out of the factories and through the dealers and then into the hands of the consuming public.
>
> The road to sound consumer credit is not a broad highway with direction

signs which point out with certainty what is applicable under all conditions to all commodities and at all times. It is a road that must be traveled with judgment, intelligence, fairness and flexibility. It is a road that requires understanding and discriminating appraisal of a customer's character, capacity and capital—and if these principles are followed wisely and well, with consumer credit we can create sales and profit and render an incalculable service to every consumer.

The words Lundell wrote and the force and skill of his delivery were a revelation to Dietz. Looking back at the incident in later years, he said, "Right then and there I recognized his broad executive promise."

The years of the Lundell Decade were ones of continuing growth and prosperity for C.I.T., in spite of many cross-currents and massive forces for change that were at work both inside and outside the corporation to shape its course. Consider the statistical record:

	Net Income (Millions)	Earnings Per Common Share	Receivables Outstanding (Billions)	Volume of Receivables Purchased (Billions)
1960	$45.1	$2.34	$2.2	$4.62
1961	45.1	2.39	2.2	4.00
1962	47.6	2.46	2.3	4.60
1963	47.4	2.47	2.6	5.19
1964	49.2	2.56	2.7	5.66
1965	50.7	2.64	2.8	5.92
1966	55.3	2.76	3.0	5.98
1967	60.5	2.97	3.0	5.53
1968	60.6	3.05	3.3	6.30
1969	62.6	3.15	3.6	6.03

During the period, the annual rate of dividends paid per share to the common stockholders increased from $1.30 to $1.80, or nearly 40%.

In the foregoing, the amounts stated for 1960 and 1961 on a per-share basis are adjusted for a 2-for-1 split in the common stock that became effective on November 22, 1961.

As the era began, most sectors of the U.S. and Canadian economies were making a strong comeback from the low levels of the 1958–59 recession. C.I.T.'s industrial financing operations scored an excellent gain in 1960, with volume rising for the year to $861.5 million from $653.1 in 1959. Outstanding receivables in this category also increased by $150 million during the year, to reach a record $731.8 million. The factoring subsidiaries did not do as well, but their business was off only slightly from 1959.

Beginning in 1960, both the factoring companies and C.I.T. Corporation, the industrial financing subsidiary, launched a strong entry into the accounts receivable business, often referred to as "commercial financing." This is a form of lending on the collateral of producers' and dealers' receivables, closely akin to the original business of the C.I.T. enterprise. It will be recalled that conventional factoring requires "notification" to the purchaser of goods that his debt is payable directly to the factor because the factor has "bought" the obligation, with all the collection and credit risk responsibilities this involves. Accounts receivable financing, however, represents making a loan at a discount from the face amount of the invoice and does not make necessary notification to the debtor of the transaction nor payment by him to the financing company. His payments are made in accordance with normal trade practice to the seller of the goods. The latter must make good to the financing house whether or not the debtor fulfills his obligation.

There were clouds over the automobile financing side of the business. For one thing, the motor industry and many of its customers had not yet recovered from the sharp setback that had reduced car sales in 1958 and 1959. The situation, in the first stockholders' report to be signed by Walter Lundell, was explained in this way:

> In view of the unsettled economic conditions in many areas, our automotive financing subsidiaries found it necessary to become more selective in their purchasing policies during the year. Because of reduced profit margins, the financial condition of many automobile dealers became impaired and a large number withdrew from business. This added to the keen competition for desirable accounts. The dollar volume of retail financing also was reduced by the general decline in used car prices and the greater number of sales of compact cars, which, being lower priced, are financed for lesser amounts than standard models.

Another threat of even greater significance than the economic problems facing the auto marketers had become a reality. This followed the announcement by the Ford Motor Company, at the beginning of 1959, that it was planning to reenter the automobile financing business through the establishment of a wholly-owned financing subsidiary.

This came as no surprise whatsoever to the C.I.T. management. As far back as 1949, Ford had successfully pressed C.I.T. to join it in the appeal to the U.S. Supreme Court that lifted certain onerous restraints imposed by the 1938 antitrust consent decrees on both Ford and C.I.T. The case also won for Ford the right to organize its own financing subsidiary if it chose to do so.

By the middle of the 1950's the interests of C.I.T. (and to a lesser extent Commercial Credit) and Ford had reached a turning point. In the highly competitive auto sales race of the time, Ford felt itself to be at a marketing disadvantage in that, in almost all areas, GMAC maintained somewhat lower rate structures to dealers and the public than did any of the independent companies. The reason for this, they also agreed, was the plain fact that GMAC was not under compulsion to earn any given return on its equity capital, as were the independents, since it had no stockholders except General Motors Corporation. The latter's primary interest obviously was to maximize the sale of its products and reap the huge financial returns that resulted, rather than to emphasize the earning power of its "captive" financing arm.

During the early and middle 1950's, the Ford management held several meetings with C.I.T.'s representatives on the issue of C.I.T.'s agreeing to meet GMAC's rate schedules, whatever they might be. At a final meeting in Detroit in 1958, which Dietz himself attended, the Ford insistence on the adoption of GMAC's rate schedules was rejected outright by the C.I.T. representatives. At these discussions, C.I.T. was frank in explaining why it would be impossible for it to permit an outside force—a competitor, in fact—to make its management decisions on such vital matters as its rate structure and earnings capability. Ford later talked with Commercial Credit and received a similar response.

Ford Motor Credit Corporation was organized in August 1959. A former C.I.T. executive was its president and another was vice president—sales. Dietz had this to say on the subject of the Ford action to his stockholders:

On January 13, 1959, we wrote to stockholders commenting on the announcement by the Ford Motor Company that it was planning to enter the new car financing business. Since that letter was written, the Antitrust and Monopoly Subcommittee of the United States Senate has announced it will conduct hearings on "increasing monopolization in automobile financing" and that this investigation will be directed at the proposed establishment by Ford of a financing affiliate as well as at the long-standing ownership of a finance affiliate by General Motors Corporation.

The United States Department of Justice likewise has announced that it is investigating the antitrust aspects of the Ford program and the activity of General Motors in automobile financing. In addition, several members of Congress have introduced bills to prohibit any automobile manufacturer from engaging in the finance business.

In the legislative attack on General Motors and Ford, C.I.T. was allied with the remainder of the independent finance company industry, which had been its adversaries in the earlier antitrust proceedings.

Because of the pending legislative proceedings, Ford Motor Credit opened only three branch offices in 1959 and nineteen in 1960, but the pace picked up rapidly thereafter. However, in spite of the inroads of this new competitor, C.I.T. continued to service thousands of Ford products dealers, as well as those of the other car and truck manufacturers.

The legislative efforts to block Ford's plan and force a divorcement of GMAC from General Motors were inconclusive. In 1964 Chrysler Motors organized Chrysler Credit Corporation (renamed "Chrysler Financial Corporation" in 1967). The independent finance companies and the nation's thousands of banks that were engaged in automobile financing thus were brought face-to-face with captive finance competition from each of the "Big Three" motor car manufacturers.

Walter Lundell, as president, was also designated chief executive officer of the corporation effective January 1, 1962, with Henry Ittleson, Jr., assuming the board chairmanship. Arthur O. Dietz, preparing for his retirement, took the title of chairman of the executive committee until his retirement from that office at the year-end.

Another name moved toward the corporation's highest echelon of management as a part of this realignment. It was that of Walter S. Holmes, Jr., who had joined the company in the position of controller at the beginning of 1959. In 1960, his responsibilities were broadened and he was named a vice president. At the annual meeting held on April 24, 1962, he was elected to the board of directors and became a member of the executive committee, giving up the controller's function shortly thereafter.

Walter Holmes was born in the village of South River, New Jersey, in 1919, but he grew up in Philadelphia. He majored in accounting and received his bachelor's degree from Lehigh University. His first post-college jobs were with two public accounting firms in Philadelphia and New York. During this period, he also earned a master's degree in business administration at New York University through after-business-hours study. In 1947, he was employed by RCA Corporation as an accountant and rose to the position of controller of RCA prior to accepting an offer that came to him from Lundell to become C.I.T.'s controller.

Walter S. Holmes, Jr.

The record of the remainder of the decade was primarily one of consistent and successful growth through diversification. The story of that tremendous accomplishment will be the subject of the next chapter. The internal corporate events of those same years will be dealt with first.

Retail automobile financing made a strong showing in the 1962–64 period, recovering from a very disappointing volume figure of only $611.7 million, the lowest in more than a decade, posted for 1961. (Another sales slump had hit the auto manufacturers in that year.) For those three years, C.I.T.'s motor retail bookings were successively $808.1 million, $912.5 million and $925.6 million.

While industrial financing and leasing—more about the latter a bit later—were tempered somewhat by the cyclical economic conditions that prevailed during the fifties and early sixties, they did not experience the wide fluctuations of automotive financing operations. Rather, in both the United States and Canada these receivables grew continuously from year to year, becoming an ever-larger part of the company's total business. This is the record of the rapid strides made in this area beginning with the mid-fifties:

INDUSTRIAL FINANCING AND LEASING RECEIVABLES

	Volume Acquired (Millions)	Year-end Outstandings (Millions)
1954	$164.9	$151.5
1955	209.4	199.0
1956	337.9	303.9
1957	372.8	377.2
1958	355.9	429.0
1959	471.2	599.8
1960	573.0	718.1
1961	483.4	736.3
1962	691.4	400.4
1963	659.0	389.8
1964	649.4	415.0
1965	655.2	427.0
1966	750.1	514.3
1967	784.0	489.2
1968	880.7	542.4
1969	1.147.2	698.8

Contracts to provide financing services on a nationwide basis for many major corporations helped to swell these tables, although there was no slackening in the company's efforts to obtain and hold the business of local and regional contractors, suppliers, distributors and dealers of every size. Among other major clients of this period were Montgomery Ward & Company, Georgia-Pacific Corporation, American Radiator and Sanitary Corporation, Brunswick Corporation, Certain-Teed Products Corporation, Johns-Manville Corporation and McKesson & Robbins, Inc.

Although there has been only limited reference to credit losses in this narrative, except for the period of the 1929–32 depression, it must be recognized that losses are an intrinsic element in the extension of credit to both consumers and businessmen. Inescapably, they are as much a part of doing business as taxes, rent, payrolls and all the other basic components of the corporate expense account.

C.I.T. men have always been extraordinarily good credit men. This expertise extends not only to the exercise of experienced and hard-boiled judgment in the approval and granting of loans but also to the seasoned and practiced ability to collect—or "salvage," to use the traditional C.I.T. term—the maximum when some extensions of credit inevitably go bad. It can reasonably be argued that the company won its leadership position in both the consumer and industrial financing fields through two fundamental forms of managerial excellence. These were, first, the consistent capability of its management and staff to deal effectively with both the hazards of granting credit and of collecting the money back, and second, a constant innovation in developing new credit areas and outdoing all competitors in putting ever-larger numbers of creditors and amounts of new business on the books.

The Billie Sol Estes case of the early 1960's was perhaps the most publicized and traumatic test of the company's ability to react to a severe credit exposure and to "salvage" the utmost, within the limits of legality and business decency, from the exposure of its investments to loss.

In 1951, at the age of 26, Billie Sol Estes came out of the West Texas foothills to the metropolis (for that region) of Pecos. He was nearly penniless. Backed only by superb self-confidence and an evangelical salesman's skills, he plunged into the chemical fertilizer, farm implement and well- and ditch-digging businesses in that booming territory. Within three years, he was selected by the U.S. Junior Chamber of Commerce as one of the nation's ten outstanding young men. Locally, he was believed to have already made at least his first million.

Estes was motivated by an insatiable desire for wealth and therefore the need for more and more credit to finance his empire-building projects. He became the largest distributor of chemical fertilizer (anhydrous ammonia) in Texas by obtaining credit in seven-figure amounts from his supplier, Commercial Solvents Company. He also entered the grain storage business, which no doubt helped to support the latter line of credit. This meant obtaining rental payments from the federal government for the storage of grain of local farmers in bonded warehouses he owned. The grain was collateral against government loans the farmers had received. To this income he added high earnings from the yield of cotton acreage he controlled. The production of cotton was rigidly restricted by federal allotments, but Estes had found a way to obtain the assignment of their acreage allotments from farmers as far away from West Texas as Georgia and Alabama, although such assignments seemingly were prohibited by federal law.

C.I.T. entered the Billie Sol Estes picture about 1957 when it agreed to finance the purchase of a number of the four-wheeled, transportable anhydrous ammonia tanks that this high-riding tycoon—"the biggest man in West Texas"—was buying to provide to the farmers who were his fertilizer customers. The tanks held the anhydrous ammonia under pressure as a liquid and were taken into the fields where it was applied as a gas. It was the lifeblood of the area's cotton crops.

The Estes account became the pride of C.I.T.'s field management in that area. Not only were his tank purchases placed on the books but other purchases, primarily grain storage buildings, were also financed. The account seemed to be an excellent one, but C.I.T.'s New York management became restive as the investment in Estes' affairs grew. For one thing, he flatly refused to provide any financial statements, considering such requests "insults." By 1961 all but $700 of the $138,000 of the 1958 Estes advances on tanks had been repaid, as had $219,000 of the 1959 volume of $363,000. The decision was made, however, not to extend any more credit to Billie Sol. Combining the tank balances with other Estes' loans for tractor, farm equipment and building purchases through these years, Estes' outstanding obligations to C.I.T. remained in the range of $450,000. This seemed to be sufficient credit to extend to such an obvious promoter as Estes. Still the anhydrous ammonia tank business poured in, but now the purchasers were individual agriculturalists of the area. Estes did not appear to be involved in any way.

On a Sunday evening in May 1961, a C.I.T. executive in New York who was closely associated with the Estes dealings received a call from one of his key credit men in the Dallas office. This man reported that he had been offered a "future" job heading up a finance company that Estes' tank supplier was planning to establish. In the meantime, he said he was promised a $400 monthly "tax-free" cash retainer while continuing to work for C.I.T. The first $400 was given to him in cash, in a sealed envelope he was instructed not to open until he left the meeting.

This information precipitated the immediate descent of a C.I.T. task force on the Pecos area. A vigorous effort was exerted to verify Estes' and the tank manufacturer's accounts and all purchasers properly acknowledged their indebtedness. Nevertheless, C.I.T. completely stopped doing business with the tank manufacturer and all those involved in the tank financing transactions.

During the summer and fall of 1961, there were recurring rumors in the Pecos area that many of the fertilizer tanks that had been financed locally were actually nonexistent and that Estes also had played fast and loose with the government's cotton acreage allotment regulations. The rumors were exposed as fact by the Pecos *Independent,* a local weekly Estes was attempting to outdo by starting a rival paper that had first appeared a few months earlier. On Lincoln's Birthday, 1962, the *Independent* began publication of a series of articles exposing the fertilizer tank frauds. Even though cotton farmers did not customarily need to own these tanks—they could be obtained without charge from their fertilizer suppliers—some farmers had bought as many as 180 of the units between 1959 and 1961. County filing records revealed that the total apparent purchase of tanks in West Texas in the period had run to a total of 33,500, which were mortgaged for $33.5 million. In Reeves County, where Pecos was located, 370 farmers had obligated themselves for 15,000 tanks at a cost of $14.5 million.

All the finance companies that were involved, including C.I.T., hastily sent teams of investigators into the area to check on their debtors and collateral. The true answer to the enigma was not long in emerging. Estes had gone to his friends and customers in the area and said he needed additional tanks in his business, but explained that all his credit was already committed in his many other "big deals." He asked to "borrow" their credit, having them sign mortgages for the tanks, agreeing to lease the tanks from them and pledging to make payments on the leases that would equal their mortgage payments. For their cooperation, he would pay them a fee of 10% of the face value of the transaction—money they would receive scot-free "for virtually nothing."

The purchasers never saw the tanks and neither did anyone else. Most of them simply did not ever exist. With the compliance of his tank supplier, Estes was simply cashing the fraudulent mortgages on nonexistent tanks to get more and more money for his far-flung enterprises from the finance companies that discounted the paper. *The New York Times* reported that in twenty-two months, the Superior Manufacturing Company of Amarillo, operated by an Estes' confederate, was paid $20 million for phantom tanks and turned $18 million of this over to Estes.

C.I.T.'s highest investment in the Estes situation approximated $5 million. Most of it was recovered, from seizure of various assets, from creditors' payments, from recoveries through the trustee appointed by the court to liquidate Estes' affairs and from recoveries under its employees' fidelity bonds. It was established that two employees had violated their trust by accepting favors from Estes, including cash, and helping to cover up his manipulations.

Walter Lundell reported to C.I.T.'s stockholders on this unhappy experience with this statement in the report of the proceedings at the 1963 annual meeting:

> Concerning the matter of certain defaulted obligations of a number of farmers and ranchers in West Texas, which has been publicized as the

Estes situation, those present were reminded that it was stated in our Report to Stockholders, dated April 24, 1962, that our total net investment in these receivables originally approximated $5,000,000. At March 31, 1962, this investment was written down, by the use of existing reserves, to an amount which the Management believed to be collectible, and this belief has been substantiated by subsequent events. It was further stated that possible losses in this situation would have no adverse effect on earnings after the March 31, 1962 date. This appraisal proved to be accurate. We have already had substantial recoveries and are continuing in our efforts to collect from debtors. The Corporation's total credit losses in 1962, including the write-offs in the Estes situation, were less than in the previous year, and losses to date in 1963 are lower than in 1962.

While a few recoveries continued to be secured, by the mid-1970's C.I.T.'s total write-off from the Estes episode was about $1.25 million, 75% of the exposure having been recovered.

After numerous investigations by the U.S. Department of Justice, the Texas State Attorney's office, committees of both houses of Congress and others, Billie Sol Estes was indicted in 1964, with certain confederates, for conspiracy and using the mails to defraud. He was convicted and sentenced to fifteen years in federal prison. After serving six years as a model prisoner in Leavenworth Penitentiary, and the Sandstone, Minnesota, and La Tuna, Texas, federal correctional facilities, he was paroled in July 1971 and returned to farming in the West Texas area.

C.I.T.'s pursuit of the maximum recovery of collectible funds is also demonstrated by the company's involvement in the "Black Tom Case."

At 2:08 A.M. on the morning of Sunday, July 3, 1916, a series of cataclysmic explosions occurred on four barges storing high explosives at the piers of the National Storage Company, Black Tom Island, in New York Harbor off Jersey City. A wide area of the New Jersey and New York waterfronts was devastated and there were many fatalities and injuries. The shock waves were felt in Camden and Philadelphia 90 miles from the blasts, and over the five states of New York, New Jersey, Connecticut, Pennsylvania and Maryland. Jersey City sustained more than $15 million in damages. More than $300,000 worth of glass window breakage occurred in Manhattan, including, tradition says, windows in the C.I.T. headquarters at 61 Broadway.

The ammunition on the barges was destined for the Allied Armies in Europe and the explosions were determined to be the act of German espionage agents, a clear transgression of the neutrality of the United

States. Two of the plotters were apprehended and given long prison terms.

The Versailles Treaty at the end of World War I called for heavy reparations payments from the German government to compensate those among the victorious nations who themselves, or whose citizens, had sustained determinable financial losses as a result of German military action. Claims for Black Tom damages were first-class possibilities in this respect.

A client of the independent factoring firm of Fredk. Vietor and Achelis, the Daugherty Silk Mills, had a large inventory of raw silk stored in a Passaic, New Jersey, warehouse, where its plant also was located. It is a reasonable speculation that this silk was intended for the production of parachutes. In any event, both the silk inventory and portions of the plant suffered severe damages from the nearby explosions and fire that followed.

The Achelis firm had inventory liens on the destroyed silk and other collateral claims on the Daugherty firm. When the latter went into bankruptcy in the 1920's, the factors took over the Black Tom claims as well as other security that was theirs. Awards from the German reparations commitments were adjudicated by a Mixed Claims Commission of the U.S. government, sitting in Washington. In 1928, an award of $200,000 was made to the Achelis firm, plus accrued interest that brought the total amount due them to $280,000.

It will be recalled that Fredk. Vietor and Achelis was acquired by C.I.T. in February 1929, including the asset represented by the Black Tom award. Disbursements were received regularly through government channels, as German reparations payments were made, until September 1932 when Hitler repudiated the payment of any further World War I obligations of the Reich. Up to that time, $200,000 had been collected on the Achelis claims.

It took another World War and another Allied victory to force the German government into a renewal of payments on its World War I reparations debts. Thus, in February 1953 the Federal Republic of Germany agreed to pay $97.5 million in principal and interest on these still-existing claims, with the total obligation to be discharged in 26 annual instalments, running to 1978.

Throughout all this time, both C.I.T. and its factoring executives and attorneys had vigorously and unremittingly pursued and defended their rights to the Black Tom claims. Enormous files of documents were built up as proceeding after proceeding in the U.S. and abroad attempted to deal with the complex issues.

The upshot of all this is that C.I.T. is continuing to collect approximately $3,300 per year from the Black Tom claims that originated more than a half-century earlier and, as this is written, will do so for some years to come.

At the beginning of 1964, Meinhard and Company and Commercial Factors Corporation were merged to form a new subsidiary, Meinhard-Commercial Corporation. This reduced from three to two the number of factoring units, William Iselin & Co. retaining its separate status. Charles L. Harding, Jr., who had headed Meinhard, became chairman and chief executive of the combined company, with Walter M. Kelly, of Commercial Factors, as president. The merger resulted in considerable cost savings and the creation of a much stronger operating organization.

Aided by the entry into commercial (also known as "accounts receivable") financing, the factoring companies were turning in excellent performances, booking increased amounts of business from year to year and producing higher profits. Their business volume grew as follows: (in billions) 1960—$1.223; 1961—$1.292; 1962—$1.376; 1963–$1.550; 1964–$1.898; 1965–$2.107. Having crossed the $2 billion mark in 1965, C.I.T.'s factoring volume has remained above that figure for the next decade, scoring continued increases.

Other developments in 1964 included the establishment of the corporation's first data processing center in space on lower Park Avenue, New York, which became available as a result of the merger of the two factoring companies. Meinhard-Commercial Corporation was moved into the C.I.T. headquarters building at 650 Madison Avenue.

As part of management's active program to diversify through acquisitions, 500,000 shares of the company's common stock were purchased both privately and on the open market during 1963–64 at an average price per share slightly under $40. It was the intent that these shares would be held available to exchange for those of companies to be acquired.

In their 1965 report to stockholders, Ittleson, Jr., and Lundell noted the passing of another milestone in the company's history:

> Shortly after the first of this year, C.I.T. passed the one hundred billion dollar mark in the total volume of financing acquired since the corporation was founded in 1908. Half of this entire amount was recorded in the past ten years. The achievement of this significant milestone in our corporate career of service to business and the consuming public gives promise that C.I.T.'s growth will continue and that its opportunities for service will expand.

As to 1966, the national economy is functioning at a high level, demand is strong in all areas of our operations and we have confidence that a good year lies ahead for your Corporation.

As 1967 opened, the United States was becoming increasingly involved in the Vietnam War. Lundell responded to the social unrest created by the war at the 1968 annual meeting of stockholders. He voiced a hope that peace was not far off but added:

At last year's meeting I said that C.I.T. was on the moving edge of growth, that we were pushing ahead on traditional as well as new fronts, and that we regarded conditions as more favorable in many respects than had been the case in the recent past.

At the present time, it is quite evident that much of the future of our nation and business will depend upon the over-riding question of war or peace. One can only hope that next year at this time peace will prevail and that all our resources of men and wealth can be channeled into productive efforts of peace. However, in the transition which will eventually take place, there will be many dislocations and resulting adjustments putting strains on our economy.

Certainly, too, any evaluation of the future must give recognition to the impact of the social unrest that is sweeping the nation and the responsibility the private sector must bear in the full achievement of a just society. A clear call has come to all business, asking for a response that must take many forms if an equal break in life is to be offered the large numbers of our fellow citizens who are economically and socially deprived today. They must be made qualified to fill productive jobs. There must be a vast improvement in the environment where they spend their lives. They must be given access to the opportunities, the encouragement, the financial means and credit and an initial helping hand from those more fortunate. In the long run, we must qualify them to make it on their own in the spirit of individual enterprise that has always contributed to the American Way for most of us.

C.I.T. is committed to accepting the responsibilities of good corporate citizenship in this effort. Our various subsidiaries, each in its own way, have programs under way that will give significant numbers of the disadvantaged group training and jobs. At the same time, we are attempting to find ways that C.I.T. funds can be prudently put to work for the betterment of the economic structure of the Negro community.

Complicated as all these problems may be, in the face of these crosscurrents and many others, we are still wholly confident that a flexible and responsive organization such as ours will continue to grow and prosper.

Taking a longer view, on only the present level of profitability, we can expect to add from $250 to $300 million in retained earnings to our capital structure during the next decade. This addition to our equity position, conservatively leveraged, means that by 1978 we should have the potential for employing in profitable investments upwards of $1.5 billion more than we now have available. The process of finding the best opportunities to employ these funds effectively is certain to produce significant basic changes that will enhance our opportunities for both internal and external growth.

Corporate change of another sort was occurring, of course, as the 1960's unfolded. Important management figures departed from the scene and new names were constantly being added to the company's executive masthead. The following paragraphs record these personnel changes:

● Charles S. Sargent, Jr., was employed by William Iselin & Co. in 1935, following his graduation from Harvard. An effective and innovative salesman, he earned a series of promotions until he became president and chief executive of the Iselin company in 1960. He also was elected a director of C.I.T. Financial in that year. He led the Iselin

subsidiary through a series of successful years until late in 1972, when he was asked to take over the leadership of C.I.T.'s larger factoring company, Meinhard-Commercial, as its president. One month after this, he met his death in an accident, cutting short a career that held promise of still greater accomplishments.

• Arthur L. B. Richardson became vice president and general counsel on August 3, 1961, succeeding Melbourne Bergerman as the latter approached retirement. He was elected a director in December 1962 and corporate secretary, suceeding Stanley Ecker, at the beginning of 1965. The latter retired from all active service one year later. A graduate of Harvard College and the George Washington University Law School, Richardson had been associated for many years with Sylvania Electric Products, Inc., rising to the position of senior vice president responsible for legal, public relations, purchasing and industrial relations activities.

• Richard H. Lund, previously assistant controller, succeeded Walter Holmes as controller on May 15, 1962, after two years with the company. He was later named a vice president and vice president–finance after relinquishing the controller's function. He joined the board of directors in 1973 and was appointed to the executive committee in 1975. A certified public accountant, he had had extensive public accounting experience.

- Ardell T. Everett, who had been an officer of the Prudential Insurance Company, became president of Patriot Life Insurance Company on October 27, 1962. Subsequently, he assumed responsibility for all of C.I.T.'s life and casualty-property damage insurance activities as their chairman. He was elected to the C.I.T. board of directors in 1966, serving until his retirement in 1974.

- Walter Holmes was elevated to the executive vice presidency of the corporation on January 1, 1965. This was one step from the office of president and chief administrative officer, to which he was elected in June 1968, Walter Lundell having moved to the position of chairman of the board.

- Alfred DeSalvo, after extensive investment banking experience and service for six years in the C.I.T. treasurer's department, was elected treasurer in 1964, when "Chuck" Dow relinquished that particular office. He became a vice president a year later and has continued to direct the company's massive daily borrowing and funding operations.

- After 26 years of service with the company, including executive assignments in the Universal C.I.T. organization, as president of Canadian Acceptance Corporation and with the parent company, Charles S. Jensen became president of the industrial financing and leasing subsidiaries, C.I.T. Corporation and C.I.T. Leasing Corporation, in 1962. He was elected a director of C.I.T. Financial Corporation in 1964 and a C.I.T. vice president and member of the executive committee on October 28, 1965. He assumed executive responsibility for all of the company's consumer and industrial financing operations in 1972 and was named executive vice president, with the same supervisory duties, on October 1, 1975.

- When Jensen left the presidency of Canadian Acceptance Corporation in 1961, he was succeeded by another C.I.T. veteran, Clarence E. Trudeau. He started with the company in 1939 as a sales representative in New York. After military service, he returned to C.I.T., in the industrial financing area, in 1946, became head of the Philadelphia division and was transferred to the Canadian company, as a vice president, in 1955. He was well prepared to take over as chief executive when Jensen returned to the United States and guided the Canadian company during the period of growth it has enjoyed throughout the following years. He served first as president and then as chairman of the board.

- Alan Rude's career continued to advance within the company's

consumer financing operations during this period. In December 1964, he moved from president of Universal C.I.T. Credit to chairman of that subsidiary, as well as its chief executive. He was succeeded as Universal C.I.T.'s president by Henry C. Watkins, who had been executive vice president, having had a career with C.I.T. that began in 1936 on his graduation from college. Rude was elected a C.I.T. Financial vice president in 1965 and a member of the executive committee. He had responsibility for supervising all consumer financing activities until his retirement in 1969. Again Watkins succeeded him, becoming a director of C.I.T. Financial Corporation and vice president—consumer financing. Watkins in turn retired on June 30, 1972.

    ● Another historic milestone with respect to the composition of the board of directors occurred at the stockholders' meeting on April 25, 1967. Morton J. May and Sydney M. Shoenberg did not stand for reelection to the board, being joined in this decision by Thomas May and George E. Warren. Morton May and Shoenberg had been directors of the company since its organization in 1908, a span of 59 years, which may approach a record for such corporate affiliations. Thomas May had been a director for 57 years. Warren, an independent investment adviser, had joined the board in 1950. All four were designated honorary directors. The deaths of both Morton May and Thomas May occurred in the following year, and George Warren passed away in 1969.

The "official" association of Edwin C. Vogel with C.I.T. Financial Corporation as an officer and director came to a close when he withdrew his name for reelection to the board at the stockholders' meeting on April 22, 1969. Walter Lundell addressed the meeting in this tribute to him:

> Mr. Vogel is one of those few men, close associates of the late Henry Ittleson, who were responsible in a very special way for establishing the corporate foundation on which the modern C.I.T. Financial Corporation has been built, and for helping to guide it through the several decades in which it won a foremost place among the financial institutions of the United States.
>
> Moreover, Mr. Vogel has, up to this very moment, continued to contribute the fullest measure of farsighted and discerning counsel, enthusiasm, encouragement, personal support, and when necessary, criticism, I might say to all of our programs and projects.

This business statesman, who had played such a vital role in guiding C.I.T. to its position of eminent stature and reputation in the nation's financial and industrial life, remained an active and valuable influence in the position of honorary director. The corporation's managers found reliance in his counsel and interest in the corporation's affairs until his death in 1973.

• In order that he might retire approximately one year before his normal retirement date, Arthur L.B. Richardson tendered his resignation as vice president, general counsel and corporate secretary to be effective at the close of 1975. He was succeeded as general counsel and secretary by Alan B. Lerner, who had been his close associate and designated successor.

Alan Lerner had joined C.I.T. in 1960 and for a number of years handled the legal affairs of the consumer financing companies. He also effectively represented the company on federal government matters including the critical bank holding company issue. He was named general attorney of C.I.T. Financial Corporation in 1971 and became closely involved with the administration of legal matters for National Bank of North America in addition to his other responsibilities.

———

Death came to Arthur O. Dietz on November 28, 1967. He had continued as an active member of the board of directors until his final illness. In these words of tribute he was mourned by his fellow directors:

> His passing has closed a lifetime of abundant achievement and usefulness to his fellow men and forty-eight years of devoted service to this Corporation, including a quarter century as its President or Chairman. In the truest sense, the modern C.I.T. Financial Corporation stands as a monument to the career, vision and indomitable character of Arthur O. Dietz.
>
> His loss from among our number brings greatest personal grief to each member of this Board, as we recall and honor the strength of mind and purpose and the warmth of friendship and generous understanding that he gave in full measure and for so many valued years to our association. We have been greatly privileged to have shared his comradeship and the example of his inspiring and courageous leadership.

Years earlier, when Arthur Dietz retired as an officer of the corporation, the board of directors had established in his honor a fund of $25,000 to grant five $5,000 college scholarships to graduates of the public school system of St. Paul, his birthplace. The grants were awarded by a selection committee of representative local citizens on the basis of the "personal character, promise of useful service to society and scholastic accomplishment" of the aspirants. As the Arthur O. Dietz Honorary Scholarships were awarded annually from 1963 to 1967, the man they honored lived to know of all of the holders and to convey to them his congratulations, his pride in them and the high hopes he held for their future careers.

33

—Of Diversification

Blind chance often governs the destinies of great business enterprises, just as it does those of great or lesser men.

Chance intervened in shaping the destiny of C.I.T. Financial Corporation on a Sunday evening in the spring of 1939, when the doorbell rang at a house in Larchmont, New York, that Mr. and Mrs. Louis Surut had rented for the summer.

The couple had just taken the property for a second summer because Mr. Surut so greatly enjoyed the boating on nearby Long Island Sound. However, the owners had the house listed for sale, and the Suruts had frequently been disturbed during their first summer's rental by visits from prospective purchasers and real estate agents wishing to make inspection tours. Therefore, when they renewed the lease for their 1939 stay, the Suruts insisted on a provision that they were not required to show the property during their tenancy.

They were addressing invitations for their daughter's graduation from the Horace Mann School when the knock came. The caller was a local real estate agent who was accompanied by two people. He explained that he had tried to reach the Suruts by telephone to ask if he could show his prospects through the house but had been unable to do so. Thus, he said, he had taken the liberty of bringing his clients unannounced.

When Mr. Surut remonstrated at the intrusion, the real estate man introduced those with him as Mr. and Mrs. James Picker—"local people, almost neighbors of yours," who had long admired the property and "were not just 'idle lookers' but people who are really interested." He added that Mr. Picker was the founder and owner of Picker X-Ray Corporation, a well-known local industrial organization.

The Suruts felt it would be rude to send the callers away and invited them in. The Pickers were impressed with the house and most complimentary about the way the present occupants had decorated it. The two families found they had many interests and friends in common, so the Suruts graciously invited the Pickers to stay for refreshments after they had toured the house.

A day or two later, Mrs. Picker telephoned to thank Mrs. Surut and invited her and her husband to dinner. From this, the two families, as Larchmont neighbors, became fairly friendly and for a while the Pickers' only son dated the Suruts' daughter.

Mr. Surut died in 1950 and Mrs. Surut lost track of the Pickers. In due course she remarried. Her husband was Arthur O. Dietz of C.I.T. Financial Corporation, who was a widower. In the summer of 1957, Mr. and Mrs. Dietz planned to spend a part of their vacation at Lake Saranac, in northern New York State. When they arrived at the inn there, they were disappointed in the accommodations assigned to them and at the reception they received. They considered moving on immediately, but then decided to have dinner and at least stay the night.

They first went to the cocktail lounge, and as they entered, Mrs. Dietz saw Mr. and Mrs. Picker, who were sitting alone at a table. The Pickers also recognized her immediately, and after the introductions of the Pickers and Dietz, Picker insisted the Dietzes join them at their table.

A pleasant interlude followed. After a time, while Mrs. Dietz and Mr. Picker were on the dance floor, Mrs. Picker, recognizing Mr. Dietz's reputation as an outstanding business leader, spoke seriously to him and said that she and her husband would welcome his advice.

Their problem, she said, was what the future of Picker X-Ray Corporation was to be. She told Dietz that her husband was 75; that he and their only son, Harvey, owned the business outright and that they were aware that this fact introduced serious estate and tax problems. As Harvey Picker described the situation later: "We had carefully conserved cash so that we could pay the necessary estate taxes on my father's death. However, if he and I were to die within a relatively short period of time of each other, the company would be forced to pay out over half its total capital in estate taxes. This would virtually wipe out its available working capital."

Mrs. Picker said, "We are wondering if we should sell the company. What do you think, Mr. Dietz?" (As a matter of fact, the Pickers were then having preliminary negotiations concerning the possibility of "going public" or selling to the Bell & Howell Company.)

Dietz's interest was immediately quickened, for he knew the Picker company to be a most successful one, even though no figures were publicly available since it was privately owned. He asked the Pickers a number of questions that evening. He then said that he thought he might have a few ideas for them and would get in touch with them soon again.

The next morning, the Dietzes made their departure from Saranac for Saratoga, New York, and more satisfactory accommodations. Once at Saratoga, however, Dietz telephoned Stanley Ecker and set in motion an investigation of the Picker business and an evaluation of the possibilities that C.I.T. might want to purchase it.

C.I.T.'s appraisal of the Picker purchase was a painstaking one, for ownership of such a company, grounded in scientific technology and production, would be a radical departure from the company's financially oriented corporate character. Everything that resulted from this effort, however, seemed to substantiate Dietz's initial intuitive reaction that the investment would be an excellent one for C.I.T.

Harvey Picker favored a sale to C.I.T. He put it this way in retrospect: "I had run the company for nearly twenty-five years with loyal friends and colleagues. I felt I owed too much loyalty to these employees to have their jobs jeopardized by a possible dissolution of the company on my death or the possible forced sale to an undesirable owner. It wasn't fair to those people with whom my father and I had worked for all those years to have the financial strength of the company depend on my surviving my father by more than seven years. This then led to the decision to merge the company."

The agreement of purchase was announced on August 1, 1958. The consideration was 341,000 shares of C.I.T. common stock, valued by the market on that date at $18.5 million. James Picker continued as chairman of the company and Harvey as president and chief executive officer. The latter also joined the C.I.T. board of directors. The announcement of the transaction said that the Picker organization "would function as a completely autonomous unit within the diversified C.I.T. family of companies. Its personnel, policies and traditions will be continued without change." The spirit of that policy has been consistently

observed since the inception of C.I.T.'s ownership of the company.

The Picker business had been founded by James Picker, the operator of a small pharmacy, in 1915. He had come to this country in 1901 as a penniless immigrant with just a smattering of knowledge of pharmacy.

He landed a $5-a-week job as delivery boy and porter for a Manhattan druggist and through hard work and frugality was able to buy the store a dozen years later.

His store was located near Mt. Sinai Hospital in New York City, where pioneering work was being done in the formative days of x-ray diagnosis. He began to stock x-ray plates, supplied by Eastman Kodak, for sale to this institution. The sales that resulted induced him to begin soliciting similar business from other hospitals and physicians in the New York City and Long Island area.

He soon sensed a second need of these customers for a wide and steadily increasing variety of radiological accessory devices, most of which were being produced by small machine shops and other experimenters and thus were hard to come by. James Picker decided to become a reliable and available source of this equipment, expanding far beyond his activities as primarily a plate supplier.

The ambitious young man established that business through seven-days-a-week, around-the-clock service to his customers. He sold himself to them as a "one-stop" source for all their requirements for x-ray plates, accessories, sundries and supplies. He then published the first complete catalog of x-ray supplies, with firm delivery guarantees and quoted prices on everything. He not only sold equipment, he devised many improvements in the crude items of the day and induced his suppliers to manufacture the better products to his specifications. Among these were lead rubber gloves, to protect radiological operators from x-ray "burns," on which he held the patent. Another was the development of equipment and a technique for one of the first safe methods for administering the drug employed in gall bladder visualization. He also pioneered in the replacement of flammable x-ray film, which had been responsible for several tragic fires, with safety film. In due course, he also became a sales agent for basic x-ray apparatus itself.

In 1929, just as the world-wide depression struck, Picker bought the crippled Waite and Bartlett X-Ray Manufacturing Company, located in Long Island City, New York. The early years were a tremendous struggle. Here is the account of this period by an early Picker employee:

> The manufacturing division was established in the very early days of the Depression and this division lost money for four years. They got into the black during the fifth year and have always made more money each year ever since. To begin with, they did not have much operating capital and a lot of time was spent going around and picking up machinery at auction sales. They obtained their desks that way, getting secondhand wooden desks with swivel chairs for as little as $5 a set. During the early days, they had to design their equipment for sale in such a way that it could be manufactured on the machinery they had been able to pick up at distress prices. They couldn't afford castings in those days. When they finally sold the original machinery 20 years later, it brought more trade-in value than they had paid for it originally.

And another employee recalled:

> You know what else? All during the Depression years following the crash, when other firms were dumping people right and left, Mr. Picker never let a single employee go! Said we were all in the same boat, sink or swim. We loved him for it and for countless other examples of his personal concern for all of us. Let a man—or his wife or child—get sick and he'd drop everything to get the best medical help available . . . cost be damned.

While the Waite and Bartlett organization had encountered financial difficulties, it had an outstanding technical reputation when James Picker rescued it. Harry Waite had invented and held all the basic patents that made x-ray apparatus safe from electrical hazards for operators or patients. These safeguards, based on Waite's basic principles, are still employed in all medical, dental and industrial x-ray units. Picker also recognized and expanded on Waite and Bartlett's capacity for designing and producing equipment that was sturdy and reliable.

As a result of Picker's business ability and leadership, success came rapidly. The manufacturing business was moved to a modern plant at Cleveland, a nationwide network of sales agents and distributors was organized, and the Picker name rapidly became a by-word in the radiological field. In World War II, the company was the principal supplier of mobile field x-ray units to the U.S. and Allied forces. This contribution to the war effort was the outgrowth of a letter Harvey Picker wrote to the U.S. Surgeon General soon after the hostilities in Europe had broken out and before the entry of the United States into the war. He offered to make available without cost to the government the services of the entire Picker engineering department to develop any units that it was believed would be needed if the U.S. entered the conflict.

The offer was accepted. Picker's only stipulation was that they be permitted to bid on any contracts for the field unit they were to design but that the award should still go to the lowest bidder. Picker not only carried out the engineering work on the unit at its own expense but also produced a prototype on the same basis. When bids were received, the company was the lowest bidder and received the contract. For several years, it was the government's sole supplier, but when the services felt they should have a second source of supply, Picker trained the second supplier, whose price for the unit was fixed higher than Picker's.

The demand for these rugged units was enormous. Prices held to the original bid, but economies were made possible by rapidly increasing production even in the face of wartime inflation. Thus, profits flowed to the Picker company at a rate that distressed James Picker. He acted with characteristic altruism and simplicity. He simply voluntarily returned to the United States treasury the more than $4 million in profits he did not feel he should retain!

He is quoted as having said at the time: "I did not want to make a profit on men dying. With our fellow Americans and allies being killed in the war, the least we could do was to see that we Pickers did not profit from it." Harvey Picker served for five years on active duty with the U.S. Navy, being mustered out in 1945 as a lieutenant commander.

When Harvey returned from service, he soon assumed the responsibilities of chief executive of the company. Under his direction, it became the nation's largest manufacturer of radiological equipment, introducing such design improvements as automatic controls, effective image amplifiers and the first ceiling tube mounts. He also led the company into the field of clinical nuclear apparatus and later ultrasound diagnostic equipment. The early recognition by Picker of the importance of these fields to medical diagnosis enhanced the company's growth. It holds a leading position in both these areas of advanced technology.

When C.I.T. acquired the Picker organization, it operated manufacturing and engineering facilities in the United States and Canada, with extensive sales and service organizations to back this production capacity. In addition, it had sales representatives in more than seventy other countries. In the medical field, it produced radiological and nuclear equipment and supplies and was experimenting in the development of ultrasound devices for tissue diagnosis. It also produced a broad line of x-ray and radioisotopic devices for use in industry to test and analyze materials and parts. From 1958 to 1966, after the C.I.T. merger, the Picker organization increased its annual sales from $41.5 million to $101.8 million, while net profits rose from $2.2 million to $4.6 million. C.I.T. recovered its entire investment in the company in less than eight years after the purchase.

It is intriguing to speculate what train of circumstances might have come to pass if Mrs. Surut had not permitted the Pickers to inspect her Larchmont house in 1939 or if chance had not intervened a second time to bring the Pickers and the Dietzes together in that Saranac cocktail lounge in 1957. The successful Picker acquisition, through which C.I.T. has contributed materially to medical progress and human welfare, marked the launching of the most sweeping diversification program in C.I.T.'s history. Without it as an excellent beginning, who can say what the course of events might have been?

Another major purchase was closed less than a month after the Picker signing. This involved the North American Accident Insurance Company, with headquarters in Chicago. The consideration was $14.5 million in cash. North American was a seventy-two-year-old writer of life, health and accident insurance, with its life insurance in force at the time exceeding $150 million. It was qualified in all states and was regarded as a conservative institution for which growth had been restrained by its limited depth of management and capitalization.

It was C.I.T.'s announced intention to provide the North American organization with the backing to make it an important factor in the life insurance field. (North American's name was changed to the North

American Company for Life, Accident and Health Insurance on January 1, 1960.) Its development was to be carried out in combination with Patriot Life, which was also increasing its direct life business under the program initiated earlier.

However, on May 2, 1966, Patriot Life was sold. This eliminated many areas of unavoidable duplication with the North American Company, which had far outstripped Patriot in size and earning power. Among these areas were the need to maintain duplicate licensing in the several states as well as parallel and often competing agency organizations, together with the demands on management involved in operating two companies. Lundell said that the North American Company, with more than $1.7 billion of life insurance in force, would henceforth receive the undivided attention of management in the acceleration of its expansion on a nationwide basis.

Not all of the management's aggressive program of diversification depended on purchases of outside entities. In 1960–63, four entries into new fields of endeavor were organized within the company. In 1959, C.I.T. Service Leasing Corporation was launched to lease fleets of automobiles and trucks to business and institutional organizations. This company met with an excellent nationwide reception and has proved to be a thriving source of income virtually from the outset. A parallel motor fleet leasing operation in Canada has been equally successful.

Another project apparently offering much promise was initiated in April 1960 by C.I.T. and the American Express Company. Given the name Unifinanz A. G., and capitalized at $5 million, the company was initially organized to conduct a general financing business in countries of Western Europe, duplicating the U.S. and Canadian operations of C.I.T. Each of the partners owned 50% of the company. The press statement announcing the plans for the enterprise stated:

> The remarkable industrial expansion of Western Europe is creating increased opportunities for consumer and industrial credit facilities. Although European nations have very efficient installment credit structures, our surveys indicate there is a place for the employment of additional amounts of capital and facilities to serve both business and the consuming public.
>
> We expect to work with European manufacturers and distributors, as well as American companies, in financing the installment sales of their products in European markets. The increased movement of funds from nation to nation, in the form of capital investment and trade, has been accelerated by the relaxation of many previously existing barriers to the free flow of commerce. We intend that the new company shall have a

significant role in advancing the internationalization of commercial operations.

This was an endeavor that did not work out in practice, for a variety of reasons, including foreign exchange problems and difficulties in securing satisfactory managerial talent. Two operating units were formed, Universal Kredit Bank, G.N.B.H. in West Germany and Unifinance in Great Britain. C.I.T. purchased the interest of American Express in the joint venture in October 1963. In 1967, the German unit was sold to the Singer Company and the British subsidiary subsequently was liquidated.

In 1960, C.I.T. Leasing Corporation was organized to engage in the leasing of all kinds of industrial and income-producing equipment except motor vehicles. This company shared the management, staff and divisional office facilities of C.I.T. Corporation and has enjoyed outstanding success. It pioneered in developing many forms of leasing that, under certain sets of circumstances, offer benefits and attractions to industrial equipment users that conventional instalment financing arrangements do not. In the first ten years, C.I.T.'s leasing operations booked a volume of business exceeding $800 million. The variety of equipment covered by C.I.T. leasing arrangements in this period was almost limitless. Included were commercial transport aircraft, diesel locomotives, electronic data processing systems, railway passenger and freight cars, marine cargo containers, materials handling equipment, heavy trucks and tractors, company automobile fleets, production machinery, inland and seagoing ships, road-building and construction equipment. A similar and even broader list would be required to describe the capital goods items for which instalment financing, rather than leasing, was arranged.

During this same period, one of the major fields of interest and endeavor for The C.I.T. Foundation, Inc., the corporation's charitable arm, had become the strengthening and advancement of the nation's smaller colleges. These institutions were sorely needed as greatly increased numbers of students seeking post-secondary educational opportunities threatened to overwhelm the educational system in the late fifties and early sixties. To encourage and give recognition to the self-improvement efforts of small, unaccredited institutions to achieve recognition as "accredited" colleges, the Foundation offered to make a $5,000 contribution to each privately supported, four-year liberal arts or business college that earned accreditation. To obtain this grant, the institution also was required to raise an additional $5,000 from business contributors, usually from its immediate geographical area.

This unique program developed a close relationship between the C.I.T. organization and many of these often-struggling institutions. In probing for other ways to assist them, it became clear to the interested C.I.T. people that one of their basic needs was for additional housing facilities. These would permit them to admit more students, secure additional income and bulwark their frequently precarious financial condition.

Almost two years was spent in seeking a practical solution for this pressing problem. It was evident, because of the very large amount of funds that would be required to provide buildings on many campuses, that a philanthropic approach could not work. The buildings would have to pay for themselves. A compact was made with the Aluminum Company of America by which C.I.T. and Alcoa sought to develop a standardized, systematized design approach. Something like "mass production" of college living space was the goal. A prominent architectural group was retained and a design concept completed, but it soon became apparent that local conditions and needs made a standardized design unworkable. The C.I.T.–Alcoa relationship was terminated. Similarly, the acceptance by the college market of residential home-builders' designs, offering low construction costs, was tested but found inadequate.

Finally, an answer to the needs of many institutions emerged early in 1963. C.I.T. Educational Buildings, Inc., a subsidiary organized to engage in the college housing construction market, established an affiliation with a nationwide building design and construction company, Tandy Industries, Inc., of Tulsa, Oklahoma. Under this program, institutions could have dormitories, dining halls and other income-producing buildings designed and produced according to their own specifications, with all costs of the program being combined in a single "package." C.I.T. would be the owner of the buildings, erected on college-owned land, and would collect semi-annual rentals for a maximum period of fifteen years after the buildings were occupied. At the end of the lease period, the institutions would receive quitclaim deeds to the buildings without making any further payments.

No outlays would be made by the institutions until the buildings were occupied and payments were flowing in from room rentals or fees collected from the students. Thus, there was no drain on any other funds of the colleges. Yet the buildings were provided for their use, allowing them to increase their enrollments and offer education to more students.

As years passed, the same program has been applied to the construction and leasing of buildings for private voluntary hospitals. Often, these buildings are used for housing aged or convalescent patients or for physical or mental rehabilitation programs. In recent years, with college and university enrollments stabilizing or declining, the market for student facilities has lessened. The hospital market consequently has become the major source of business for the C.I.T. Buildings subsidiary. Since the inception of the program, projects with a total cost exceeding $100 million have been completed.

The opening of the decade of the sixties saw C.I.T.'s management reach another decision that was to be of the greatest importance to the future of the company's consumer financing operations. This was to make a frontal, resolute entry into the personal instalment loan business. There was an obvious parallel between the company's basic business of financing instalment purchases by the consuming public and the making of cash loans to relatively the same broad segment of the population who bought "on time." Yet, as this narrative has shown, a number of opportunities and proposals to move into the direct loan business had been presented over the years, but none had been permitted to gain more than temporary headway, if they were acted upon at all.

As late as November 1956, a recommendation by a group of Universal C.I.T. executives to launch a beginning into the small loan field through the medium of establishing certain test offices was met with this policy statement: "We are not at this time going to try to build up a large-scale loan operation, nor set up pilot offices."

The idea was not allowed to die, however. By the middle of 1958, a fairly large volume of loans was being booked in certain offices and states, with the automobiles owned by the borrowers serving as collateral. In early September of that year, having received the approval of Dietz and Ittleson, Jr., Walter Lundell called a meeting of his managerial staff and announced that the company would "engage in the business of direct loans and take steps to increase our loan portfolio to realize, more fully, the potential income available." The obtaining of licenses to qualify the branch network to make such loans in all states was authorized. An "ultimate objective" of building a portfolio of $50 million in personal loans was established. At the end of 1958, C.I.T.'s U.S. loan portfolio totaled only $6.1 million, less than one-tenth of that of any of its independent sales finance company competitors.

Against these figures, Henry C. Watkins, then a regional manager, wrote as follows to his superiors:

I do feel that Universal C.I.T. is at a distinct disadvantage with other major competitors in the finance field because of their large loan portfolios producing such a high yield. The more I examine this loan picture and the returns available, the more I am sold that we have got to get going in this loan field with a great deal more speed than we are at present.

The building of this business was centered on regular mailings to individuals on the Universal C.I.T. lists of present and past customers, augmented on occasion by mailings to other lists of credit card holders and the like. Newspaper advertising was tried in some areas and the field staff was given some training and considerable stimulation toward soliciting loan business on a person-to-person basis. Street signs and office posters identifying C.I.T. with the loan business were ordered. Gains began to be made. Although in the past, the enthusiasm of Arthur Dietz for the business had been moderate at best, by late in 1959 the *Wall Street Journal* reported in an interview with him:

> He also reported further gains in the company's small loan business, which was given renewed emphasis during the recent recession when auto lending slid off. Such loans are now offered in 250 of C.I.T. Financial's 400 offices around the country, located in 32 states where the company is licensed to do such business. Personal-loan volume is expected to exceed $20 million this year and to hit between $50 million and $60 million next year, Mr. Dietz said.

While the program of building the loan business from within continued to make steady strides, a new approach came into being in 1960. This was begun by the purchase, in May of that year, of Home Finance Service, Inc., a chain of 36 exclusive loan offices in Louisiana, Mississippi and Georgia.

In the summer of 1962, a second personal loan company was bought. This was an eleven-office chain with $4.5 million in assets operating in Indiana under the name Family Finance, Inc.

Less than a year later, Time Finance Company, another personal loan organization, was brought into the C.I.T. orbit by an exchange of stock. This was a sizable organization of 77 offices operating in Kentucky, Ohio, Illinois, Indiana, Tennessee, Virginia and West Virginia, with loan outstandings of more than $26 million and a certain amount of dealer-originated sales financing business. The consideration, in terms of the current market price of the C.I.T. common shares exchanged, was approximately $17 million.

To move forward and complete the narrative of loan-company acquisitions, two more major transactions occurred, in 1967 and 1970, in addition to a number of purchases of one- or two-office situations.

The 1967 acquisition was the largest in the loan-company purchase program. Laurentide Finance Corporation of America, operating 133 local offices in California, Oregon and Nevada and holding loans outstanding of $80 million, was bought for a cash consideration of $8 million from Canadian interests. Practically all of the new offices were located in communities where Universal C.I.T. had not been represented. The Laurentide organization operated autonomously for a time but in due course was absorbed into the C.I.T. office system.

In a most important respect, the Laurentide acquisition differed from any of the earlier personal loan company purchases. All of these had been healthy, going concerns with effective management organizations in place. In the case of Laurentide, however, the company had encountered serious operating difficulties and for several years had been losing money for its owners. Their disenchantment with its operations was the reason they wished to dispose of it.

C.I.T.'s management was completely aware of what it was buying and drove a hard bargain, despite the great attractiveness of acquiring such an extensive network of local offices in an excellent market. Once the purchase was made, the difficult task of restructuring and rebuilding the business was undertaken and brought to a very successful conclusion after several years of great effort. Roy L. Cook, a veteran member of the Universal C.I.T. organization, played the primary role in this accomplishment.

The company's important Canadian personal loan operations, which had expanded steadily through internal development, received strong reinforcement in October 1970. The branch network of Canadian Acceptance Corporation was more than doubled in number by the addition of 96 Canadian offices of General Acceptance Corporation, a substantial loan and discount finance company, which retained its U.S. offices. In addition to the Canadian branches, C.I.T. obtained the 16 units "G.A.C." had operated in Puerto Rico, where C.I.T. already had well-established operations. In all, C.I.T.'s loan portfolio was expanded by $50 million in Canada and $9.5 million in Puerto Rico.

In the twelve-year span from 1958, when the building of its personal loan business began, to the end of 1970, C.I.T. increased its personal loan portfolio more than a hundredfold—from $6 million to $700 million. The purchase program had immediately brought in nearly $200 million in receivables outstanding. But vigorous internal efforts, backed by a tremendous investment in recruiting personnel, heavy promotional outlays and a continuing drive to obtain additional offices to reach more prospective clients, were responsible for more than two-thirds of the growth. The company had become one of the largest factors in the consumer loan business in the United States and Canada. Late in 1974, the personal loan portfolio passed the $1 billion mark and was by a large margin the major component of C.I.T.'s business and consumer financing and leasing division.

As internal diversification and expansion continued in the 1960's, so did growth through additional acquisitions of a widely varying character. With the Picker investment a proven success, by the beginning of the sixties, the key management group of Ittleson, Jr., Lundell and Ecker, with the encouragement of Dietz and Vogel, initiated a calculated but in no way precipitous program of entry into new areas of corporate diversification.

The rationale for this decision was at least twofold. As one of the participants later recalled, there was partly the subconscious (or at least unadmitted) recognition that the establishment of Ford Motor Credit and Chrysler Credit, as well as the unremitting intensity of bank competition, increased the vulnerability of the company's reliance on its massive automobile sales financing operations. This insight is the more remarkable because the years 1964 and 1965 were to be among the best in the company's history in the amount of new retail auto business placed on the books. In both years, the volume of this financing exceeded the $1 billion level.

The second motivation was a determination to maximize the employment of the company's available raw material—money. With earned surplus being increased, through retention of earnings, at an annual rate of $20 million to $25 million per year, leveraged borrowing capability on an ultraconservative basis was rising at an annual rate of well over $100 million. To the extent that these available funds could be put to work in the corporation's existing lines of business, this was all to the good, but despite the steady growth of these activities, they could not absorb nearly all of the readily available resources.

This borrowing power, if allowed to remain unused, might be compared to idle plant capacity in a manufacturing enterprise. The Picker venture having turned out so well, it was an obvious course to seek out additional opportunities for putting funds to work outside the company's traditional lines of financing and insurance as well as within them.

The management let it be known in various quarters of the banking and investment world that C.I.T. was prepared to consider additional acquisitions of either a financial or manufacturing character. These would take the form of cash purchases preferably, but exchange-of-stock transactions were not to be ruled out if the situation in question appeared to offer a reasonable opportunity to inject additional working capital on a profitable basis.

Proposals of many kinds began to flow in as word of this readiness to "take a look" at any worthwhile acquisition was circulated. Initially, Stanley Ecker's office became the clearinghouse for such offers, and over a period of perhaps five years, more than 200 candidates for purchase were given serious consideration.

The first transaction to be brought to a successful conclusion under this program was the purchase of Gibson Greeting Cards, Inc., for $36.5 million in cash in March of 1964. The original printing and publishing business out of which Gibson grew had been established in Cincinnati in 1850, making it the nation's oldest active greeting card manufacturer.

The company got its start when the family of George Gibson, a Scottish lithographer, emigrated to the United States and traveled inland by the Erie and other canals until they settled in Cincinnati. They had with them on their journey a small French-made lithography press. Four sons, aged 12 to 23, decided to settle there, while the father, mother and two daughters went on to St. Louis. Using the press, the boys established the business of Gibson & Company, lithographers.

They printed such items as stationery with patriotic designs and messages, honor and reward cards for schools and Sunday schools, Valentine novelties and the like. The company branched into the jobbing of the products of others by distributing the popular Currier & Ives prints during the 1870's and then began to make its own prints. It also took on the jobbing of the first line of actual Christmas and New Year's greeting cards, which had first been developed by L. Prang & Company, a Boston color lithographer, about 1866. Within five years, Prang was selling five million such cards a year.

Soon after they began distributing Prang's products in the Ohio-Kentucky area, the Gibsons began designing and producing their own cards. In 1883, Robert Gibson, who had been 14 when the company was established and who was the business manager of the four, bought out his brothers and was the sole proprietor of the company until his death in 1895. The name of the company was later changed to the Gibson Art Company. A history of the company goes on:

> The second generation of Gibsons came into the picture just about the time that a rash of cheap imitative imports was undercutting the domestic market. Even Prang was forced to abandon his greeting card activities and concentrate on more profitable areas.

> The Gibson corporation weathered this period of decline, however, and saw a rebirth of the greeting card industry in the country after 1907. From that time until 1920 the growth of the industry was gradual, but with the ending of World War I the demand for greeting cards rose sharply, and many new companies entered the field. The resulting competition led to important innovations in printing processes, art techniques and decorative or "finishing" treatments. Gibson, for instance, popularized the so-called French fold—one sheet of paper folded in half twice— which remains as today's most utilized greeting card form.

> By 1930 the greeting card business was firmly established in the United States, and it came through the Depression in better shape than most industries. One reason for this was that while many people couldn't afford expensive presents on special occasions, they could afford greeting cards. The post-World War II period has brought increasingly sophisticated printing, embossing and finishing techniques, making for better and better cards with every passing year.

At the time of the C.I.T. purchase, Gibson was the third largest organization in the U.S. greeting card business and had reported sales of more than $26 million for 1963, with net earnings of $1.8 million. It was engaged not only in the production of conventional lines of greeting cards for all seasons but also in distributing foreign language cards, special designs of cards for supermarkets and discount stores and a full line of gift wrappings.

The impact of C.I.T.'s ownership on the expansion of Gibson's business was demonstrated within a few months when, in November 1964, Cleo Wrap Corporation was acquired through an exchange of stock. Ownership of Cleo Wrap was obtained for 52,500 C.I.T. common shares, which had a market value at the time of approximately $1.9 million. The Cleo Wrap business, located in Memphis, broadened the Gibson line of products and has been an excellent contributor to Gibson's profitability. C.I.T. funds have made possible several plant expansions and the installation of ultra-modern production equipment.

As with its other acquisitions, C.I.T. maintained the existing Gibson organization in place after the purchase. Maxwell C. Weaver, who had headed the company for a number of years, continued as president and later chairman of the board until his 1970 retirement. He was also elected to the C.I.T. Financial board of directors.

34

— Into Banking
and Other Endeavors

The largest investment, and that with the greatest future consequence in the execution of the external diversification program, was initiated in February 1965 when C.I.T. made a public tender offer for all of the shares of the Meadow Brook National Bank. With these shares trading in the $24 range, C.I.T. offered to pay $31.75 per share for each of the 3,645,000 outstanding shares, which would bring the total consideration to $106.7 million if all shares were tendered.

At the time, Meadow Brook was a leading suburban bank in the New York metropolitan area, with most of its operations centered on Long Island. It had 66 branch offices. Its deposits of $754 million and assets of $869 million at the 1964 year-end made it the 45th largest bank in the nation. It had earned $5.9 million in 1964, for an 18% increase over the previous year.

The decision to make an open bid for tenders to the bank's stockholders, was reached by the C.I.T. group only after lengthy debate and soul-searching.

There were many forces at work in this situation. First of all, the idea of obtaining a stake in the commercial banking business had become a very appealing one to C.I.T.'s managers. As Henry Ittleson,

Jr., put it in a later interview, "I told A.O.D. we were losing so much business to the banks—they were going into so many of our lines of business that they wouldn't touch in the past—such as auto financing, accounts receivable and construction equipment financing, all kinds of loans collateralized just by machinery and equipment—that I thought that if we could buy a bank on a good basis, we ought to do it. If we did so, we would no longer be dependent solely on our mode of getting the business for we would also have the bank's mode of getting it. Dietz agreed." As for Lundell, he was an enthusiastic supporter of the idea, with only Ecker being a possibly stronger advocate.

For any bank with a broad base of ownership, it would have been virtually impossible to initiate purchase negotiations without expecting immediate leaks that would be likely to drive up the price of the stock and perhaps affect the market action of C.I.T.'s securities as well. Moreover, it was recognized that any bank's management or major stockholders would probably be reluctant to engage in serious discussions, leading to a commitment to sell the shares they controlled, without disclosing the fact to their general shareholder body. Thus, secrecy within the C.I.T. organization seemed essential until a decision could be reached to make an offer.

But the idea of being labeled as "raiders" by making a purchase offer without the sanction of the management involved also seemed repugnant to the C.I.T. executives. They did not intend to unseat or disrupt the management of any institution they might purchase, any more than they had done with the other organizations they had acquired and smoothly meshed into their overall corporate structure. They wished only to make an open offer, at a fair price, that the owners of the bank's shares individually could accept or reject as they saw fit.

Early in 1964, while these considerations were being discussed within C.I.T.'s innermost management circles, Ecker received a telephone call from an investment house specializing in bank securities. This was in response to the general interest C.I.T. had expressed in considering additional company purchases. The caller told Ecker that a certain bank in the Detroit area might be available.

Ecker replied that C.I.T. would prefer to buy a New York area institution because it would be "easier to watch." Also, New York was the nation's money center, seemingly offering greater growth possibilities than would most regional environments. A proposal then followed that the Meadow Brook Bank be considered.

This suggestion seemed to have possibilities and one brief meeting was arranged with Sidney Friedman, chairman of the bank. Friedman expressed no interest whatsoever in going forward with any discussions. On the heels of this meeting, word was leaked by a source that has never been identified that C.I.T. was considering the purchase of Meadow Brook. Meadow Brook's stock began to move up in price and representatives of the daily press as well as certain investment analysts began calling C.I.T. officials to check on the rumor.

As there had been no decision to pursue the matter further, in view of Friedman's attitude, Henry Ittleson, Jr., issued this statement:

> C.I.T. has not made any offer for stock of Meadow Brook National Bank either directly or through anyone else, nor does it intend to make any such offer. Neither C.I.T. nor any of its subsidiaries presently own, nor have we ever owned, any shares of this bank.

That forthright denial quieted all rumors. However, as a result of the leak, coupled with the outcome of the Friedman meeting that indicated the bank's management would oppose an offer, Lundell and his associates then dropped any thoughts of buying the bank.

Months passed and nearly a year later the same bank stock specialist expressed the belief that, with certain changed circumstances, Meadow Brook's management would be unlikely to oppose an attractive offer. Furthermore, he was close to a group that held some 300,000 of the bank's shares, or nearly 10% of those outstanding, which would like to dispose of them.

The C.I.T. officials again appraised the potential of the purchase of Meadow Brook and decided to make another try for a meeting with the bank's management. This attempt came to nothing.

Their study of the situation had shown that Meadow Brook National Bank traced its beginning to the founding of the First National Bank of Merrick (Long Island) in 1924. It was initially capitalized at $25,000, local residents putting up the money. The leader of the group was Frank Wolfe, a vice president of a large New York City bank. The bank flourished until the Bank Holiday of 1933, when only a rescue effort by the Reconstruction Finance Corporation enabled it to reopen its doors.

The bank then had two presidents within a year. With the position vacant, Augustus B. Weller, who had been a bond salesman and worked in advertising and who was a local civic leader, was invited to take the presidency. He had no banking experience whatever.

The bank then had six employees and a total annual payroll of $9,800. Weller's first move, despite the shaky condition of the finances, was to raise salaries. "I wanted to get rid of their 'public be damned' attitude," he said in later years.

"Gus" Weller was an iconoclastic banker in many other ways, but the institution flourished under his homespun leadership. In 1949, with the economy of Long Island booming and the population soaring, he decided on a policy of growth through mergers and acquisitions. The first was with the First National Bank and Trust Company of Freeport. The name selected for the new institution was "Meadowbrook" Bank. Two months later, the form "Meadow Brook" was adopted for reasons of historical accuracy. These were the first two English words to appear on a map designating the area of Long Island. The map, otherwise in Dutch, was prepared in 1657.

Weller moved forward boldly, opening scores of new branches and putting through a series of mergers that numbered seventeen in the sixteen remaining years of his presidency. Most important of these were the simultaneous acquisitions of the Queens National Bank and Colonial Trust Company in 1960. Both of these institutions were located within New York City, giving Meadow Brook the distinction of being the first suburban bank to establish itself in the metropolis. In 1962, Meadow Brook became the dominant bank in Suffolk County when it absorbed the sizable Bank of Huntington.

During Weller's regime the bank's ranking, in terms of assets, among all banks in the nation had moved upward from 7,002nd place to 43rd. It was in 1964 that Weller retired and was succeeded by Sidney Friedman, who had been Meadow Brook's general counsel as a member of its law firm. Friedman had had extensive experience in dealing with the liquidation of insolvent banks during the 1930's as a member of the staff of the Reconstruction Finance Corporation.

Whether Friedman and his associates would oppose a tender offer or not and before any new leaks could occur, C.I.T.'s executives decided to go ahead with their plans. A special meeting of the board of directors was called overnight for the morning of February 25, 1965. The terms of the tender offer, as they had been worked out by the management, were approved.

A telephone call was immediately placed to Friedman, notifying him of C.I.T.'s projected action and an announcement of the tender plans was released to the Dow Jones news service and the press. The next day's financial pages carried major stories announcing C.I.T.'s desire to enter the banking business.

The *Wall Street Journal* published this report of the bank management's initial reaction:

> Meadow Brook National Bank's management yesterday advised stockholders to withhold any acceptance of C.I.T. Financial Corp.'s offer to purchase the bank's shares until after a directors' meeting of the bank to be held Sunday.

C.I.T., the large diversified finance company, offered Wednesday to purchase all of the 3,645,134 outstanding shares of Meadow Brook at a net price of $31.75 a share. Before the C.I.T. offer was made known, the bank's stock traded over the counter at $25.25 bid and $25.75 asked. Yesterday the stock was quoted at $28.75 bid and $29.50 asked. This was up 25 cents from Wednesday's closing bid price.

In an interview yesterday a spokesman for Meadow Brook's management, didn't give any clue to directors' feelings about the offer. He said, "Right now none of the bank's management has any feelings about this, and they'll be careful not to express any until next Sunday's meeting." Bank officials on Wednesday said they were "surprised" by the offer.

However, two insurgent directors elected to the bank's 19-man board early in 1964 said they were in favor of accepting C.I.T.'s offer. These two directors representing minority stockholders are Dudley L. Miller, a New York City lawyer, and Jack Lyons, identified as associated with the Bloomingdale family interests.

Mr. Miller said, "The price is very fair and it ought to be carefully considered by the directors Sunday." He said he hadn't yet spoken to Meadow Brook's management to assess their reaction to the offer.

Mr. Lyons said, "We expect to tender the substantial holdings of the Bloomingdale interests." He declined, however, to recommend this position to other stockholders. "Every stockholder has to decide for himself whether to accept this offer and no one—not even the bank's management—has the right to take the position of investment adviser in this matter."

Spokesmen for two large securities houses said they think the offer by C.I.T. is "generous." C.I.T. itself said reaction was "favorable" from broker-dealers. "Brokers have called us and asked for forms by which they can accept the offer," said a C.I.T. spokesman.

C.I.T. said it plans to buy all Meadow Brook shares tendered if tenders total at least 3 million shares. The offer will expire March 19 but may be extended until April 16, C.I.T. said.

At their Sunday meeting, the bank's directors decided to tender their own shares but withheld any recommendation either for or against the offer to the general stockholder body. However, the financial press immediately agreed that the directors' personal acceptance, combined with the large block already committed, virtually assured the success of the C.I.T. tender.

This proved to be the case. By March 21, C.I.T. announced that it was tabulating acceptance forms as rapidly as possible and that at least 60% of the outstanding shares had already been tendered. It extended its offer to April 30 and announced that it would accept all the shares that had been tendered. By April 30, 90% of the shares had been tendered and a further extension of the offer to June 1 was made. Eventually, the number of shares received by way of the tender offer reached 97%. By the end of 1972, all of the stock had been acquired by C.I.T.

To a newspaperman's question as to why the tender-offer route of purchase had been adopted, a C.I.T. spokesman gave this answer:

> There were two, about equally important reasons for asking for tenders of the bank's stock from the shareholders. In the first place, this was by far the most practical and expeditious way to establish our ownership of the bank, as we hoped to do. Secondly, it was the democratic way.
>
> By offering each stockholder the opportunity to decide freely for himself whether he wished to sell his investment in the bank or to hold it, we avoided imposing our will, or the will of any majority, on a minority group. By seeking tenders, we permit each individual stockholder to express and exercise his own preference in the matter.

In a special message to C.I.T.'s stockholders when the tender offer had been made final, Walter Lundell prophetically said this:

> We have every confidence that this investment will prove to be an excellent one for your Corporation. It will contribute to our future earning power, to our diversification and to the profitable employment of more of our available resources. We intend to operate the Bank as an autonomous member of the C.I.T. family of companies, with its present management organization and experienced staff. We will also devote our best efforts toward maintaining the Bank as the fine institution it has been in the past and toward aiding it to make ever-greater contributions to the business and industrial life of the many communities it serves.

Early in March, to allay any misgivings among the bank's officers and staff as to the impact on them of the C.I.T. purchase, Lundell addressed a letter of reassurance addressed to Friedman as chairman of the bank. Copies of this were distributed to every employee. Lundell said:

> I want to assure you that each present employee of the Bank will be retained in the employment of the Bank for a minimum of one year from the date when our ownership may become effective, subject only to the right of the Board of Directors of the Bank, in the necessary exercise of its responsibilities, to terminate any employee for sufficient cause. This statement does not imply that there will be any change in the above pol-

icy at the end of the one-year period. Recognizing that the fine personnel organization of the Bank is its most important asset, we believe that the maintenance of the present staff relationships is essential if the Bank is to continue to operate with the same success that is has enjoyed in the past.

With the acquisition an accomplished fact, Friedman carried on as chairman and chief executive and the employment of all other individuals was continued in accordance with Lundell's pledge. All members of the bank's board of directors also held their seats. Five C.I.T. officers—Ittleson, Jr., Lundell, Holmes, Dow and Richardson—were added to the board.

Friedman continued to direct the affairs of the bank and played a major part in its growth both internally and through the acquisition of other banks until his retirement at the close of 1972. He was named to the C.I.T. Financial board of directors soon after the bank acquisition became effective.

The magnitude and complexity of the Meadow Brook transaction did not interfere with progress in other phases of the acquisition program. To enlarge and diversify the place of Canadian Acceptance Corporation in the economy of Canada, at the end of June 1965 C.I.T. made an offer to purchase for a cash consideration of $8 million all of the stock of Holt, Renfrew and Company, Limited, one of Canada's oldest and leading quality apparel, fur and specialty retailing organizations. The company, which had been founded in 1837, operated eight metropolitan stores in principal cities and ten branch shops in suburban shopping centers and major hotels. Its 1964 sales had been a record $18.2 million.

The management of Holt, Renfrew endorsed the offer and announced they would tender the large share of the outstanding stock that the officers and directors personally controlled. The transaction was successfully completed before the end of the summer.

To complete the Holt, Renfrew story at this point, C.I.T., through Canadian Acceptance, invested considerable amounts of funds in the expansion of the business over the next few years, opening additional stores, modernizing others and increasing the volume of sales and profitability of the enterprise. However, by 1971 it was apparent that the store chain occupied a role of only minor significance in the overall and continually expanding C.I.T. business as it was the company's sole retailing component and had only limited prospects for further expansion. Yet it was a valuable and attractive property and was certain to command an excellent selling price if it were to be offered to a buyer primarily engaged in retailing in the United States and/or Canada. Thus, Holt, Renfrew was sold at an excellent profit to Carter Hawley Hale Stores, Inc., the prominent U.S. retailing organization.

In the last half of 1965, negotiations were going forward for the purchase of another major manufacturing enterprise. This one was brought to a successful conclusion unlike many others that failed for one reason or another. The company was All-Steel Equipment, Inc., headquartered in Aurora, Illinois, a major producer of metal office furniture and electrical installation components and fittings. The Goldman, Sachs investment banking firm and a major Chicago bank were the intermediaries in arranging the transaction.

The plan to acquire all of the stock—closely held and unlisted on any exchange—of All-Steel for a cash price of $35.5 million was announced on January 10, 1966. Lundell welcomed the development with a statement that All-Steel would be "an important acquisition for C.I.T. in terms of sales and earning power. We have great confidence in the future of the business and the contribution it will make." The following years have borne out that prediction.

In addition to its main plant at Aurora, employing more than 1,000, the company operated another major unit at South Bend, Indiana, through a subsidiary known as RACO. RACO is the nation's leading producer of switch, outlet and junction boxes, with allied fittings and tools, for the electrical contracting industry. All-Steel is one of the three principal companies in office furniture manufacturing. In subsequent years, through the use of funds made available by C.I.T., a second furniture plant and warehouse was constructed at Hazelton, Pennsylvania, and the company's operations were expanded into Canada, where a substantial operation now exists.

Originally bearing the awkward name of Allsteelequip Company, the enterprise had been founded in Aurora in 1912 by three men, George Hurteau, Axel Nelson and Charles H. Lembcke, who each put up $1,000 to provide the firm's capital. All three had worked for the well-known Lyon Metal Products, Inc., of Aurora, today a major competitor of All-Steel. Hurteau had been plant superintendent, Nelson a punch press foreman and Lembcke a shipping clerk.

They soon had ten people working in their small, meagerly equipped plant. Its products were simple electrical cut-out boxes, shop tote boxes and other metal containers, turned out largely on custom orders from customers.

After a falling out, his partners barred Lembcke from the plant at the beginning of the 1914 Christmas holiday. Lembcke's answer was to recruit Axel F. Erickson, a Lyon foreman, as his production man and to secure the financial backing of John Knell, the well-to-do president of the Aurora Brewing Company, to buy out his recalcitrant associates. Knell became an active participant in the business, as its president.

With Knell's resources and credit standing, the struggling business forged ahead rapidly. A new and better plant was occupied in 1917, the beginning of a sales force was organized and lines of steel factory equipment and components produced for other manufacturers were constantly broadened. These included stoker housings, water cooling cabinets, kitchen cabinets, food lockers and miscellaneous sheet metal parts for General Electric, International Business Machines and others. The RACO organization was purchased in 1933, greatly strengthening the electrical fittings business.

From its production of cabinets and lockers, All-Steel gravitated into the office file cabinet business. Since its file customers also had needs for desks and other office furniture, All-Steel began to supply them by buying these items from other manufacturers. At the start of World War II, the company was preparing to launch the production of its own desk and chair designs.

During the war, all civilian production was shelved for the job of turning out military materiel—ammunition boxes, fuse casings, metal lockers and the like. With the return of peace, however, All-Steel brought forth its original steel desk line in 1947, offering an unrivaled interchangeability of parts. Soon, chairs, bookcases, telephone stands, credenzas and other office furnishings were added.

Lembcke had retired in 1933, but Knell continued at the helm of the company, as president, until 1955. He was succeeded in that year by Karl P. Grube, vice president-engineering, who had been with the company since 1948. Grube was an aeronautical engineer with a proven record in that industry.

In 1963, all of All-Steel's Aurora operations and offices were concentrated in one place through the construction of a wholly modern headquarters and plant immediately south of the city's municipal limits.

Following the customary pattern, the existing management team of All-Steel at the time of the purchase was not disturbed and a highly compatible relationship with the rest of the C.I.T. organization was developed. Grube, president and later chairman of the company until his retirement in 1973, became a member of the C.I.T. board of directors.

There were transactions of major importance that were never completed during the Lundell Decade as well as those that were.

The purchases of General Felt Industries, Inc., a large manufacturer of carpet padding and other felt products, and of American Optical Company were two transactions brought close to fruition in the early sixties but which foundered for a combination of reasons.

In September 1967, an agreement in principle was announced by C.I.T. and Grosset & Dunlap, the major book publishers, through which C.I.T. was to purchase all of the shares of the publishing firm for a $46 million cash consideration. Seventy percent of the Grosset & Dunlap shares were held by five other large publishing houses: Book-of-the-Month-Club, Inc., Crowell, Collier and Macmillan, Harper & Row, Little, Brown & Company and Random House. Included in the proposed purchase was Bantam Books, the large paperback publisher, which was a Grosset & Dunlap subsidiary.

The announcement stated that the agreement was subject to "preparation of a definitive contract and fulfillment of certain conditions." Among the latter was the appraisal by C.I.T. legal representatives of the potential liability represented by certain lawsuits that were pending against Grosset & Dunlap. The outcome of these investigations was disappointing. There also was a growing conviction in the minds of Lundell and his associates that the popular publishing field was not for them. They saw publishing's reliance on personal flair and judgment approaching a kind of genius and felt that the individuals guiding such an enterprise would be most difficult to integrate with C.I.T.'s financially oriented management philosophy. After several months, it was decided to withdraw from the initial agreement.

The next aborted effort occurred just before and over the July Fourth holiday weekend of 1968. Late in June, the Hughes Tool Company, the oil-drilling equipment and aircraft manufacturing concern controlled by the reclusive and unpredictable Howard Hughes, had publicly offered to buy at least two million shares, or more than 42% of those outstanding, of the American Broadcasting Companies, Inc. The broadcasting company's board and management reacted angrily to this proposal. Leonard H. Goldenson, the president, declared the company would fight the Hughes offer in the courts.

As it happened, Goldenson and Walter Lundell had met on several occasions and had pursued friendly talks about a possible C.I.T.-ABC relationship. These had not focused on an outright merger of the two corporations but had been centered more on the possible purchase by C.I.T. of certain ABC nonbroadcasting subsidiaries. It was thought, for example, that a particular magazine subsidiary might offer opportunities for C.I.T., through mailing lists, to promote the direct sale of its life and health insurance and perhaps the consumer loan business.

The sudden Hughes bid triggered an immediate renewal of the

Lundell-Goldenson discussions, but now they were focused on an out-right merger. The ABC group unhesitatingly expressed their prefer-ence for C.I.T. over Hughes as a partner. There was much good will and enthusiasm on both sides during hastily called meetings over the holiday weekend, including an unusual Sunday meeting of as many C.I.T. directors as could be reached.

However, the specter of Hughes and the absolute impossibility of predicting his response to a proposed C.I.T.–ABC merger hung over the negotiations. Some members of the C.I.T. group were unalterably opposed to inviting a knockdown public contest with Hughes. There was also the prospect that, no matter what agreements the C.I.T. and ABC managements would arrive at, Hughes might not withdraw his bid for ABC shares and could conceivably end up as a third, and unwelcome, partner. Finally, there was the proposal of the ABC side that it should be the surviving company in the merger, even though under the terms proposed the C.I.T. stockholder group would hold by far the largest investment in the new enterprise. In the end, the combi-nation of these adverse considerations outweighed all possible favora-ble factors. At noon on Monday, July 8, C.I.T. and ABC issued this terse announcement, the first public acknowledgment that their talks had been under way:

> The Board of Directors of ABC Companies, Inc. and C.I.T. Financial Corporation have decided not to proceed at this time with negotiations looking toward a combination of their businesses.

The summer of 1968 had hardly ended when another C.I.T. merger development struck the financial world with stunning force. Just after the noon hour on Friday, September 27, Xerox Corporation and C.I.T. announced that a "combination" of Xerox and C.I.T. was being negotiated, that the managements of both companies regarded the transaction with favor and that approval of the boards of directors of both companies would be sought.

Business Week termed the merger-to-be "the largest in corporate his-tory and the biggest stock market transaction in history." Terms of the agreement called for Xerox to offer one of its shares, trading at a cur-rent market price of about $276, for each 3⅞ shares of C.I.T. com-mon. C.I.T. had been selling at about $48 prior to the offer and the exchange terms would place a new market value, in terms of the price of Xerox shares, of $71.42 on the stock. C.I.T.'s shareholders would receive a total of $1.5 billion in Xerox stock for their company. The market value of their holdings prior to the offer was about $900 million.

Trading in C.I.T. stock was halted on Friday, prior to the announcement of the offer. When it opened on the following Monday, the price quickly rose above $59 a share. Xerox shares fell in price, dropping below $270.

Xerox, of course, had been one of the prime stock market favorites because it had dominated the photocopying business for more than a decade and had grown in sales volume at a rate almost without precedent. It had also diversified into the information transmission, education and aerospace fields. The price of its stock had increased more than 1000% between 1963 and 1968.

The attractions of the merger to those with C.I.T. interests were simple and straightforward ones. There would be an immediate substantial enhancement in the market value of their investments because the Xerox offer would give them the equivalent of $70 or more in Xerox stock for each C.I.T. share (against a market value of less than $50 a share for their holdings before the offer was made). Secondly, they would be joining forces with an organization generally thought to have as excellent a growth record and growth prospects as those of any major U.S. corporation.

For the Xerox side, C. Peter McColough, its president, put the case this way in the initial public announcement of the proposed transaction:

> Xerox today has more significant opportunities for worldwide growth and diversification than ever before. A merger of Xerox and C.I.T. would provide a much broader base than we now enjoy, thus enabling us to accelerate our plans in several promising fields. I refer to such fields as education, health, more advanced and complex systems of graphic communications and fields related to information systems and services. The merger also would permit us to participate in C.I.T.'s most significant function, that of serving the economy's ever-increasing need to finance consumers, industry, transportation systems, educational facilities and other fields.
>
> Furthermore, C.I.T., which is a widely diversified financial institution, has steadily increased its earnings for 16 consecutive years and is engaged in many activities which are consistent with the objectives of Xerox. I sincerely believe this merger would mark the beginning of a new, progressive era in the history of both companies.

Wall Street analysts pointed out that the addition of C.I.T.'s resources of $3.7 billion, as shown on the corporate balance sheet but which did not include another $2 billion in unconsolidated assets of the banking and manufacturing subsidiaries, to Xerox's $800 million would create one of the largest industrial corporations in the American economy. Revenues on an annual basis would top $1.5 billion and earnings $160 million. On a *pro forma* basis, it was pointed out that the merger would add approximately $1.25 a share to the $4.45 Xerox actually had earned in 1967.

The transaction was the brainchild of a free-lance financial consultant specializing in mergers, Jonathan De Sola Mendes, working with Robert S. Johnson, who had just left C.I.T., after seven years as a vice president closely involved with the diversification program, to join a New York investment house.

They decided the two companies would be an excellent match and that a move by Xerox could be made financially attractive to the owners of both. Early in 1968, the partners took their proposal to the Xerox chief executive, laying out a broad and detailed plan for handling it. The Xerox people studied this material for several weeks and then signified their interest in meeting with their C.I.T. counterparts and moving forward if possible.

The proposal and the fact that Xerox was interested was then transmitted to Lundell, as chairman and chief executive. Henry Ittleson, Jr., and Walter Holmes, who had assumed the presidency in July. Lundell agreed to meet with McColough and that first meeting occurred on September 20. The first Xerox offer, based on the analysis by Mendes and Johnson, was an exchange of $4^1/_5$ C.I.T. shares for each Xerox share. Lundell rejected this and asked for a much more favorable price. Without undue haggling, it appeared that a compromise of 3% C.I.T. shares for one Xerox share could be acceptable to both parties.

These negotiations took just a week. The transaction-to-be was announced on the following Friday after that first Friday meeting. This was fast work, but the talks did not need to be extended while each company studied the other because both companies enjoyed unquestioned financial status and reputation.

Technicians representing every aspect of corporate management and operations were put to work by both companies to hammer out the detailed plans for the merger. The press followed the merger prospects of the two companies with continuous stories, and the financial advisory professionals turned out numerous analytical studies on the subject.

The end came as suddenly and unexpectedly as the beginning. On November 13, a Wednesday, the following joint announcement was made:

> Termination by mutual agreement of all negotiations that might lead to a merger of Xerox Corporation and C.I.T. Financial Corporation was an-

nounced today by C. Peter McColough, president and chief executive officer of Xerox and L. Walter Lundell, chairman of the board and chief executive officer of C.I.T.

It was stated that no further comment will be available from either corporation.

. . . And none was. The press launched a frenzied effort to get the facts on why the transaction had foundered and there was a riot of speculation. Some "observers" concluded that Xerox had initiated the breakoff, and there were about as many guesses that C.I.T. was responsible. The individuals involved had pledged themselves to keep their motives and their final discussions confidential, and this pledge has never been violated.

As for the price of C.I.T. common stock, the highest it reached during the Xerox period was 60 on the first trading day after the news broke. The price remained in the 54-57 range during the following weeks and closed at 55⅜ on the day before the termination was announced. After a halt in trading prior to the announcement of the end of negotiations, it opened at 47⅜ on November 15.

35

Building a
Major Bank

The acquisition of Meadow Brook National Bank in the spring and summer of 1965 was one of the most momentous forward strides ever to be taken by C.I.T., both in terms of the size of the investment and the contribution made to the management's diversification grand plan. However, it was only a beginning.

When the bank became part of C.I.T., it was operating 66 branches, almost all on Long Island, with scattered representation in Queens and Brooklyn in New York City. Its assets exceeded $870 million. Earnings in the prior year of 1964 had been $4.2 million. The headquarters was in West Hempstead, Long Island, and the bank was known as an unequivocally "retail" operation, serving a mixed suburban-rural clientele.

With the financial backing and leadership that C.I.T. began to contribute as soon as its control was established, the bank's resources grew within a five-year span to $2.2 billion at the end of 1970. The number of branches had nearly doubled to 115. Net earnings for the year were $20.3 million. The headquarters had been moved in 1968 to its own premises in a 24-floor building at 44 Wall Street, in the center of the Manhattan financial district. The bank was well on its way, by reason

The 44 Wall Street Building

of additional management personnel and changes of direction, to becoming an established national and indeed international institution.

The first important move under the C.I.T. aegis was the merger of the Bank of North America into Meadow Brook. North America was essentially a Manhattan-based institution, with a total of 16 branches and assets of more than $400 million. Its acquisition thus made a major contribution to the movement of the C.I.T. bank into the New York City money center.

North America had its beginning in 1924 in midtown New York City as an "industrial" bank, the Modern Investment and Loan Corporation. This type of bank was one organized under New York State laws as a specialized consumer-loan institution, despite the name that was applied to the classification. A number of other industrial loan organizations were taken over by the bank in following years. In 1958, a small New York City commercial bank with an imposing name—Bank of North America—was purchased and the name adopted for the entire institution. More mergers with commercial banks in Brooklyn, Queens and on suburban Long Island followed.

The merger of Meadow Brook and North America was completed early in May 1967. C.I.T. issued to North America's stockholders a total of 338,358 shares of a new issue of $100 preferred stock, convertible into C.I.T. common at a rate of one preferred share for 2½ shares of common. The convertibility offer extended to the end of 1976. The consideration, expressed as a cash equivalent, was approximately $34 million.

One of the immediate results of this acquisition was to lay the groundwork for a new name for the bank. From the beginning, "Meadow Brook" had possessed a certain bucolic ring for C.I.T's executives. An early search for a name more appropriate to their aspirations for the bank had been initiated. When it became apparent that Bank of North America was to be acquired, the public's reaction to this name was tested and found to be very good. Thus, the name *National* Bank of North America was proposed. The name change occurred concurrently with the merger. It was suitably introduced and promoted along with the adoption of a new identifying symbol, a stylized eagle in flight.

Two more important acquisitions were launched in 1969 and completed in 1970. These involved Trade Bank and Trust Co., a sizable New York City institution, founded in 1922, and First National Bank in Yonkers, a Westchester County (New York) bank.

Trade Bank had six offices, predominantly in mid-Manhattan, and assets of $260 million. C.I.T. preferred stock was exchanged for Trade Bank common at a rate of one share for each 2½ Trade shares. The stock would be convertible into C.I.T. common until 1979 at a rate of one share of preferred for 2½ of the common. The dollar value of the consideration was approximately $30 million.

The Yonkers Bank provided National Bank of North America with a firm foothold in the wealthy Westchester suburban area. It had eleven offices and assets of $140 million. It had been founded in 1933 by local interests after the banking facilities of the community had been seriously curtailed by closings that followed the Bank Holiday. In this transaction, four shares of Yonkers stock were exchanged for 1½ C.I.T. common shares plus ½ share of $100 convertible preferred stock, equivalent in cash to a total price of approximately $16 million.

While the three consolidations added a total of 33 new branches to the National Bank of North America network, inward growth was preceding at a rapid pace. Sixteen new offices had been opened through 1970 and a goal of opening at least 10 new offices a year had been established.

The most important staff contribution made to the bank by C.I.T. was the transfer in February 1966 of John H. Vogel from the position of vice president–administration of C.I.T. Financial to the executive vice presidency of the bank. He had been a member of the C.I.T. organ-

John H. Vogel

ization for thirty-two years. The first thirty of these were spent with
Meinhard & Company, which he had joined at 17 as a messenger in the
mail room. While working upward in the Meinhard factoring firm, he
studied at nights and earned his bachelor's diploma from New York
University in 1939 and a master's degree in business administration in
1941. He became a vice president of Meinhard in 1951 and later served
as a director and secretary of the company as well.

As executive vice president of Meadow Brook, Vogel supervised all
loan and credit operations. He became a director of National Bank of
North America in 1968, following the 1967 merger. He assumed the
bank's presidency on January 1, 1970, and two years later became
chief executive officer, succeeding Sidney Friedman, who continued as
chairman of the institution for another year. When Friedman's retirement became effective at the close of 1972, Vogel also replaced him as
a director of C.I.T. Financial Corporation.

Spurred by C.I.T.'s financial support and ambitious planning for the
institution, the Vogel-Friedman leadership, in less than a decade, totally refashioned the character and scope of National Bank of North
America. Many seasoned banking executives were brought in by the
various mergers and by active recruiting efforts that attracted both men
and women with proven records and high promise. National and inter-

national divisions were developed. The national division's officers blanketed continental U.S. with their marketing efforts. Accounts of many of the country's largest and most prestigious corporations were secured and profitably developed.

The corps of international banking experts that was organized has won the bank a recognized position in most of the world's money centers. The bank has financed the mining and shipment of gems from Latin America to European diamond cutting centers. In Latin America, it has also provided funds to governments for road-building programs, housing projects and other developmental projects. Among the products on which loans have been made to further international trade have been beef from Australia, sunflower seeds from Yugoslavia and manufactured goods from Japan. Giant oil tankers and other marine units also have been financed, in the construction stage or as collateral while in service. Shipments by U.S. manufacturers and agriculturalists to almost every nation in the world also have been funded.

Other divisions that were organized or greatly strengthened after the C.I.T. purchase were an equipment leasing division, a trust department, a real estate division, and a stock transfer and dividend- and interest-paying administrative unit.

Another C.I.T. policy was of major importance to the continued expansion of the bank. Until 1973, the parent company took no dividends from the bank, allowing these to be retained to strengthen the institution's capital structure. This policy added $128 million to the bank's capital. Approximately 50% of annual earnings were paid out in dividends, the remainder continuing to be added to equity capital.

The addition of a commercial banking subsidiary to the C.I.T. corporate galaxy produced the anticipated benefits of significantly broadening the company's diversification base and providing a new and major source of earning power. It also introduced another fundamental influence on the essential corporate character of C.I.T. Financial Corporation.

For generations, the banking system of the United States had been closely regulated, and this supervision had been intensified after the debacle of the 1933 bank closings. National banks were governed by the Comptroller of the Currency. Each state had the power and duty to oversee those banks holding its state charters and did so through its banking department. The Federal Reserve Board and Federal Deposit Insurance Corporation also had broad regulatory powers. The Bank Holding Company Act of 1956 had forbidden corporations holding 25% or more of the stock in *two or more* banks from engaging in any business activities "not closely related to the business of banking . . . as to be a proper incident thereto." Corporations holding such an investment in only *one* bank, however, were exempted from this prohibition.

The rationale for the bank holding company legislation included the fear that if the affairs of a group of banks with one ownership were to become entangled with other extraneous corporate activities, the safety of depositors' funds might be jeopardized by exposures that the non-banking affiliates might create. The restriction was also looked upon as a safeguard for banks against raiders from outside the system who might attempt to build banking "empires." Finally, it reflected a belief that the historical separation of powers between the suppliers of funds (the banking system) and the users of funds (industry and commerce) should be preserved.

At the time of the passage of the legislation, the so-called one-bank holding companies that were exempted were only a minor factor in the banking system. Merchandising organizations of great financial strength, such as Montgomery Ward and Macy's, operated small banks for convenience. Some colleges controlled local banking institutions for investment purposes. Other banks were owned by labor unions and fraternal organizations. Well-to-do families or investors, especially in smaller communities, often had large interests in a local bank, through personal holding companies, along with the other business enterprises. It had seemed unnecessary to the framers of the 1956 legislation to disturb or regulate these established and unobjectionable relationships.

There were about 600 one-bank holding companies in the mid-sixties when C.I.T. acquired Meadow Brook. Generally, the exempted one-bank holding companies had a common character—those with a controlling (or at least a 25%) interest were not themselves banks or bankers. However, a new factor entered the picture in late 1967 when Union Bank of California reorganized *itself* into a one-bank holding company by creating an overlaying corporate unit above the bank. One of the main objectives was to allow the company to engage in new fields of activity that might otherwise have been prohibited to the bank itself. Such activities could include services of a financial nature, perhaps mortgage banking, auto leasing, insurance or many others, as well as totally nonfinancial interests such as manufacturing or merchandising.

There appeared to be little or no thought within the banking fraternity that a move into manufacturing or other completely extraneous pursuits was desirable. The significance of the Union Bank move, however, was immediately apparent to its leading competitors as they

watched other financial institutions performing services for business
and consumers that they felt completely equipped to handle. The one-
bank holding company route could free commercial banks from the
tight fetters under which they long had chafed. By the end of 1968, 57
banks were moving to transform themselves into one-bank holding
companies. Most of these were among the largest institutions in the
nation: Bank of America, the largest; First National City Bank of New
York; Crocker-Citizens National Bank, San Francisco; First Pennsylvania Banking and Trust Co., Philadelphia; Wachovia Bank and Trust
Co., Winston-Salem, and so on. In all, they controlled some $80 bil-
lion in deposits, or 20% of the national total.

This growth of one-bank holding companies was of immediate concern to the federal authorities and members of Congress. In the fall of
1968, Chairman Wright Patman, of the House Banking and Currency
Committee, threatened to take steps to stop the trend. Various bills that
would impose restraints on the movement into one-bank holding companies were introduced.

Obviously, any legislation or new regulations that would affect
one-bank holding companies, the old breed as well as the new, would
intrude on the relationship between C.I.T., its bank and its other pa-
tently nonfinancial operations. Walter Lundell took note of this with
the following remarks at the 1969 annual meeting of stockholders:

> A subject under discussion in Washington at present is the regulation of
> so-called one-bank holding companies. C.I.T. Financial Corporation is
> such a company, for we do control one bank—National Bank of North
> America. Several bills are pending before Congress, including one spon-
> sored by the Administration, that would restrict non-banking activities of
> one-bank holding companies. The proposed legislation, if enacted,
> would have an influence, which cannot be determined at this time, on
> broad areas of the nation's financial community, including many hun-
> dreds of commercial banks which have formed, or which propose to or-
> ganize, one-bank holding companies. In addition, over the years, there
> have been some 600 companies, of which C.I.T. is one, which have ac-
> quired a bank, although their principal business is not that of banking. As
> we see it, the problems and need for regulating these two essentially dis-
> similar types of one-bank holding companies are quite different, with the
> newer, bank-dominated holding companies representing a development
> concerning which careful appraisal may be indicated.

> We at all times have conducted ourselves with respect to National Bank
> of North America with scrupulous attention to the laws now on the books
> and we believe any equitable new legislation should protect our present
> position. However, at this point, we cannot predict what course the legis-

lation will actually take. One form of the legislation could require us to divest ourselves of National Bank of North America or, as an alternative, withdraw from our manufacturing and merchandising activities. We are staying in close touch with the Washington situation and will be sure that C.I.T.'s interests are fully represented to those who are developing legislation in this area.

On December 31, 1970, after lengthy hearings in both houses of Congress, much public discussion and eventual passage by the House and Senate, President Nixon signed into law the amendments to the Bank Holding Company Act. This law extended the administrative supervision of the Board of Governors of the Federal Reserve Board to the activities of one-bank holding companies.

All bank holding companies, of any size, were required to register with the board and be subject to its authority. A "grandfather clause" (for which C.I.T.'s spokesman had contended vigorously) permitted companies to continue any activities in which they were engaged on June 30, 1968, whether these were in compliance with the new amendments as being banking-related or not. However, the Board was given the authority to order the termination at any time of affiliations permitted under the "grandfather clause" if it found such action was necessary to "prevent undue concentration of resources, decreased or unfair competition, conflicts of interest or unfair banking practices." A period of time to accomplish such divestitures was provided. The board was also given broader authority to approve the entry by bank holding companies into entirely new activities if they are determined to be " . . . so closely related to banking or managing or controlling banks as to be a proper incident thereto."

In the annual report to stockholders for 1970, President Holmes summarized the impact of this legislation on C.I.T.'s operations in this way:

> In summary, we are permitted to continue all activities in which we have been engaged since before June 30, 1968, subject to approval of the Federal Reserve Board. This provision covers all of our major business activities. In the future we may also engage in any new activities the Federal Reserve Board determines to be "a proper incident" to the banking business, and expand our non-banking activities in which we were engaged prior to the 1968 date through internal development but not by acquisitions. Subject to regulatory requirements, we may own more than one bank in the State of New York. Should the Federal Reserve Board at any time require divestiture of any of our activities, we would have a ten-year period to accomplish this.

The management continues to believe that as a regulated bank holding company we shall have ample authority and opportunity to operate and expand C.I.T.'s diversified business activities.

That appraisal has proved to be an accurate one with the passage of time. No divestitures have been required of C.I.T. The management has not been forced to make the difficult choice of giving up the bank or the "nonrelated" subsidiaries, which would have been primarily the manufacturing companies. However, all further expansion into new nonfinancial fields or any that could not win Federal Reserve Board approval was effectively ended. The area of growth by the Picker-Gibson-All-Steel acquisition route was over.

36

The Historic
Change of Course

With the passing of the busy years of the 1960's, the unspoken doubts in the minds of Lundell and Ittleson, Jr. emerged into the open with respect to the company's traditional reliance on retail automobile financing as its principal source of earnings. In later years, neither could state with precision when their discussions on this subject began or who initiated them. One thing is completely certain, however; whatever early doubts they may have held at the time the Ford and Chrysler credit companies came into being in due course hardened into certainties.

The actions by Ford and Chrysler, which brought increased pressures on rate structures, were by no means the only reasons for the growing disenchantment with auto financing in the councils at C.I.T. There was the unrelenting and ever-growing bank competition that also increased pressure on profit margins. There was the disappearance of the "independent," second-tier motor manufacturers that has been corded previously. There were the long-term and almost continuous increases in borrowing and handling costs resulting from economic inflation. Intensifying the impact of the latter were the tight limitations on rate increases and other possible offsetting adjustments imposed by the regulatory and tax changes that had been taking place over the years at both the state and federal levels.

Walter Holmes, as he moved upward to the executive vice presidency late in 1964, had been an early participant in the Lundell-Ittleson discussions. He directed the preparation of many projections based on various probabilities and assumptions that reinforced with facts what had been only misgivings. Paralleling these were the studies concerning the underutilization of the company's capital base, which led to the acquisition program in manufacturing and banking.

From the standpoint of the volume of new retail auto business booked, 1965, the motor industry's first nine million passenger car year, had narrowly topped 1964 and was the second best year in C.I.T.'s history (being exceeded only by 1957). The year's total was $1.012 billion. With the auto manufacturing industry's sales sagging somewhat in the following years, retail financing volume likewise declined: 1966, $972 million; 1967, $879 million; and 1968, a slight comeback to $889 million as sales improved.

It was at this point that the decision was reached to undertake a massive turnaround in the company's most fundamental corporate purposes. Automotive retail and wholesale financing were to be—the word of the time—"curtailed" in order to channel funds and the energies and management skills of the consumer and industrial financing division into more profitable areas with greater growth potentials. There were a number of such areas—personal loans, the rapidly growing business of mobile home and second mortgage real estate financing, and the whole broad range of financing and leasing income-producing industrial and transportation equipment and machinery.

At first, the watchword was "selective" curtailment. This was indeed the initial pattern but the term also served to avoid creating premature and undue alarm within the dedicated and committed motor financing staff. Many of these employees had given all their business lives and built their careers almost exclusively on what they knew and what they had accomplished in serving the automobile industry.

The selective approach called for funds to be withdrawn in an orderly manner and sales efforts to be discontinued in both specific territories and specific situations. The territorial exclusions were based on prevailing rates if they were inadequate because of competitive or regulatory reasons, or on local economic conditions if these caused undue collection efforts or loss exposures. An individual analysis of the profitability of each dealer account was made. Where a dealer's business was unsatisfactory from the standpoint of the return to C.I.T. that it generated, he was invited to take his patronage elsewhere. None of these actions were taken precipitously, however. The car manufacturers were given due notice of C.I.T.'s plans, dealers received early warnings if they were to be affected, and all concerned were allowed as much time as they needed to make other arrangements if C.I.T.'s service was to be withdrawn.

The stockholders also were given notice of this new policy in the 1969 annual report. The brief statement read:

> With profit margins in automobile financing becoming increasingly narrow, we embarked during the past year on a program to curtail our retail and wholesale motor vehicle financing operations. The funds that thus became available are being deployed to areas of greater profitability, including direct consumer loans and a broad spectrum of industrial and leasing activities.

The company's operating results for 1970 strikingly reflected the results of this change of direction. Retail motor volume was cut by more than two-thirds, from $646 million in 1969 to $203 million, while the portfolio of retail auto receivables outstanding dropped during the year from $806 million to $424 million. The amount invested in financing dealers' stocks of unsold cars—"wholesale financing"—fell to a virtually nominal $8 million from $193 million. The total volume of motor wholesale financing handled was cut by more than $1 billion, from $1.345 billion in 1969 to $246 million in 1970.

The business downturn, attended by the severe collapse of stock prices in the spring of 1970, high unemployment and the "money crunch," which affected all segments of the nation's economy, handicapped the C.I.T. organization's efforts to replace the loss in automotive volume and outstandings with other forms of financing. Personal loan extensions were off for the first time in more than a decade, although only by $10 million to $623 million. Even so, for the first time in the company's history, the personal loan portfolio moved ahead of the retail motor portfolio. Outstanding personal loan receivables at the end of 1970 aggregated $700 million against retail motor receivables outstanding of $424 million. Personal loans represented 21% of the total portfolio and retail auto receivables slightly more than 13%. Ten years earlier, the latter had represented almost half the total portfolio. Mobile homes and other miscellaneous forms of consumer financing, as well as factoring and commercial financing, also showed declines. Industrial financing and leasing were hit hard, declining from $699 million in the previous year to $533 million.

Nevertheless, net income increased to $66 million from 1969's

$62.4 million and the gain on a per-common-share basis was from
$3.15 to $3.27. A turnaround in business conditions and a better outlook for C.I.T. was signaled by the fact that the fourth quarter of the
year was the best in the company's history up to that time.

In explanation of the strong profit showing, despite a decreased volume of business and a reduced portfolio of earning assets, the 1970
annual report stated:

> The increase in earnings from financing-factoring-leasing operations dur-
> ing the past year, despite the lower levels of both receivables outstanding
> and volume of receivables acquired, indicates the initial success of our
> corporate strategy to concentrate our efforts and our financial resources in
> types of business that offer the greatest opportunities for profitability.
> However, there were many cross-currents that contributed to this end re-
> sult. . . . Operating expenses were reduced by $5.6 million in 1970
> despite inflationary pressures. This was due to changes in our organiza-
> tional structure and methods of operation, as well as the vigorous effort
> throughout the organization to increase productivity and rigidly control
> all operating expenses.

The report went on to point out with satisfaction that the increased
earnings were secured despite a higher level of interest rates than in the
previous year, which increased interest expense by $5.9 million, and a
$7.9 million increase in provision for losses. Concerning the latter, it
said, " . . . losses were higher than we have experienced in recent
years [but] . . . they remain well within the range of normal expectations for a period of economic downturn and rising unemployment
such as the nation experienced in 1970."

Obviously, the change in corporate direction was working well.

The original concept and decision to deploy some $1¼ billion of the
company's resources out of automobile financing and into other lines
of endeavor were those of Lundell and Ittleson, Jr., but it became the
responsibility of Walter Holmes and his close associates to carry these
out to their ultimate conclusion. As has already been noted, the son of
the founder ended forty-five years of day-to-day association with the
corporation's affairs when he relinquished the office of chairman of the
board in February 1967, becoming honorary chairman. In turn, Walter
Lundell retired as chairman and chief executive officer in July of 1970.
Holmes, who had been president since 1967, then took over the reins
as chief executive.

As though in preparation for his retirement from active service,
which was to come a year later, Walter Lundell had given an accounting of his stewardship of the C.I.T. enterprise to the stockholders in
attendance at the 1969 annual meeting, saying:

On the urban affairs front—where business is taking its stand alongside the governmental and institutional sectors in attempting to alleviate the ills of poverty, discrimination and the failure of society to develop human potentials—we are continuing our programs described to our stockholders last year. These include special employment programs for disadvantaged individuals, a work-study program and an actual schooling project at our Home Office. Here, young people who lack essential educational qualifications are being given classroom training that will equip them to handle office work. The first class graduated two weeks ago with Mr. Holmes presenting the graduation certificates and delivering the graduation address.

We are also providing financial support for recognized programs and organizations active in the urban affairs area.

In conclusion, I would like to stress that we who are your Management keep before us at all times the realization that there is one constant in business to which we must always be alert and prepared to deal with effectively. That is the constant represented by the forces of change. In our forward planning for C.I.T. Financial Corporation, we recognize there are many strong currents running today that must be fully reckoned with as we chart and then pursue the course of our corporate affairs.

Looking back a decade for a moment, we can observe how this philosophy of altering the course of the business of C.I.T. to take advantage of any given set of emerging opportunities has paid off. Ten years ago, we were just entering the manufacturing business through our acquisition of the Picker company, which has been such a fine investment over the years. Ten years ago—in 1959—a beginning was just being made in the personal loan business and we held only $17 million in personal loan receivables at the end of that year. Our portfolio of personal loans at the end of last month, as you have just seen, has reached a record $515 million, a 30-fold increase over the 1958 figure.

Five years ago, our other manufacturing companies and National Bank of North America were just coming into the fold. Our educational buildings and major equipment leasing programs were just getting under way. Today, all of these are most important elements in the C.I.T. picture and I hesitate to think what our business situation would be today without them.

In the face of all the powerful emerging and accelerating forces of change throughout our society, a successful business performance demands great flexibility, honest skepticism and large measures of courage and creativity on the part of many people. We intend that the C.I.T. organization will continue to honor and give every encouragement to these qualities wherever they may be found.

When Lundell's retirement became a fact, Walter Holmes paid the following tribute to him in the annual report to stockholders for 1970:

Mr. Lundell's association with C.I.T. began in 1927 and through the ensuing years he did so much to shape the present-day C.I.T. that it would be impossible to record all of his many contributions. During the decade in which Mr. Lundell served as C.I.T.'s chief executive officer, a great expansion in the scope of activities and resources of the Corporation was achieved, together with an increase of more than twenty million dollars in the level of annual net earnings. Your company was transformed from one primarily engaged in instalment sales financing to the broadly diversified organization it is today. I am proud to express our highest measure of gratitude to Mr. Lundell for his unique contributions of leadership and service to C.I.T. over so many years.

Holmes, as president, was now C.I.T.'s chief executive and Todd G. Cole was second in command as executive vice president. The succession had been carefully planned. When Lundell and Holmes had their first discussions in the latter weeks of 1958, Lundell was seeking the right incumbent for the position of controller. Although he was always alert to possible broader potentials in his associates, it was primarily the need to strengthen the company's tax and accounting functions that concerned him as he reviewed the candidates for the controllership.

Holmes had a different view of the job for which he was under consideration. When Lundell, in the course of their interviews, asked him "What position here at C.I.T. would you like to have in the long run?", Holmes had a one-word reply—"Yours." And it will be recalled that he soon entered on the track of general management responsibilities—corporate vice president in 1960, a member of the board of directors and the executive committee in 1962 and the executive vice presidency in 1968.

The second addition to prepare for the next generation of senior management took place in April 1969. In reading the financial news, Lundell had noted that Todd G. Cole, vice chairman, chairman of the finance committee and a director of Eastern Air Lines, had resigned his offices with that air carrier. Lundell had a casual acquaintance with Cole and a high regard for his record in the air transport business and his standing in the financial community. Before joining Eastern in 1963, Cole had been associated with Delta Air Lines for 23 years beginning as controller, then chief financial officer and finally executive vice-president–administration with broad management responsibilities.

Lundell knew a bank executive who was a rather close friend of Cole's. He telephoned that gentleman, inquired about Cole's future plans and suggested that Cole might be interested in talking with him. With the banker as the intermediary, the meeting was arranged and in due course Cole accepted Lundell's offer that he come with C.I.T. as

vice president and assistant to the president. Before the end of 1969, he was elected to the C.I.T. board of directors and became financial vice president. In 1971, he was named to the number two position in the company as executive vice president. The presidency followed in June 1973, Holmes assuming the chairmanship of the board, which had been vacant since Lundell's retirement.

Cole's qualifications were most valuable ones. A native Louisianan, he attended Louisiana State University, won a law degree and also became a certified public accountant through night study. He was broadly acquainted and highly respected in all financial quarters.

Thus, it was the Holmes-Cole team that was to guide C.I.T. destinies as the 1970's began and the most radical change of course in the company's history gathered momentum.

It is virtually impossible to decide which assignment that they faced was the more difficult and unprecedented—to dismantle the nation's largest and historically most profitable automobile financing apparatus, or to develop and execute successfully a marketing effort that would have the immediate effect of replacing the abandoned sources of income with an increasing flow of profits.

Any thought that the automotive cutback was to be dealt with on a selective or limited basis had been given up. As the program developed, it became the clear intention of the management virtually to eliminate the line of business that had provided the major sustenance of the company's earning power for more than a half-century. Only in a few special areas of circumstances, the Puerto Rican market being one, was C.I.T. prepared to remain a significant factor in the automobile financing market. The Puerto Rican exception was based on the company's unusually favorable operating experience there and the key role it occupied in the island's economy.

It should be emphasized that the retirement from auto financing had almost as harsh an impact on the operations of the insurance subsidiaries as it did on the consumer financing units. The principal business of Service Fire Insurance Company, as has been noted, was the writing of policies to cover physical damage on financed vehicles—a protection for both the owner and the finance company. The decline in retail auto financing was attended by a correlated drop in Service Fire's business. Similarly, the North American Company for Life and Health Insurance derived the largest part of its business from credit life insurance purchased by auto instalment buyers to discharge any remaining debts that might be owed if they were to die. Thus, the loss of a billion dollars of retail automobile financing meant an almost equal drop in the North American Company's life insurance writings.

Both of the insurance subsidiaries therefore experienced a period of severe readjustment. With its former source of premium volume virtually wiped out, the Service Company began to seek completely new underwriting opportunities. The North American Company, which had been steadily building its ordinary life and group life businesses, was somewhat less affected. Normally, credit life insurance is purchased by the borrower, at his option, when a personal loan is arranged. Thus, the concurrent growth of C.I.T.'s consumer loan operations served to replace much of the credit life insurance business lost through the auto financing withdrawal.

The elimination of so much automobile financing activity involved wrenching personnel experiences. Offices that had produced sufficient volume and income from auto operations in some cases were not adaptable for personal loan or consumer financing functions and had to be closed. Automobile financing, with its large investments in dealer inventories and relatively high average outstanding balances in consumer accounts, had required close supervision of local offices by a large regional management structure. With the decline of the auto business and the growth of the more straightforward activity of making direct personal loans, a substantial part of the regional superstructure could be eliminated. Inevitably, at both the regional and local levels there were some individuals, mostly long-time veterans, who found it impossible to adapt to the new order. Thus, although the program was administered with maximum care and consideration, early retirements and other personal adjustments had to occur. The latter included a number of transfers to other units within the corporate family. The number of employees on the rolls of the financing and leasing companies dropped by four hundred during the two years 1971–72, even though the total volume of financing receivables acquired increased by more than $300 million.

A complete restructuring of the U.S. consumer financing operations then was launched, being completed in 1972. A new overall entity was created and named C.I.T. Financial Services, Inc. This was based on the existing Universal C.I.T. Credit Corporation, into which were merged the smaller consumer finance units that had previously operated separately and with considerable autonomy. These were Laurentide Finance Corporation, Home Finance Service, Inc. and Time Finance Company.

In the program of redirecting the corporation's largest operating unit, Holmes had the support not only of Cole but of a team of other senior associates who performed superbly. Henry C. Watkins had moved to vice president–consumer financing of the parent company in addition to serving as chairman of the U.S. consumer financing unit. His principal associate was Glen E. Jorgensen, a 35-year veteran who had touched all the bases in his rise through the Universal C.I.T. ranks, to the presidency of the subsidiary. These two bore the administrative brunt of dealing with the massive challenges of the redirection program. In Canada, Clarence Trudeau, as president of Canadian Acceptance Corporation Limited, performed with similar leadership effectiveness.

Their task was a two-pronged one: to close down the motor operations with a minimum disruption of the organization while simultaneously expanding all other sources of income to the utmost. The new policy also demanded that the industrial financing, factoring and leasing subsidiaries exert the same maximum energies to find opportunities to employ the company's huge supply of available funds in "areas of greater profitability" (as the 1969 annual report put it). This was spearheaded by Charles S. Jensen, Watkins' counterpart at the C.I.T. Financial level as vice president–industrial financing and chairman of the industrial financing and leasing companies. He was elevated to the position of executive vice president, overseeing the same corporate areas, in 1975. The administrative leadership of these companies' programs came from their president, Chester C. Goss, who had joined the

C.I.T. organization as an industrial financing new-business man immediately following World War II.

On the factoring side, it was Richard S. Perry, with more than a quarter-century of service, who was responsible for William Iselin's share of the effort. He had been named executive vice president of that company in 1969 and president in 1972. Reinald R. Kaufmann, who had been a member of the company's factoring organization since its very inception in the 1920's, headed Meinhard-Commercial Corporation during this period until his retirement in 1974, when he was succeeded by John O'D. Feeks, a veteran executive of the company.

With the economy still lagging through most of 1971, the volume of so-called diversified receivables—all the nonmotor classifications—that was acquired during the year equaled the 1970 figure. The decline in the automobile portfolio continued, as planned, so that there was an overall reduction in the receivables portfolio during the year from $3.19 billion to $2.92 billion. There was a strong gain in earnings, however, attributable primarily to a decline in short-term interest rates, as a result of the economic slowdown, and the continuing favorable effects of the automotive withdrawal. Net income for the year was $78.7 million, a 20% increase over the preceding year, with earnings per share up $0.56 to $3.81.

The company-wide endeavor to replace and eventually exceed the earnings surrendered by the automotive withdrawal program continued to bear fruit in the following years. The same can be said for the companies comprising the financing-factoring-leasing division. They were successful in building back the portfolio of receivables outstanding to the pre-1970 level and then moving on to higher ground for the corporation's earning assets. This is shown in the graph on the following page.

The corporation's new directions continued to benefit earnings year by year. In 1972, net profits rose to $86.1 million ($4.15 per common share) and $89.1 million ($4.28 per common share) in 1973.

Once again, the record provided abundant proof, as *Fortune* had found forty years earlier, that the judgment of its executives was C.I.T.'s chief asset, with the results of the exercise of that judgment serving as a testimonial to the organization's soundness and flexibility.

RECEIVABLES OUTSTANDING—YEAR-END AMOUNTS*

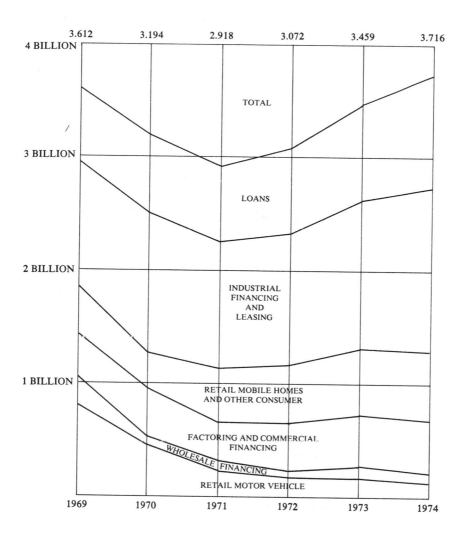

*Automotive wholesale receivables have been eliminated for all years, as these have practically no significance from an earnings standpoint and their replacement was never intended. They totaled $193.1 million at the end of 1969 and $7.3 million at the end of 1974.

37

The New Leadership

Except for the first Henry Ittleson with his youthful years in the May Company, Walter Holmes and Todd Cole were the first principal officers of C.I.T. who had won their spurs as corporate managers outside the company before entering on their C.I.T. careers. Over the decades, not only had the topmost executives been C.I.T. career men but also their entire management corps, with rare exceptions, had spent nearly their entire business lives in the company's service. The composition of the board of directors had paralleled this. Until Walter Lundell invited Robert W. Purcell, chairman of the board of the International Basic Economy Corporation, to join the board in 1968, there had never been a director who was not an officer of the company or one of its subsidiaries, a representative of one of its investment banking firms or of the founding May-Shoenberg interests.

With their consistent record for willingness to innovate and to be iconoclastic with respect to traditional ways of doing things, C.I.T.'s earlier managers had never been ingrown or insular. Yet, as rightfully should be expected when a change of command occurs, the Holmes-Cole combination brought their own tone and character to the process of corporate management. They honored the company's past, they regarded themselves as guardians of its traditions, but from the beginning their management style was completely their own and was not patterned on that of those who actually had lived that past and created those traditions.

With so much of their and the organization's energies being absorbed in the restructuring of the consumer financing operations, they nevertheless maintained intimate familiarity with the ongoing activities of each one of their operating subsidiaries. For each, they established constantly advancing objectives for growth and profitability and they were satisfied only when these were attained or exceeded in the allotted time span.

The first requirement to undergird this program was a series of periodic actions, in the pattern of the past, to maintain the organization's working capital at an optimum level.

The commercial paper market, from which C.I.T. derived short-term funds at any given time of $1 billion or more, experienced a wrenching blow in the spring of 1970. The Penn Central Railroad, with $87 million of commercial paper debt outstanding, went into bankruptcy, defaulting completely on these obligations as well as its other debt. This disaster touched off a flight by fearful investors from the "paper" of many issuers, including such well-known names as the Chrysler Financial Corporation. Since the Chrysler Corporation subsidiary was unable to replace its current obligations as they fell due, with new commercial paper borrowings, the parent company was forced to appeal to a consortium of banks for aid. The banking group responded by increasing the financing subsidiary's credit lines by $400 million, to $1.1 billion, enabling it to cover its obligations. Similar action by the banking community also enabled other "paper" issuers to survive the sudden squeeze in the short-term market.

In the case of C.I.T., however, the panic in the commercial paper market had the opposite effect. As investors drew back their funds from borrowers concerning whom they had misgivings, they sought to reinvest their money with C.I.T. and a few other issuers who had an impregnable reputation for soundness. Thus, during the period of the great drought in the overall commercial paper market, C.I.T. was offered more funds than it could possibly use. Despite the disappearance of billions of dollars from the commercial credit market as a whole, C.I.T.'s standby bank lines of more than $800 million with over 400 U.S. banks were never touched—a record that has continued up to this narrative's conclusion.

Further recognition of C.I.T.'s standing in the money market came early in 1972 when Standard & Poor's Corporation, the authoritative corporate credit rating institution, upgraded their rating of C.I.T.'s bonds from "A" to "AA". The "AA" rating is the highest established for any financially oriented company. This action was taken, the rating service said in its announcement, "in view of C.I.T.'s conservative debt ratios and long-term performance in affording its bond-holders above-average protection."

The first longer-term public financing since 1967 was an issue of $100 million of six-year 6⅞% debentures sold in January 1971. This was followed by the sale of $100 million of eight-year 7⅝% debentures in November 1973 and another $100 million of eight-year 8.85% debentures in December 1974. In July 1975, $150 million of twenty-year 9½% debentures were issued and $25 million in Canadian funds was raised through the private placement of a fifteen-year 9½% note.

Two increases in the common stock dividend were made during the period of rising earnings after 1970. The annual rate was increased to $2.00 per share with the July 1, 1971, disbursement and to $2.20 beginning on April 1, 1973. The last prior increase to $1.80 per share had become effective on April 1, 1968.

In the tradition begun by Vogel and Ecker, the C.I.T. management had always placed emphasis on maintaining the closest possible relationships within the investment community. Those engaged in investment analysis or the management of investors' funds had always found an open door awaiting them at the C.I.T. executive offices. Dietz and Lundell and others made many formal appearances before security analysts' groups in addition to informal, more personal contacts.

Holmes and Cole continued this policy with great vigor, primarily to tell the story of the successful redirection of the company's business out of automobile financing and the development of its other operations to replace the motor business. Their program, which also gave visibility to the company's new management team, took a number of forms. In many principal cities, leading bankers served as hosts for luncheon meetings at which the guests were the principal businessmen of each community. At these, Holmes and Cole informally told the C.I.T. story, emphasizing the company's involvement in the financial and industrial life of each immediate area, and participating in lively discussion periods on economic and business topics.

Similarly, the C.I.T. investment banking firms, Dillon, Read and Company and Kuhn, Loeb and Company, arranged a series of dinner meetings in various cities to which the leaders of the financial communities in each city were invited. Holmes and Cole were the speakers at these meetings and their remarks were augmented by film presentations illustrating their company's broad diversification. They also traveled to all the major financial centers of Western Europe for similar appearances and to visit financial organizations there. They have continued regular presentations before security analysts' groups and hold quarterly meetings at the C.I.T. headquarters with analysts specializing in the affairs of financial organizations. The publication of an annual financial supplement to the annual report has been inaugurated. This contains detailed data of interest to professionals but which are regarded as too comprehensive for inclusion in the annual report. The availability of senior officers for individual interviews with analysts also continues.

Another program to strengthen the corporation's ties with the community at large, and particularly the financial sector, was one that brought a number of able individuals to the board of directors who had not had previous associations with C.I.T. The first of these "outside" directors was Robert W. Purcell, who had become a director in 1967. He was followed in 1970 by Robert B. Anderson, an international business consultant and attorney who had been Secretary of the Treasury and Secretary of the Navy in the Eisenhower administration. Herman J. Schmidt, vice chairman of Mobil Oil Corporation, and Christopher F. Edley, an attorney and executive director of the United Negro College Fund, became directors in 1974. Albert V. Casey, chairman of the board and president of American Airlines, Inc., was elected in 1975.

A policy also had been adopted making retirement of "outside" directors mandatory at the age of 72. For those with employment associations with the company, retirement from the board is concurrent with retirement from active service, except for retiring chief executive officers to whom the age-72 standard is applicable.

———————

Another chapter in the chronicle of the individuals who built the modern C.I.T. enterprise came to an end on August 25, 1973, when Henry Ittleson, Jr., died suddenly while vacationing in Europe. He had continued as a director and as honorary chairman of the board after his retirement in 1968 from the board chairmanship and day-to-day responsibilities. His association with the corporation, which began with the showdown with his father in 1922, had extended over a period of fifty-one years.

In part, Walter S. Holmes, Jr., paid tribute to the man and his career in these words, spoken at a memorial service in New York City on September 27, 1973:

Outside these walls as the dusk of the fall season moves across the land, the influence of Henry Ittleson, Jr., is present in thousands of homes where employees of C.I.T. Financial Corporation are returning to their families. Many individuals have been architects and builders of the C.I.T. organization as it exists today. But each one of us who has been associated with him in the task would certify that C.I.T.'s place in the economic life of this nation would be a different and far less significant one, were it not for the impact on its destiny, over a period of more than 50 years, of Henry Ittleson, Jr.

Masked by his selflessness and rejection of the limelight, Henry was a visionary and a creator. He chose to give the impression that he dealt in cold facts and let the numbers speak for themselves but this was not really the case. His analytical ability, his intuitive grasp of the logic and import of future events, his probing intelligence, his courage and determined commitment to what he knew to be the right—these were assets of enormous importance to C.I.T. that were never reflected on its balance sheet. Working with and through others—and always letting them have the credit—he was the pilot who set our Corporation on course for many abundantly fruitful voyages, who brought it through many storms, shoals and other perils and who kept a steady watch from the quarterdeck on every movement of vessel and crew.

He did not expect change simply to happen. He insisted that it be the result of penetrating analysis and planning. Frequently, he was the sponsor of a proposed change of course. At other times, he acted effectively as the devil's advocate, probing new proposals in order to establish beyond doubt that they were not just temporary or ill-conceived expedients but soundly based concepts that would best serve the long-term interests of all parties involved—our customers, our employees, our creditors and our stockholders.

Often, tough and challenging debates resulted, but once he was convinced of the undeniable merits of a given course of action, Henry's support and dedication to it were wholehearted. He would always devote his total efforts to the achievement of the agreed-upon goal.

Always a provident man who judged the risks vigilantly, he was not essentially a caretaker or conservator. He *was* throughout his life a builder. He built many homes and enjoyed bringing beauty and material excellence into being. He built the C.I.T. Headquarters Building a few blocks from here. Those who know the C.I.T. Building can find in it an uncompromising expression of his lifelong dedication to practical esthetics and quality.

He was a builder in another sense: his great love of beauty, gifted eye and recognized expertise equipped him to be the builder of a collection of paintings of rare excellence. As an early patron of artists who have won high esteem, he made his influence felt on the world of art, as on the other spheres to which he committed his efforts and interest.

He was a proud and jealous guardian of the reputation and stature of C.I.T. in the financial world and before the public. He would countenance no acts or words that—as he so often put it—were "out of the question for C.I.T." He was a businessman's businessman, respected for his ability and integrity, a man who moved with dignity and honor among his peers.

We, in the discharge of our responsibilities, in the execution of the tasks he has left for us to carry on, in our adherence to the ideals and purposes that his life exemplified, in the very business of living our own lives day by day, will each of us be living memorials to Henry. He left his mark on us and we are better for it, as the world is better for his life's work.

For sixty-five years, the Ittlesons, father and son, had wielded an incalculable influence on the course of the affairs of C.I.T. Financial Corporation. It truly remains a living memorial to them both.

38

Into the
Mid-Seventies

An early action taken to broaden staff services at the parent-company level was the inauguration of a company-wide marketing program, the first in the organization's history. It was recognized that sales representatives of the corporation's many subsidiaries were all in a position to use their customer relationships and broad penetration of the U.S. and Canadian markets to uncover leads whereby other C.I.T. companies might sell their services on a competitive basis to the same customers.

For example, an agent handling a company's employee group life policy might act as an intermediary so that his All-Steel counterpart in the same territory might be asked to bid on an office furniture purchase the client was planning. Or a user of C.I.T.'s fleet leasing services might be introduced to an opportunity to factor his receivables or obtain C.I.T. financing to purchase needed factory equipment. By familiarizing all of the corporation's sales forces with what other C.I.T. subsidiaries had to offer, the possibilities for creating additional sales opportunities have continued to expand.

To implement this program, the third member of the Ittleson family was brought into the senior management group of the company. H. Anthony Ittleson, only son of Henry Ittleson, Jr., and grandson of the founder, was named vice president—marketing in 1971. He had been a member of the organization since his graduation from Brown University. Despite his family ties, he had learned the finance business from the bottom up. He worked for the company during college vacations, but made his permanent start as a field collection man in the Philadelphia office of C.I.T. Corporation, checking and collecting industrial accounts, in 1961. He then was assigned to both credit and sales duties of increasing responsibility in Denver, Los Angeles and New York City. In 1968, he became a vice president of C.I.T. Corporation, working in its national financing and leasing division.

He organized a Marketing Council made up of key representatives, mostly from the younger management generation of each major subsidiary and staff department. Through it, "Tony" Ittleson marshaled a series of projects and innovations designed to coordinate the sales and promotional-advertising-distribution activities of all the C.I.T. companies to the maximum. As he continued to direct this program, he was elected a director of National Bank of North America in 1972 and of C.I.T. Financial Corporation in 1973. In that same year, he also assumed executive responsibility for the corporation's public relations and advertising departments.

One of the most immediate and pressing problems to be faced by the Holmes-Cole management was to rectify the deterioration in earnings that had taken place in the manufacturing and merchandising division during the late '60's. From a record profit of $10.7 million in 1966, profits for the next four years were successively $7.5 million, $8.5 million, $5.0 million and a low of $3.2 million for 1970. At this point, the management made no bones about the fact that the stockholders were not receiving an adequate return from the corporation's investment in its manufacturing subsidiaries.

The poor 1970 results require some explanation. Not only were the manufacturing companies suffering with the rest of the economy from the recession that began in 1969, but Picker, often the most profitable unit, was exposed to a twelve-week strike of its production employees. In addition, a lengthy truckers' strike that brought most over-the-road transport in the Midwest to a standstill hit the C.I.T. manufacturing division with special force. With its main plants located at Cleveland, Cincinnati, South Bend and Aurora, operations were severely handicapped both in receiving production materials and in shipping finished products.

Much management effort was thrown into reversing the trend of manufacturing earnings. In 1972, the Picker organization was restructured and all managerial functions concentrated at the Cleveland plant.

New products were introduced, primarily designed to ease the work loads of radiological technicians and reduce the exposure time to which patients are subjected during x-ray examinations.

An integrated management approach was instituted at Gibson, replacing what had been four separate operating or profit centers. New products, including candles and paper specialties, were introduced. A major expansion was undertaken at the Cleo Wrap plant in Memphis, which had been a particularly profitable operation. More than 175 million rolls of gift wrappings were produced in 1971, and it was planned to more than double this production. All-Steel's operations remained affected by the sluggish business conditions that had discouraged the expansion of business facilities requiring new furnishings, but both expansion and modernization of manufacturing, warehousing and marketing facilities were initiated.

In addition to the major manufacturing facility built at Hazelton, Pennsylvania, showrooms were enlarged, modernized or established for the first time in major metropolitan centers, and a strong entry was made into the Canadian market. Additional capital expenditure programs were carried out at both the Aurora All-Steel plant and the RACO plant at South Bend.

Results for the following year reflected both better economic conditions and the results of these programs to improve products and services to customers and raise manufacturing and distribution efficiencies. Sales in 1972 increased only $4 million to $366 million, but the division's earnings rose 36% to $10 million from 1971's $7.4 million. This showing was accomplished despite the fact that Holt, Renfew, the Canadian merchandising chain, had been sold in January 1972 and thus made no contribution to the year's figures. In 1971, it had added sales of $28 million and earnings of $668,000 to the division's totals.

In 1973, the manufacturing operations were plagued by delays and shortages in obtaining raw materials and components, the result of the strong comeback in general business conditions in that year. In addition, they operated under price restraints imposed by the federal government's "Phase II" program to control inflationary pressures. Nevertheless, both gains in sales to $411 million and net profits to $10.8 million were achieved, the latter topping the prior record year of 1966.

With restructuring programs of all companies in place and the termination of price controls on April 30, 1974, that year's results yielded a convincing demonstration of the success of the four-year effort to rebuild the earning power of the manufacturing units. Sales moved ahead a full $50 million to $461 million and earnings rose to $12.1 million.

Manufacturing operations provided 13% of the corporation's earnings, compared with 4% at the low point in 1970.

Robert L. Strawbridge, who had been executive vice president of Houdaille Industries, had joined C.I.T. in 1968 as vice president–manufacturing and merchandising. He later acted as president of Picker Corporation for several years during that company's restructuring program. His contribution to the advance of the manufacturing division's earnings to record levels was recognized at the close of 1974 when he returned to the position of vice president of the parent company, supervising all manufacturing and merchandising activities, and was elected to the board of directors.

As has already been noted, the insurance division experienced a heavy impact from the decrease in automotive financing operations, since much of the premium volume of both the life insurance and casualty insurance subsidiaries had been generated through the writing of retail auto financing contracts. Thus, this division also required close management attention in the years following 1970.

Although fluctuations in the securities markets and in general interest rates always influence the income of insurance companies, the steps that were taken to mitigate the loss of the automotive-related business can be credited with a large share of the earnings gains that were scored by the insurance division. The combined net profit figure of $11.4 million in 1970, increased to $11.5 million in 1971; $13.1 million in 1972; $14.8 million in 1973, and $15.2 million in 1974.

One of the first actions taken occurred in early 1971 when the life-health and casualty companies were consolidated under one management, introducing important economies. The headquarters of the Service Fire company was moved from New York City to the North American Life and Health headquarters in Chicago. This was followed by changing the name of the Service company to the "North American Company for Property and Casualty Insurance," bringing both companies under one banner to make possible combined marketing programs.

In 1971, the North American Life and Health company inaugurated a new marketing approach that was to become a most successful business builder. This was called "mass merchandising" and involved selling group life insurance policies to business, professional, labor and other organizations and associations acting as a common bond for their members. The policies written were equivalent to the employee group life insurance plans offered by many employers. Among the organizations for which such group policies have been written during the ensuing years are university alumni, medical organizations, police and firemen's associations, airline pilots, secondary school teachers, professional engineers, university faculty and administrative personnel, civil servants and newspaper employees, as well as many others.

The unflagging efforts to expand the North American Life company's agency representation and its sales of individual or ordinary life policies resulted in the passing of a significant milestone in the first quarter of 1972. Ordinary life insurance in force went over the $1 billion mark, and growth toward the $2 billion figure has continued. Also, the company has become one of the nation's leading marketers of term insurance, providing less expensive coverage against life's hazards than policies that build cash values. It has attained a rank among the 100 largest of the nation's 1,500 stock life insurance companies.

On the casualty insurance side, an aggressive entry was made into the writing of insurance on major risks as a participant in pools or syndicates comprised of many insurance carriers, who thus share in underwriting such large exposures. These joint coverages are placed on industrial and commercial buildings, refineries, aircraft and marine hulls, major construction projects and similar risks. C.I.T.'s consumer credit operations also continued to contribute sizable volumes of premium income from the property damage insurance placed on mobile homes and recreational vehicles financed by retail buyers.

One of the important actions taken to help build the company's personal loan portfolio was a program initiated "experimentally" in 1970 to offer federal income tax payers a computerized service, backed by trained personnel, for completing their returns. This was so successful that the service has expanded widely to most U.S. loan offices in subsequent years. Not only does the service establish customer relationships that may lead in the future to the use of C.I.T.'s financing facilities by those served, but also the immediate need for funds to make income tax payments generates "on-the-spot" loans.

In the same year, C.I.T. Financial Services launched a major spot radio campaign, over more than 1,000 stations, to promote its personal loan and other consumer services, including the tax program. Since that time, in both the U.S. and Canada, local and national advertising programs have been conducted with consistency.

In 1973, a major investment was made in opening new consumer financing offices to intensify coverage of the most promising markets in every section of the country. At the same time, a program was initiated to modernize, with a standard decor, the interior appearance of all existing offices. During the year, at a rate of more than one a week, 60 new offices were opened, bringing the total number to 978 operating in the United States and Canada. Fifteen more branches were opened in 1974, and in 1975 the 1,000 mark was crossed. Three new divisional offices were established by C.I.T. Corporation in the major regional business centers of Indianapolis, Louisville and Miami to service the mounting volumes of industrial financing and leasing being put on the books. This brought the number of "Corp" offices to 30, a gain of four division centers since 1970.

A fully-staffed Real Estate Division was organized in 1973, after a painstaking study of the potential for employing funds in short- and medium-term mortgage loans to owners or developers of commercial or residential properties, as well as other forms of financing in the realty market. Even though the real estate construction industry experienced a severe recession beginning in 1974 because of scarce money supplies and very high interest rates, this new venture made good gains and rapidly built up a multimillion dollar portfolio of earning assets.

Another development of 1973 was the entry of C.I.T. Corporation, Canadian Acceptance Corporation and both factoring companies into international operations. C.I.T. Corporation and Canadian Acceptance became the U.S. and Canadian members, respectively, of Leaseclub, which, with eleven member organizations in the industrial nations of Western Europe, was Europe's largest association of equipment leasing companies. The organization had been founded ten years earlier. This was an outgrowth of the conferences Holmes and Cole had with financial and investment leaders in Europe earlier in that year. Through their memberships, the C.I.T. companies were placed in positions to offer service and guidance, through their European affiliates, to domestic manufacturers and distributors wanting to lease products to European clients and to provide financial accommodations and marketing counsel to European lessors wishing to do business in the U.S. and Canada.

William Iselin & Co. became a member of Factors' Chain International, an organization of member factoring companies in seventeen nations of Western Europe, South Africa, Israel and Canada. This gave Iselin the opportunity to service its domestic clients' accounts receivable created through sales to foreign customers and to perform credit and collection services for other members of the organization with respect to accounts of their clients in the United States.

Meinhard-Commercial Corporation became affiliated with the Foreign Credit Insurance Association, which was organized under the auspices of the United States Export-Import Bank to promote foreign trade by U.S. business interests. Through this organization,

Meinhard-Commercial financed accounts receivable due domestic manufacturers and distributors from their foreign customers.

A significant change in direction also occurred during these years in the marketing objectives of what was originally C.I.T. Educational Buildings, Inc. As the college-age population declined in the final years of the decade, the demand for additional dormitory space virtually disappeared. In the meantime, however, C.I.T. Educational Buildings had found a second market—providing similar income-producing buildings for voluntary community hospitals. These projects usually took the form of specialized additions, such as buildings for the extended care of convalescing patients who did not require full hospital facilities, facilities for the care of the aged, physical rehabilitation units and the like. However, some primary-care buildings also were produced. In due course this medically related type of construction became almost the entire business of the subsidiary. As a result, its name was changed in 1973 to C.I.T. Buildings Corporation.

Another achievement of historical significance to the company's consumer financing operations became a reality during 1975. This was the linking of all the 850 U.S. loan offices of C.I.T. Financial Services into a single sophisticated data processing system, regarded as one of the largest and most advanced being employed by any organization outside the United States government. Named the CITation System, the installation completes all calculations and record-keeping entries formerly done manually at the branch level. It then feeds these into the Eastern Air Lines Computer Center at Miami, Florida, operated by Eastern personnel under a contract with C.I.T. The records on each individual account are stored in the airline's computer for instantaneous referral back to terminals in each branch, as may be required. All of the company's accounting and control records for each branch and region of C.I.T. Financial Services also are built up and stored for split-second reference.

The system, in its original conformation, involved more than 45,000 miles of communication lines, 1,200 different computer programs, 600,000 separate instructions to the computer and the storage of more than one million records, such as individual customer accounts.

The massive undertaking to design and implement this system had its beginnings as far back as the early sixties. Other consumer financing organizations and related businesses had adopted so-called real-time computerized methods of keeping records, which were closely followed and studied by the C.I.T. management. A full-time data processing task force was organized for this purpose. The technology was advancing so rapidly, however, that it was repeatedly concluded that a plunge into the data processing maelstrom would best be deferred, in view of the financial, operational and organizational commitments that would be demanded.

Prior to the actual launching of the CITation project, the management came close to recommending a move into real-time data processing of the consumer credit operations in 1966. A staff report strongly recommended this, but for a series of reasons, it was decided to defer the issue at that time. The future proved that this was a fortunate decision. Had a real-time system been designed and installed then, it would have been centered on the company's automotive financing operations and their extensive dealer-servicing involvements, rather than direct personal loan procedures. Thus, the system would have been ill-suited for the direction in which the company's business was to focus in the seventies. In addition, computer technology was due to advance rapidly in the next several years in speeding up the transmission of data. In the language of the computer art, a 1966 system would have been a "slow" one, while the system eventually installed qualified as a "fast" one.

Eventually, discussions on the possibility of using the extensive, ultramodern facilities and great technical expertise of the Eastern Airlines organization were explored intensively. Cole's extensive experience and familiarity with the airline's computer capabilities as a former senior officer of Eastern, contributed greatly to facilitating the C.I.T.-Eastern interchanges.

Finally, in the spring of 1972, both the Financial Services and parent company managements decided that the time to move forward had arrived. On June 29, 1972, the board of directors ratified an action by management to enter into a contract with Eastern for the development of the desired real-time system. The price for the project would be in excess of $6 million, with allowance for possible price increases to more than $8 million. Terminals and other communication equipment would cost more than $4 million and other costs, largely internal, were estimated at $2 million. The total investment in the system therefore could exceed $14 million. The board approved the recommendation. Actual work to produce the system immediately began on a forced-draft schedule to reach fruition three years later. At the inception of the program in 1972, a schedule was established for the system to become operative at 8 A.M. on October 31, 1974. This deadline was beaten by seventeen hours. The system began functioning at 3 P.M. on October 30, 1974.

As with any such complex enterprise, numerous shakedown problems were encountered throughout the stages of experimentation and installation. These were surmounted, however, by the teamwork between the C.I.T. data processing personnel, headed by Robert B. Parsons, Jr. (formerly an Eastern executive and vice president–systems administration of C.I.T. since 1971), the C.I.T. financial services operating staff under the leadership of Charles L. Wingfield, executive vice president of that subsidiary, and the Eastern staff assigned to the C.I.T. project.

With the early "bugs" overcome, the CITation System promptly demonstrated its great cost-reducing capacity and its ability to provide welcome simplification and expediting of company's recording and accounting functions, for the benefit of customers and company personnel alike. Moreover, it created a company-wide communications network providing the potential for instantaneous message contact, via the link-up of the system's computer terminals, between any two or more company locations.

The long series of annual increases in earnings that the business and consumer financing division had contributed to total corporate earnings came to an end in 1973. After 1969's $35.2 million, they rose to $37 million in 1970, $45.1 million in 1971, and $50 million in 1972. In 1973, they declined to $47.1 million. The year's annual report attributed this result to a $44 million, or 80%, increase in interest costs because short-term interest charges soared to "unprecedented levels" during the year. "Charges to customers were adjusted wherever legally and competitively possible [but] . . . there is a time lag before such adjustments have an effect on the overall yield of our portfolio," the report continued. "Profit margins of the Business and Consumer Financing Division can therefore be expected to narrow during periods of rising interest rates and to widen during periods of declining rates."

"Operating costs were maintained under effective control in 1973, although increases reflecting expansion of our operations and inflation were incurred. Our collection experience was excellent, resulting in abnormally low credit losses," the report later stated.

As noted earlier, the corporation's combined net profits continued their series of increases in 1973. This occurred because of the higher contributions of the other three divisions, the banking division making the best showing.

Still higher money costs, plus less favorable credit loss experience than the unusually good results in the preceding year, resulted in a further decrease in the financing division's earnings in 1974, a sharp drop to $39.4 million from the $47.1 million return in 1973. Overall interest expense increased to an average rate of 8% for the year, against 7.4% in 1973. This involved an increased outlay for borrowed money totaling $37 million on top of the prior year's increase of $44 million.

Provision for credit losses in 1974 also rose, from $16.2 million in 1973 to $27.4 million.

Although all three of the other divisions turned in better performances than in 1973, these failed to completely offset the decline of more than $7 million in the business and consumer financing net. Thus, consolidated earnings for 1974 fell, amounting to $91.7 million, compared with 1973's $94.4 million.

The annual report said this: "Earnings for the year were second only to the peak attained in 1973, but the decline did bring to an end a record of 22 consecutive years of annual gains beginning in 1952 and extending through 1973."

From an earnings standpoint, beginning in 1970, the greatest advance scored by any of the corporation's four divisions was that of the banking division—the National Bank of North America. From 1969's $15.7 million, these rose to $19.8 million in 1970 and $20.2 million in 1971. With interest rates declining sharply in 1972 (the prime bank rate reached a low of 4¾%) and poor money-market conditions also affecting the bank's return from its investment portfolio, there was a decline in earnings to $18.1 million in 1972. An excellent recovery to $21.6 million was made in 1973, followed by a rise to $25 million in 1974. The share contributed by the bank to overall corporate earnings had increased from 18% in 1969 to 27% in 1974.

Many developments contributed to these gains. During the latter half of 1970, there occurred the acquisition of Trade Bank and Trust Company and the First National Bank in Yonkers. Also during that year, the bank opened seven new offices and received regulatory approval for twelve more. An intensive employee recruiting, training and upgrading program continued.

An increase of 10%, to $2.54 billion, was registered in the bank's assets in 1971, while deposits crossed the $2-billion mark for the first time. That year also saw a number of commitments made to programs primarily directed to the solution of critical social problems of the nation. A $5.6 million loan was made to finance an experimental housing project in Macon, Georgia, the first of its kind in the eastern United States. This was a part of "Operation Breakthrough" of the federal Department of Housing and Urban Development, directed at helping solve the nation's critical shortage of adequate housing, particularly for minority families. The bank joined with a number of other New York City institutions to form the city's first Minority Enterprise Small Business Investment Company. This was organized to complement the efforts of individual banks to assist minority small businessmen by

providing loans and technical assistance. The bank also joined Min-
banc Capital Corporation, a national organization, to supply capital to
minority-owned banks.

In October 1972, The National Bank of Far Rockaway was acquired
through an exchange of stock involving 31,250 C.I.T. shares and consolidated with National Bank of North America. In conjunction with
this transaction, the shares of all remaining minority stockholders (2%
of the original total outstanding) were acquired for $43 a share, com-
pared with the original 1965 tender price of $31.75 a share. With this
purchase, the total amount C.I.T. had invested in its bank-acquisition
program was $197.2 million, in addition to retained earnings by the
bank that at the end of 1974 aggregated $124 million.

Another development of interest was the appointment of the bank, in
July 1972, as the principal transfer agent and dividend disbursing agent
for the common and preferred stock of C.I.T. Financial Corporation.
Two major New York banks had previously performed these services
and their transfer to National Bank of North America had been delayed
until the latter's equipment capability could be built up. The addition
of the equipment and volume of activity required to service C.I.T.'s
40,000-plus stockholders enabled the bank to enlarge its corporate trust
department's capacity and take on assignments in this area from other
companies.

In both 1972 and through the first half of 1973, the earnings of all
banks had been under pressure as a result of the federal government's
anti-inflationary policy to restrain the prime rate and other lending of
banks. At the same time, interest rates in the open market, such as
those paid to time depositors and on certificates of deposit, escalated
rapidly, increasing the banks' cost of funds. With the lifting of the ar-
tificial restraints in the latter part of 1973, despite the continuation of
"voluntary" guidelines affecting loans to small borrowers, bank earnings improved. The 1973 and 1974 results of National Bank of North
America reflected this trend.

By the end of the latter year, the bank's total assets went above $3
billion, for an increase of more than $1¼ billion since 1969. Deposits
rose to $2.5 billion, a gain of more than $1 billion in the same period.
The bank's relative capital position was one of the strongest among all
the nation's money center banks. Equity capital amounted to $205 mil-
lion, a 1-to-12 ratio to deposits. During the year, the bank established
its first branches in New York City's fifth borough, Staten Island, the
only one where it had not been represented. Including all boroughs,
Long Island and Westchester County, branches were opened at a one-
a-month rate, bringing the total to 135 locations at the year-end.

The bank's correspondent relationships with other institutions throughout the United States and abroad had continued to expand, reaching a total of more than 600 banks in 60 countries during 1975.

Messrs. Holmes and Cole could rightfully state, as they did in the 1974 annual report, that in that year the bank "registered a dollar increase in earnings exceeding all previous annual gains and further strengthened its financial position."

39

Continuum

As C.I.T. Financial Corporation approached the biblical span of threescore and ten years, the fundamental credo of the institution, as expressed by its Founder nearly two generations earlier, was still embodied in his words:

"I have a confident word about the generality of our function, and that is this: habits and customs may change; markets may shift from one economic level to another; products may enjoy wide use for a few years and be superseded by entirely new and better products; but credit—the commodity in which we deal—is ever in demand. In our field it is our primary job to control and safeguard its use, because only then will it grow with the growing needs of an expanding nation."

Each of the corporation's leaders—Henry Ittleson (whose words these were), Arthur Dietz, Walter Lundell and Walter Holmes—recognized the heavy responsibility of stewardship contained in that statement. Equally, the historical record testifies to the incalculable number of other individuals who followed their leadership and consciously or unconsciously have demonstrated an unqualified commitment to that same obligation to justify C.I.T.'s economic existence through the prudent, innovative and constructive administration of its resources. These were members of the board of directors, officer-executives and the many other loyal and trusted men and women at all levels of the organization who, each in his or her own time and in his or her own way, have contributed to the achievements chronicled here— and the many more that are not.

The record stands. It is a unique one, just as C.I.T., with its specialized diversity of business interests and functions, is a unique organization on the American business scene. The $100,000 investment of the original stockholders in 1908 has grown to a figure for stockholders' equity exceeding $800 million. In the first year, the volume of financing business transacted was $738,000. The average annual volume in the 1970's was well over $4 billion, plus another $1.5 billion in loans by National Bank of North America. In 66 years through 1974, the institution had funded more than $146.5 billion of credit extensions to the consumer and industrial sectors of the United States and Canadian economies.

In the same period, it had net earnings of $1.577 billion and had paid dividends to its common stockholders of $906 million. If he had retained his investment, a purchaser of 100 common shares, priced at $30 a share at the first public offering in April 1924, would have owned 2,100 shares at the end of 1974, as a result of splits and stock dividends. His original capital investment of $3,000 thus would have grown in market value to some $67,000 in that time. He also would have received $101,788 in cash dividends.

There have been two propulsive forces behind the C.I.T. organization and the writing of this record. The first is the unflinching confidence of its managers in themselves and in the economies and industrial strength and genius of the United States and Canada. The second is their readiness to challenge things as they are at any point in time. This was the formula that Henry Ittleson was applying when he put his first piece of business on the books on February 26, 1908, discounting invoices for the Providence Jewelry Company totaling less than $100 and thus pioneering in a new form of mercantile credit. It is the formula the management of C.I.T. found still applicable 67 years later when it entered into two 15-year leasing transactions with subsidiaries of American Electric Power Company, Inc., one of the nation's largest public utility holding companies. The leases covered 1,500 triple-hopper railroad cars. This huge armada of rolling stock is being used to transport coal from the utilities' own mines to their generating stations to provide new supplies of electrical power in the nation's energy crisis. The twin transactions involved a total commitment by C.I.T. of $40 million, making this commitment one of the largest in the company's history.

Constant innovation. Constant evolution. Henry Ittleson had said of it, "I earnestly believe that as our country continues its progress, C.I.T. will constantly enlarge its fields of activity, its usefulness and the diversity of its operations," and he built an enterprise with a staff of four in a three-room office into a major nationwide financial institution.

Arthur Dietz saw C.I.T. as "An organization dedicated to the principle that the administration of credit requires the same high order of imagination, judgment and courage that has spurred the progress of science, production and distribution in America during this century," and through foresight and personal leadership, he welded the destinies of C.I.T. to the growth and ever-increasing prosperity of the nation's number one industry, automobile manufacturing, for four decades.

Walter Lundell said, "It is our function, in this money-oriented economy, to utilize our large amounts of capital funds and our borrowing capacity in whatever creative ways will provide both maximum safety and maximum profitability, in what we hope will be a judicious combination. Our expert, seasoned finance and insurance organization of more than 10,000 people and our far-flung network of local offices give us the capability to continually develop our present financing, leasing and associated insurance activities and to pioneer in new fields wherever we discern opportunities for innovation." Acting on this grand design, he guided C.I.T. into banking and a carefully planned and executed diversification program that gave his company a new character, bulwarking its earning power by reason of the broad base of operations from which its income is derived.

Walter Holmes devised the term "managed change"—defining it in these words: "C.I.T. Financial Corporation has been a growing company because it has always been a changing company. There has been only one basic corporate objective—by operating flexibly and innovatively, to put money to work profitably. Over the years, the company has deployed its large inventory of highly liquid working capital in scores of directions, picking and choosing its investment goals in response to—or in anticipation of—the opportunities and changes its management discerned in the economic environment." He applied these principles to the dynamic expansion and consolidation of all that had occurred before, building a major banking institution, strengthening and securing the consumer and industrial financing operations, giving increased scope to insurance potentials and bringing the manufacturing subsidiaries to new levels of profitability.

It is not the duty of the historian to predict the future. But the ever-increasing dimensions of service that C.I.T. Financial Corporation is capable of rendering to its clients and customers, and thus to the economic life of the society within which it functions, are presaged by all that is recorded in its history. Abiding traditions, eagerness to seek and embrace the new and the better, unassailable financial strength and reputation, and an organization of proud, experienced and highly competent people—from these ingredients C.I.T. Financial Corporation will fashion a future that holds the promise of being as remarkable as its past.

Appendix

I
Corporate Headquarters
C.I.T. Financial Corporation
and Predecessor Companies

1908–1912	Security Building Suite 310–316 St. Louis, Mo.
1912–1915	723 Railway Exchange Bldg. St. Louis, Mo.
1915–1918	818–820 Adams Building 61 Broadway New York, N.Y.
1918–1922	347 Madison Avenue New York, N.Y.
1922–1926	902 Liggett Building 41 East 42nd Street New York, N.Y.
1926–1957	One Park Avenue New York, N.Y.
1957–	650 Madison Avenue New York, N.Y.

II
Members of the Board of Directors
(Dates in parentheses show termination of service)

Commercial Credit and Investment Company

1908
Louis D. Beaumont (1942)
Henry Ittleson (1948)
David May (1927)
Morton J. May (1967; Honorary, 1967–68)
Dudley C. Shoenberg (1909)
Moses Shoenberg (1925)
Sydney M. Shoenberg (1967; Honorary, 1967–75)

1909
Joseph E. Shoenberg (1910)

1911
Tom May (1967; Honorary, 1967–68)

Commercial Investment Trust

1915
Harmon August (1932)

Commercial Investment Trust Incorporated

1921
Phillip W. Haberman (1953)
Claude L. Hemphill (1959)
Edwin C. Vogel (1969; Honorary, 1969–73)

1923
Henry Goldman (1937)

Commercial Investment Trust Corporation

1924
Joseph A. Bower (1946)
Frank W. Collins (1940)
Arthur O. Dietz (1967)
Henry Ittleson, Jr. (1973)
William A. Phillips (1937)
William A. Reed (1929)
E. G. Wilmer (1927)

1925
Frederick A. Franklin (1934)
Robert G. Paine (1926)

1928
Robert G. Blumenthal (1933)
Ralph H. Bollard (1946)
Edward M. Newald (1934)
Thomas Vietor (1933)

1930
Frank Altschul (1944)
Arthur Lehman (1935)

1931
Stanley B. Ecker (1965)

1932
Lincoln Cromwell (1947)
Arthur Iselin (1947)

1934
Francis T. Lyons (1936)

1935
Johnfritz Achelis (1956)
Dudley Cates (1943)
John I. Snyder (1946)

1936
Lewis L. Strauss (1946)

1938
Vincent Cullen (1949)
Fred Meissner (1956)

1941
Ernest Kanzler (1966)
George H. Zimmerman (1970)

1944
Hugh B. Baker (1964)

C.I.T. Financial Corporation

1946
Robert Lehman (1960)
Sydney D. Maddock (1957)
John M. Schiff
George R. Urquhart (1957)

1947
Melbourne Bergerman (1962)
Jarvis Cromwell (1951)
Charles S. McCain (1952)

1948
Fred W. Hautau (1952)
Leo H. Spanyol (1963)

1949
Ellis H. Carson (1954)

1950
George E. Warren (1967; Honorary, 1967–71)

1951
Frederic H. Brandi
Morton Goodspeed (1960)

1952
L. Walter Lundell (1974)

1953
Emil C. Chervenak (1966)
C. John Kuhn (1960)

1956
Charles L. Harding, Jr. (1969)
Walter M. Kelly (1965)

1957
Charles W. Dow (1971)
Joseph S. Fechteler (1966)
Thomas E. Lenihan (1962)
Alan G. Rude (1969)

1958
Harvey Picker

1960
Charles S. Sargent, Jr. (1972)

1962
Walter S. Holmes, Jr.
Arthur L. B. Richardson

1965
Charles S. Jensen
Maxwell C. Weaver (1970)

1966
Ardell T. Everett (1974)

Sidney Friedman (1973)
Karl P. Grube (1973)

1967
G. Russell Clark (1970)
Robert W. Purcell

1969
Todd G. Cole
Henry C. Watkins (1972)

1970
Robert B. Anderson

1973
H. Anthony Ittleson
Richard H. Lund

1974
Christopher F. Edley
Herman J. Schmidt
Robert L. Strawbridge

1975
Albert V. Casey

Notes

PAGE

CHAPTER 2

8   Copy of letter from Henry Ittleson in possession of author, from family records.

9   Allen Bush, *A Centennial History of the Jews of Colorado 1859–1959,* p. 97.

11 Louis S. Frank, quoting Henry Ittleson regarding his interview with David May. Taped interview with author, August 1971.

15 *Ibid.*

CHAPTER 4

21 *Gould's St. Louis Directory for 1908,* Gould Directory Company, p. 382.

22 Commercial Credit and Investment Company, Minutes of Meeting of the Board of Directors, June 9, 1908.

CHAPTER 9

51 Edwin R. A. Seligman, *The Economics of Instalment Selling* (Harper & Brothers, 1927), p. 46.

53 Commercial Investment Trust, Minutes of Meeting of Trustees, October 16, 1916.

CHAPTER 10

61 Louis S. Frank interview, August 1971.

63 *New York Times,* September 20, 1953, Section II, p. 3.

63 Arthur O. Dietz, interview with author, October 1962.

CHAPTER 11

70 *Automobile Topics,* May 20, 1916, p. 125.

71 Frank Emerson Wright, *The Financing of Automobile Instalment Sales* (A. W. Shaw Company, 1927), pp. 70–72.

73 George W. Norris, Proceedings of the Annual Meeting of the Chamber of Commerce of the United States, Washington, D. C., May 12, 1926.

74 James L. Wright, *Nation's Business,* March 1926, p. 66.

75 *New York Times,* December 4, 1926, p. 12.

76 *New York Times,* November 1, 1927, p. 17.

76 Debate between Creighton J. Hill and Henry Ittleson as quoted in *New York Times,* February 12, 1926, p. 41.

79 Text of Haberman address before the Contemporary Club in possession of author.

79 *New York Times,* June 20, 1926, p. 9.

80 *New York Times,* December 4, 1927, Section II, p. 6.

81 *New York Times,* December 6, 1927, p. 26.

81 Louis S. Frank, *What Would Happen If Credit Should Stop,* Commercial Investment Trust, 1926.

CHAPTER 12

86 Henry Ittleson, Transcript of Proceedings, Organization Meeting of National Association of Automobile Finance Companies, December 10, 1924, from C.I.T. archives.

CHAPTER 13

93 *Instalment Selling,* Dillon Read & Co., New York, November 1928, p. 12.

CHAPTER 14

99 Edwin C. Vogel, taped interview with author, January 5, 1972.

101 Henry Ittleson, Jr., taped interview with author, June 20, 1972.

CHAPTER 15

107 *New York Times,* December 6, 1925, Section II, p. 20.

107 *New York Times,* December 17, 1925, p. 34.

108 *New York Times,* November 20, 1925, p. 29.

114 *New York Times,* July 14, 1926, p. 29.

114 *Instalment Selling,* Dillon Read, p. 15.

114 *New York Times,* February 12, 1928, Section II, p. 14.

CHAPTER 17

125 *New York Times,* October 31, 1929, p. 3.

125 *New York Times,* December 1, 1929, Section II, p. 20.

CHAPTER 18

130 Deed of Trust creating Commercial Investment Trust Corporation Employees Relief Fund, June 27, 1930, p. 2.

133 Jarvis Cromwell, taped interview with author, July 1974.

137 Clyde William Phelps, *The Role of Sales Finance Companies in the American Economy,* Commercial Credit Company, p. 67.

137 Milan V. Ayers, *Time Sales Financing,* October 1938, p. 3.

137 Reavis Cox, *Economics of Instalment Buying* (Ronald Press, 1948), p. 281.

138 *Harvard Business Review,* July 1956, p. 55.

139 *Fortune,* January 1933, p. 70.

140 Vogel, address before the Annual Meeting of the United States Chamber of Commerce, C.I.T. archives.

PAGE

142   *New York Times,* May 10, 1931, Section II, p. 18.
143   Henry Ittleson, Jr., interview, June 20, 1972.

CHAPTER 19

149   Leo H. Spanyol, interview with author, June 1963.

CHAPTER 20

153   Joseph G. Myerson, interview with author, March 1973.
154   Sydney D. Maddock, taped interview with author, February 8, 1974.
155   A. B. Jamieson, *Charter Banking in Canada* (Ryerson Press, 1953), p. 79.

CHAPTER 21

162   Allan Nevins and Frank Ernest Hill, *Ford: Decline and Rebirth* (Charles Scribner's Sons),
      p. 62.

CHAPTER 22

165   *The Canadian Acceptance Story,* Canadian Acceptance Corporation Limited, December
      1972, pp. 4–7.
167   Sydney D. Maddock interview, February 1974.

CHAPTER 23

174   *Automotive Daily News,* quoted in the *Wall Street Journal,* December 4, 1936, p. 5.
174   Robert P. Shay, "New-Automobile Finance Rates, 1924–62," *The Journal of Finance,*
      September 1963, p. 483.
174   *New York Times,* December 4, 1936, p. 27.
175   *Cleveland Press,* February 26, 1937, p. 8; February 24, 1937, p. 11; March 5, 1937.
175   Cleveland Better Business Bureau, Inc., March 1937.
175   Text of Resolution, Legislature of the State of New York, enacted March 6, 1939.
176–177   *Automotive Daily News,* February 13, 1937, p. 1.
182   Edsel Ford letter to branch managers, C.I.T. archives.

CHAPTER 25

199   Sydney D. Maddock interview, February 1974.

CHAPTER 26

209   Alan G. Rude, letter to the author, March 16, 1975.

CHAPTER 27

217   *Fortune,* September 1947, pp. 87–88.
223   Robert P. Shay, "Regulation W: Experiment in Credit Control," University of Maine *Bulletin,* April 1953, pp. 170–171.

CHAPTER 28

229   Hudson Hoagland, *Selective Giving,* Ittleson Family Foundation, p. 63.
234   *In Memoriam; Henry Ittleson, January 27, 1871–October 27, 1948,* C.I.T. Financial
      Corporation, pp. 10–11.

CHAPTER 30

247   *Architectural Forum,* January 1958, pp. 91–92.
252   Henry Ittleson, Jr., interview, June 1972.

CHAPTER 31

264   L. Walter Lundell, "The Future Commitments of Consumer Financing," before the Na-
      tional Consumer Finance Association, October 3, 1961.

                                    CHAPTER 33

287–289 Mrs. Arthur O. Dietz, taped interview with author, June 8, 1972.
288   Harvey Picker, letter to author, April 17, 1975.
289   *Ibid.*
291   Edwin R. Goldfield, interview with L. E. Strang, June 17, 1959.
291   William Bruning, *James Picker: A Man of Many Parts,* Picker Corporation, 1963, p. 19.
302   Chris Fitzgerald,"A Million and a Half Sentimentalists Every Day," Cincinnati,
      November 1968, pp. 68–69.

                                    CHAPTER 34

305   Henry Ittleson, Jr., interview, June 20, 1972.
306   Augustus B. Weller, interview with author, September 1965.
307   *Wall Street Journal,* February 26, 1965, p. 19.
309   *Commercial and Financial Chronicle,* March 25, 1965, p. 4.
314   *Business Week,* October 5, 1968, p. 34.

                                    CHAPTER 36

332   Walter S. Holmes, Jr., interview with author, October 11, 1973.

                                    CHAPTER 39

356   Henry Ittleson, "A Current Appraisal of Instalment Financing," address at the Annual
      Meeting of National Association of Sales Finance Companies, Chicago, September 29,
      1937, p. 16.
358   Arthur O. Dietz, Annual Meeting of Stockholders, C.I.T. Financial Corporation, April
      26, 1960.
358   L. Walter Lundell, Annual Meeting of Stockholders, C.I.T. Financial Corporation, April
      23, 1968.
358   Walter Holmes, Jr., presentation to the New York Society of Analysts, October 25, 1971.

The author is especially grateful to Mrs. Rose L. (Cohn) Brown, of St. Louis, whose family
narrative *Colorado Days* was an invaluable source of information on the early days of Henry
Ittleson and his family in Kansas and Colorado. Mrs. Brown is a niece of C.I.T.'s Founder.

Index

ABOUT THE AUTHOR

WILLIAM L. WILSON was responsible for public relations and corporate advertising activities of C.I.T. Financial Corporation from 1946 to 1973, holding the title of vice president–public relations for most of that period. He continued his association with the corporation until his normal retirement date in 1975, devoting much of his time to researching and writing this book. In actuality, the period of research began soon after he joined the C.I.T. organization. He had established a corporate historical archives collection and also arranged to tape-record interviews with key officers prior to their retirement from the company.

He has had personal associations with nearly all those who appear in leading roles in this history, beginning with Henry Ittleson, the Founder, and the latter's earliest co-workers, Claude L. Hemphill and Phillip W. Haberman. For a period of years in each case, he worked closely on a day-to-day basis with Arthur O. Dietz, L. Walter Lundell and Walter S. Holmes, Jr. while they were C.I.T.'s chief executives.

In addition to the conduct of his public relations and advertising responsibilities, Wilson was responsible for the establishment of The C.I.T. Foundation, Inc., directing its activities for more than twenty years, and C.I.T. Buildings Corporation, for which he developed the original concept of financing the construction of self-liquidating buildings for non-profit institutions.

Prior to joining the C.I.T. organization he was a public relations and industrial relations executive in the aircraft industry and had done newspaper and magazine editorial work. He is a graduate of Dartmouth College and lives in Princeton, N.J.